CATCHING THE WOLF OF WALL STREET

ALSO BY JORDAN BELFORT

The Wolf of Wall Street

CATCHING THE WOLF OF WALL STREET

by Jordan Belfort

BANTAM BOOKS

CATCHING THE WOLF OF WALL STREET
A Bantam Book / March 2009

Published by Bantam Dell
A Division of Random House, Inc.
New York, New York

Book design by Glen M. Edelstein

Library of Congress Cataloging-in-Publication Data
Belfort, Jordan.
Catching the Wolf of Wall Street / by Jordan Belfort.
p. cm.
ISBN 978-0-553-80704-2 (hardcover) – ISBN 978-0-553-90601-1 (ebook)
1. Belfort, Jordan. 2. Securities fraud. 3. Stockbrokers–United States–Biography.
4. Wall Street (New York, N.Y.) I. Title.
HV6766.B45A3 2009
332.6'2092–dc22
[B] 2008047665

Printed in the United States of America
Published simultaneously in Canada

www.bantamdell.com

10 9 8 7 6 5 4 3 2 1
BVG

To my love, Anne Koppe, for being such a good sport

AUTHOR'S NOTE

This book is a work of memoir; it is a true story based on my best recollections of various events in my life. Where indicated, the names and identifying characteristics of certain people mentioned in the book have been changed in order to protect their privacy. In some instances, I rearranged and/or compressed events and time periods in service of the narrative, and I re-created dialogue to match my best recollection of those exchanges.

PROLOGUE

CROCODILE TEARS

September 2, 1998

You'd think that anyone who was facing thirty years in jail and a hundred-million-dollar fine would be ready to settle down and play things straight. But, no, I must be some sort of glutton for punishment, or maybe I'm just my own worst enemy.

Whatever the case, I'm the Wolf of Wall Street. Remember me? The investment banker who partied like a rock star, the one whose life was sheer insanity? The one with the choirboy face, the innocent smile, and the recreational drug habit that could sedate Guatemala? You remember. I wanted to be young and rich, so I hopped on the Long Island Railroad and headed down to Wall Street to seek my fortune–only to come up with a brainstorm that inspired me to bring my own version of Wall Street out to Long Island instead.

And what a brainstorm it was! By my twenty-seventh birthday, I had built one of the largest brokerage firms in America. It was a place where the young and the uneducated would come to get rich beyond their wildest dreams.

My firm's name was Stratton Oakmont, although, in retrospect, it should have been Sodom and Gomorrah. After all, it wasn't every firm that sported hookers in the basement, drug dealers in the parking lot, exotic animals in the boardroom, and midget-tossing competitions on Fridays.

In my mid-thirties, I had all the trappings of extreme Wall Street wealth–mansions, yachts, private jets, helicopters, limos, armed bodyguards, throngs of domestic servants, drug dealers on speed dial, hookers who took credit cards, police looking for handouts, politicians on the payroll, enough exotic cars to open my own exotic-car dealership–and a loyal and loving blond second wife named Nadine.

Actually, you may have seen Nadine on TV in the 1990s; she was that wildly sexy blonde who tried to sell you Miller Lite Beer during *Monday Night Football.* She had the face of an angel, although it was her legs and ass that got her the job; well, that and her perky young breasts, which she had recently augmented to a C-cup, after giving birth to the second of our two children. A son!

Nadine and I were living what I had come to think of as *Lifestyles of the Rich and Dysfunctional*–a sexed-up, drugged-up, hyped-up, over-the-top version of the American Dream. We were careening down the fast lane, at 200 miles per hour, with one fingertip on the steering wheel, never signaling, and never looking back. (Who would want to?) The wreckage of the past was astonishing. It was far too painful to look back; it was much easier just to plunge forward and keep speeding down the road, praying that the past wouldn't catch up with us. But, of course, it did.

In fact, I was teetering on the brink of disaster after a small army of FBI agents raided my Long Island estate and led me away in handcuffs. It had happened on a warm Tuesday evening, the week before Labor Day, less than two months after my thirty-sixth birthday. And when the arresting agent said to me, "Jordan Belfort, you've been indicted on twenty-two counts of securities fraud, stock manipulation, money laundering, and obstruction of justice..." I had pretty much tuned out. After all, what was the point of hearing a list of the crimes I knew I'd committed? It would be like taking a sniff from a milk container labeled *spoiled milk.*

So I called my lawyer and resigned myself to spending the night in jail. And as they led me away in handcuffs, my only solace was getting to say one last good-bye to my loving second wife. She was standing in the doorway with tears in her eyes and wearing cutoff jean shorts. She looked gorgeous, even on the night of my arrest.

As they escorted me past her, I stiffened my upper lip and whispered, "Don't worry, sweetie. Everything will be okay," to which she nodded sadly and whispered back, "I know, baby. Stay strong for me, and stay strong for the kids. We all love you." She blew me a tender kiss and snuffled back a tear.

And then I was gone.

BOOK I

CHAPTER 1

THE AFTERMATH

September 4, 1998

Joel Cohen, the disheveled assistant United States attorney for the Eastern District of New York, was a world-class bastard with a degenerate slouch. When I was arraigned the following day, he tried to convince the female magistrate to deny me bail on the grounds that I was a born liar, a compulsive cheater, a habitual whoremonger, a hopeless drug addict, a serial witness-tamperer, and, above all things, the greatest flight risk since Amelia Earhart.

It was a helluva mouthful, although the only things that bothered me were that he had called me a drug addict and a whoremonger. After all, I had been sober for almost eighteen months now, and I had sworn off hookers accordingly. Whatever the case, the magistrate set my bail at $10 million, and within twenty-four hours my wife and my attorney had made all the necessary arrangements for my release.

At this particular moment, I was walking down the courthouse steps into the loving arms of my wife. It was a sunny Friday afternoon, and she was waiting for me on the sidewalk, wearing a tiny yellow sundress and matching high-heeled sandals that made her look as fresh as a daisy. At this time of summer, in this part of Brooklyn, by four o'clock the sun was at just the right angle to bring every last drop of her into view: her shimmering blond hair, those brilliant blue eyes, her perfect cover-girl features, those surgically enhanced breasts, her glorious shanks and flanks, so succulent above the knee and so slender at the ankle. She was thirty years old now and absolutely gorgeous. The moment I reached her, I literally fell into her arms.

"You're a *sight* for sore eyes," I said, embracing her on the sidewalk. "I missed you so much, honey."

"Get the fuck away from me!" she sputtered. "I want a divorce."

I felt a second-wife alarm go off in my central nervous system. "What are you talking about, honey? You're being ridiculous!"

"You know *exactly* what I'm talking about!" And she recoiled from my embrace and started marching toward a blue Lincoln limousine parked at the edge of the curb of 225 Cadman Plaza, the main thoroughfare in the courthouse section of Brooklyn Heights. Waiting by the limo's rear door was Monsoir, our babbling Pakistani driver. He opened it on cue, and I watched her disappear into a sea of sumptuous black leather and burled walnut, taking her tiny yellow sundress and shimmering blond hair with her.

I wanted to follow, but I was too stunned. My feet seemed to be rooted into the earth, as if I were a tree. Beyond the limousine, on the other side of the street, I could see a dreary little park adorned with green-slat benches, undernourished trees, and a small field covered by a thin layer of dirt and crabgrass. The park looked as sumptuous as a graveyard. My misery made my eye hang on it for a moment.

I took a deep breath and let it out slowly. *Christ, I needed to grab hold of myself!* I looked at my watch . . . *didn't have one* . . . I had taken it off before they slapped the cuffs on me. Suddenly I felt terribly conscious of my appearance. I looked down at my abdomen. I was one giant wrinkle, from my tan golf pants to my white silk polo shirt to my leather boating moccasins. I hadn't slept in how many days? Three? Four? Hard to say–I never slept much anyway. My blue eyes burned like hot coals. My mouth was dry as a bone. My breath was–wait a minute! Was it my breath? Maybe I scared her off! After three days of eating grade-D bratwurst I had the worst case of dragon breath since–didn't know when. But, still, how could she leave me now? What kind of woman was she? *That bitch!* Gold-digger–

These thoughts roaring through my head were completely crazy. My wife wasn't going anywhere. She was just shell-shocked. Besides, it was common knowledge that second wives didn't bail on their husbands the moment they got indicted; they *waited* a bit so it wasn't so obvious! It couldn't be possible–

–just then I saw Monsoir smiling at me and nodding his head. *Fucking terrorist!* I thought.

Monsoir had been working for us for almost six months now, and the jury was still out on him. He was one of those unnerving foreigners who wore a perpetual grin on his face. In Monsoir's case, I figured it was because his next stop was to a local bomb factory, to mix explosives. Either way, he was thin, balding, caramel-colored, medium height, and had a narrow skull shaped like a shoe box. When he spoke, he sounded like the Road Runner, his words coming out in tiny beeps and bops. And unlike my old driver, George, Monsoir couldn't shut up.

I walked to the limousine in a zombielike state, making a mental note to thrash him if he tried to make small talk. And my wife, well, I would just have to humor her. And if that didn't work, then I would start a fight with her. After all, ours was the sort of wildly rocky, dysfunctional romance where knock-down, drag-out brawls brought us closer together.

"How are you, boss?" asked Monsoir. "It is *berry, berry* good to have you back. What was it like inside the–"

I cut him off with a raised palm: *"Don't*–fucking–speak, Monsoir. Not now. Not ever," and I climbed into the back of the limousine and took a seat across from Nadine. She was sitting with her long, bare legs crossed, staring out the window into the rancid gullet of Brooklyn.

I smiled and said, "Taking in your old stomping ground, Duchess?"

No response. She just stared out the window, a gorgeous ice sculpture.

Christ–this was absurd! How could the Duchess of Bay Ridge turn her back on me in my hour of need? The Duchess of Bay Ridge was my wife's nickname, and depending on her mood it could cause her to either flash you a smile or tell you to go fuck yourself. The nickname had to do with her blond hair, British citizenship, over-the-top beauty, and Brooklyn upbringing. Her British citizenship, which she was very quick to remind you of, created a rather *royal* and refined mystique about her; the Brooklyn upbringing, in the gloomy groin of Bay Ridge, caused words like *shit, prick, cocksucker,* and *motherfucker* to roll off her tongue like the finest poetry; and the extreme beauty allowed her to get away with it all. At five-seven, the Duchess and I were pretty much the same size, although she had the temper of Mount Vesuvius and the strength of a grizzly bear. Back in my younger and wilder days, she was pretty quick to take a swing at me or pour boiling water over my head, when the need arose. And, as odd as it seemed, I loved it.

I took a deep breath and said in a joking tone, "Come on, Duchess! I'm very upset right now and I need a bit of compassion. *Please?*"

Now she looked at me. Her blue eyes blazed away above her high cheekbones. "Don't fucking call me that," she snarled, and then she looked back out the window, resuming her ice-sculpture pose.

"Jesus Christ!" I muttered. "What the hell has gotten into you?"

Still looking out the window, she said, "I can't be with you anymore. I'm not in love with you." Then, twisting the knife in deeper: "I haven't been for a long time."

Such despicable words! The audacity! Yet for some reason her words made me want her even more. "You're being ridiculous, Nae. Everything will be fine." My throat was so dry I could barely get the words out. "We've got *more* than enough money, so you can relax. *Please* don't do this now."

Still staring out the window: "It's too late."

As the limousine headed toward the Brooklyn–Queens

Expressway, a combination of fear, love, desperation, and betrayal overtook me all at once. There was a sense of loss that I had never experienced before. I felt completely empty, utterly hollow. I couldn't just sit across from her like this–it was absolute torture! I needed to either kiss her or hug her or make love to her or *strangle her to death*. It was time for strategy number two: the knock-down, drag-out brawl.

With a healthy dose of venom, I said, "So let me get this fucking straight, Nadine: *Now* you want a divorce? Now that I'm under fucking indictment? Now that I'm under house arrest?" I pulled up the left leg of my pants, exposing an electronic monitoring bracelet on my ankle. It looked like a beeper. "What kind of fucking person are you? Tell me! Are you trying to set a world record for lack of compassion?"

She looked at me with dead eyes. "I'm a good woman, Jordan; *everyone* knows that. But you mistreated me for years. I've been done with this marriage for a long time now–ever since you kicked me down the stairs. This has nothing to do with you going to jail."

What a bunch of horseshit! Yes, I had raised a hand to her once–that terrible struggle on the stairs, eighteen months ago, that despicable moment, the day before I got sober–and if she had left me *then*, she would have been justified. But she didn't leave; she *stayed*; and I *did* get sober. It was only now–with financial ruin lingering in the air–that she wanted out. Unbelievable!

By now we were on the Brooklyn–Queens Expressway, approaching the Brooklyn–Queens border. Off to my left was the glittering island of Manhattan, where seven million people would dance and sing their weekend away, unconcerned with my plight. I found that wholly depressing. Off to my immediate left was the armpit of Williamsburg, a flat swath of land loaded with dilapidated warehouses, ramshackle apartments, and people who spoke Polish. Just why all those Poles had settled there, I hadn't the slightest idea.

Ahhh, *a brainstorm*! I would change the subject to the kids. This, after all, was the common bond we shared. "Are the kids okay?" I asked softly.

"They're fine," she answered, in a rather cheery tone. Then:

"They'll be fine no matter what." She stared out the window again. The unspoken message was: "Even if you go to jail for a hundred years, Chandler and Carter will still be okay, because Mommy will find a new husband faster than you can say *Sugar Daddy*!"

I took a deep breath and decided to say no more; there was no winning with her right now. *If only I had stuck with my first wife!* Would Denise be saying now that she didn't love me anymore? *Fucking second wives;* they were a mixed bag, especially those of the trophy variety. For better or worse? *Yeah, right!* They only said that for the sake of the wedding video. In reality, they were only there for the better.

This was payback for leaving my kind first wife, Denise, for the blond-headed scoundrel seated across from me. The Duchess had been my mistress once, an innocent fling that spiraled way out of control. Before I knew it, we were madly in love and couldn't live without each other, couldn't *breathe* without each other. Of course, I had rationalized my actions at the time–telling myself that Wall Street was a very tough place for first wives, so it wasn't really my fault. After all, when a man became a true power broker, these things were expected to happen.

These things, however, cut both ways–because if the Master of the Universe took a financial nosedive, then the second wife would quickly move on to more-fertile pastures. In essence, the gold digger, aware that the gold mine had ceased to yield the precious ore, would move on to a more *productive* mine, where she could continue to extract ore, undisturbed. Indeed, it was one of life's most ruthless equations, and right now I was on the ass end of it.

With a sinking heart, I shifted my gaze back to the Duchess. She was still staring out the window–a beautiful, malevolent ice sculpture. At that moment I felt many things for her, but mostly I felt sad–sad for both of us, and even sadder for our children. Up until now they had lived a charmed life in Old Brookville, secure in the fact that things were just as they should be and that they would always stay that way. How very sad, I thought, how very fucking sad.

We spent the remainder of the limo ride in silence.

CHAPTER 2

THE INNOCENT VICTIMS

The village of Old Brookville stands on the sparkling "Gold Coast" of Long Island, an area so magnificent that up until a short time ago it had been strictly off-limits to Jews. Not literally, of course, but for all practical purposes we were still considered second-class citizens, a clique of slippery peddlers who'd risen above their station and needed to be observed and controlled lest they overrun the area's first-class citizens–namely, the WASPs.

Actually, these weren't just any old WASPs but a small subspecies of WASP known as "the blue blood." Numbering only in the thousands, the blue bloods, with their tall, thin frames and fancy clothes, had natural habitats that included world-class golf courses, stately mansions, hunting and fishing lodges, and secret societies. Most of them were of British stock, and they took great pride in tracing their genealogies back to the time of the *Mayflower*. Yet, in evolutionary terms, they were no different from the massive dinosaurs that had ruled the Gold Coast 65 million years before them: They were on the verge of extinction–victims of increased death taxes, property taxes, and a steady dilution of the intellectual gene pool, as generations of inbreeding yielded idiot sons and daughters who wreaked financial havoc on the great fortunes their blue-blooded ancestors had taken generations to build. (The magic of Charles Darwin working overtime.)

In any event, this was where the Duchess and I now lived and where I had assumed we would grow old together. Now, however, as the limousine pulled through the limestone pillars at the edge of our six-acre estate, I wondered.

A long circular driveway, bordered by immaculately trimmed box hedges, led to our ten-thousand-square-foot stone mansion finished in French chateau style, with gleaming copper turrets and casement windows. At the end of the driveway, a long cobblestone walkway led to the mansion's twelve-foot-high mahogany front door. As the limo pulled up to it, I decided to take one last shot with the Duchess before we went inside. I got down on my knees and placed my hands on either side of her thighs, which were crossed. As always, her skin felt silky smooth, although I resisted the urge to run my hands down the full length of her bare legs. Instead, I looked up at her with puppy-dog eyes and said:

"Listen, Nae, I know this has been tough on you"–tough on *you*?–"and I'm really sorry for that, but we've been together for *eight* years, sweetie. And we have two *amazing* kids! We'll get through this." I paused for a moment and nodded my head for effect. "And even if I *do* go to jail, you and the kids will always be taken care of. I promise you."

"Don't worry about us," she said coldly. "Just worry about yourself."

I narrowed my eyes and said, "I don't get it, Nadine. You make it seem like you're totally shocked about all this. When we first met it wasn't like I was being nominated for the Nobel Peace Prize. I was being smeared and vilified by every newspaper in the free world!" I cocked my head to the side, at an angle that implied logic, and continued: "I mean, I guess it would be one thing if you married a doctor and then found out, after the fact, that he'd been defrauding Medicaid for the last twenty years. I guess *then* you *would* be justified! But, now, given the circumstances–"

She cut me right off. "I had no idea what you were doing"*–oh, I guess the two million in cash in my sock drawer never made you suspicious!*–"none at all. And after they took you away, that Agent Coleman interrogated me for five hours–*five fucking hours*!" The last three words she screamed, and then she pushed my hands off her thighs. "He told me that *I* would go to jail too, unless I told him everything! You put me at risk; you put me in *danger.* I'll never forgive you for that." She looked away, shaking her head in disgust.

Oh, shit! Agent Coleman had traumatized her. Of course, he had been totally full of shit, but, still, she was holding me responsible. Yet perhaps that boded well for our future together. After all, once the Duchess realized that she wasn't at risk, she might have a change of heart. I was about to explain that to her, when she turned back to me and said, "I need to get away for a while. The last few days have been stressful on me, and I need to be alone. I'm going to the beach house for the weekend. I'll be back on Monday."

I opened my mouth, but no words came out, just a tiny gasp of air. Finally I said, "You're leaving me alone with the kids under house arrest?"

"Yes!" she said proudly, and she opened the rear door and popped out of her seat in a huff. And just like that she was gone–marching toward the mansion's massive front door, with the hem of her tiny yellow sundress rising and falling with each determined step. I stared at the Duchess's fabulous behind for a moment. Then I jumped out of the limousine and followed her into the house.

On the mansion's second floor, three large bedrooms were on the east end of a very long hallway, and a fourth bedroom, the master bedroom, was on the west end. Of the three east bedrooms, our children occupied two, and the third was used as a guest room. A four-foot-wide mahogany staircase swept up in a sumptuous curve from a grand marble entryway below.

When I reached the top of the stairs, rather than following the

Duchess into the master bedroom, I turned east and headed for the kids' rooms. I found them both in Chandler's room, sitting on her glorious pink carpet. They were dressed in their pajamas, playing happily. The room was a little pink wonderland, with dozens of stuffed animals arranged just so. The drapes, the window treatments, and the goose-down comforter on Chandler's queen-size bed were all done in "Laura Ashley style," a palette of mellow pastels and floral prints. It was the perfect little girl's room, for my perfect little girl.

Chandler had just turned five, and she was the spitting image of her mother, a tiny blond model. At this particular moment, she was engaged in her favorite pastime–arranging a hundred fifty Barbie dolls into a perfect circle around her, so she could sit in the center and hold court. Carter, who had just turned three, was lying on his stomach just outside the circle. He was thumbing through a picture book with his right hand, his left elbow resting on the carpet and his tiny chin resting in his palm. His enormous blue eyes blazed away behind eyelashes as lush as butterfly wings. His platinum-blond hair was as fine as corn silk and had tiny curls on the back that shimmered like polished glass.

The moment they saw me they jumped up and ran toward me. "Daddy's home!" screamed Chandler. Then Carter chimed in: "Daddy! Daddy!"

I crouched down and they ran into my arms.

"I missed you guys so much!" I said, showering them with kisses. "I think you got even *bigger* in the last three days! Let me look at you." I held them out in front of me, and I cocked my head to the side and narrowed my eyes suspiciously, as if I were inspecting them.

They both stood tall and proud, shoulder to shoulder, their chins slightly elevated. Chandler was big for her age, Carter small, so she was a good head and a half taller than him. I compressed my lips and nodded my head gravely, as if to say, "My suspicions were confirmed!" Then I said accusingly: "I was right! You *did* get bigger! Why, you little sneaks!"

They both giggled deliciously. Then Chandler said, "Why are you crying, Daddy? Do you have a boo-boo?"

Without me even knowing it, a trickle of tears had made their way down my cheeks. I dried them with the back of my hand and then offered my daughter a harmless white lie: "No, I don't have a boo-boo, silly! I'm just *so* happy to see you guys, it made me cry tears of joy."

Carter nodded in agreement, although he was quickly losing interest. He was a boy, after all, so his attention span was limited. In fact, Carter lived for only five things: sleeping, eating, watching his *Lion King* video, climbing on the furniture, and the sight of the Duchess's long blond hair, which soothed him like a ten-milligram Valium. Carter was a man of few words, yet he was remarkably intelligent. By his first birthday he could work the TV, VHS, and remote control. By eighteen months he was a master locksmith, picking Tot Loks with the precision of a safecracker. And by two years old he had memorized two dozen picture books. He was calm, cool, and collected, entirely comfortable in his own skin.

Chandler, on the other hand, was the exact opposite. She was complex, curious, intuitive, introspective, and never at a loss for words. Her nickname was the CIA, because she was constantly eavesdropping on conversations, trying to gather intelligence. She had spoken her first word at seven months, and at the age of one, she was speaking full sentences. At two, she was having full-blown arguments with the Duchess, and she hadn't stopped since. She was difficult to cajole, impossible to manipulate, and had an unusually keen sense for seeing through bullshit.

And that created problems for me. My ankle bracelet could be explained away as some sort of advanced medical device, something that the doctor had given me to make sure my back pain never returned. I would tell Chandler that it was a six-month therapy regimen, and I was to keep the bracelet on at all times. She would probably buy that for a while. However, being under house arrest was going to be much more difficult to conceal.

As a family, we were constantly on the move—running and doing and going and seeing—so what would Chandler think about my sudden compulsion to not leave the house? I ran it through my mind and came to the quick conclusion that, in spite of everything, the Duchess could still be counted on to cover for me.

Then Chandler said, "Are you crying because you had to pay people back money?"

"Whuh?" I muttered. That dirty little Duchess! I thought. How could she! *Why* would she? To try to poison Chandler against me! She was waging a psychological war, and this was her first salvo. Step one: Let the children know Daddy's a big fat crook; step two: Let the children know there are other, *better* men, who aren't big fat crooks, who will take care of Mommy; step three: The moment Daddy goes to jail, tell the children Daddy abandoned them because he doesn't love them; and, finally, step four: Tell the children that it would be appropriate to call Mommy's new husband Daddy, until *his* gold mine dries up, at which point Mommy will find an even newer daddy for them.

I took a deep breath and conjured up another white lie. I said to Chandler, "I think you misunderstood, sweetie. I was busy working."

"No," argued Chandler, frustrated at my denseness. "Mommy said you took money from people and now you have to pay it back."

I shook my head in disbelief and then took a moment to regard Carter. He seemed to be eyeing me suspiciously. Christ–did he know too? He was only three, and all he cared about was the fucking Lion King!

I had a lot of explaining to do, and not just today but also in the days and years to come. Chandler would be reading soon, and that would open up a whole new can of worms. What would I say to her? What would her friends say to her? I felt a fresh wave of despair wash over me. In a way, the Duchess was right. I had to pay for my crimes, although on Wall Street everyone was a criminal, wasn't that true? It was only a question of degree, wasn't it? So what made me worse than anybody else–the fact that I'd gotten caught?

I chose not to follow that train of thought. Changing the subject, I said, "Well, it's really not important, Channy. Let's play with your Barbie dolls." And after you go to sleep, I thought, Daddy is going to head downstairs to his study and spend a few hours figuring out a way to kill Mommy without getting caught.

CHAPTER 3

EVAPORATING OPTIONS

We were somewhere on the Grand Central Parkway near the Queens–Manhattan border when I finally lost patience with Monsoir.

It was Tuesday morning, the day after Labor Day, and I was on my way to my criminal attorney's office in Midtown Manhattan with my electronic monitoring bracelet on my left ankle and this babbling Pakistani behind the wheel. Yet, despite those hindrances, I was still dressed for success, in a gray pinstripe suit, crisp white dress shirt, red shepherd's check necktie, black cotton dress socks–which, on my left ankle, concealed the electronic monitoring bracelet–and a pair of black Gucci loafers with tassels on them.

Dressing for success; that had seemed important this morning, although I was certain that even if I wore a diaper and a bow tie, my trusted criminal attorney, Gregory J. O'Connell, would still tell me that I looked like a million bucks. After all, this morning's first order of business would be to hand him a check in that very amount: one million bucks. That was a priority, he'd explained, because there was a better than fifty-fifty chance that the U.S. Attorney's Office would be making a motion to freeze my assets this week. And lawyers, of course, need to get paid.

It was a little after ten a.m., and the morning rush hour had just ended. Off to my right I could see the low-slung hangars and terminals of LaGuardia Airport, looking as grimy as usual. Off to my left I could see the burgeoning Greek paradise of Astoria, Queens, which had a higher concentration of Greeks per square foot than anyplace on earth, including Athens. I had grown up not far from here, in the Jew paradise of Bayside, Queens, a neighborhood of safe streets that was now in the process of being overrun by well-heeled Koreans.

We had left Old Brookville thirty minutes ago, and, since then, the closet terrorist hadn't kept his mouth shut. He'd been going on and on about the criminal justice system in his beloved Pakistan. On most days I would have simply told him to shut the fuck up. But on this particular morning I was too worn out to throttle him. And that was the Duchess's fault.

True to her word, the blond-headed scoundrel had flown the coop on me that weekend, spending three days and nights in the Hamptons. I was pretty sure she had crashed at our beach house at nighttime, but I hadn't the slightest idea what she had done during the day and, for that matter, whom she had done it with. She didn't call once, painting a clear picture that she was *busy! busy! busy!* prospecting for a new gold mine.

When she finally walked in the door, Monday afternoon, she said only a few words to me–something about the traffic being brutal on her way back from the Hamptons. Then she went upstairs to the kids' rooms, smiling and laughing, and took them outside to the swings. She didn't seem to have a care in the world–making it a point, in fact, to amplify her cheeriness, ad nauseam.

She pushed them at an overly merry clip and then took her shoes off and went skipping around the backyard with them. It was as if our two lives no longer intertwined in any way whatsoever. Her very callousness had sent my spirits plunging to even lower depths. I felt as if I were in a dark hole, suffocating, with no escape.

I hadn't eaten, slept, laughed, or smiled in almost four days now, and, at this particular moment, with Monsoir's inane ramblings, I was contemplating slitting my own wrists.

Now he started speaking again. "I was only trying to cheer you up, boss. You are actually a *berry* lucky man. In my country they cut your hand off if they catch you stealing a loaf of bread."

I cut him off. "Yeah, well, that's real fucking fascinating, Monsoir. Thanks for sharing." And I took a moment to consider the pros and cons of Islamic justice. I came to the quick conclusion that, given my current circumstances, it would be a mixed bag for me. On the plus side, the Duchess wouldn't be acting so tough if I could force her to wear one of those head-to-toe burkas around town; it would stop that blond head of hers from sticking out like a fucking peacock. Yet, on the minus side, the Islamic penalty for white-collar crime and serial whoremongering had to be pretty severe. My kids and I had recently watched *Aladdin,* and they were ready to cut the poor kid's hand off for stealing a ten-cent grapefruit. Or was it a loaf of bread? Either way, *I* had stolen over a hundred million bucks, and I could only imagine what the Islamic penalty was for that.

Although, had I really *stolen* anything? I mean, this word *stolen* was somewhat of a mischaracterization, wasn't it? On Wall Street we weren't actually thieves, were we? We simply talked people out of their money; we didn't actually *steal* it from them! There was a difference. The crimes we committed were *soft* crimes—like churning and burning, and trading on inside information, and garden-variety tax evasion. They were *technical* violations more than anything; it wasn't blatant thievery.

Or was it? Well, maybe it was... maybe it was. Perhaps I *had* taken things to a new level. Or at least the newspapers thought so.

By now the limousine was making its way over the great arc of the Triborough Bridge, and I could see the gleaming skyline of Manhattan off to my left. On clear days, like today, the buildings seemed to rise up to heaven. You could literally feel the weight of them. There was no doubt that Manhattan was the center of the financial universe, a place where movers and shakers could move and shake, where Masters of the Universe could congregate like Greek gods. And every last one of them was as crooked as me!

Yes, I thought, I was no different than any other man who owned a brokerage firm–from the blue-blooded WASP bastard who ran JPMorgan to the hapless white-bread schnook who ran Butt-Fuck Securities (in Butt-Fuck, Minnesota), we all cut a few corners. We *had* to, after all, if nothing more than to stay even with the competition. Such was the nature of contemporary perfection on Wall Street if you wanted to be a true power broker.

So, in reality, none of this was my fault. It was *Joe Kennedy's* fault! Yes, he had started this terrible wave of stock manipulation and corporate chicanery. Back in the thirties, Old Joe had been the original Wolf of Wall Street, slashing and burning anyone in his path. In fact, he'd been one of the chief instigators of the Great Crash of '29, which plunged the United States into the Great Depression. He and a small handful of fabulously Wealthy Wolves had taken advantage of an unsuspecting public–making tens of millions of dollars short-selling stocks that were already on the verge of collapse, causing them to plummet that much lower.

And what had his punishment been? Well, unless I was a bit off on my history, he became the first chairman of the Securities and Exchange Commission. *The audacity!* Yes, the stock market's chief crook had become its chief watchdog. And all the while, even as he served as chairman, he continued to slash and burn from behind the scenes, making millions more.

I was no different from anybody else–no damn different!

"You're different than everybody else," said Gregory J. O'Connell, my nearly seven-foot-tall criminal lawyer. "That's your problem." He was sitting behind his fabulous mahogany desk, leaning back in his fabulous high-backed leather chair, and holding a copy of my not-so-fabulous indictment. He was a good-looking man, in his late thirties or early forties, with dark-brown hair and a very square jaw. He bore a striking resemblance to Tom Selleck from *Magnum, P.I.,* although he seemed much taller to me. In fact, leaning back the way he was, his head and torso seemed a mile long. (Actually, he was only six-four, although anyone over six-three seemed seven feet tall to me.)

Magnum plowed on: "Or at least that's how the government views you, as well as your friends in the press, who can't seem to get enough of you." His voice was a deep tenor, his advice offered in the same theatrical way Enrico Caruso might offer it, if he were so inclined. "I hate to say it," continued the towering tenor, "but you've become the poster child for small-stock fraud, Jordan. That's why the judge set your bail at ten million, to make an example of you."

With a hiss: "Oh, really? Well it's all fucking bullshit, Greg! Every last drop of it!" I popped out of my black leather armchair, elevating myself to his eye level. "Everyone on Wall Street's a crook, *you* know that!" I cocked my head to the side and narrowed my eyes suspiciously. "I mean, what kind of lawyer are you, anyway? I'm fucking innocent, for Chrissake! Completely fucking innocent!"

"I know you are," said my friend and lawyer of four years. "And I'm Mother Teresa, on my way to Rome for a pilgrimage. And Nick over there"–he raised his chin toward the room's third occupant, his partner Nick De Feis, who was sitting in the black leather armchair next to mine–"is Mahatma Gandhi. Isn't that right, Nick?"

"It's Mohandas," replied Nick, who had graduated at the top his class at Yale. He was about the same age as Greg and had an IQ around seven thousand. He had short dark hair, intense eyes, a calm demeanor, and a slender build. About my height, he was a greater wearer of blue pinstripe suits, heavily starched collars, and WASPy wingtip shoes, the sum of which made him look very intelligent. "Mahatma's not actually a name," continued the Yaleman. "It's Sanskrit for great soul, in case you were wondering. Mohandas was–"

I cut him off with: "Who gives a fuck, Nick? I mean, sweet Jesus! I'm facing life in prison and you two bastards are jabbering away in Sanskrit!" I walked over to a floor-to-ceiling plate-glass window that shoved an awesome view of the concrete jungle of Manhattan down your throat. I stared out the window blankly, wondering how the fuck I ended up here—and knowing exactly how.

We were on the twenty-sixth floor of an art-deco-style office building that rose up sixty stories above Fifth Avenue and 42nd Street. It was an area of Manhattan known as Bryant Park, although it used to be known as Needle Park, when two hundred heroin-addicted hookers, back in the seventies, had proudly called it home. But the park had long since been reclaimed and was now considered a fine place for working-class Manhattanites to enjoy a serene lunch, a place where they could sit on green-slat benches and breathe in the noxious fumes of a hundred thousand passing automobiles and listen to the blaring horns of twenty thousand immigrant cabbies. I looked down at the park, but all I could see was a swath of green grass and some ant-size people, none of whom, I figured, were wearing ankle bracelets. I found that very depressing.

Anyway, this particular building—namely, 500 Fifth Avenue—was an especially fine place to keep a law office. In fact, that was something that had instilled great confidence in me when I'd first met Nick and Greg four years ago, confirming a gut feeling I'd had that these two young lawyers were quickly on the rise.

You see, at the time, the law firm of De Feis O'Connell & Rose wasn't one of New York's marquis names. Rather, they were up-and-comers, two sharp young lawyers who'd made a name for themselves at the U.S. Attorney's Office (prosecuting crooks like me) and who'd only recently made the leap into private practice, where they could earn some *real* bucks (defending crooks like me).

The firm's third partner, Charlie Rose, had died tragically of a malignant brain tumor. But the gold-plated sign on the office's walnut front door still bore his name, and there were numerous pictures of him on the walls of the reception area, the conference room, and the walls of both Nick's and Greg's offices. It was a sentimental touch not lost on me. In my mind, the message was clear: Nick and Greg were extremely loyal guys, the very sort of guys to whom I could entrust my freedom.

"Why don't you take a seat?" said a soothing Magnum, extending his mile-long arm toward my armchair. "You need to calm down a bit, buddy."

"I am calm," I muttered. "I'm real fucking calm. What the hell do I have to be nervous about, anyway? The fact that I'm facing three hundred years?" I shrugged and took my seat. "That's not so bad in the general scheme of things, is it?"

"You're not facing three hundred years," replied Magnum, in the tone a psychiatrist would normally use to coax a suicidal jumper off the edge of a bridge. "At worst, you're facing thirty years...or maybe thirty-five." Then he paused, pursing his lips like an undertaker. "*Although* there's an excellent chance the government's gonna try to supersede you."

I recoiled in my seat. "Supersede me? What are you talking about?" Of course, I knew exactly what the fuck he was talking about. After all, I had been under criminal investigation for the better part of my adult life, so I was an expert in these matters. Still, I thought that somehow, if I made *supersede me* sound like an entirely outlandish concept, it would make it that much less likely to happen.

"Let me clarify things," said the Yale-man. "Right now you're being charged with securities fraud and money laundering, but only on four stocks. Chances are they'll try to add on other charges—or *supersede you,* as the term goes. Don't be surprised if they try to indict you on the rest of the companies you took public. There were thirty-five in all, right?"

"More or less," I said casually, entirely numb at this point to the sort of bad news that would make the average man pee in his pants. Besides, what was the difference between thirty years and thirty-five? They were both life sentences, weren't they? The Duchess would be long gone, and my children would be completely grown up—married, most likely, with children of their own.

And what would be *my* fate? Well, I would end up one of those toothless old men, the sort of worthless wino who embarrasses his children and grandchildren when he shows up at their doorstep on holidays. I would be like that old jailbird Mr. Gower, the druggist from *It's a Wonderful Life.* He had once been a well-respected man in his community, until he poisoned an innocent child after receiving a telegram that his son had died in World War I. Last time I'd watched the movie, Mr. Gower had just been sprayed in the face with a bottle of seltzer and then kicked out of a bar on his ass.

I took a deep breath. *Christ*–I had to rein in all these stray thoughts! Even in good times my mind had a habit of running away from me. I said, "So tell me what my options are here. I mean, the thought of doing thirty years in jail doesn't exactly thrill me."

"*Wellllllll*," said Magnum, "the way I see it–and feel free to chime in here, Nick–you have three options. The first is to fight this thing to the end, to go all the way to trial and win an acquittal." He nodded his head once, letting the word *acquittal* hang in the air. "And if we *do* win, then that'll be that. This will all be behind you, once and for all."

"No double jeopardy," I added, feeling both proud and disturbed at my expertise in criminal law.

"Exactly," offered the Yale-man. "You can't be tried twice for the same crime. It'll be a case people talk about for years. Something that'll make Greg and I *big wheels around town*." Then he paused and smiled sadly. "But I strongly advise you against that course. I think it would be a big mistake to take this thing to trial. And I say this as your friend, Jordan, not as your attorney."

Now Magnum took over: "Understand, buddy, as a law firm we make much more money advising you to go to trial–probably ten times as much in a case like this. A trial as complicated as this would drag on forever–more than a year, probably–and the cost would be astronomical: ten million plus."

Now the Yale-man chimed in: "But if we *do* go to trial and you end up losing, it's going to be a total disaster. A disaster of biblical proportions. You'll get thirty years plus, Jordan, and–"

Magnum, overlapping: "–and you won't do your time in a federal prison camp, playing golf and tennis. You'll be in a federal penitentiary, with murderers and rapists." He shook his head gravely. "It'll be hell on earth."

I nodded in understanding, keenly aware how the feds housed their criminals. It was according to time: the more time you faced, the higher your security risk. Anything under ten years, with no violence in your background, and you qualified for a minimum-security prison. (Club Fed, so to speak.) But if your sentence was greater than ten years, they locked you in a place where a jar of Vaseline was more valuable than a truckload of weapons-grade plutonium.

Greg plowed on: "Now, as your friend, I would be *very* upset knowing you were locked in a place like that, especially when there were other options open to you—better options, I would say."

And Magnum kept right on talking, but I tuned out. I was already aware that going to trial wasn't an option. I knew that contrary to what most people thought, the sentences meted out for financial crimes were far worse than those for violent crimes. It was all in the amount: If investor losses exceeded a million dollars, the sentences were severe. And if investor losses topped a hundred million—as in my case—sentences were off the charts.

And there was more, starting with the fact was that I was guilty as sin. It was something Nick knew, Greg knew, and I knew too. For their part, Nick and Greg had represented me since the beginning—since the summer of 1994, when I'd made the fatal mistake of smuggling millions of dollars to Switzerland.

I had been under intense regulatory pressure at the time, starting with the SEC, which had become obsessed with my brokerage firm, Stratton Oakmont. I had started the place back in the fall of 1988, quickly discovering a wildly lucrative niche in the securities markets selling five-dollar stocks to the richest one percent of Americans. And *just like that,* Stratton became one of the largest brokerage firms in America.

In retrospect, things could have turned out much differently. Just as easily, I could have gone down the path of the straight and narrow—building a brokerage firm to rival Lehman Brothers or Merrill Lynch. As fate would have it, one of my first mentors, a true genius named Al Abrams, had a rather aggressive take on what constituted a violation of the federal securities laws. And Al was a careful man, the sort of man who kept ten-year-old pens in his drawer so when he backdated documents the ink would hold up to an FBI gas chromatograph. Al spent the better part of his day anticipating the moves of nosy securities regulators and covering his tracks accordingly.

And he was the one who'd taught me.

So, like Al, I had been careful too, covering my tracks with the zest and zeal of a sniper deep behind enemy lines. From the earliest days of Stratton, I was well aware that every trade I made, and every deal I consummated, and every word I spoke on the telephone would one day come under the microscope of a securities regulator. So, whether my actions were legitimate or not, they had damn well better appear to be that way.

In consequence, I had driven the SEC up the wall after they sued me in the fall of 1991, expecting an easy victory. They even went as far as setting up shop in my own conference room to try to intimidate me. Alas, things did not go as they planned: I ended up bugging my own conference room and setting the thermostat at alternating extremes–freezing them out in winter and burning them out in summer. Then I hired their ex-boss, a man named Ike Sorkin, to protect me, defend me, and undermine their investigation at every juncture. Meanwhile, between 1991 and 1994, I was making $50 million a year, as each of these young investigators (all of whom were making $30,000 a year) resigned in frustration and disgrace, and with terrible cases of frostbite or dehydration, depending on the season.

Eventually, I settled my case with the SEC. "Peace with honor," my lawyer had called it, although, to me, it was a total victory. I agreed to pay a $3 million fine and then walk off quietly into the sunset. The only problem was that I just couldn't bring myself to leave. I had become intoxicated with wealth and power, hooked on an entire generation of young Long Islanders calling me king and the Wolf. The buzzword of the day was instant gratification, and the ends justifying the means was the instrument of its assurance. And *just like that,* Stratton spiraled out of control. And I along with it.

By the early nineties, the Wolf of Wall Street was bearing his fangs. He was my devilish alter ego, a persona far removed from the child my parents had sent out into the world. My sense of right and wrong had all but vanished, my line of morality having moved toward the dark side in a series of tiny, almost imperceptible steps, which together landed me firmly on the wrong side of the law.

The Wolf was a despicable character; he cheated on his wife, slept with hookers, spent obscene amounts of money, and viewed securities laws as nothing more than shallow obstacles to be hurdled in a single bound. He justified his actions using absurd rationalizations, as he buried Jordan Belfort's guilt and remorse beneath obscene quantities of dangerous recreational drugs.

And all the while the government kept coming. Next it was NASDAQ, refusing to list any company in which the Wolf was the largest shareholder. The Wolf's solution–as insane as it now seems–was to smuggle millions of dollars to Switzerland, using their legendary bank-secrecy laws to try to turn himself into the invisible man. Through a series of shell corporations, numbered accounts, and expertly forged documents, the plan seemed perfect.

But from the very start it also seemed to be jinxed. The problems began when my chief money courier was arrested in the United States with half a million in cash, and the problems ended (in disaster) when my Swiss banker was arrested a few years later, also in the United States, at which point he began cooperating against my money courier.

Meanwhile, a young FBI agent named Gregory Coleman had become obsessed with the Wolf, vowing to take him down. In what would turn into a game of cat and mouse that became legendary within the FBI, Coleman followed my paper trail halfway around the world and then back again. And, finally, after five years of dogged legwork, he had connected enough dots to secure an indictment.

So here I was, six days post-arraignment, a victim of my own recklessness and Coleman's persistence. And there was Magnum, moving onto option two, which was a plea bargain. "...And while I can't promise you an exact sentence, I don't think it'll be more than seven years, or maybe eight at the most." He shrugged. "Let's use eight to be conservative."

"No fucking way!" I snapped. "Let's use *seven* and be optimistic, for Chrissake! They're *my* years—not *your* fucking years—so if I want to use seven of them, that's my fucking prerogative!"

The Yale-man said, "Okay, seven years is a fair number to work with. It's eighty-four months, before deductions, and—"

I cut off the Yale-man: "Ah, good, let's talk about my deductions! And feel free to exaggerate if you like. I promise I won't sue for malpractice."

They both smiled dutifully, and then the Yale-man continued: "The first deduction is for *good time.* You get fifteen percent for each year served. So, that's fifteen percent off eighty-four months—" He looked up at Magnum. "You got a calculator?"

"Forget the calculator," sputtered I, the math whiz. "It's seventy-one and a half months. But let's call it seventy-one, just to be fair. What's next?"

The Yale-man went on: "Well, you get six months in a halfway house, which is *almost* like being home. That brings you down to sixty-five months."

Now Magnum chimed in: "And then there's the drug-treatment program, which"—he let out a chuckle—"given your past history you'd definitely qualify for." He looked over at Nick. "He could probably *teach* the course, Nick, right?"

"One would think," replied the Yale-man, with a starchy shrug. "You'd make an excellent teacher, Jordan. I'm sure you'd make the class very interesting. Anyway, you get twelve months off for the drug program; so now you're down to fifty-three months."

Magnum said, "You see what I'm saying here, Jordan? It's not nearly as bad as you thought, right?"

"Yeah, one would think," and I took a moment to consider my fate. Four and a half years—well, it was certainly better than going to trial and risking becoming Mr. Gower. I would serve my time in Club Fed, playing tennis and golf, and be released around my fortieth birthday. I would have to pay a hefty fine, of course, but I still had enough money squirreled away to emerge from jail a wealthy man.

And then all at once it hit me: *I might even be able to sell this package to the Duchess!* Perhaps she would stay if she knew I was facing only four and a half years . . . although I could reduce that a bit, tell her that I was facing only four years. How would she know I was lying? Maybe I should say forty-eight months. Which sounded shorter? Probably forty-eight months, or maybe I would say forty-seven months and then follow it up with "That's less than four short years, baby!"

Wow, what a pleasant ring that had to it! *Less than four short years, baby!* It would be no more than a hiccup, something that could happen to any man of power. Yes, I would explain that to the Duchess, and she would understand. After all, I had been a terrific provider over the years. So why should she waste her time searching for a new gold mine when the gold mine she already had would be back in operation in *less than four short years, baby*!

". . . could always cooperate," said Magnum, raising his eyebrows two times in rapid succession. "Now if you go down *that* road, you might not even spend a day in jail; you could get straight probation. Although you'd probably have to do a year or so."

I had been too busy fantasizing about the backstabbing Duchess, so I'd missed the first half of what Magnum said. Apparently he had now moved on to option three: cooperating, also known as ratting. Call it what you will, I chose to ignore the latter part of Magnum's sentence prediction, and I said, with a trace of hope in my voice: "I won't have to do even a day in jail?"

Magnum shrugged. "I said it's a possibility. Not a guarantee. Once you become a cooperating witness, the sentencing guidelines are thrown out the window. The judge could do whatever he wants. He could give you probation, he could give you a year, or, theoretically, he could throw the book at you. Now, in your case, you have Judge Gleeson, who's the perfect judge for this sort of thing. He understands the importance of cooperation, so he'll be fair with you."

I nodded slowly, sensing daylight. "So he's pro-defense?"

"No," replied Magnum, bursting my bubble. "He's not pro-defense, and he's not pro-government. He's straight down the middle. He pretty much dances to his own tune. He's one of the smartest judges in the Eastern District, so no one's gonna pull the wool over his eyes, not you *or* the U.S. attorney. But that's a positive, because if you do the right thing, John will be fair with you. That much I can promise.

"By the way, don't call him John in the courtroom, unless you want to be held in contempt." He smiled and winked. "Just call him Your Honor, and you'll be fine."

Now the Yale-man chimed in: "Greg knows John as well as anybody. They used to work together at the U.S. Attorney's Office. They're friends."

Wait a second. *Did he just say friends? My lawyer is friends with the judge!* It was music to my ears.

It all made sense now. I had always known that Magnum was the perfect lawyer for me. I'd even looked past the fact that standing next to him made me feel like a shrimp. And in the end, look how well things had worked out! By sheer coincidence, my lawyer was friends with the judge, which meant he would wink at the judge *ever so subtly* just as the judge was about to announce my sentence, at which point the judge would nod back at Magnum *just as subtly* and then say, "Jordan Belfort, in spite of the fact that you stole a hundred million bucks and corrupted an entire generation of young Americans, I'm sentencing you to twelve months' probation and a one-hundred-dollar fine."

Meanwhile, the Duchess would be sitting in the courtroom—dressed to the nines and counting her lucky stars that she had decided to abandon her search for a new gold mine. After all, the Wolf's gold mine was about to reopen for ore extraction, simply because his lawyer was *friends with the judge*!

I smiled warmly at Magnum and said, "Well, this is some pretty good news, Greg." I shook my head slowly, breathing a sigh of relief. "Why didn't you say you were friends with the judge in the first place? It's a terrific development. *Really* terrific, if you catch my drift!" I winked at Magnum conspiratorially and rubbed my thumb and first two fingers together, as if to say, "Just tell me how much cash you need to pay off the judge!" Then I winked again.

"Whoa, whoa, whoa!" exclaimed Magnum, in a tone deep enough to wake the dead. "John is not like that! He's completely legitimate. He's the kind of judge who might end up on the

Supreme Court one day. Or at least the Court of Appeals. Either way, he won't do anything improper."

Fucking killjoy! I thought. My own lawyer won't go to bat for me. Instead, he's trying to take the wind out of my sails. I resisted the urge to tell him to go fuck himself, and I said, "Well, I wouldn't want to do anything to jeopardize anyone's career aspirations. Anyway, I don't think I'd make a very good cooperating witness, so it's a moot point."

Magnum seemed taken aback. "Why do you say that?"

"Yeah!" added a stunned Yale-man. "I couldn't disagree with you more. You'd make an excellent cooperating witness. Why would you think otherwise?"

I let out a deep sigh. "For a lot of reasons, Nick, not the least of which is that I'm at the very top of the food chain. Anybody I cooperate against will be a lesser figure than me. Not to mention the fact that most of the people the government would be interested in are my best friends. So, tell me, how the fuck am I supposed to rat out my best friends and maintain even one ounce of self-respect? I wouldn't be able to walk around Long Island with my head up. I'd be a leper." I paused, shaking my head in despair. "And if I decide to cooperate, I have to come clean about all my crimes, tell them everything, right?"

They both nodded.

I said, "That's what I thought. So, basically, I'll be pleading guilty to the whole ball of wax, which means my fine is gonna be enormous. I'll be totally wiped out"–which would mean bye-bye, Duchess–"starting from scratch again. I don't think I could handle that right now. I've got a wife and kids to think about. I mean, what's better: spending four years in jail, while my family lives in the lap of luxury, or spending a year in jail, while my family wonders where their next meal's coming from?"

"It's not so cut-and-dry," replied Magnum. "I mean, yes, you'd definitely be pleading guilty to everything. That's the way it works when you cooperate. But, no, you won't be wiped out. The government would leave you with something to live on–maybe a million bucks or so. But everything else would go: the houses, the cars, the bank accounts, the stock portfolios–everything."

There were a few moments of silence. Then Nick said with great warmth: "You're a young guy, Jordan. And you're also one of the smartest guys I've ever met." He smiled sadly. "You'll rebuild. Mark my words: You will rebuild your fortune. One day you'll be back on top again, and nobody in their right mind would bet against you."

"He's right," added Greg. "If you think this is the end for you, you're seriously mistaken. This is the beginning. It's time to start your life anew. You're a winner. Don't ever forget that." He paused for a brief instant. "Yeah, you've made some mistakes along the way, some big mistakes. But that doesn't take away from the fact that you're a winner. Next time you'll do things right. You'll be older and wiser, and you'll build your foundation on stone instead of sand. And then no one will be able to take it away from you. Nobody."

He nodded his head slowly, sagely. "And as far as ratting out your friends goes, I wouldn't be so concerned with it. If the shoe were on the other foot, every last one of them would turn on you. Right now you gotta do what's right for you and your family. That's all that matters. Forget the rest of the world, because they would certainly forget about you." Now he changed his tone to one of nostalgia. "You know, we used to have a saying in the U.S. Attorney's Office: The Italians sing on Mulberry Street, and the Jews sing on Court Street. In other words, people in the Mafia don't cooperate, they don't 'sing' on other mobsters. But it's all a load of crap now. With RICO, the sentences start at twenty years and they go up from there. So the mobsters sing too. The Jews sing, the Italians sing, the Irish sing. Everyone sings."

He shrugged his wide shoulders. "Anyway, the bigger problem I see with cooperating is Joel Cohen, the assistant U.S. attorney–the AUSA–on your case." Magnum let out a great sigh. Then, in staccato-like beats, he said, "Joel–Cohen–can–not–be–trusted. I repeat: He–can–not–be–trusted. He–is–a–bad–egg."

Then Nick chimed in: "Greg's right about that. We've had some bad experiences with Joel in the past. See, the way it works when you cooperate is, the AUSA is supposed to write a letter to the judge, saying how helpful you've been and what a great witness you've been, and so on. Now, Joel, by law, will have to write the letter, but here's where it gets tricky. You see, what he actually writes is up to him. If he wants to stick it to you, he can color the letter in a negative way. Then you're up shit's creek."

"Well, fuck that!" I muttered. "That's a disaster in the making, Nick." I shook my head in amazement. "And, no offense, but I don't need the two of you to tell me that Joel Cohen is an asshole. I could tell that just by looking at him. I mean, did you hear that scumbag at my bail hearing? If it were up to him they would nail me to a crucifix."

"But it's not up to him," argued Magnum. "In fact, it probably won't even be Joel who writes your letter when the time comes. See, if you cooperate, it'll drag on for four or five years, and you won't get sentenced until after your cooperation is through. There's an excellent possibility Joel will have already left the office by then–joining the ranks of us humble defense attorneys."

We spent the next few minutes debating the pros and cons of cooperating, and the more I learned about it, the less it appealed to me. No one would be off-limits; I would be forced to cooperate against all my old friends. The only exceptions would be my father, who'd been Stratton's Chief Financial Officer (he hadn't done anything illegal, anyway), and my longtime assistant Janet* (who'd done illegal things but was so low on the totem pole that no one would care). Greg assured me that I could get both of them "passes."

What bothered me most, though, was the thought of cooperating against my ex-partner, Danny Porush, who had been indicted along with me and was still sitting in jail, trying to make bail. And then there was my oldest friend, Alan Lipsky. He was also under indictment, although his case was only partially related to mine. I couldn't imagine cooperating against Alan. We had been best friends since diapers. He was more a brother to me than my own brother.

Just then came an insolent burble from Greg's telephone. His secretary said rather casually, "Joel Cohen is on line one. Would you like to take it or should I tell him you'll call back?"

---

*Name has been changed

At that very moment, inside the twenty-sixth-floor corner office of De Feis O'Connell & Rose, you could have heard a pin drop. The three of us just sat there, staring at one another, mouths agape. I said it first: "That rat bastard! He's superseding me already! Holy shit! Ho-lee fuc-king shit!"

Magnum and the Yale-man nodded their heads in agreement. Then Magnum put a forefinger to his lips and said, "Shhhh," and he picked up the phone. "Hey, Joel, howaya?... Uhn-huhn... Uhn-huhn. Right, well, it just so happens I have your favorite person sitting right in front of me.... Yeah, that's right. We were just talking about what a blatant miscarriage of justice this whole thing is." Greg winked at me confidently and then leaned back in his seat and began rocking. He was a mighty warrior, ready to take on the insolent Joel Cohen. Magnum could crush him with a single gust. "Uhn-huhn," continued Magnum, rocking back and forth. "Uhn-huhn... Uhn-huhn–" And then all at once his face dropped, and he stopped rocking in his fabulous black leather throne, as if the finger of God had descended upon him. My heart skipped a beat right before Magnum said, "Whoa, whoa, whoa, Joel. Settle down. Don't be doing anything rash here. You can't be serious about that. She's not the sort of–Uhn-huhn... Uhn-huhn... Well, I'll talk to him about it. Don't do anything until I get back to you."

She? I thought. What the fuck was Magnum talking about! She who? She Janet? Were they after Janet? That made no sense. Janet was merely an assistant. Why would they want her? A visibly shaken Magnum hung up the phone and uttered the five most poisonous words I'd ever heard in my life. He said, without a trace of tone, "They're indicting your wife tomorrow."

There were a few moments of eerie silence, and then all at once I popped out of my armchair and screamed, "*What!* No fucking way! How can they do that? She hasn't done anything! How can they indict the Duchess?"

The Yale-man threw his palms up in the air and shrugged. Then he opened his mouth to say something, but no words came out. I turned back to Magnum and said in a tone of ultimate despair, "Oh, shit... Oh, my God... Oh–my–fuc–king–God!"

"Calm down," said Magnum. "You gotta calm down. Joel's not

going to do anything yet. He promised he'd wait until I spoke to you."

"Spoke to me about what? I–I don't get it. How could they indict my wife? She didn't do anything."

"According to Joel, they have a witness who says she was in the room with you when you were counting money. But listen to me: The facts aren't really important. Joel doesn't have an interest in indicting Nadine. He made that clear to me. He just wants you to cooperate; that's the beginning and the end of it. If you cooperate, your wife gets a pass. Otherwise, they're going to arrest her tomorrow. It's your call." With that, Magnum looked at his wristwatch. It was one of those purposely understated, superexpensive jobs, with a chocolate-brown leather band and a pearl-white face. Had to set him back $20,000, I figured, but it was the sort of watch that was supposed to say, "I'm so successful and confident that I don't need to wear a gleaming gold wristwatch to project an image of success and confidence." Magnum added, "He gave me until four o'clock to get back to him; that's four hours from now. Tell me what you want to do."

Well, it was plainly obvious that I had no choice. I would have to cooperate now, regardless of the consequences. After all, I couldn't let Joel indict my wife. Not in a million years.

Wait a second! All at once a series of delicious thoughts came bubbling up into my brain, starting with: How could the Duchess leave if she were under indictment too? She would be stuck with me then, wouldn't she? We would be like two peas in a pod. I mean, what man in his right mind would take on the burden of an indicted woman with two children?

Yes, the Duchess might be a world-class piece of ass, but two young children and a federal indictment hanging over her head would make her much less enticing to the average gold mine.

In fact, I would have to say that virtually all gold mines–or at least the more productive ones–would quickly close their shafts to a woman burdened with such dire circumstances. She would become a cautionary tale in her own right, a young woman with more baggage than the lost-luggage warehouse at Kennedy Airport.

So, yes, that was the answer then; there was no other way: I would let the Duchess go down in flames with me. I would let her get indicted too. She would have no choice then but to stay married to me. It was my only logical move. It was my only *rational* move. I looked Magnum in the eye and twisted my lips subversively, and I said, "You call that rat bastard right now and tell him to go fuck himself." I paused for a moment and watched every last ounce of color drain from his long, handsome face. Then I added, "And then after *that,* you can tell him that I'll cooperate." With that, Magnum expelled a giant gust of air, as did the Yale-man. I said, "I mean, I really don't care anymore, even if I end up going to jail for twenty years. I just really don't give a shit."

It was pure, unadulterated irony. My wife had dumped me in my darkest and most desperate hour, yet I was still willing to fall on my sword to protect her. Talk about the world being upside down.

Magnum nodded slowly. "You're doing the right thing, Jordan."

"You are," added Nick. "It'll work out in the end."

I looked at the Yale-man and shrugged. "Maybe it will, Nick, or maybe it won't. Only time will tell. Either way, I *am* doing the right thing. That much I know for sure. Nadine's the mother of my children, and I won't let her do a day in jail, not if I can help it."

CHAPTER 4

A LOVE-HATE RELATIONSHIP

Later that evening, a few minutes before midnight, I was lying beneath my white silk comforter, alone with my thoughts. I felt completely lost, like a man without a country, a man without purpose. And I also felt like a man who had been set adrift into a vast ocean of white Chinese silk. Oh, yes, the Duchess had decorated this room to the nines–in fact, the whole house had been decorated to the nines, but especially this room, which was now fit for a king, and as such a mockery of the fallen Wolf.

What was I now? How far had I fallen? I was under house arrest and being dumped by a gold-digging Duchess: a British Brooklynite who had the face of an angel, the temper of Mount Vesuvius, and the loyalty of a starving hyena.

I took a deep breath and tried to grab hold of myself. Christ, I was a wreck! I sat up and looked around the room. I was stark naked, totally exposed. I crossed my arms, as if embarrassed. I squinted. Jesus, it was dark in here. The only light was coming from that flat-panel TV screen suspended on the wall, above the limestone fireplace. The volume was on mute, so the room was eerily silent. I could hear the sound of my own shallow breathing, as well as the *thump thump thump* of my own broken heart.

And just where *was* my dear heartbreaking wife? Well, that was still somewhat of a mystery to me. Supposedly she was in Manhattan, out with the girls. At least that's what the note said—some nonsense about having to attend her friend Gigi's thirtieth birthday party, which I distinctly remembered celebrating three months ago, in June. Or maybe I was just paranoid and the back-stabbing Duchess could still be trusted.

I had found the note lying on the kitchen counter, beneath a $1,400 Winnie the Pooh ceramic cookie jar (a collector's item of some sort, bought at auction), with the words *Dear* and *Love* conspicuously absent from the salutation and the closing. It was like a note between two strangers—one named Jordan, the other Nadine—neither of whom loved or respected the other. Just reading it had sent my spirits plunging even lower.

On a more positive note, however, since leaving Magnum's office I had pretty much come to terms with my cooperation, or at least I'd rationalized it to the point of palatability. Yes, I would provide the government with whatever info they wanted, but I would be clever about it—providing it in such a way as to protect my friends. When necessary, I would feign ignorance; when plausible, I would feign memory lapses; and, most importantly, when I reached a crossroads or found myself at a fork in the road, I would steer the government down the trail that led away from my friends. Hopefully, with a little bit of luck, the people I cared about most would cooperate too, and I would be spared having to betray them.

Meanwhile, the Duchess would be *thrilled* I was cooperating. One of her chief gripes was that I had put her at risk, and now I could tell her that risk was no longer a possibility. Of course, I would omit the fact that I actually *had* put her at risk. I was no fool, after all, so what was the point of giving her fresh ammo against me? It would be much more productive to focus on the positive aspects of my cooperation: namely, that I wouldn't have to do even a day in jail and that even after I paid my fine we—*we!*—would still have enough money left over for the rest of our lives. And while those were small exaggerations–actually, the last one was a fucking whopper–it would be many years before the Duchess found out. So I would worry about it then.

Just then I heard the sound of gravel kicking up in the driveway. The backstabbing Duchess was finally home, ready to inflict more emotional pain on me. A few moments later I heard the front door slam and then some very angry-sounding footsteps ascending the sumptuous spiral stairs. The footsteps didn't seem to belong to a hundred-twelve-pound blond-headed Duchess; they seemed to belong to an agitated water buffalo. I laid flat on my back and braced myself for the torture.

The door swung open and in walked the Duchess, wearing a light-blue wrangler's ensemble. Jesus! Despite the fact that the Duchess had taken a limousine home, she looked like she'd just arrived by stagecoach from the Western frontier. All she was missing was a cowboy hat and a pair of six-shooters. As she moseyed her way over to her side of the bed, I took a moment to regard her. She was wearing a long, stonewashed denim skirt with tiny white cowgirl ruffles on the bottom and a fabulous slit that ran up the front. I wasn't much of an expert on women's skirts, but I had a sneaky suspicion that few women on the Ponderosa could have afforded this one. She wore a short-sleeve light-blue cotton blouse, very low cut in the front and very tight in the waist, accentuating the natural V of her body as well as her surgically enhanced C-cups.

Without saying a word, the Western Duchess reached beneath a burnt-apricot-colored lamp shade on the end table and flicked on the light. I rolled onto my right side and stared at her. She really knew how to put herself together. I couldn't begrudge her that even now.

I looked down . . . ahhh, the cowboy boots! Those were familiar. They were tan and white, with cherry-red toe caps and sterling-silver tips. I had bought them for her last year, in a fit of euphoria, while I was on a golf trip in Texas. They had set me back $13,000. At the time they'd seemed liked a bargain. Now I wondered.

Just then she cocked her blond head to the right and removed a sterling-silver earring and placed it on the end table with great care. Then she cocked her head to the left and removed the left earring and placed it beside the other. I forced a smile and resisted the urge to say, "Eh, baby, how was prospecting tonight? Find any precious ore?" With great love and tenderness in my voice, I said, "Hey, sweetie. How was Gigi's party?"

"Okay," she said, with a surprising pleasantness. "Nothing special," and she turned to face me and nearly lost her balance, at which point I realized that the wrangling Duchess had more to drink this evening than just sarsaparilla. In fact, she was stone-cold drunk.

"Are you okay?" I asked, holding back a smile and getting ready to catch her if she fell. "You need any help, sweetie?"

She shook her head no. With a bit of a wobble, she sat down on the edge of the mattress. Then, all at once, faster than you would know it, she swung her cowboy boots onto the bed, rolled onto her side, and plopped her left elbow down beside me. She rested her left cheek in the palm of her hand and looked into my eyes and smiled. She said, "How'd it go with your lawyer today?"

Very interesting, I thought, making a mental note to thank the Mexican genius who'd invented tequila, as well as the bartender who had been gracious enough to serve the Duchess one too many this evening. This was the closest the Duchess had come to me in almost a week. And she looked rather beautiful right now, in the burnt-apricot glow of the lamp shade. Those big blue eyes of hers, which were now glassier than a mirror, were gorgeous. I took a deep breath to relish her scent, which was an interesting mixture of Angel perfume and premium-grade tequila. I felt a pleasant tingling sensation–a rush of fire in the loins! *Perhaps,* I thought, *perhaps tonight.* I felt an uncontrollable urge to jump her bones right now, before she sobered up and started to torture me again. But I resisted the urge and said, "Really good, sweetie. Actually, I have some terrific news for you."

"Oh, yeah? Whuz that?" she asked, and she began rubbing my cheek with the palm of her hand. Then she ran her fingers through my hair with great tenderness.

I couldn't believe it! The Duchess had finally come to her senses! She was going to make love to me this very fucking instant and then everything would be okay again. It had always been that way with us. Things could be bad for a while, but not much longer than that. In the end, we would always make love and then all would be forgotten.

Should I jump her right now? I wondered. How would she react? Would she be angry with me or would she respect me? I was a *man,* after all, and the Duchess understood such things. She was wise to the ways of the world, especially when it came to men, and even more especially when it came to their manipulation...

...although to jump her now would not be the prudent thing to do. First I needed to put a good spin—no, a *great* spin—on my legal problems. I needed her to feel entirely confident that my gold mine was about to open once more for unfettered ore extraction.

I took a deep breath, coagulating all the loose ends of my bullshit story, and I went for broke. "First of all," I said, with great confidence, "I know you were worried about all that crap Coleman spewed at you, and I just wanted you to know that none of that—not even one drop of it—was ever a possibility." And that would be lie number one. "You and I both know that you never did anything wrong"—and that would be lie number two, considering she actually *had* witnessed me counting money, as Joel Cohen had alleged—"and, of course, the government knows that too. Coleman just said that to scare you and to make things difficult for me. That's it."

She nodded slowly. "I know that," she replied. "I mean, it bothered me when he first said it, but I never actually believed it."

You didn't? Hmmm, okay, then! Ignorance is definitely bliss. I nodded in agreement and soldiered on: "Yeah, of course I know. It was all bullshit, Nae"—and here comes lie number three—"the whole damn lot of it. But, either way, it's all a moot point now. You see, Joel Cohen called Greg today; in fact, he called him right while I was sitting in the room, and he told him that what he really wanted—what he was really looking for—was for me to cooperate. That's it." I shrugged. "Apparently, I know so much about what's going on in the stock market that I could save the government years of heartache, not to mention countless dollars." Hmmm, I really liked the way that sounded. It made me sound smart, vital, important, altruistic, a necessary participant in the fight against greed and corruption on Wall Street; not like the cooperating rat I was about to become! I decided to milk that line of thinking for all it was worth. "Anyway, Joel said that if I *did* cooperate, if I was willing to help the government make sense of everything, I probably wouldn't have to spend even a day in jail. That's how valuable the knowledge I have is." I nodded a single time, wondering if I had shot myself in the foot by using the word *probably,* so I added, "I mean, I already spent three days in jail, which is long enough, don't you think?" I smiled innocently.

She nodded slowly but remained silent. I noticed a tear running down her cheek. I wiped it away with the back of my hand. A good sign, I thought. Wiping away a woman's tears brought you one step closer to her heart and, for that matter, her loins. It was a biological phenomenon. When a strong man wiped away a woman's tears, she could refuse him nothing.

Emboldened by the Duchess's tears, I continued with relish: "But it gets even better, Nae. You see, if I cooperate, I won't get sentenced for four or five years, and any fine I might"–*might*–"have to pay wouldn't be due until then. I mean, don't get me wrong, it's gonna be a pretty hefty fine, but it's not something that's gonna wipe us"–*us*–"out. We'll still be very rich when it's all over." And there goes the biggest lie of all, the whopper, which was lie number four.

In fact, if the government were to leave me with a million dollars, as Magnum had indicated, the Duchess and I would be broke in three months. But I had rationalized that too, which was why I now added, "But however much money they leave us"–*us*–"with, it's not like I'm gonna retire or anything. I mean, in a few months from now, once all this commotion dies down, I'm gonna start trading stocks again." I paused, not quite liking the way that sounded. "I mean honestly, of course. I'm talking big stocks, not small stocks. I'm not going back to all the craziness and everything." I found myself desperately searching for an exit ramp. "Anyway, I could probably make five or ten million a year just trading for my own account, totally legitimately, without any risk."

I studied her face for a moment. She seemed to be sobering up a bit. Hmmm, I wasn't sure if that was good or bad, but I sensed a window of opportunity slamming shut. It was time to stop selling the future and to go for the close. I said confidently, "That's it, Nae. That's the whole ball of wax. I know it sounds too good to be true, but that's the way it is. I guess I should just count my lucky stars that the government is so desperate for the information I have." Now I paused, and I shook my head gravely. "Anyway, the only thing I was really upset about was that I might have to give them information about my friends." I smiled and shrugged, as if to say, "There's a silver lining here!" Then I said, "But, according to Mag–I mean, Greg, all my friends are going to cooperate too." I shrugged again. "So in the end that won't really be a factor." I edged myself closer to her and began running my fingers through her hair.

She smiled and said, "Well, that's really good news, honey. I'm really happy for you."

You? Did she just say *you*? Shit–that was bad! She should be happy for us, not just me! I was about to correct her when she added, "And I wouldn't be too worried about your friends. Other than Alan Lipsky, every last one of them would sell you down the river in two seconds flat. There's no loyalty on Wall Street. You always told me that, right?"

I nodded but didn't say a word. In fact, I had heard enough and spoken enough. Once more, the Duchess and I were back on the same page, which is to say, it was time to attack. I reached over and grabbed her around the waist and pulled her close to me. Then I grabbed her by her cute Western tie and yanked her head toward me.

And then I kissed her.

It was a slow wet kiss, an altogether loving kiss, which ended quicker than I'd hoped, when she pulled away and said, "Stop it! I'm still mad at you."

It was time to take charge. "I need you," I groaned, reaching my hand up the slit of her dress, heading for the Promised Land. By the time I reached the top of her thigh, the heat was so terrific I was ready to come on the sheets.

So I pounced, throwing my full weight on top of her. I began kissing her ferociously. She tried to wriggle free, but she was no match for me. "Stop!" she whined, with a hint of a giggle. "Stop it!"

I hung on the giggle and pulled up her denim skirt, revealing her pretty pink vulva with its tiny Mohawk of blond peach fuzz. Ahh, I had always marveled at what a terrific vagina the Duchess had! It was the most delectable vagina I'd ever seen, and considering I'd slept with almost a thousand hookers, my opinion counted for something. But all that hooker business was in the past now. All I wanted was the Duchess–now and forever!

I slowed my tempo a bit, and I looked her in the eyes and said, "I love you, Nae. I love you so much." My eyes began welling up with tears. "I've always loved you, from the first moment I laid eyes on you." I smiled at her warmly. "I missed you so much this week. I can't even begin to tell you how empty I've felt." I pushed her hair back with my hand and went for the close: "Make love to me, baby. Make love to me right now, nice and slow."

"Fuck you!" she sputtered. "I fucking hate you! You wanna fuck me? Fine–then go ahead and fuck me! Fuck me hard, because I fucking hate you. I hate your guts, you selfish little prick! You don't give a shit how I feel. All you care about is yourself." She started grinding into me with contempt, purposely keeping out of tempo with me. It was as if she was trying to let me know that, in spite of me being inside her, she still wasn't mine.

I was shocked. And I was devastated. But, most of all, I was upset that she had called me little–a little prick, to be exact. The Duchess knew I was self-conscious about my height!

But I refused to get angry. Instead, I grabbed her cheeks and nailed her with a kiss, holding my lips to hers as I desperately tried to get some rhythm going. But it was difficult. She was moving her blond head from side to side, like an infant refusing a spoonful of applesauce, and she was swerving her hips in an exaggerated circular motion.

With a bit of anger slipping out around the edges, I snapped, "Hold still, Nadine! What's wrong with you!"

Her poisonous response: "Fuck you! I hate you–I fucking *hate* you!" She grabbed my cheeks and said, with venom: "Look in my eyes, Jordan. Look in my eyes right now."

I looked. She continued: "Don't ever forget what went down with this marriage; don't you ever fucking forget." Her blue eyes were like glassy death rays. "This is the last time I'm ever gonna fuck you. This is it; you can mark my words. You're never gonna have me again, so you better enjoy it while it lasts." And she started grinding into me with deep, rhythmic thrusts, as if she were trying to make me come, right on the spot.

Jesus Christ! I thought. She'd turned the corner on her tequila high! She couldn't possibly mean what she was saying, could she? How could such a beautiful face spew out such venom? It made no sense. I knew the right thing to do would be to climb off her, to not give her the satisfaction of making me come while she was telling me how much she hated me... but she looked absolutely gorgeous in the burnt-apricot glow of the lamp shade. *So fuck it!* I thought. It was impossible to figure women out, and if she was genuinely serious about this being my last time, I better make it count or at least make myself come quickly, before she changed her mind and said that the last time was the last time... and with a single deep thrust I tried my best to hit the base of her cervix and... *bang!*... just like that I came inside her. I screamed, "I love you, Nae!" to which she screamed, "I fucking hate you, you asshole!" and then I collapsed on top of her.

And there we lay for what seemed like a very long time, which turned out to be around five seconds, at which point she pushed me off and started crying hysterically. Her body was shaking volcanically, as she said through terrible, gut-wrenching sobs, "Oh, my God! What did I do? What did I do?" She kept repeating those same four words, as I lay next to her, frozen in horror.

I tried to put my arm around her, but she pushed it away.

Then came more sobs, and then she said something that I would never forget for the rest of my life. "It was blood money!" she sobbed. "It was all blood money!" She could barely get the words out through her sobs. "I knew it all along, and I did nothing. People lost money and I spent it. Oh, God–what did I do?"

All at once I found myself growing intensely angry. It was her reference to blood money, the thought that everything we shared—including my own success—was somehow tainted. It was as if our entire marriage had been a farce, as if nothing around me was real and genuine. I was a man of parts, the sum of which didn't equal a whole. I was surrounded by wealth and beauty and ostentation, yet I felt poor and ugly and hopelessly embarrassed. I longed for simpler days. I longed for a simpler life. I longed for a simpler wife.

Making no effort to hide my displeasure, I went right back at her. "Blood money," I sputtered. "Give me a fucking break, Nadine! I work on Wall Street; I'm not a fucking mobster." I shook my head in disgust. "Yeah—I cut a few corners, just like everybody else, so get a fucking grip!"

Through terrible sobs, from deep in the breadbasket: "Oh, God, you corrupted everyone—even my own mother! And I . . . I . . . just stood there and . . . and watched . . . and . . . and . . . spent . . . the . . . the . . . blood . . . mon . . . ney!" She was sobbing so uncontrollably that her words were coming out one at a time.

"Your mother?" I screamed. "You know how good I've been to your mother? When I met her she was getting thrown out of her fucking apartment for not paying her fucking rent! And I took care of your idiot brother and your idiot fucking father, and your sister and you and everybody else, *God damn it!* And this is what I get in return?" I paused, trying to collect myself. I was crying too now, although I was so angry my own tears were lost on me. "I can't fucking believe this," I screamed. "I can't fucking believe this! How the fuck could you do this now? You're my wife, Nadine. How could you do this now?"

"I'm sorry," she sobbed. "I'm sorry. I didn't mean to hurt you." She was shaking like a leaf. "I didn't mean to . . . I didn't mean to," and she rolled off the bed, onto the $120,000 Edward Fields carpet, and she curled up in the fetal position and continued to cry uncontrollably.

And that was that.

I knew right then and there that I had lost my wife forever. Whatever bond the Duchess and I had once shared had now been severed. Whether or not I would ever get to make love to her again was still a matter of question, and, in truth, I couldn't have cared less. After all, I was facing much bigger problems than where to get my rocks off.

In fact, just down the hall were our two young children, the innocent victims in all this, who were about to wake up to one of the cruelest realities of life:

Nothing lasts forever.

CHAPTER 5

OCD AND THE MORMON

The next morning, I was back in the limousine again.

This time, however, the closet terrorist wasn't driving me through the gloomy groin of western Queens; rather, he was driving me through the rancid gullet of western Brooklyn. In fact, we were making our way through a demographic nightmare known as Sunset Park, a neighborhood *so* ethnically diverse–loaded with Chinese and Koreans and Malaysians and Vietnamese and Thais and Puerto Ricans and Mexicans and Dominicans and Salvadorans and Guatemalans, along with a handful of remarkably dim-witted Finns, who were too slow on the uptake to realize that the rest of their Finnish brethren had fled for their lives thirty years ago, when the ethnic hordes invaded–that, staring out the side window, I felt like we were driving through the parking lot of the United Nations after a missile strike.

Yes, this part of Sunset Park was, indeed, a shithole. It was a flat swath of dirt and asphalt punctuated by dilapidated warehouses, deserted storefronts, rotting piers, and bird poop. Downtown Manhattan–where I would ultimately be heading this morning–

was just a few miles to the west, on the other side of the polluted East River. From my current vantage point, in the limo's right backseat, I could see the swirling waters of the river, the towering skyline of Lower Manhattan, and the glorious arc of the Verrazano-Narrows Bridge, stretching to the not-so-glorious borough of Staten Island.

According to plan, at precisely nine a.m., Monsoir pulled in front of a grimy underground parking garage on the south side of a grimy two-way street. As I climbed out of the limousine, I said, "Stay put until I beep you, Monsoir," and while I'm gone don't be blowing up any bridges, I thought. Then I slammed the door in his face and walked down a short flight of steps to the lower level of the parking garage.

I heard a familiar voice: "Jordan! Over here!"

I turned to my right, and there was Special Agent Gregory Coleman. He was standing in front of a typical government-issue car, which is to say: four doors, no dents, perhaps two years old, and made in America. In fact, it was a 1997 maroon Ford Taurus with lightly tinted windows and no siren. He was leaning against the rear passenger-side door with his arms crossed, the pose of the victorious warrior.

Standing beside him, with a kind smile on his face, was his partner-in-training, Special Agent Bill McCrogan. I had met McCrogan only once, on the night of my arrest, and for some inexplicable reason I had liked him. He seemed too kind to be an FBI agent, although I was certain that once Coleman got through with him he wouldn't be so kind anymore. McCrogan was a few inches taller than Coleman, the better part of five-ten, and he looked about thirty. He had a thick thatch of curly brown hair, broad features, and an entirely average build. Over his pale-blue eyes he wore a pair of wire-rimmed glasses that made him look God-fearing. A Mormon, I figured, probably from Salt Lake City or Provo, or maybe even the hills of Idaho... although who really gave a shit.

Coleman, on the other hand, looked Italian or Greek, although I had him figured as a German, because of his last name. Yes, he was probably from the hills of Bavaria. He was about the same height as me, a little over five-seven, and he weighed no more than one-sixty. He was broad in the chest, but not overly so. His features were fine and even, although they were a bit on the pointy side and seemed to ooze suspicion, especially at me. He had short brown hair, parted to the side, and there were a few strands of gray by his ears. But those must have been the result of him chasing after me for the last five years, which would be enough to make any man gray. He had smooth olive skin, an aquiline nose, a high forehead, and the most piercing brown eyes imaginable. They looked sharper than a hawk's. He was about my age, which meant that the bastard had been on my tail since he was in his late twenties! Christ–what kind of man could become so obsessed with bringing someone else to justice? I mean, really, how bad a case of OCD did this guy have? And why had he become OCD-ed with me? What a fucking shame that was.

"Welcome to Team USA!" said Agent OCD, smiling broadly and extending his right hand, the wrist of which sported a black plastic watch with a circular face and a suggested retail price somewhere below $59.99.

I shook his hand warily and searched his face for irony. But all I found was what appeared to be a genuine smile. "Thanks," I muttered, "but I figured you'd be gloating a bit." I shrugged. "I mean, I wouldn't blame you if you did."

The Mormon chimed in: "Gloating? He's been miserable since the day he caught you! It was the chase he loved"–he looked at Agent OCD–"right, Greg?"

OCD rolled his eyes and shook his head. "Yeah, whatever," and he smiled at me once more, except *this* smile was peppered with sadness. "Anyway, I'm glad you finally decided to join the good guys. You're doing the right thing here. You really are."

I shrugged again. "Yeah, well I feel like a bit of a louse."

"You're not a louse," he shot back.

"Definitely not," added the Mormon, with a toothy Mormon smile. "You're much worse than a louse!" And he laughed a warm Mormon laugh and then extended his God-fearing hand for a Mormon handshake.

I smiled at the kindhearted guy and shook his hand dutifully. Then I took a moment to regard my two new friends. They both wore dark blue suits, crisp white dress shirts, conservative blue neckties, and black lace-up shoes. (Typical G-man's ensemble.) They looked pretty good, actually; everything fit together nicely, and their suits had been pressed to near perfection.

Either way, my ensemble was terribly smarter than theirs. I had felt it was important to look good on my first day of ratting, so I'd chosen my outfit carefully. I was wearing a $2,200 single-breasted navy serge suit, a white oxford dress shirt with a conservative button-down collar, a solid navy crepe de chine necktie, and black lace-up shoes. But unlike their shoes, which were clodhoppers, mine were made of buttery-soft napa leather. In fact, they had been custom-made in England for $1,800. *Good for me!* I thought. I had them beaten hands down in the shoe department.

And in the watch department too.

Indeed. For today's festivities I was sporting my $26,000 Swiss Tabbah, with its chocolate-brown leather band and oversize white rectangular face. It was the sort of ultrafine Swiss watch that reeked of wealth to those in the know yet would come off as nothing special to people in Coleman and McCrogan's income bracket. It had been a clever move on my part, to leave the Bulgari home in its cage this morning. After all, why make my new friends jealous, or did they now have the right to grab my watch right off my fucking wrist and put it on theirs? (The spoils of war, so to speak.) Hmmm . . . I would have to ask Magnum about that.

The Mormon and I were still shaking hands, when he added, "In all seriousness, though, you *are* doing the right thing here, Jordan. Welcome to Team USA!"

"Yeah," I replied, in a tone laced with irony. "I'm doing the only thing I can do, right?"

They both pursed their lips and nodded slowly, as if to say, "Yes, threatening to indict a man's wife leaves him few options, now, doesn't it!" Then Coleman said, "Anyway, I'm sorry about all this cloak-and-dagger stuff, but we think some of your old friends might try to have you followed. So we're gonna drive you around the streets of Brooklyn for a while to shake off any tails."

Wonderful! I thought. Agent OCD must have information he's not sharing with me–like somebody wants me dead! It had never occurred to me that I might get assassinated over this cooperation business, but now that I thought about it, it would make perfect sense to a lot of people, wouldn't it? In fact, maybe I should just assassinate myself right now and save everyone else the trouble. Of course the Duchess would be thrilled about that, wouldn't she? She would dance on my grave, chanting, "It was blood money! It was blood money!" and then she would light a ceremonial fire and set our marriage certificate ablaze.

Christ, I had to get a grip here! I needed to focus. I needed to keep that blond-headed scoundrel out of my thoughts. It was these two rat bastards I needed to focus on. I took a deep breath and said, "Who do you think might be after me?"

OCD shrugged. "I don't know. Who do *you* think might be after you?"

I returned his shrug. "I don't know. I guess everybody, right?" I paused for an instant, then added, "Or everybody except my wife. I mean, she couldn't give a shit where I am, or where I'm going, for that matter, as long as I'm not going near her."

"Really?" said OCD. "Why do you say that?"

"Because she fucking hates me! That's why I say that!" And because last night she told me she would never let me stick it inside her again, I said to myself.

"Huh," he muttered. "That surprises me."

"Oh, yeah? Why is that?"

OCD shrugged once more. "I don't know. The night you were arrested it seemed like she really loved you. In fact, I asked her if she loved you and she told me that she did."

"It's true," added the Mormon.

I narrowed my eyes, as if confused. "Why would you guys ask my wife that? I mean, isn't that a little off the beaten trail?"

"Wellllll," chirped OCD, "you'd be surprised what we get out of a wife if she's disgruntled. In fact, sometimes the wife will be scream-

ing, 'My husband has cash hidden in the basement! He cheats on his taxes!' right as I'm escorting the husband away in handcuffs." OCD chuckled at that. "But not your wife. She didn't say anything."

"Not a thing," added the Mormon. "I mean, I could be mistaken, but I think your wife still loves you."

"I hate to break up the party," mused Coleman, "but we need to get the show on the road. Anyway, this place smells like, uh..."

"Dog shit?" I offered.

"Yeah, pretty much," he replied, opening the rear passenger door and motioning for me to climb in. "Just lay across the backseat and try to keep your head down, okay?"

I stared at OCD for a good few seconds, wondering if he was alluding to the possibility of a sniper being outside, waiting to blow my head off. But I dismissed the thought as being ridiculous; after all, if someone wanted to assassinate me, there would be more convenient times than when I was under the protection of two FBI agents.

So I climbed in with a confident shrug, and just like that we were on our way–driving through the rancid gullet of Sunset Park. We made a series of rights and lefts, along with an occasional U-turn, as they went about shaking off imaginary tails. Meanwhile, we engaged in only idle conversation, with all three of us aware that it would be inappropriate to discuss anything meaningful without my lawyer present.

To my surprise, they both seemed genuinely concerned over the breakup of my marriage, especially the impact it might have on my children. I found my spirits rising as they repeated the story of how the Duchess had professed her love for me on the night of my arrest. Furthermore, they were both convinced that once the initial shock had passed, she would want to stay married. But I knew they were wrong; they didn't know the Duchess like I did. She had decided to move on, and that was that.

By the time we hit the Brooklyn Bridge, my spirits had plunged lower than ever. I was running out of time now, quickly approaching the point of no return. FBI headquarters was less than five minutes away.

Yes, I thought, there were some pretty dark days up ahead; of that much I was certain. The only question was how deep did the rabbit hole go? I took a deep breath and tried to steel myself, but it was no use.

Soon enough I would be singing on Court Street.

CHAPTER 6

THE BASTARD AND THE WITCH

The New York field office of the FBI occupied the twentieth, twenty-first, and twenty-second floors of a glass-and-concrete tower that rose up forty-two stories above Lower Manhattan. The area, which was known as Tribeca, for "triangle below Canal Street," was the part of town that included Wall Street, the federal courthouses, the World Trade Center, and the least respected of all government institutions: the Immigration and Naturalization Service.

I walked down a long narrow hallway in the building's subbasement, with Coleman and McCrogan on either side of me. Coleman had just finished explaining how we were in the part of the building that was used for debriefings.

I nodded dutifully and kept on walking, resisting the urge to ask him if the FBI considered the word *debriefing* to be synonymous with *interrogation.* Either way, I had no doubt that many things had *gone on* down here that hadn't exactly jived with the Bill of Rights. (Probably some light torture, some sleep deprivation, and garden-variety habeas corpus violations.) But I decided to keep those stray thoughts to myself, and I just kept nodding and walking–maintaining a neutral expression–as they escorted me into a small debriefing room at the end of the hall.

Inside the room, three people were sitting in cheap black armchairs around a cheap wooden conference table. There were no windows in this room, just fluorescent lights emitting a blue tubercular glow. The walls were completely bare, painted a disturbing shade of hospital white. On one side of the table sat my trusted lawyer, Gregory J. O'Connell, aka Magnum, smiling broadly, looking as towering and dapper as ever. He was wearing a gray pinstripe suit, a white dress shirt, and a red striped tie. He looked right at home down here, a former prosecutor himself, who now had the pleasure of defending the guilty.

Across from Magnum sat a man and a woman, the former of whom I knew from the day of my arraignment, when he'd said all those kind things at my bail hearing. His name was Joel Cohen, and a little over two years ago he had teamed up with OCD to bring me to justice, succeeding where a half-dozen AUSAs before him had failed.

In essence, as sharp and as dedicated as OCD was, he had needed an equally sharp counterpart within the U.S. Attorney's Office to handle the legal end of things. OCD on his own could only investigate; he needed a bastard like Joel Cohen to prosecute me.

At this particular moment, the Bastard was leaning forward in his armchair with his bony elbows resting on the desktop. He was staring at me with narrowed eyes, licking his chops inwardly, no doubt. He wore a cheap gray suit, a cheap white dress shirt, a cheap red tie, and a sinister expression. He had a short mop of curly brown hair, a high forehead, a fleshy nose, and a pasty-faced complexion. He wasn't bad-looking, though; he just looked unkempt, as if he rolled out of bed and came straight to the office. But that was by design, I figured. Oh, yes, the Bastard was trying to make a statement–that now that we were in *his* world, the price of your suit, the reputation of your dry cleaner, and the fashion sense of your barber didn't matter a lick. It was the Bastard who had the power, and I was his prisoner–regardless of appearance. The Bastard was of average height and weight, although he had that aforementioned degenerate slouch, which made him appear shorter. I had no doubt that he held me in as much contempt as I held him. Right now, in fact, he had a look on his face that so much as said, "Welcome to my underground lair, prisoner! Let the torture begin!"

The room's third occupant was a mousy little creature named Michele Adelman. She was sitting to the Bastard's left. I had never met her before, but her reputation preceded her. Her nickname was the Wicked Witch of the East, something she'd earned due to her uncanny likeness—both physically and personality-wise—to that conniving old hag from *The Wizard of Oz.* And since Michele (and Joel) worked as assistant U.S. attorneys for the *Eastern* District of New York, the nickname made that much more sense.

The Witch was a squat five foot two, with a great mane of dark frizzy hair, dark beady eyes, thin maroon lips, and an abbreviated chin. I could only imagine how mousy she'd look if she picked up a block of Swiss cheese between her paws and started nibbling on it. And I could only imagine how witchlike she'd look if she straddled a broomstick and took a cruise around the debriefing room. She wore a dark blue pantsuit and a stern expression.

"Good morning!" said Magnum. "I'd like to introduce you to two people whom you're going to be spending quite a bit of time with over the next few months." He motioned to the Witch and the Bastard, who both nodded dutifully. Then he said, "Jordan, this is Joel Cohen, whom I believe you've had the pleasure of meeting before"—I reached over and shook the Bastard's hand, wondering if he might try to slap a handcuff on me—"and this is Michele Adelman, whom I don't think you've had the pleasure of meeting before," and now I shook the Witch's hand, wondering if she might try to turn me into a newt.

"Anyway, I want everyone to know that Jordan is fully committed to his cooperation." Magnum nodded a single time. "He plans on being both honest and forthright at all times, and I can assure that the information he has is *invaluable* in your fight against crime and injustice on Wall Street." And Magnum nodded once more.

What a load of crap! I thought. *I mean, really!*

"That's good," replied the Bastard, motioning for me to take a seat next to Magnum. "We all look forward to your cooperation, Jordan, and I speak for all those present when I say that we hold no ill feelings toward you"–out of the corner of my eye I could see OCD rolling his eyes, as he and the Mormon took seats on either side of the Witch and the Bastard–"and that if you do the right thing here you'll be treated fairly."

I nodded gratefully, not believing a word he said. OCD would treat me fairly; he was a man of honor. But not the Bastard; he had it out for me. The Witch, however, I wasn't sure about it. According to Magnum, she hated all men–including OCD and the Bastard–so I would be of no special interest to her. My problem was the Bastard. Hopefully he would leave the office before I got sentenced. Then everything would be okay.

With great humility, I said, "I believe you, Joel, and like Greg said, I'm totally committed to my cooperation. Ask whatever you want, and I'll answer as best I can."

"So did you sink your yacht for the insurance money?" snapped the Witch. "Let's hear the truth."

I looked at the Witch and offered her a dead smile. On the table was a tall pitcher of water with six glasses next to it, one of which was half full. What would happen if I threw the glass of water on the Witch? She'd probably scream, "Help me! I'm melting! I'm melting!" But I decided to keep that thought to myself, and all I said was, "No, Michele. If I wanted to sink it for the insurance money, I wouldn't have done it with myself and my wife on it."

"Why?" countered the Witch. "That would be the perfect alibi."

"And it would also be a perfect way to get himself killed," snapped OCD. "He got caught in a storm, Michele. Go read *Yachting* magazine. It's in there."

With great confidence, Magnum said, "I can assure all those present that Jordan did not sink his yacht for the insurance money. Right, Jordan?"

"Absolutely," I replied. "But I won't deny that I hated the thing. It was a hundred and seventy feet of floating heartache. It was constantly breaking down, and it burned through money faster than Haiti." I shrugged innocently. "Anyway, I was glad it sank." Would they really make me tell them the story of the yacht sinking? It really *had* been an accident. The only thing I'd been guilty of was poor judgment, which at the time had been slightly impaired. I was under the influence of enough drugs to sedate Guatemala, so I pressured the captain to take out the boat into the middle of a Force 8 gale, to quell my drug-induced boredom.

"Anyway," said Magnum, "you have your answer, Michele. It was an accident." I nodded in agreement, feeling confident in our first exchange. It had been entirely innocuous, and Magnum and I had handled ourselves beautifully, neutralizing the Witch's spell. Or so I'd thought, until the Bastard said, "And when the boat was sinking, isn't it true that you called Danny Porush and told him that you had ten million dollars in cash buried in your backyard, and that if you and your wife died he should dig it up and make sure it went to your children?"

I looked around the debriefing room and all eyes were on me, including Magnum's. OCD had a wry smile on his face that so much as said, "You see, Jordan, I know things about you that you had no idea I knew!" The Mormon, however, had a rather mischievous smile on his face that so much as said, "I'd be willing to split the ten million with you if you hand me a treasure map and keep the others out of it!" But the Witch and the Bastard both bore grim expressions that so much as said, "Just go ahead and lie to us and see what happens!"

Ironically, I had no idea what they were talking about. In fact, I was now astonished for three reasons: first, because I hadn't buried even ten dollars in my backyard, much less ten million; second, because there was no way of proving it, short of taking OCD into my backyard with a pick and a shovel and digging up six acres of some very expensive Bermuda grass; and, third, because the way the Bastard had phrased his question, he'd insinuated that the information had come from Danny Porush himself, which meant he was cooperating too.

And that was both good and bad. On the bright side, it meant that I wouldn't have to cooperate against him, which was something Magnum had predicted. But on the not-so-bright side,

Danny had been my right-hand man, which meant everything I said would be cross-checked for accuracy. I would have to be extremely careful with that; outright lies would have to be avoided. It would simply be too easy to get caught. Omissions of fact were my only hope. After all, withholding information could just as easily be a lapse of memory.

With a hint of disdain, I replied, "That's the most ridiculous thing I ever heard, Joel." I shook my head and let out a cynical chuckle. "You know, I don't know where you're getting your information from, but I promise you that it's completely bogus." I looked at OCD. His expression was neutral, his hawk eyes slightly narrowed, as if he was sizing me up. I looked him right in the eyes and said, "Trust me, Greg; whoever told you that is yanking your chain. Think about it for a second: Who in their right mind would bury ten million dollars in their backyard? I would've had to dig the hole in the middle of the night and then resod my lawn before sunup. And I'm not exactly the manual-labor type. In fact, the last time one of my lamps blew a bulb, I threw out the lamp." I stared right into the bastard's eyes.

"You have a very competent lawyer," Joel sputtered, "so I'm sure he's explained to you that if you get caught lying, or try to deceive us in any way whatsoever, we have the right to rip up your cooperation agreement and throw it in the garbage can." He flashed me a dead smile. "That means you'd be sentenced without the benefit of a 5K letter, which translates into about thirty years in a–"

Magnum cut the Bastard off with, "Whoa, whoa, whoa, Joel! Settle down! Jordan is fully aware of his obligations, and he has every intention of living up to them."

The Bastard shrugged. "And I'm not saying he won't," he shot back. "But it's my legal obligation to inform him of the *terrible fate* that would befall him"–*and how happy it would make me,* his tone implied–"if he were sentenced without the benefit of a 5K letter." The Bastard looked me right in the eye and added, "And remember that all the information you provide us with can be used against you if you should change your mind and decide to go to trial."

"I'm fully aware of that," I said calmly. "Greg explained all this to me yesterday. But you don't have to worry: I won't put you in a position where you'd have to ruin my life, Joel." Try as I might, the last few words slipped out with a healthy dose of irony.

"You know, I think this might be a good time to confer with my client," said Magnum. "Would you give us a few moments?"

"No problem," said the Bastard, rising from his armchair. He smiled at the Wicked Witch of the East, who rose from her seat too, followed by OCD and the Mormon. Then, in single file, they exited the room and closed the door behind them. The moment they were gone, I popped out of my chair and snarled, "This is total horseshit, Greg, total fucking horseshit! You were right about him; he's a real *fuckhead*! And the other one, Michele Adelman—Jesus! What a cunt *she* is! Someone oughtta give her a fucking broomstick and tell her to fly herself back to Oz!"

Magnum nodded in agreement, slowly rising from his chair until he was a good two heads above me. With a friendly smile, he said, "First of all, I want you to calm down. Take a deep breath and count to ten; then, when you're done, we can talk about the ten million buried in your backyard."

I looked up at Magnum, whose head now seemed to be scraping the fluorescent bulbs. "Will you please sit down!" I demanded. "You're too fucking tall. I lose my perspective when we're both standing." I motioned for him to take a seat.

"You're not that short," he replied, staring down at the top of my head, as if I were a midget. "I think you have a complex." He reached down and placed his large hand on my shoulder. "In fact, when all this is over, I think you should seek help."

I expelled a gust of air. "Yeah, well, I'll take it up with the prison shrink when I'm not busy getting butt-fucked by Bubba the Bull-queer." I shook my head in frustration. "Anyway, I didn't bury any money in my backyard, Greg, or anywhere else, for that matter."

"That's fine," said Magnum, taking his seat. "You have nothing to worry about, then. Joel has to write you the 5K letter, even if he doesn't believe you. He can only withhold the letter if he catches you in an outright lie. But you *are* going to have to give him a financial statement." He paused for a brief instant. "And it's going to have to include any cash you might have. If something should *surface* down the road"–he rolled his eyes–"it would be very bad for you; very, very bad. How much cash are you sitting on right now?"

"Not much," I replied. "Maybe a million, slightly less."

"That's it?"

"Yeah, that's it. Maybe you're forgetting about all the cash I smuggled overseas. Why the fuck do you think I'm sitting here, for a traffic violation?"

"I understand you smuggled money overseas, but that doesn't account for all of it." He paused and rolled his long, rangy neck, eliciting half a dozen dull vertebral cracks. Then he said, "Listen, I'm just playing devil's advocate here, trying to anticipate what Joel might think, and I think he might be skeptical."

I shook my head in consternation. "Let me explain something, Greg: For the last four years I didn't actually own a brokerage firm. I was just controlling them from behind the scenes, right?"

He nodded.

"Right, so follow me for a second: Since *I* didn't actually own the brokerage firms, it was *me* who was getting shares in hot new issues, and it was *me* who was kicking back cash to the owners." I paused, searching for a simple way to explain to Magnum (who wasn't a crook) how things went down in a crooked world. "In other words, in the early nineties, back when I *owned* Stratton, *I* was the one who was getting the cash kickbacks. But after I was thrown out of the brokerage business and was operating from behind the scenes, the whole process reversed itself, and *I* was the one who was paying the kickbacks–paying off the owners of the brokerage firms. You understand?"

He nodded again. "Yes, I do," he said confidently. "That makes perfect sense to me."

I nodded back. "Good, because it happens to be the truth." I shrugged. "Anyway, I don't even have the million dollars. My mother-in-law is holding it for me."

"Why is that?" asked Magnum, taken aback.

How naive! I thought. Magnum was a fine lawyer, but he didn't think like a true criminal. I would just have to educate him. "Because the night I was arrested, I thought Coleman would come back with a search warrant. So I told Nadine to give the cash to her mother for safekeeping. But I can get it back anytime I want. You think I should?"

"Yes, you should. And if the subject of cash comes up again, you should offer that information proactively. Remember, as long as you're honest, you can't get into trouble." He reached into his suit-jacket pocket and pulled out a single sheet of yellow legal paper that had been folded lengthwise, into thirds. Then he smiled and raised his eyebrows three times in rapid succession and placed the sheet of paper on the conference table. He slipped on a pair of reading glasses and unfolded the precious document and said, "This is the list of people you said you have information on. There are ninety-seven names on it, and some of them are pretty damn juicy." He shook his head. "Did you really commit crimes with all these people?" he asked incredulously. "It seems almost impossible."

I pursed my lips and nodded slowly. Then I sat down beside him and took a moment to study this esteemed list, which read like a who's who of Wall Street villains. And accompanying the villainous Wall Streeters were some corrupt politicians, some crooked police officers, a corrupt judge or two, a handful of mobsters, and some accountants and lawyers and CEOs and CFOs, and then a dozen or so civilians—people who weren't actually in the brokerage business but had acted as my nominee, which was Wall Street lingo for *front man.*

With a sinking heart, I said, "What a fucking shame this is." I scanned the list, shaking my head in despair. "This is really ugly, Greg, really fucking ugly. I thought you were gonna leave some of these names off, some of my friends like Lipsky... and Elliot Lavigne... and... uh, Andy Greene?"

He shook his head slowly. "I couldn't do it," he said gravely. "It would make matters worse. If I left one of your friends off the list, it would pique the government's interest that much more."

I nodded in resignation, knowing that Magnum was right. Only yesterday, when we'd made the list, it'd seemed like no big deal. We'd even had a few laughs over it, finding humor in how people from all walks of life could be corrupted by the allure of fast money on Wall Street. It seemed that greed, in the shape of instantaneous profits, knew no strangers. It crossed over all ethnic lines, infecting all age groups. On the list were blacks, whites, Asians, Hispanics, Indians (dots, not feathers), Indians (feathers, not dots), the young, the old, the healthy, the infirm, males, females, homosexuals, bisexuals, you name it. It seemed that no one could resist the temptation of making hundreds of thousands of dollars with no risk. What a sad commentary, I thought, on the state of twentieth-century capitalism.

Five minutes later, the list was still lying on the conference table, although it had a much larger audience now. The Bastard, the Witch, OCD, and the Mormon were back in the room, all of them hunched over in their armchairs, staring down at the list as if it were the Holy Grail.

"This is a pretty inclusive list," marveled the Bastard. Then he looked up and smiled a reasonably friendly smile at me and said, "If this is a sign of things to come, Jordan, then everything should work out very well for you." He looked down at the list again and kept muttering, "Very well, indeed... this is excellent..."

I smiled dutifully and tuned out. And as the Bastard kept fawning over my list, I found myself wondering what he would be thinking right now if I'd left all the hookers on the list. There must have been a thousand of *those,* or at least five hundred. What would the Witch think of that? Would she try to cast an impotence spell on me? She had heard the stories, no doubt, of how we Strattonites classified our hookers like stocks–with the best hookers being Blue Chips and the skankiest hookers being Pink Sheeters (the Pink Sheets was where stocks of little or no value were listed). And somewhere, occupying some murky middle ground, were the NASDAQs, who were either fallen Blue Chips or had never been hot enough to qualify for true Blue Chip status.

"... best place to start is from the beginning," said the Bastard, who'd finally stopped his muttering. He picked up a cheap Bic pen and said, in a dead-serious tone: "Where did you attend grade school?"

"P.S. One Sixty-nine," I replied.

He nodded a single time, then scribbled down my answer on a yellow legal pad. "And that was in Bayside?"

"Yes. Bayside, Queens."

He scribbled that down too and then stared at me, as if he were expecting me to say more. But I didn't. I remained silent, waiting for him to ask the next question.

"Feel free to expand on your answers," the Bastard said. "Less is not more in this situation." He smiled thinly.

I nodded in understanding. "Sure," I said, and I said no more.

I wasn't even trying to give the Bastard a hard time; it was just that, over the years, I'd been trained to give brief answers during legal inquisitions. In point of fact, I had been deposed no less than fifty times–mostly by the NASD (in customer arbitrations), but also by the SEC and the Senate Ethics Committee, the latter of which had been conducting a bribery investigation into one of their less esteemed senators.

Whatever. I'd been conditioned to give only yes or no answers–to offer no extraneous information based on what I *thought* my interrogator wanted to hear. And while I was aware that the ground rules were different now, old habits died hard.

A few more moments of silence passed, then the Bastard finally said, "You were an A student in grade school?"

"Yes," I said proudly. "Straight A's all the way."

"Any disciplinary problems?"

"None to speak of, although I *did* get in trouble once for pulling a girl's hat off her head on the way home from school." I shrugged. "It was in the third grade, though, so it didn't end up on my permanent record." I thought back for a moment. "You know, it's funny, but I can trace pretty much every problem I've ever had in my life back to a female." Or, more accurately, I thought, to the pursuit of pussy.

There was silence, and then more silence. Finally I took a deep breath and said, "Do you want me to tell you the story of my life? Is that what you're looking for?"

"Yes," the Bastard answered, nodding his head slowly, "that's exactly what we're looking for." He put his pen down, leaned back in his seat, and said, "I'm sure some of the last few questions seemed a bit ridiculous to you, but I assure you they're not. When you're on the witness stand, the defense is going to try to paint you as a career criminal, a born liar who'll say anything to get himself off the hook. And wherever they think there's dirt–even if it's in your childhood–that's where they'll dig. They'll use whatever they find to try to discredit you."

"Joel's correct," added Magnum. "They'll dredge up anything and everything. And the way the prosecution counters that is by disclosing your misdeeds to the jury before the defense even gets a chance. In other words, *we* air your dirty laundry proactively, as if it's no great secret, entirely irrelevant to the proceedings."

"Exactly," chirped the Bastard. "We leave the defense nowhere to go."

Now OCD chimed in: "What we *can't* afford are surprises. That serves none of our purposes. We need to know the most intimate details about your life–anything and everything you've done for as long as you can remember."

And now the Witch said, "And that includes not only your drug use but also your fondness for prostitutes, both of which have been duly noted in the press," to which the Bastard added, "And both of which are certain to be exploited by a good defense attorney."

After a few moments of awkward silence, I said, "That's all fine and good, but I was under the impression"–I resisted the urge to stare directly into Magnum's eyes and shoot death rays at him–"that people rarely go to trial in these cases, that they usually plea-bargain. Or, if not that, cooperate."

The Bastard shrugged. "For the most part, that's true, but I wouldn't count on it. In the end, there's always one holdout, someone who takes it all the way to trial."

Everyone nodded in unison, including Magnum, who was now in the process of revising history. Well, fuck it! I thought. It was time for the chips to fall where they may. "You know," I said casually, "I might be only thirty-six years old, but I've had a very full life. This could take a very long time."

OCD smiled wryly. "I've been trying to make sense of your life for the last five years," he said. "I, personally, have as much time as it takes."

"Yeah, let's hear it," added the Bastard.

"It's your only hope of getting a reduced sentence," snapped the Witch.

I ignored the Witch and looked at the Bastard and said, "Fine; since you've already brought up the subject of Bayside, let's start there. It's as good a place to start as any, considering that's where most of the early Strattonites came from." I paused, thinking back for a moment. "And even the ones who didn't actually come from Bayside ended up moving there after the firm got started."

"Everyone moved to Bayside?" the Bastard asked skeptically.

"Not everyone," I replied, "but *most* everyone. You see, moving to Bayside was a way of proving your loyalty to the firm, a way of showing that you were truly a Strattonite. I know it sounds slightly absurd–that moving to a certain neighborhood could make that much of a statement–but that was how it was back then. We were like the Mafia, always looking to keep outsiders out." I shrugged my shoulders. "When you worked at Stratton, you socialized only with other Strattonites, and that's what living in Bayside was all about. You were blocking out outsiders, proving that you were part of the cult."

"You're saying Stratton was a cult?" sputtered the Witch.

"Yes," I said calmly. "That's *exactly* what I'm saying, Michele. Why do you think it was so hard to penetrate?" Now I looked at OCD. "How many doors you think you knocked on over the years–just a ballpark?"

"At least fifty," he replied. "Probably more."

"And every last one of them was slammed in your face, right?"

"Pretty much," he said wearily. "No one would talk to me."

"A big part of that was that everyone was making so much money, no one wanted to upset the applecart." I paused, letting my words sink in. "But it was more than that: What was at the very *core* of it was protecting the Stratton way of life. That's what everyone was doing: protecting the Life."

"Define 'the Life,'" said the Bastard, with a hint of sarcasm.

I shrugged. "Well, among other things, it meant driving the fanciest car, eating at the hottest restaurants, giving the biggest tips, wearing the finest clothes." I shook my head in amazement. "I mean, we did *everything* together. We spent every waking moment together. And not just at work, but at home too." I looked at the Witch, staring into her black-as-night eyes. "That's why Stratton was a cult, Michele. It was all for one and one for all, and lots for oneself, of course. And there were no outsiders around–ever." I looked around the room. "Understand?"

Everyone, including the Witch, nodded.

The Bastard said, "What you're saying makes sense, but I thought most of your early recruits came from Long Island, from Jericho and Syosset."

"About half of them did," I replied quickly. "And there's a reason for that, but we're jumping ahead here. It would be best to take things in order."

"Please," said the Bastard. "This is very productive."

I nodded, gathering my thoughts. "So back to Bayside, then. It's rather ironic, considering that when I was a teenager I swore I'd leave Bayside as soon as I struck it rich. I was about fifteen when I first realized there was a different kind of life out there–a better life, I thought at that time–meaning, a life of wealth and affluence. Remember, I didn't grow up with money, so extravagances like mansions, yachts, private jets–things that people now associate me with–were all completely foreign to me then. Bayside was strictly middle class, especially the part I was raised in." I smiled nostalgically. "It happened to be a wonderful place to grow up. There wasn't an ounce of crime there, and everyone knew everyone. Everyone had moved there from the Bronx or from other parts of Queens, from neighborhoods that had . . . you know . . . *turned.* My parents moved there from the South Bronx, from a place that's a real shithole now–and you're not writing any of this down, Joel."

"Anything I write down, I have to turn over to the defense, whoever that ultimately might be." The Bastard smiled conspiratorially. "So, in my particular case, less is more. Anyway, just keep talking; I have an excellent memory."

I nodded. "All right. Well, my parents moved to Bayside to spare me the heartache of growing up in the Bronx. We lived in a six-story apartment building in one of those planned communities that were springing up like hotcakes back then. And it was beautiful; there were grassy fields to play ball on, playgrounds, concrete walking paths, trees for tree houses, bushes for hide-and-seek. But, most importantly, there were hundreds of kids, which meant there were lots of future Strattonites to recruit from. And they were all getting good educations"–I paused, reconsidering my words–"although the education part was sort of a double-edged sword."

"Why is that?" asked OCD, who seemed to be getting a kick out of me.

"Well," I said, "by the time we hit our teens we were educated enough to know how *little* we actually had. In other words, we knew that, yeah, maybe we weren't starving like the kids in Africa, but there was definitely more out there." I paused for effect. "That's how everyone in my neighborhood thought. There was a sense of unlimited hope–or a sense of entitlement, you might call it–that one day we would all strike it rich and move out to Long Island, where the real money was, where people lived in houses and drove Cadillacs and Mercedes."

"Alan Lipsky grew up in the same apartment building as you, didn't he?" asked OCD.

"Yes," I said, "on the same floor. And Andy Greene, who you probably know as Wigwam, lived only a few blocks away. Although no one called him Wigwam back then; he didn't actually go bald until the eleventh grade." I shrugged. "He didn't get his first toupee until he was in his junior year of college. That's when he became Wigwam." I shrugged again, wondering if Andy Greene would be sitting in this very room in the not-too-distant future. After all, he had been the head of Stratton's Corporate Finance Department, responsible for finding deals to take public and getting them cleared at the SEC. He was a good man, although he would be devastated if he had to go to jail and was forced to take his toupee off–despite the fact that he had the worst toupee this side of the former Iron Curtain.

"Anyway," I said, "Alan lived in apartment Five-K and I lived in

Five-F, and we've been best friends since diapers. I'm sure you're all aware of the fact that I provided Alan with training and financing and that I showed him how the game works." Everyone nodded. "And, in return, he and Brian paid me upward of five million a year in royalties, in sort of a quid pro quo. But I'm jumping ahead again; that happened many years later."

The Bastard nodded. "You said before that you never had any disciplinary problems growing up: You had no arrests? No history of juvenile delinquency?"

I shook my head no, wanting to smack the Bastard for insinuating that I'd been a bad seed from the start. But all I said was, "I was a good kid, a straight-A student, just like I said." I thought for a moment. "And so was the rest of my family. My oldest two first cousins both went to Harvard and graduated at the top of their classes. They're both doctors now. And my older brother–I think you know, Joel–he's one of the most well-respected health-care lawyers in the country. He used to play poker with some of your friends in the U.S. Attorney's Office, although he left the game once my investigation started heating up. I guess it was too uncomfortable for him."

The Bastard nodded deferentially. "I never met your brother, but I've heard only the *best* things about him. It's amazing you two are even related."

"Yeah," I muttered, "it's a total fucking miracle. But we *are* related, and I was just like him when we were younger. Maybe our personalities were different–I mean, I was the outgoing one and he was the introvert–but I was just as good a student as him. Probably even better. School came ridiculously easy to me. Even after I started smoking pot–back in the sixth grade–I was *still* getting straight A's. It wasn't until tenth grade that the drugs started catching up with me."

OCD recoiled visibly. "You started smoking pot in sixth grade?" he asked.

I nodded with a twisted sense of pride. "Yeah, Greg, when I was eleven. My friend's older brother was a pot dealer, and one night Alan and I slept over our friend's house and his brother turned us on." I paused, smiling at the utter insanity of having smoked pot at the age of eleven. "Anyway, pot wasn't as strong back then, so I only caught a minor buzz. I didn't end up bouncing off the walls, like I did as an adult." I let out a tiny chuckle. "Anyway, I continued dabbling with pot for a couple more years, but it never caused me a problem. My parents still thought everything was okay."

I paused and took a moment to study everyone's expressions, which were at various stages of incredulity. I continued my story: "I think the first time they noticed something was wrong was when I was in eighth grade, when I got a ninety-two on a math test. My mother was devastated. Before that, I'd never gotten anything below a ninety-eight, and even *that* would cause a raised eyebrow from her. I remember her saying something like, 'Is everything okay, honey? Were you sick? Was something bothering you?' " I shook my head at the memory. "Of course, I didn't tell her that I'd smoked two fat joints of Colombian Gold before the test and that I was finding it difficult to add two plus two that afternoon." I shrugged innocently. "But I do remember her being very concerned about that test, as if, somehow, getting a ninety-two would reduce my chances of getting into Harvard Medical School." I shrugged again. "But that was how my mother was; she was an overachiever who held us to a very high standard." I lit up. "In fact, just a few years ago, she became the oldest woman in New York State to pass the bar. She practices law on Long Island now, doing everything pro bono." Ah, a way to redeem myself with the Witch! I thought. "She defends battered women, ones who can't afford a lawyer," and I looked into the Witch's beady eyes, hoping to win her over with my mother's fabulous deeds.

Alas, the Witch remained impassive, entirely unmoved. She was a tough son of a bitch. I decided to kick it up a notch. "You know, back in the day, Michele, my mother was a successful CPA, when there were very few professional women in the workplace." I raised my eyebrows and nodded my head quickly, as if to say, "Pretty impressive, eh?" Then I stared at her, waiting for her expression to soften. Still nothing. She just kept staring back at me, shooting daggers. After a few moments, I looked away. She was so poisonous that I now found myself looking to the Bastard for salvation, hoping he would approve of my mother, in spite of the Witch's insolence. I said to the Bastard, "She's a genius, my mother. A truly wonderful lady."

The Bastard nodded, apparently buying into the righteousness of my mother, although there was also a hint of "Who gives a fuck?" in his body language. But then, with great sincerity, he said, "Well, it sounds like she's a really great lady," and he nodded his head some more.

"Yeah, she really is great," I said. "And then there's my father, who I'm sure you're all familiar with." I smiled ruefully. "He's also a CPA, and a genius in his own right, *althoughhhh . . .*" I paused, trying to find the right words to classify my father, Max, whose Stratton nickname was Mad Max, due to his wildly ferocious temper.

Mad Max was a serial chain-smoker, a great advocate of premium Russian vodka, a human ticking time bomb, and a surprisingly dapper dresser. Mad Max played no favorites; he hated everyone equally. "Well," I said with a mischievous smile, "let's just say that he's not as benevolent a creature as my mother."

With a hint of a smile, OCD asked, "Is it true he used to smash brokers' car windows if they parked in his spot?"

I nodded slowly. "Yeah," I said, "and if he was in a bad mood he would go to work on your body and fenders too. Then he'd have your car towed." I shrugged. "But the brokers still parked in his spot anyway. It became just one more way of proving your loyalty to the firm: Suck up a beating from Mad Max and then you're truly a Strattonite."

There were a few moments of silence, then the Bastard said, "So when did you first start breaking the law? How old were you?"

I shrugged. "That depends on how you define breaking the law. If you consider the consumption of dangerous recreational drugs breaking the law, then I was a criminal at age eleven. Or if it's cutting school, then I was an *arch*criminal at age sixteen, because I cut most of the tenth grade.

"But if you want to know the first time I did something that *I* considered illegal–something that I was doing day in and day out–I would say that it was when I started selling ices on Jones Beach."

"How old were you?" asked the Bastard.

"Almost seventeen." I thought for a moment, back to my beach days. "What I would do was walk around the beach with a Styrofoam cooler, selling ices, blanket to blanket. I'd walk around screaming, 'Italian ices, Chipwiches, Fudgsicles, frozen fruit bars–Milky Ways and Snickers,' and I'd go on and on, all day. It was the greatest job ever, the absolute *greatest*! In the morning–like at six a.m.–I would go down to this Greek distributor where all the Good Humor trucks went, in Howard Beach, Queens, and I'd load up on ices and ice cream. Then I'd pack the coolers in dry ice and head to the beach." I paused, relishing the memory. "And I made a bloody fortune doing it. On a good day, I'd clear more than five hundred dollars. Even on a slow day I'd *still* clear two-fifty, which was ten times what my friends were making.

"That's where I first met Elliot Loewenstern; we hustled ices together on the beach." I motioned to my villains, thieves, and scoundrels list. "I'm sure you're all familiar with Elliot. He's on there somewhere, pretty close to the top." I shrugged, not the least bit concerned about implicating Elliot Loewenstern. After all, I knew that Elliot, whose nickname was the Penguin–due to his long, thin nose, his compact potbelly, and his slightly bowed legs, which caused him to waddle around like a migrating penguin–would cooperate if he were facing anything more than a few hours in jail. In fact, I'd seen him crack under police questioning when the stakes were considerably lower. It was during our ice-hustling days, and he was facing only a fifty-dollar fine for vending without a license. But rather than paying the fine and keeping his mouth shut, he ratted out every other vendor on the beach, including me. So, yes: If OCD and the Bastard secured an indictment against the Penguin, he would be singing on Court Street with the relish of Celine Dion.

I was about to continue with my tale, when the Bastard said, "I find it a bit odd that after everything you've done you still consider selling ices breaking the law." He shrugged his bastardly shoulders. "Most people would consider it an honest way for a kid to make a buck."

Interesting, I thought. The Bastard had raised a very profound issue–namely, what constitutes breaking the law? Back in the day, virtually everyone I knew (both peers and adults alike) had considered my ices-hustling to be completely righteous. In fact, I'd received accolades from one and all. Yet, the simple fact was that it *was* illegal, because I was vending without a license.

But was it *really* illegal? Weren't some laws not really meant to be enforced? After all, we were just trying to make an honest buck, weren't we? In fact, we were enhancing the beachgoing experience for thousands of New Yorkers, who otherwise would have had to walk all the way up to the boardwalk (which was full of splinters) and wait in line at the concession stand, which was manned by a grim-faced adolescent who probably spit on their food the moment they turned their backs. So one could definitely make the case that Elliot and I had been doing "good," despite the fact that, technically speaking, we were breaking the law.

"Well, the short answer," I said to the Bastard, "is that we *were* breaking the law. We were vending without a license, which, for better or worse, is a Class B misdemeanor in New York State. And to take it one step further, we were also guilty of income-tax evasion, because we were making twenty grand a summer and not declaring a dime of it. And to take it even *further,* when I turned eighteen, I started selling puka-shell necklaces as a side item. I figured, hey, as long as I'm walking around the beach selling ices, why not take advantage of the underserved costume-jewelry market?" I shrugged a capitalist's shrug. "So I went down to the jewelry exchange in Manhattan's Chelsea district and bought a couple of thousand puka necklaces and then hired junior high school kids to walk around the beach with them. I had three kids working for me, and they charged four dollars a necklace. Meanwhile, my cost was only fifty cents apiece, so even after I paid the kids fifty bucks a day, I was still netting two hundred for myself. And that was on top of my ices money!

"But, of course, I hadn't taken out workman's comp, nor was I taking out taxes for them. Not to mention the fact that I had them vending without a license. So now it wasn't only *me* who was breaking the law, but I was corrupting a bunch of innocent fourteen-year-olds as well.

"I even got my mother into the act. I had her waking up at five a.m. to butter bagels, which I sold between the hours of nine and eleven, before the sun was high enough to stimulate ices demand. And then there were all the sanitary laws we were violating by preparing food in an uninspected plant, although my mother *did* keep a very clean household, and she *was* kosher. So I don't think anyone ever got sick.

"But, hey, it was all in the name of good old-fashioned capitalism, so I wasn't *really* breaking the law, was I? It was all very harmless, all very commendable." I looked at the Bastard and smiled. "Like you said, Joel, it was a very honest way for a kid to make a buck." I paused, letting my words sink in. "Anyway, I could go on and on here, but I think you get the point: Everyone, including my own law-abiding parents, thought selling ices was the greatest thing on earth. The act of a budding entrepreneur!

"But is there really any such a thing as a righteous crime? When did I cross the line with the ices? In the very beginning, when I chose to vend without a license? Or was it when I recruited the junior high school kids? Or was it with my mother? Or choosing not to pay taxes..."

I took a deep breath and said, "Understand: You don't start *out* on the dark side of the force, unless, of course, you're a sociopath, which I hope you all know I'm not." Everyone nodded. In a dead-serious tone, I said, "The problem is that you become desensitized to things; you cross over the line a *tiny* bit and nothing bad happens, so you figure it's okay to step over again, except this time you step a bit further. It's human nature to do that; whether you're an action junkie or adrenaline junkie, or even if you're not a junkie at all, and you're simply dipping your foot into a piping hot bathtub. At first you can't keep your toe in, because the water's too hot. And then, a minute later, your whole body is submerged, and the water feels just fine.

"When I went off to American University, all these things were reinforced. I started dating a girl from a very wealthy family, whose father was in the bookbinding business. His name was David Russell, and he was worth millions. Not surprisingly, he thought what I was doing on the beach was the greatest thing ever. In fact, one day he had this big party at his house, and he paraded me around, saying, 'This is the kid I was telling you about!' Then he made me tell everyone the story of how I would go down to the Greek distributor at six o'clock in the morning and load up coolers full of Italian ices and then walk around the beach hawking my ices from blanket to blanket, running from the cops when they chased after me for vending without a license. And, of course, every last one of his guests thought it was the best thing they ever heard. They even made a toast to me. 'Here's to the millionaire of tomorrow!' they all said."

I smiled at the memory. "I was only a junior in college back then, but I knew they were right. I *knew* that I'd be rich one day, and so did all my friends. Even when I worked at the beach, I always made twice as much as any other vendor. And I'm not even talking about the buttered bagels or the puka-shell necklaces. I just worked longer and harder than anyone else–even Elliot, who was a hard worker in his own right. But at the end of the day, when Elliot and I would sit down, I'd always outgrossed him by fifty percent."

I paused to catch my breath, and I took a moment to gauge the temperature of my captors. What were they thinking? I wondered. Could they possibly relate to someone like me? I was a breed apart from them. In the Witch's case, I was a species apart. Either way, they all looked dumbfounded. They were just staring at me, as if I had a screw loose or something.

I plunged forward into my first years of adulthood. "Anyway, after I graduated from college, I decided to go to dental school, because I wanted to make lots of money. It's funny how ridiculous that seems now–that I thought dentistry would be a path to wealth–but I guess all that malarkey my mother had whispered in my ear when I was growing up had had an impact on me." I shrugged. "In fact, I thought my only other option was to go to medical school, but becoming a doctor seemed like an insanely long haul. Between internship, residency, fellowship, it just seemed too far out of reach. And then I overslept for the MCATs, which pretty much sealed the deal. I mean, how was I supposed to tell my mother that I'd overslept for a test that she'd been waiting for the results from since I'd emerged from her womb? She would've been heartbroken!

"So I figured, as a good son, it was my obligation to lie to her, and I told her that I'd decided not to take the MCATs because being a doctor wasn't for me. I told her that dentistry was my calling." I shook my head slowly, amazed at how I sealed my fate all those years back. "Anyway, we're now at the part of the story where the true insanity begins: my first day of dental school." I smiled cynically. "You ever hear that old expression about all roads leading to Rome?"

Everyone nodded.

"Right–well, in my case, all roads led to Stratton, and I stepped onto the road on day one, which was orientation. We were sitting in the school's auditorium, a hundred and ten dental students, waiting to hear the first words of wisdom from the dean of the school. I remember this like it was yesterday. I was looking around the auditorium, trying to size up my competition, trying to figure out if everyone was as money-hungry as I was or if some of them were just there for the true love of dentistry, like to serve their fellow man or something." I shook my head, as if my last few words defied logic.

"The room was packed–about half men, half women. The dean was standing up front, behind a cheap wooden podium. He looked like a decent-enough guy, in his mid-fifties and reasonably well dressed. He had a full head of gray hair that made him look successful, respectable, and very dental, at least to *my* way of thinking. But he did have this sort of grim expression on his face, like he could've been moonlighting as a warden in a state penitentiary." *Like you, Joel, you mangy bastard!* "But, in spite of that, he still looked like a basically okay guy. So when he grabbed the mike off the podium, I leaned forward in my seat to listen.

"In a surprisingly deep voice, he said, 'I want to welcome everyone to the Baltimore College of Dental Surgery. You all deserve to be very proud of yourselves today. You've been accepted into one of the finest dental programs in the country.' And he paused, letting his words hang in the air. So far, so good, I thought. Then he said, 'What you're going to learn over the next four years will assure you an esteemed place in society, as well as a life of reasonable comfort. So, please, give yourselves a warm round of applause, everyone. You sure as hell deserve it. Welcome, everyone! Welcome!' and he lifted his mike in the air and everyone started clapping, right on cue.

"Everyone except me, that is. I was devastated. In fact, I knew it *right then* that I'd made a huge mistake." I rolled my neck, trying not to let the memory upset me. "It was the way he'd used the word *reasonable.* It was a fucking hedge word, for Chrissake! That bastard *knew*–he fucking *knew*–that the golden age of dentistry was over, so he couldn't bring himself to say that we'd have *absolute* comfort. Instead, he'd hedged and said *reasonable* comfort, which is an entirely different thing.

"Yet, to my utter shock, when I looked around the room, no one else seemed worried. Everyone else was fine and dandy; they were all clapping their hands merrily–*la-de-fuck-in-da!*–and they all had these expectant looks on their faces. The Dentists of Tomorrow! I'll never forget it, or at least I'll never forget the *irony* of it, because while they were busy clapping, I was on the verge of slitting my wrists." I paused and let out a deep sigh. With a hint of sadness in my tone, I said, "The truth is that I knew I'd made a mistake long before that. I knew it even as a kid.

"I mean, who was I kidding? I didn't have the patience to go through that much schooling!" I shook my head in resignation. "I was born with only half the equation: I was smart as a whip and had the gift of gab, but I lacked patience. I wanted to get rich quick; I wanted everything now. That was my downfall. And after making so much money on the beach all those summers, I had the taste of blood on my lips. I was like an accident waiting to happen. Like a high-performance race car zooming down the highway at two hundred miles an hour: Either I'd win the race or I'd crash and burn like the space shuttle. It could've gone either way."

I compressed my lips and shook my head gravely. "Well, unfortunately, my instincts had been right on target. As soon as the applause died down, the dean put the mike to his lips and said, 'I want to let you all in on a little secret: The golden age of dentistry is over.' He nodded his head a single time. 'If you're here simply because you're looking to make a lot of money, you're in the wrong place. So take my advice and leave right now, and never come back. There are better ways in the world to get rich; save yourself the heartache.' Then he said a few more things, which blew right past me, because I was too busy looking for a fire exit. Then he twisted the knife in deeper. 'Remember, your goal is to practice preventive dentistry. So if you practice your profession well, you'll be seeing less and less of your patients.' And he started nodding his head, as if he'd just let out a major pearl of wisdom. Then he started talking again, although I was done listening. In fact, I was doing a bit of talking myself at that point, saying, 'Excuse me, pardon me, excuse me...' as I walked out of the auditorium right in the middle of his speech. I remember getting some funny looks from everyone, and I also remember not giving a shit about them." I paused for effect. "That's how I became a dental-school dropout my first day. It was all the dean's fault. The only question was how to break the news to my mother."

"That's terrible!" exclaimed the Witch. "She must've been devastated!" The Witch compressed her thin lips and stared at me menacingly.

Well, well, well! I thought. The Witch had a soft spot for my mother, after all! Apparently, my mother's goodness was irresistible. I said, "Yes, Michele, my mother would have been very upset if I had told her, which, of course, I didn't." I shrugged my good son's shrug. "I mean, I loved her way too much to be honest with her. Besides, she was my mother, and I'd been lying to her since I was five." I flashed the Witch an impish smile. "So why tell her the truth now, right, Michele?"

The Witch responded with no words, just two twitches of her nose.

Christ! I shook my head quickly, trying to rid myself of her spell. "Anyway," I said, with a bit of a quiver in my tone, "I told my mother that dental school was going great, and then I hid down in Maryland for four months and worked out all day and laid in the sun. Baltimore's pretty nice that time of year, so the time passed quickly. I still had beach money left over from the summer, so I was living pretty well. In the end, I auctioned off my dental equipment to supplement things. All the drills and drill bits, the scalers, the gauze pads–they made us buy all this shit before we got started, so now I was stuck with it."

Scratching his head, OCD said, "You really auctioned off your dental equipment? Seriously?"

I nodded. "You bet I did! In fact, I posted signs all over campus so I'd draw a good crowd." I smiled proudly. "You see, Greg? I was aware of the importance of supply and demand even then. I knew that if I wanted to have a successful auction I'd need to have lots of bidders. So I advertised." I shrugged another capitalist's shrug. "Anyway, you should've seen the auction; it was a real hoot. I held it in the dental lab, surrounded by beakers and Bunsen burners. Fifty or sixty kids showed up, most of them in their white dental smocks. I wore one of those blue plastic visors, like a bookie.

"In the beginning, they were all a bit gun-shy, so I played up the theatrics a bit. I started speaking really fast, like a true auctioneer would, and then things started to roll. 'Okay, okay,' I said quickly, 'I got a beautiful high-speed hand piece, manufactured by our good friends over at Star Dental Labs. She's stainless steel, self-cooling, and spins at twenty thousand rpms a minute. She comes straight from the box, with a lifetime warranty. Just look at her–she's a real beaut!' And I held up the drill for public inspection. 'She's an absolute must,' I said. 'A must for any dentist who's serious about providing his patients with first-class dental care. Brand-new, she'll set you back nine hundred fifty dollars. Do I have an opening bid of two hundred dollars...Do I have two hundred... I'm looking for two hundred...'

"And some kid with a ferocious mop of red hair and horn-rimmed glasses raised his hand and said, 'I'll take it for two hundred!' to which I said, 'Excellent! We have an opening bid of two hundred dollars from the very smart man in the white smock and horn-rimmed glasses. Do I have a bid of two-fifty now...I'm looking for two-fifty...Does anybody have two-fifty? Sweet Jesus!

Come on, everyone! She's a steal down here! Remember, this drill is self-cooling and sprays out a jet of water to prevent heat buildup. It's state of the art all the way…' And then some Asian girl with flawless skin and the body of a fire hydrant raised her hand and said in an eager voice, 'I'll pay two-fifty!' to which I said, 'Ahhh, we have a two-hundred-fifty-dollar bid from the lovely lady in white, who knows a bargain when she sees one. Good for you, young lady!' And I went on and on until I had the whole room in a frenzy."

I paused, catching my breath. Then, with great pride, I said, "I netted over three thousand dollars that day. And it was the first time in my life I felt like a true salesman. And I was good at it. My auctioneer's rap came pouring out of my mouth as if there was no tomorrow." I smiled at the memory. "Toward the end of the auction, the dean came walking into the room, and he just stood there, staring at me. After a minute, he shook his head and walked away, too dumbfounded to comment. I'm sure it was the first auction at the Baltimore College of Dental Surgery, and I'm also sure it was the last. And it was a grand success, I might add."

By now everyone in the room was chuckling, even the Witch and the Bastard. It was a good sign, I thought, so I decided to jump right into the insanity of the meat-and-seafood business: "What I failed to mention, though, was what inspired me to hold the auction that day."

"You said you were running low on funds," said OCD.

I shrugged noncommittally. "That had something to do with it, but it wasn't what was really driving me. What happened was that, a few days before, I received a phone call from Elliot, the Penguin. I was home at the time, lying in bed and staring up at the ceiling, wondering what the fuck I was gonna do with the rest of my life. I was living in a tiny studio apartment, just outside Baltimore, and it had two pieces of furniture in it: the bed and a rotting tweed couch. The Penguin was living in Queens, and when he called me, he was in a very agitated state, almost out of breath. He said, 'I found a way to make beach money all year 'round. I'm working as a salesman for a meat-and-seafood company, and I'm clearing two-fifty a day in cash. They even gave me a company vehicle.' I think it was the last part that shocked me most. 'Really?' I said. 'They gave you a car? Jesus, that's amazing.'

" 'Yeah, it is,' he answered. 'And I can get you a job there if you want.' "

I thought back on the Penguin's words. "In retrospect, I should've realized that something wasn't on the up-and-up. Remember, Elliot didn't actually say they'd given him a company car. He said, 'company vehicle,' which is kind of an odd way to put it, you know? I mean, if you went to work at IBM and they gave you a car, you wouldn't refer to it as a company vehicle: You would say, 'IBM gave me a company car!' Still, the thought of making beach money all year 'round was so enticing that I chose not to read too much into things. Before I hung up, I asked, 'Are you sure they're gonna hire me, Elliot? I don't have any real sales experience.' "

I began chuckling. "You have no idea how ironic that question was." I started shaking my head.

"What's so ironic?" the Bastard asked tonelessly. "I don't get it."

"Well, companies like Great American Meat and Seafood–which was the name of Elliot's company–are *always* looking for salesmen. The same goes for companies like Stratton Oakmont or Monroe Parker or Kirby vacuum cleaners or any other company that employs fast-talking commission-based salesmen." I paused and took a moment to think back. Then I said, "At Stratton, we used to give our job applicants the mirror test–meaning, we would stick a mirror under their noses and wait for it to fog up. If it *did,* we hired them; if it *didn't,* it meant they were dead, which was the only reason we *wouldn't* hire them–unless, of course, they were already licensed stockbrokers. Then we *definitely* wouldn't hire them, because they knew too much. We wanted our brokers young and naive, hungry and stupid." I shrugged. "Give me someone like *that,* and I'll make them rich, with no problem. But give me someone with brains and imagination–well, that's a bit more difficult.

"But, to get back to the story, I spent a few more minutes on the phone with the Penguin, listening to him chirp about how wonderful the meat-and-seafood business was. 'It's all restaurant-quality food,' he assured me. 'Nothing but the best.'

"I mean, the whole thing sounded too good to be true, but I'd never known Elliot to be a liar. He was a bit gullible, maybe, but he definitely wasn't a liar. So I put aside my skepticism, packed up my 1973 Mercury Cougar, and drove up to New York to drop the bomb on my parents. It was February 1985. I was twenty-two at the time. I had my whole life in front of me."

CHAPTER 7

THE BIRTH OF A SALESMAN

So you just picked up and left," said the Witch, shaking her head back and forth.

"Yeah," I said casually, "that's just what I did. And I had all my worldly possessions with me, which amounted to a suitcase full of dirty clothes and the shirt on my back. And, of course, I had the three thousand dollars I'd cleared from my auction.

"In retrospect, it still amazes me how *easy* it was to pick up and leave Baltimore. My studio was on a month-to-month lease, I had no furniture to speak of, and my financial obligations were basically zero. The only bummer was that I'd be living at home with my parents again, which I can assure you is no picnic. They were still living in the same two-bedroom apartment I grew up in, which was the same apartment I swore I'd leave after I struck it rich."

I paused and scratched my chin thoughtfully. "In fact, they're still living in the same apartment today, in spite of all the money my father made at Stratton." I shook my head in amazement. "Can you imagine? I mean, I even offered to buy them a house when things were rolling, but they didn't want to move. I guess you could say they're the ultimate creatures of habit."

"So how'd you break the news to them?" the Bastard asked impatiently.

"Well, I figured it would be easier if they digested things in small chunks, so, before I left Baltimore, all I told them was that I'd dropped out of dental school; I didn't say that I landed a job as a meat-and-seafood salesman.

"I dropped that bomb on them in the living room, which was where all *important* conversations took place. My father was sitting in his favorite chair, and my mother was sitting on the couch, reading a book. For some reason, I still remember what book it was—*On Death and Dying*." I shrugged. "I don't know; my mother always liked those morbid books. My father, meanwhile, was busy watching his latest cop show and chain-smoking his lungs into complete oblivion.

"I took a seat across from my father and said, 'I need to talk to you guys for a few minutes.'

"My father looked at my mom, and he said in a slightly annoyed tone, 'Lee, will you turn down *T.J. Hooker* for a minute?' At that, my mother dropped her book and nearly ran over to the wall unit and turned down the Trinitron. That was the relationship between my parents, Mad Max and Saint Leah. The latter spent the better part of her day trying to keep the former from blowing an emotional gasket.

"I said to them, 'Dentistry is not for me, guys. I gave it a full semester, and I know for sure now that I could never be happy as a dentist.' That was a lie, of course, although I figured that if I told them that I'd dropped out the first day then they'd really be pissed. Either way, my mother was having none of it.

" 'I didn't think you'd be a dentist forever,' she said. 'I thought you'd open up a chain of dental clinics one day, or discover a new type of dental procedure. It's still not too late.'

" 'No, Mom; it *is* too late. I'm not going back,' and then I looked at my father for support. He was actually better in these situations. He loved a good crisis; they seem to calm him down somehow, even to this day. It was the small stuff that drove him crazy. I said to him, 'Listen, Dad: I don't want to be a dentist. I want to be a salesman. That's what I'm cut out for, to sell things–' And my mother popped off the couch and screamed, 'Oh, my God, Max! Not a salesman! Anything but that!' Then she turned to me and said, 'Look what you've done to me already,' and she lowered her head and pointed to a small patch of gray hair. 'This is from when you cut tenth grade and smoked marijuana all day with that awful Richard Kushner.' Then she pointed to a wrinkle on her forehead and added, 'And this is from when you grew marijuana in the closet and said it was a science project! And now you're dropping out of dental school to become a salesman!'

"I was slowly losing patience with her. With a bit of edge in my tone, I said, 'I'm not going to dental school, Mom, and that's final!'

" 'No, it's not final!'

" 'Yes, it is final!'

"And back and forth we went, until, finally, Mad Max stepped in. 'Will you two stop it!' he screamed. 'I mean, Jesus!' And he shook his head in disbelief. Then he looked at my mother and said, 'He's not going to dental school, Leah. What's the use?' And then he looked at me and smiled warmly. With a hint of a British accent, he asked, 'What type of salesman would you like to be, son? What do you see yourself selling?' "

"Your father's British?" asked OCD. "I didn't know that." OCD's tone dripped with surprise, as if someone had given him some very bad information.

"No, he's not actually British," I replied. "He just speaks with a British accent when he's trying to act reasonable. That's my father's other persona: Sir Max. It's his lovable alter ego. See, when Mad Max becomes Sir Max, he puckers up his lips and speaks with a hint of British aristocracy. It's pretty remarkable, actually, considering he's never even visited England." I turned the corners of my mouth down and shrugged, as if to say, "Some things simply defy logic and aren't worth pondering." Then I said, "But Sir Max is the best. He never loses his temper. He's totally reasonable in all situations."

"So what did you tell Sir Max?" asked the Bastard.

"Well, at first I hemmed and hawed a bit–talking about the possibility of selling medical supplies or dental supplies, something that would fit in with my degree. Then, as if it were an afterthought, I brought up the subject of Elliot Loewenstern and meat and seafood. My mother, of course, immediately began torturing me, using her own brand of Jewish guilt, which is your run-of-the-mill Jewish guilt mixed with passive-aggressiveness and sarcasm.

" 'My son, the meat salesman!' she started muttering. 'That's just wonderful! He drops out of dental school to peddle meat. A mother should only *be* so lucky.' She added a few more choice words, and then the phone started ringing and Sir Max morphed back into Mad Max, and started cursing, 'That motherfucking goddamn piece-a-shit phone! Who the hell has the gall to call this house on a goddamn Tuesday afternoon? Inconsiderate bastard! The fucking gall!' And my mother jumped off the couch and ran to the phone like Jesse Owens, as she pled with my father: 'Calm down, Max! Calm down! I'm getting it–I'm getting it!' But Mad Max was still mumbling curses under his breath: 'That rat bastard! *Who* calls the house on a goddamn Tuesday afternoon?' "

With mock seriousness, I said, "My father *really* hated it when that phone rang! I'm telling you: Nothing drove him crazier."

"Why?" asked OCD.

I shrugged. "For the most part, it had to do with my father being resistant to change. He hates it in any shape or form. In fact, for the last thirty-six years he's had the same address, the same phone number, the same dry cleaner, the same auto mechanic–he even has the same Chinese laundry service! And he knows all the owners on a first-name basis, so he'll say things like, 'Pepe* over at the dry cleaner said this, or Wing* at the Chinese laundry said that, or Jimmy* over at the Sunoco station said something else.' It's totally unbelievable." I shook my head back and forth, emphasizing the point. "When the phone rings, it brings an unwanted stimulus into his environment, creating the potential for change. Whether the call brings good news or bad news doesn't matter to him; he flips out either way." I shrugged again, as if this was just another

*Name has been changed

expected happening at Chez Belfort. Then I said, "Now, under *normal* circumstances, the worst thing my mother can say after she picks up the phone is, 'Max! It's for you!' But once Mad Max picks up the phone, he'll become Sir Max again, using his British accent. 'Oh, how may I help you? *Righty-o, then! Cheerio, my friend!*' And he'll stay Sir Max until he hangs up the phone, at which point he'll turn right back into Mad Max again and curse his way back to his chair, then fire up another Merit.

"Anyway, when my mother answered the phone that day, it wasn't for my father. It was for me, and, of all people, it was the Penguin. So my father started muttering, 'That cocksucking phone! It's always the same with it. And this fucking Penguin character! What rock did he crawl out from underneath? That stupid Penguin, waddling fool . . .' "

By now we were all in hysterics. The Bastard recovered first. "So did Mad Max go ballistic about the meat business?"

"Not at all," I replied. "The moment I hung up, I told them I'd landed a job as a meat-and-seafood salesman, which caused Saint Leah to start flipping out, which then caused Sir Max to reemerge." I paused for a moment, then said, "No, my problems didn't start until the next morning, when the Penguin pulled up in front of my building in his company vehicle, which turned out to be a Toyota pickup truck. 'What the fuck is that?' I snapped. 'Don't tell me this is the company vehicle you were talking about!'

" 'Yeah, ain't she a beaut?' he replied, and then he popped out of the truck, dressed in jeans and sneakers, and he waddled over and put his arm on my shoulder. Then he stared at the truck and said, 'Whaddaya think?'

" 'It's a real piece-a-shit!' I snarled, and then I noticed a big white freezer box on the back on the truck. 'What the fuck is that, Penguin? It looks like a coffin!' I saw a trail of gray dry-ice smoke rising up from out of one of the corners of the box. 'And what the fuck is that?' I said, pointing to the smoke.

"Elliot flashed me a knowing smile, then he held up an index finger and said, 'Here! I'll show you,' and he went waddling over to the passenger side and opened the lid of the freezer box. 'Check out the food,' he chirped proudly, and he started pulling out boxes, one by one, and showing me the food. Each box was the size of an attaché case, and it had a different cut of meat in it or a different type of fish. And there was everything–filet mignon, shrimp, lobster tails, lamb chops, pork chops, veal chops, fillet of sole, salmon steaks, crab legs. He even had prepared foods, like chicken Kiev and chicken cordon bleu. I'd never seen anything like it.

"By the time he was done, we were literally surrounded by more than two dozen boxes, and I was more confused than ever. There was something bothering me, but I couldn't place my finger on it. 'How do we get the restaurants to buy from us?' I asked. 'Are our prices cheaper? Do we have better food?'

"The Penguin looked at me deadpan and said, 'Who said anything about selling to restaurants?' "

I looked at the Bastard and shook my head. With a hint of a chuckle, I said, "I think I knew everything right then and there, and all that came afterward was merely incidental. When I didn't run back upstairs and reapply to dental school, I sealed my fate." I shrugged. "The next decade of my life–meaning, the very insanity of Stratton Oakmont–was now a foregone conclusion."

The Bastard leaned forward in his seat, obviously intrigued. "What makes you say that?" he asked.

I thought for a moment. "Well, let's just say that, right then and there, I knew what I was getting myself involved in. I knew it was a"–I avoided using the word *scam,* not only because the meat-and-seafood business wasn't an outright scam but also because I didn't want my captors thinking of me as a career scam artist. Better they should view Stratton as a blip in an otherwise semi-law-abiding life–"bit of a hustle," I said carefully. "Or maybe even *more* than a bit. But I figured, since the food was so good, how much harm could I cause?"

I shrugged at my own rationalization. "Anyway, it was about a twenty-minute ride to the warehouse, and on the way Elliot explained the ins and outs to me. Everything was being sold door to door, either to homes or to businesses but never to restaurants. The food wasn't priced that way. 'We sell at retail, not wholesale,' the Penguin informed me. And while he didn't come right out and say it, he inferred that our prices weren't cheap. 'It's all about convenience,' he kept chirping. 'We deliver restaurant-quality food right to their door. And we'll even pack their freezers for them!' He kept repeating the last part, even called himself a professional freezer packer, as if that made up for the fact that he was overcharging everyone.

"Whether it did or didn't, by the time we reached the warehouse I had a pretty good idea of what was going on at Great American Meat and Seafood: There were no territories, no brochures, no existing customers to service, no salary of any kind; it was straight commission. 'We're cold-calling machines,' he chirped, as we pulled into the warehouse. 'That's why we make so much money.'

"My job interview took place inside a ramshackle office at the front of the warehouse. It lasted eight and a half seconds, at which point I was hired. I hadn't heard of the mirror test back then, so I just assumed that I'd gotten the job because I was a friend of Elliot's. I didn't know they'd hire anyone with a pulse." I shrugged innocently. "And then came the training program, which consisted of two days in a truck with Elliot. I sat in the passenger seat, observing, as he drove around aimlessly, knocking on people's doors, trying to sell the food. The rap he used was that he was a truck driver who had an overorder on his truck, and he couldn't get back to the freezer; so he was willing to sell everything at cost, lest the food thaw out and he lose everything.

"And, to support his claim, each box had an inflated price marked on it. As he was selling, he would point to the prices and say, 'I'll take fifteen dollars off *this* box, and fifteen dollars off *that* box...' and then he'd smile at his customer and add, 'Hey, I'd rather sell everything at cost than let the food thaw out, right?' "

"He was outright *lying* to his customers!" snapped the Witch.

I smiled inwardly. "Yes, Michele, he was outright lying to his customers. And I'll tell you that it definitely shocked me at first. It seemed totally sleazy, what he was doing. Totally slimy. But, of course, the Penguin had a rationalization for it. In fact, he had rationalizations for everything.

"We were somewhere on the South Shore of Long Island when I broached the subject with him. Elliot was behind the wheel, searching for 'virgin territory,' which was Penguinspeak for a neighborhood where no one had heard the pitch before. It was early afternoon, and I'd seen him do his spiel about half a dozen times so far, although he hadn't sold a box yet. I said to him, 'I can't believe what a scam this is, Elliot. Are you sure this is even legal?'

"Elliot looked at me as if I'd just fallen off a turnip truck and said, 'Look who's talking, you fucking hypocrite! Aren't you the guy who used to pinch the bottom of the ices cup to get extra scoops out of the barrel?' And he expelled a gust of air. 'This is no different, pal. Besides, people can't even get this food in the supermarket.'

"I shook my head and said, 'Yeah, yeah, I understand that the food is great and everything, and I'm really happy about that, but it doesn't change the fact that you're a lying sack of shit!' I paused for a moment, then added, 'And as far as my pinching the bottom of the ices cup, I only did it because the cups were stacked upside down. So when I picked one up, it got pinched automatically.'

" 'Yeah, sure,' chirped the Penguin. 'It was all an accident. You could've stacked the cups right side up. No?' He rolled his eyes at me. 'Anyway, what I'm doing with the prices goes on everywhere. Seriously. Just walk into any jewelry store or electronics store and check it out yourself. *Everyone* does this shit.' "

I paused, letting Elliot's words hang in the air. Then I said, "There's no denying that he had a point. You see it in jewelry stores all the time: They inflate their price tags and then mark things down right in front of you so you think you're getting a good deal." I paused again, then: "And all this business about an overorder isn't much different than all those stores you see advertising 'going-out-of-business sales.' Most of them have been advertising the same going-out-of-business sale for the last ten years, and in ten more years they'll *still* be going out of business!"

I took a deep breath and continued: "Anyway, we spent most of the first day working middle-class neighborhoods, knocking on people's doors and ringing their bells. And the rejection was absolutely staggering. Doors were being slammed in our faces left and right, with people telling us to basically drop dead. By two o'clock, Elliot was getting negative. He started whining to me, 'Nobody wants the food today.'" I shook my head and let out a few chuckles. "It was sad to see. I mean, the poor bastard was on the verge of tears! At the beach, everyone loved us; we were almost like celebrities there. But here we were being treated like lepers.

"Still, the Penguin somehow managed to unload twelve boxes that day, and the next day he unloaded sixteen." I nodded slowly, still impressed at his persistence. "One thing I can tell you about the Penguin is that he's a relentless bastard. He kept waddling from door to door, knocking and knocking until his knuckles were bleeding, even as he snuffled back the tears. But he was averaging three hundred dollars a day in commission, so it was worth a few tears. I mean, that was a lot of money back then, especially to a kid who'd just dropped out of dental school. So, fuck it, I thought. In spite of knowing it was a little bit of a hustle, I figured I'd give it a whirl."

I paused and looked at OCD. "You wanna guess what happened next?"

OCD smiled and shook his head a few times. "I could only imagine."

"Actually," I said, "you probably couldn't, because no one at the Great American could. You see, since price seemed to be everyone's biggest objection, I figured, why not try selling to rich people? Or, better yet, to rich people I *knew.* The problem was that I didn't really know any rich people–except for the father of my girlfriend from college, David Russell. But that was a sticky situation, because he and his wife had just gotten separated and I didn't know where he was living. She, I knew, was still living in the mansion up in Westchester, but I couldn't just go knocking on her door. She never really liked me, although I can't imagine why." I looked at the Witch and said, "What's not to like, Michele, right?"

The Witch didn't speak or smile; she simply raised her thin left eyebrow high on her forehead, as if to say, "Are you fucking kidding me?" I shrugged and said, "Well, I guess she had her reasons. But, that aside, I did the next best thing and went to her next-door neighbor." I nodded a single time, implying the righteousness of my decision. "Yes," I said proudly, "I pulled my Toyota pickup truck right up to her neighbor's enormous front door and hopped out and started knocking. I remember it like it was yesterday. The house was an enormous white colonial with forest-green shutters; and the front door was bigger than the one that led into the Emerald City. It was painted barn red and had a thousand coats of lacquer on it. And I kept rapping on it until, finally, after a minute, a kind-looking sixtyish woman, with gray hair and granny glasses, came to the door and said, 'Can I help you, young man?'

"I offered her a sad smile and said, 'Maybe you can, ma'am. My name is Jordan, and I deliver meat and seafood to some of your neighbors in the area. I have an overorder on my truck today, and I can't get back to the freezer. I'm willing to sell you everything at cost.' I flashed her my big blue puppy-dog eyes and added, 'Is there any way you can help me out, ma'am?'

"She stared at me for a few seconds, and then, in a tone ripe with skepticism, she said, 'Which neighbors do you deliver to?' Without missing a beat I answered, 'To the Russells next door.' Suddenly it occurred to me that she might actually call over there, so I quickly added, 'Actually, it was to Mr. Russell–to David, as he liked to be called,' and then I compressed my lips and nodded sadly. 'But, you know, with all that's going on over there with the divorce, they haven't been buying much meat lately.'

"The woman was very sympathetic to that, so her tone immediately softened. 'I can only imagine,' she said sadly. 'It's a terrible thing, divorce.' Then, suddenly, she perked up and asked, 'Well, what do you have on the truck today?' I lifted an index finger and said, 'Hold on, I'll be right back,' and I ran out to the truck, grabbed one of everything, and came lumbering back with a dozen boxes. I had them stacked twelve high, towering a foot over my head.

"When I reached the front door, the woman said, 'It's freezing outside; why don't you bring those into the foyer?' She motioned toward a gray marble foyer that was big enough to land a plane in. 'Uh, um, thank you,' I said, letting out a couple of obvious grunts and groans. 'These boxes are really heavy.' Then, as I walked past her, I added, 'You're right about it being freezing outside; it's absolutely brutal!' And I dropped down to my knees and let the boxes hit the gray marble floor with an exaggerated thud." I paused and took a moment to regard my captors.

They seemed shocked more than disgusted over the wonderful string of fibs I had told this kind old woman. What they had no idea of, though, was that the greatest fibs were yet to come. Of course, I knew I shouldn't plunge into the gory details of how I had convinced this kind old woman to buy all forty boxes of meat on the truck. This wasn't the sort of thing that my captors would respect, but I just couldn't seem to stop myself. I was getting an irrational joy by flashing back to the days when I was still a budding salesman. Besides, while I was busy talking about the past, I had no time to focus on the present, which is to say, the grim reality that had become my life. So I soldiered on, with relish.

"Well, I gotta tell you," I said with a bit of cockiness slipping out around the edges, "there are only a handful of defining moments in a young man's life, moments where something *so extraordinary* happens that he knows things will never be the same again." I paused for effect. "And this was one of them. I'd hustled ices on the beach before, but that wasn't really selling; it was more about working hard and having the desire to succeed. And even my little auction at dental school wasn't really salesmanship, although it was definitely one step closer.

"But when I looked up at this kind woman's smiling face, well"–I added a hint of the supernatural to my tone–"a *strange* feeling washed over me, almost magical, in fact. It was as if I knew exactly what this woman needed to hear–or, better yet, exactly what I needed to say to her to convince her to buy everything.

"I opened the first box and raised my palm toward twelve beautiful filet mignons, each individually wrapped in clear plastic. 'Black Angus filet mignons,' I said proudly, 'inch and a half thick. They've been flash-frozen and Cryovac-ed to near perfection; they'll last up to twelve months in your freezer, ma'am.' I nodded proudly, shocked at how easily the bullshit was rolling off my tongue. 'Restaurants broil these for seven minutes on each side and then serve them with béarnaise sauce.' Then I looked her right in the eye and said with the utmost conviction, 'They're so tender you can cut them with a plastic fork.' Then I moved the box to the side and went on to the next one. 'South African lobster tails,' I declared. 'Split them down the back, brush them with butter and garlic, and twenty minutes later you got yourself a surf and turf.'

"And I went on and on, spitting out a little rap about each product and then saying I had three of these on the truck or four of those on the truck. Finally, when all the boxes were open and we were literally surrounded by meat and fish, I pointed to the prices and said, 'I'll take fifteen dollars off each box, which is my absolute cost. Believe me, you can't even *get* this food in the supermarket! That's how good it is.'

"After a few moments she said, 'Well, I'd love to help you. I mean, you seem like such a *nice* young boy. But it's only my husband and me. I wouldn't have use for so much food.' She thought for a second then said, 'Besides, I hardly have any room in my freezer.' She shrugged sadly. 'I'm very sorry.'

"I looked up at her and nodded slowly. 'I totally understand that, but let me say this: I happen to be a professional freezer packer, and I'm willing to bet I can shuffle things around a bit, maybe even clean things up in the process. And not only will I pack your freezer for you, but I'm *also* willing to walk your dog and mop your floor and mow your front lawn and paint your house'–I raised both my palms toward her–'not that it needs it or anything, but what I'm trying to say is that I'll do whatever it takes to sell the food today.' I compressed my lips for effect. 'See, if my food ends up thawing out, I might lose my job, and I can't afford for that to happen. I'm trying to put myself through college.' Suddenly a wonderful thought came bubbling up into my brain. I bit my lower lip and said, 'Do you have grandchildren, by any chance?'

"Well, the woman fairly beamed at the question. I think I made her day, in fact. 'Oh, yes,' she answered with a smile. 'I have five of them; they're very wonderful.' I smiled and said, 'I'm sure they're very precious. So why not throw a great big barbecue for them? It would be a terrific excuse to get the whole family together. And then you can tell everyone about this nice young boy who came by and sold you all this wonderful food! You can even give them doggie bags to bring home.' I raised my eyebrows and nodded eagerly. 'In fact, I'll even deliver the food to them! Just call me back, and I'll come by with my truck.'

"She mulled it over for a few seconds, then said, 'Okay; I have an extra freezer in the garage. You can put it in there.'

" 'Oh, my God,' I declared. 'Thank you so much, ma'am. You saved my life! What would you like? I have all sorts of prepared foods too. I have chicken Kiev, chicken cordon bleu, crab thermidor, which happens to be especially delicious,' and it also happens to be my highest markup item, I thought.

"The woman smiled at me and said, 'I guess I'll take everything. I mean, I wouldn't want you to lose your job, right?' "

I paused and leaned back in my seat and stared at the Bastard. "And that's how simple it was. She bought the whole fucking truck from me right on the spot!" I shrugged my shoulders. "Of course, I felt a bit guilty about having lied to the woman, but the food, well, it was top-notch, not to mention the fact that I'd single-handedly inspired her to throw a family reunion. So it was all good, right?"

"Yeah, it was all good," snarled the Bastard.

I ignored his sarcasm. "Right, it was all good. In fact, it was *so* good that my first week on the job I sold two hundred and forty boxes—which was more than twice the company record. And that was how it started. From there, a bizarre chain of events led me into the stock market and then to Stratton. Let me take them in order."

The Bastard nodded a single time. "Please do."

I nodded back. "It started with the Great American office. It was as if the entire sales force suddenly caught fire. Everyone's production doubled, some even tripled. It was as if I'd raised the bar or opened a new realm of possibility as to how much money could be made if you worked hard and sold the right way. Within a week, the manager came to me and asked if I'd help train the new salesmen. The manager was P. J. Cammarata. He kept saying, 'You pumped up the office, Jordan. It's pumped beyond belief now...' and blah, blah, blah. He kept going on about how the pump was everything." I paused, shocked at how clear my memory of this was. "In retrospect, it was the only intelligent thing he ever said.

See, the pump *is* crucial; without it, a sales force withers away and dies quicker than you can imagine."

"So you agreed to train the salesmen?" asked the Bastard.

"Yes, but for selfish reasons. I was already planning on starting my own company; it was only a question of when. I figured I'd buy my own truck, go down to the meat market, and make the wholesale markup too. It's what I had done at the beach all those years, and it'd worked like a charm." I shrugged. "So I began to train the salesmen and quickly realized that I had a knack for it. In fact, I was so good at it that I could take virtually any kid off the street and turn him into a meat salesman.

"A few weeks after that, P.J. asked me if I would give a sales meeting to the office, to take the pump to the next level." I paused, thinking back for a moment. "It's rather ironic that it would be a dimwit like P.J., with his dirty jeans and tan Members Only jacket, who would instigate one of the defining moments of my life. See, above all, it's my ability to speak before the crowd—giving sales meetings to the Strattonites—that was at the heart of my success. It's what kept the pump going all those years, despite all the regulatory problems we were having."

"The meetings?" the Bastard asked open-endedly.

"Yes, the meetings. It's what separates—or, should I say, *separated*—Stratton from every other brokerage firm in America. Twice a day I would stand before the boardroom and preach to the brokers. No one on Wall Street had done that before. Occasionally a brokerage firm would bring in a guest speaker—someone like an Anthony Robbins type—but it was always a one-shot deal, not as part of a program. And that's a complete waste of time, to do it once. If you want results, you have to do it every day; and if you *really* want results, you have to do it twice a day, once in the morning and once in the afternoon. Then miracles can happen.

"But, of course, I wasn't aware of that back in my Great American days... although I *will* tell you that the first meeting I gave was a real eye-opener. It took place inside the warehouse, in Forest Hills, Queens. There were twenty salesmen there, most of them in their early thirties. They were all dressed in jeans and sneakers, trying to look like truck drivers. They were gathered around in a circle, and I was standing at the center. At first I started speaking slowly, talking about the quality of the food, how *amazing* it was, how there was nothing else like it, and how lucky our customers were to have access to it. In hindsight, I was laying the foundation for a cult, although back then I was doing it without even knowing it. And the fact that–"

OCD held up his hand. "What do you mean, 'laying the foundation for a cult'?"

I looked at OCD and said, "Let me put it this way: At the heart of any cult–whether it's Stratton Oakmont or Great American or those crazy Branch Davidians from Waco, Texas–is the fundamental belief that, in spite of what the rest of the world might be saying about them, everyone else is crazy and they're sane. And, without exception, it always starts with a belief in the justness of their cause. With Muslim extremists it's a warped interpretation of the Koran; with the Branch Davidians it's a warped interpretation of the Bible; and at Stratton it was the boardroom itself, the great equalizer in an otherwise unfair world. In other words, it didn't matter what family you were born into or how limited your education was or how low your IQ was; once you stepped into the Stratton boardroom, all that was behind you. You became equalized; you could make as much money as the most powerful CEO in America." I shrugged my shoulders, as if this were basic stuff.

"All cults draw their power by advancing a concept like that–that they have some sort of one-up on the world. With Great American it was having food you couldn't get in the supermarket, and with Stratton it was the promise of becoming rich, in spite of the fact that you were a high school dropout who deserved to be working the checkout line at Seven-Eleven." I chuckled ironically. "That's why I said before, 'Give them to me young and stupid, young and naive.' Because they make much better cult members.

"Anyway–back to my first meeting–after a few minutes of selling the salesmen on how great the food was, the words began gushing out in torrents. Perfect strings of thoughts came pouring out of my mouth. Before I knew it, I was literally preaching, going on and on in intimate detail about things that had never even occurred to me before. Yet I still sounded like I was the world's foremost expert on them: things like the difference between winners and losers, and the power of positive thinking, and being the master of your own destiny.

"Then I started getting technical, and I plunged into the art of selling–explaining how to open and close a sale; how to modulate the speed and tone of your voice to keep people interested; and the importance of being relentless, of not taking no for an answer and knocking on doors until their knuckles bled. 'You owe it to yourselves!' I said to them. 'You owe it to yourselves, you owe it to your families, and, most importantly, you owe it to the people whose doors you're knocking on, because the food is so amazing that every last person who buys from you will be eternally grateful!'

"I can't overstimate how baffled I was at my own ability to speak like this. It was completely effortless; and the gratification was *instant.* I could see it in the eyes of every salesman there. They loved it, and they loved *me.* And the longer I spoke, the more they loved me.

"Over time, I found that giving meetings filled a hole inside me. It was simply the most amazing feeling ever; you can't even begin to imagine." I smiled sadly at the memory. "But, of course, like everything else, I became desensitized to it. Eventually, even at the height of Stratton, when I was giving meetings to a football field full of brokers, I no longer got the same rush from it. So the hole grew larger." I paused, letting the implications of that sink in. Then I said, "So I turned to other things, like drugs and sex and living life on the edge. By the early nineties the word on Wall Street was that I had a death wish. But I never looked at it that way: I thought I was living life as it unfolded; putting one foot in front of the other and walking down a preordained path. But the path turned out to be the path to my own destruction, and it was being laid down by my own actions."

No responses. The debriefing room was dead silent now. In fact, you could have heard a pin drop. I continued with my tale: "I still remember the looks on the salesmen's faces as if it were yesterday. But the face that sticks out most is Elliot's. He was totally mesmerized. He looked like he was getting ready to run out of the warehouse right that second and start knocking on doors. That's how much the meeting affected him, and that's how much it affected our relationship. You see, before that, we considered each other equals, but after the meeting we had a silent understanding that *I* would be the one calling the shots now.

"It was maybe two weeks later when I approached him with the idea of opening up our own meat-and-seafood company. 'Why pay Great American twenty dollars a box,' I said, 'when we can go down to the meat market ourselves?'

"But the Penguin was *so* brainwashed, he actually said, 'But what about the food? Where are we gonna get food as good as Great American's?' "

I chuckled at the memory. "Can you imagine? I mean, this guy was so brainwashed that he'd actually convinced himself that Great American's food was so good that he couldn't go door to door without it. It was almost laughable. I mean, yeah, their food was good, but it was only *good;* it wasn't *great*! The steaks were choice, not prime, and the fish was frozen, not fresh. So I had to deprogram the Penguin from the Great American cult.

"I let him down easy–sort of. 'What the fuck is wrong with you, Penguin? The food is just average, for Chrissake! So get a fucking grip.' Then I smiled at him warmly and said, 'Listen, we'll find even *better* steaks than Great American, and we'll find fresher fish too. Then we'll hire salesmen of our own–to go door to door for *us*–and then we'll get rich!'

"That's how Elliot and I got into the meat-and-seafood business. And we had the perfect plan: It was almost summertime, so we would sell ices during the day and tie up all the loose ends of our business venture at night. And with the money from the beach, we'd finance our meat-and-seafood company. We even brought in another beach vendor to partner up with us, our friend Paul Burton." I motioned to my list again. "He's on there too," I said casually. "Paul was living with his mother at the time, in a big white house in Douglaston, Queens, and, by coincidence, the house had a big backyard, just perfect for a meat-and-seafood company. Or so we thought.

"See, despite Douglaston being a very upscale neighborhood,

Paul's house was a shithole. His mother had gotten it in a divorce, about twenty years earlier, and she hadn't put a dime into it since. It was almost like a haunted house now, and the backyard was no better. It had a freestanding garage surrounded by nothing but dirt, about a half acre of it." I smiled nostalgically. "Still, it was absolutely perfect for us. We were budding entrepreneurs, and starting out of a garage seemed very romantic. I mean, that's how Steve Jobs and Michael Dell started. Or maybe it was from out of their dorm rooms. Either way, that was how the Penguin and I financed ourselves: Billionaires of Tomorrow!

"In fact, we even went to see an accountant to make sure we hadn't *missed* anything!" I shrugged innocently. "And that's where the problems started. He was a referral from Elliot's father, who's a Hasidic Jew. The accountant was also a Hasidic Jew, and apparently he had as much experience with the meat-and-seafood industry as he did with eating pork chops. And after we explained our business plan to him, he smiled and said, 'Well, it sounds like you two are going to make a fortune together. *Mazel tov!*' And then, for good measure, he added, 'You're going to be very rich young men soon; very, very rich.'

"Well, what was there to say to that? Elliot and I took his words to mean that we were in desperate need of tax write-offs. In fact, we went straight from the accountant's office right to the Palm restaurant, where we spent four hundred fifty dollars on champagne and lobster. Then we leased ourselves two sports cars: I leased a Porsche and the Penguin leased a Lincoln Continental." I rolled my eyes at the Penguin's choice of automobile. "Then we got ourselves cell phones, despite the fact that, back then, cellular service was so ridiculously expensive that only a CEO of a Fortune Five Hundred company would dare own one.

"Still, it all made perfect sense to us: We were enterpreneurs, after all, which to our way of thinking entitled us to a few things. And with all the money we were saving by starting out in Paul's backyard, we'd earned the right to lavish ourselves with a few basic luxuries. Then came opening day, September twenty-sixth, 1985. It seemed like as good a day as any to open up a meat-and-seafood company–although Mother Nature begged to differ. Or at least that's what I surmised when Hurricane Gloria came smashing into Long Island and the eye passed right over Paul's backyard. In fact, she dumped what amounted to thirty-two inches of rain on the backyard, because it happened to be at the bottom of four converging hills. And just like that, our little meat-and-seafood company became a gigantic fucking mud pit." I shook my head in amazement. "We were out of business before we even started."

"You never opened?" the Bastard said skeptically. "But in the *Forbes* article–"

The Witch cut off the Bastard. "According to *Forbes* you were in business for quite some time." She cocked her head to the side and stared at me accusingly.

OCD shook his head. "I don't think he meant *literally,* Michele."

"Greg's right," I said, trying not to make enemies with the Witch. "Although, on a separate note, I will tell you that agreeing to the *Forbes* interview was one the biggest mistakes of my adult life. I was only twenty-eight, though, so I was a bit naive back then." I shrugged. "Anyway, I thought I'd get a chance to tell my side of the story, to set the record straight. Stratton had been in business for only two years, so no one had even heard of us. But the woman who interviewed me stuck a tomahawk in my back, coining me *a twisted version of Robin Hood, who robs from the rich and gives to himself and his merry band of brokers.*" I grimaced at the memory. "It was a nightmare, that article. A total fucking nightmare."

"You lose brokers over it?" asked the Bastard.

"No," I answered quickly, "the brokers loved bad press, especially *that* article. In fact, the day after it hit they came to work dressed in medieval garb, and they were running around screaming, 'We're your merry band! We're your band!' " I chuckled at the memory. "What bothered me about the article, though, was the picture of me they used. It was horrendous."

OCD smiled devilishly. "You mean the one with you standing next to the rusty drainpipe?" He let out an ironic chuckle. The Mormon added, "Yeah, the one where you have an evil smile!"

I shook my head in disgust. "Yeah, yeah, yeah," I muttered. "The rusty drainpipe, as if Stratton were going down the drain. I know all about it. The *Forbes* photographer fucked me over with that one; first he tricked me into going up to the roof, and then he *casually* asked me to stand next to the drainpipe." I rolled my eyes. "I didn't notice it at the time, because I was too busy worrying about my hair as he snapped a thousand and one pictures, waiting until he caught me at *just* the right moment, when I had this shit-eating grin on my face. And that was the picture they used." I shook my head at my own naïveté. "And, of course, the article poked fun at my meat-and-seafood days—point being that I had no business being in the world of high finance, that I was a lowly meat salesman and nothing more. In fact, the title of the article was 'Steaks, Stocks, What's the Difference?' "

I looked at the Witch and said, "But you happen to be right, Michele. As the article pointed out, we *did* stay in business for a while, although I wouldn't actually categorize it as being in business; it was more like playing catch-up ball or chasing your own tail." I thought back for a moment. "After the hurricane was gone, Paul's backyard was submerged under three feet of water. We spent the next two weeks digging ourselves out of the mud; then, out of nowhere, the backyard turned into a sinkhole and everything began to collapse—starting with the garage, then the patio, and then, eventually, the house itself. We called in a geologist to see if the house was on a previously unknown fault line, but it wasn't.

"And we had other problems too. We'd bought a used freezer trailer—as old as the hills—figuring we could save a few bucks. But it was wildly inefficient and sucked enough power to electrify New Jersey. And, of course, the wiring in Paul's house couldn't handle the amperage"—I searched my memory for a moment—"and I think it was in early December when we nearly burned Paul's house down." I shrugged innocently. "That's when his mother came marching into the backyard, with a rope tied around her waist so she wouldn't sink into the center of the earth, and she screamed, 'Get the fuck out! And take those stupid pickup trucks with you!' "

I smiled at the memory. "But Paul's mother was a kind woman, and she gave us a full month to find a new warehouse. That seemed pretty reasonable at the time, although it turned out to be easier said than done. We had no credit history, and our balance sheet was a disaster, so all the better landlords rejected us.

"There were six of us at that point: Elliot, Paul, and me, and our three employees, starting with big Frank Bua, who at six foot five was the spitting image of the Gerber baby with a beard; then tiny George Barbella, who stood two inches above midget status and looked like the devil himself; and then we had an intractable steriod-head named Chucky Jones,* who looked like the Norse god Thor. He was only five foot four, though, so he looked like Thor after he'd been squashed.

"Not surprisingly, each of our employees had a serious dysfunction, although, in Frank's case, it had more to do with his wife. She had a rare disease called alopecia totalis, which had caused all of her hair to fall out, even her eyebrows and eyelashes. She looked like a female Yul Brenner. George Barbella's dysfunction was that he was completely obsessed with the food, even more so than Elliot. He used to walk around complaining how our shrimps had been glazed with water, to add weight to them. 'When my customers cook them,' he'd moan, 'they turn from jumbos into micros.' " I shrugged innocently. "But glazing was standard industry procedure, so it wasn't my fault. Anyway, what he *really* should've been concerned about was the food smelling like kerosene."

The Bastard recoiled in his seat. "The food smelled like kerosene?"

"Sometimes," I replied. "Paul's garage didn't have any heat, and by the time December rolled around we were nearly freezing to death. So we bought this giant kerosene heater, which looked like a torpedo on wheels. It did a fine job heating the place, although the thing burned hotter than the sun and was noisier than an F-15 on afterburners. And every so often it would misfire–belching out a thick cloud of smoke, which got on the food. Still, it was better than freezing to death." I paused, taking a sip of water. "And then there was Chucky's dysfunction, which was, among other things, pulling his pants down in the garage and injecting himself in the ass with testosterone. But on the bright side, he had a terrific sense of humor and gave each of us nicknames: Frank Bua was the Gerber Baby; George Barbella was Tattoo, named after the midget

---

*Name has been changed

from *Fantasy Island;* and Paul Burton was Cinema Head, because he had an enormous forehead, which, according to Chucky, was large enough to project a movie on."

They already knew Elliot's nickname. I was about to offer up mine when OCD smiled and said, "Elliot was the Penguin. What was your nickname?" He narrowed his eyes shrewdly. "Let me guess: You were Napoleon, right?"

Fucking asshole! I thought. The Duchess used to call me Napoleon when she was trying to annoy me! She even made me dress up as that little bastard for Halloween once. Had OCD heard about that? I mean, was it really *that* obvious to everyone that I had a Napoleon complex? Or had he just guessed? Well, it didn't really matter.

I was about to tell OCD to fuck off when the Mormon saved me the trouble. "Look who's talking!" snapped the Mormon, and he started chuckling, as did the Witch and the Bastard. The unspoken message was: *OCD and the Wolf of Wall Street both have Napoleon complexes!* Magnum, however, hadn't laughed, refusing to mock another man's stature; after all, he was the size of two full-grown men, and to make fun of a pint-size one would have been inappropriate.

Before OCD had a chance to pull his gun on the Mormon, I said to him, "You're partially right, Greg, at least about Elliot. But his nickname wasn't just the Penguin; it was the *Suicidal* Penguin. See, we were already on the verge of bankruptcy by then, and Elliot was on the verge of suicide. So Chucky used to waddle around the office with his index finger to his temple and his thumb sticking up, as if he were getting ready to blow his own brains out. 'Hi, I'm the Suicidal Penguin,' he'd chirp, 'and I deliver meat and seafood to local restaurants. I have an overorder on my truck and can't get back to the freezer,' and he'd keep saying it over and over again, as he waddled around the garage, flapping his arms like a migrating penguin. 'Help me! Help me!' he'd chirp. 'Hurricane Gloria pissed all over me and the kerosene heater is suffocating me and the Gerber Baby's wife looks like a space alien and Cinema Head's mother is closing down our movie theater and . . .' " I started chuckling. "He was really something else,

Chucky, and then, one day–*poof!*–he was gone. Vanished like a fart in the wind. It turned out he was robbing liquor stores at night. Last I heard of him was when two NYPD detectives came by the garage, trying to ascertain his last-known whereabouts. He's probably dead by now, either that or he's doing stand-up comedy somewhere."

"So what was *your* nickname?" asked the Witch, compressing her thin lips until they all but disappeared. I smiled and said, "I got off easy, Michele. Chucky called me J.P., which was short for J. P. Morgan. See, Chucky never made fun of me. He believed in me, and he loved the meetings. After each meeting he would pull me aside and say, 'What the fuck are you doing with this business? It's beneath you. You're the sharpest guy I know, J.P. . . .' And he'd tell me to cut Cinema Head and the Penguin loose. 'They're holding you back,' he'd say. 'You're J. P. Morgan, and they're small-time bunko artists.' " I paused, thinking back on his advice. "He happened to be right on target with Paul; he was much too lazy to sell door to door. And he was also right about our company; going door to door with a pickup truck was a fool's errand, totally fucking ludicrous.

"But he was wrong about Elliot. The Penguin was a winner, in the truest sense of the word. No one worked harder than him, and he was completely loyal to me. We would go on to make a fortune together, although not in the meat-and-seafood business. It would be on Wall Street. First we needed to be taught a few more lessons in humility."

I took a deep breath and said, "It was sometime in late December when we finally hit bottom. We were literally out of money, and Paul's mother was threatening to call the sheriff. All seemed lost; all options had been exhausted. And then something incredible happened, something entirely unexpected. I'd just gotten back to the garage from another torturous day in the field, when the Penguin said to me: 'I got a strange call today from one of our meat suppliers. They asked me what terms we wanted.' He shrugged, as if confused. 'I didn't know what they were talking about, so I told them I'd think about it and get back to them.'

" 'What does *terms* mean?' I asked. 'Terms for our surrender?' to which the Suicidal Penguin shrugged his shoulders and said, 'I'm not really sure, but what's the difference? The freezer's empty, and we don't have money to buy food. We're out of business.' "

I paused, smirking at how unsophisticated we'd once been. We hadn't the slightest idea that our suppliers would be willing to ship us food on credit. It seemed like an outlandish concept that they'd be willing to go out on a limb like that, but, as I was about to learn, it was standard operating procedure: Everyone gave credit. The business lingo was *terms,* which was short for *terms for payment.*

With a hint of mischief in my tone, I said, "Once I found out that our suppliers would be dumb enough to ship us food on credit, I quickly saw a way out. It was simple: Grow like wildfire. Take on as much credit as possible and push the payment terms as far out into the future as I could. Then buy as many pickup trucks as possible, all of them with no money down–which you could do if you were willing to pay twenty-four percent interest. But I wasn't concerned about the monthly payments, because the more trucks I had on the road, the more food I would sell and the better my cash flow would be.

"In other words, since my suppliers were giving me thirty days to pay for the food while my customers were paying me every day, as long as I kept selling more and more, my cash flow would continue to improve. Even if I weren't making a dime on a sale, I would *still* be generating cash, using the thirty days of float."

The Bastard said quickly, "It's Business 101."

Yeah, right! I thought cynically. The Bastard couldn't possibly appreciate the dark art of juggling cash flow! (He was far too honest.) Perhaps he understood the simple math of it, but there were so many devilish strategies to employ, especially in the endgame, when your creditors were circling and your balance sheet was bleeding red ink faster than a hemophiliac with a gunshot wound. It would take a month to explain all the scummy nuances to someone like the Bastard.

On the other hand, Elliot and I quickly became Jedi Masters at the art and then just as quickly we crossed over to the dark side–finding every way possible to juggle cash flow. My favorite was reverse financial extortion, during which you'd turn the tables on an angry supplier by explaining to him that the only shot he had of getting paid back was to accept a small payment on an old invoice in return for extending you more credit; that one worked like a charm. And then there was the old one-signature-check trick, where I'd give a supplier a check with either my or Elliot's signature missing, which would cause the bank to return it for improper endorsement, as opposed to insufficient funds. Of course, we were always careful to alert the bank manager about this check, lest he mistakenly try to clear it and it bounced like a kangaroo.

And there were other tricks too, but none of them was the Bastard's business. So all I said was, "Exactly; it's Business 101, Joel. Before I knew it, I had twenty-six trucks on the road, a legitimate warehouse, and a whole lot of money in the bank. Of course, my balance sheet was a total wreck, although I refused to focus on that. Instead, I relished giving sales meetings to twenty-six nitwits, most of whom were addicted to either crack or smack or were certified alcoholics.

"Still, at least I was the proud owner of a seemingly successful meat-and-seafood company. And all my friends were really impressed with me; they all thought I was a first-rate entrepreneur." I shrugged innocently. "That's when I met Kenny Greene; he came to work for me in the meat business."

"Really?" said OCD. "I didn't know that."

I nodded slowly, wondering why Kenny Greene hadn't been indicted along with Danny and me. He was the third partner at Stratton, although he hadn't been associated with the firm since we'd settled our SEC case four years ago. Still, he'd been a twenty-percent partner up to that point, as had Danny (I owned the other sixty percent). He'd made tens of millions of dollars and had broken as many laws as we had. It seemed highly illogical (and also a tad unfair) that he'd escaped OCD's wrath–unless he'd been cooperating all along!

I chose to keep those thoughts to myself, and I said, "He was a referral from one of my friends from college, a guy named Jeff Honigman. He and Kenny were first cousins." I motioned to my villains, thieves, and scoundrels list. "Jeff's on there too, although most of his dirty deeds took place after he left Stratton, when he was working for Victor Wang, at Duke Securities." Once more, I motioned to the list. "Victor's on there too, somewhere close to the top, just above Kenny's name." I wondered if they were aware of what a truly depraved maniac Victor Wang was. "In fact, Victor worked for me in the meat-and-seafood business too, although only for about an hour. He was too proud and too lazy to actually take a truck out and go door to door; he just showed up to listen to one of my sales meetings. And, of course, I still remember the first time I laid eyes on Victor." I started chuckling at the memory.

The Mormon chimed in: "How could you forget, right?"

I nodded in agreement. "Right, how could *anyone* forget? He's basically the biggest Chinaman to ever walk the planet. He's got a chest the size of the Great Wall, slits for eyes, a brow ridge like a rock ledge, and a head that's larger than a giant panda's." I paused, catching my breath. "You know, I don't know if all of you have *seen* Victor, but he's the spitting image of Oddjob, from the James Bond movie *Goldfinger.* Remember Oddjob? He's the one who killed people by throwing his hat at them–"

"What's your point?" said the Bastard, shaking his head.

I shrugged. "No point, really, other than that Kenny and Victor were childhood friends who dealt drugs together back in high school–both of them, I might add, being backed by Kenny's mother, Gladys. But I refuse to give you any information about Gladys; she might try to kick my ass." I smiled ruefully. "In fact, the last time someone got under Glady's skin was at a bowling alley. I think she ended up tossing the guy for a strike. Or maybe it was in a supermarket, where she knocked out a woman in the express line. Either way, if you'd ever actually *seen* Gladys it wouldn't really surprise you." I nodded my head three times, for emphasis. "There's not an ounce of fat on her, and her gut could stop an English musket ball fired at more than twenty paces. Know the type?" I raised my eyebrows.

Nothing but blank expressions, punctuated by silence. I soldiered on: "Anyway, Gladys belongs on that list too, although I assume you're not interested in her, right?" I crossed my fingers.

"Right," the Bastard said tonelessly. "We're not interested in her. Why don't you get back to the meat business."

I nodded, relieved. "Fair enough; but just so you know, this whole Kenny–Gladys–Victor triangle leads right back to your earlier question about where the first wave of Strattonites came from. Kenny and Victor both grew up in Jericho. Kenny was a pot dealer and Victor was a coke dealer, and Gladys was their backer." I paused, then added, "But her motives were pure, of course. I mean, you know, she was just trying to keep the family afloat after Kenny's father died of cancer. It was all very sad." I shrugged, hoping Gladys could somehow hear my words and would choose not to beat me up if we crossed paths. "Anyway, out of the first wave of Strattonites, about half came from Jericho and Syosset–which are sister towns–and virtually all of them had been clients of Kenny and Victor. That's how Stratton was able to grow so quick; even before we gained a reputation as a place for kids to get rich, I had dozens of them lining up at my door. And then they'd move to Bayside to join the cult.

"But let me take things in order: Kenny worked at the meat company for only one day, at which point he crashed up one of my trucks and then never called me again, or at least not until I was out of the meat business. And Victor, as I said, never worked there at all; he just showed up once to listen to one of my sales meetings and he never came back.

"In the meantime, my business was on the verge of imploding." I shook my head slowly, preparing myself to relive the dreaded memory. "You can only play the cash-flow game for so long before it reverses itself on you. In our case, the reversal started in January of 1987. It was a ferocious winter, and sales had plunged through the floor. Cash flow, of course, had plunged with it. I gave meeting upon meeting, desperately trying to motivate the salesmen to go out and sell, but it was no use. It was too cold, and sales came to a grinding halt.

"And by the very nature of the cash-flow game, that's when the boomerang came flying back the hardest. Remember, it's Business 101, Joel. When you're growing on credit, today's bills are for things you sold thirty days ago or, in our case, sixty days ago, because we were already thirty days behind on our bills." I paused, then corrected myself. "Actually, we were ninety days behind on most of our bills, but we were no longer doing business with those companies; they'd already cut us off, so we'd been forced to move on to more-fertile pastures–meaning, new suppliers who hadn't caught wind of the fact that we didn't pay our bills.

"But that part of the game was over now too. Word was out that we were a bad credit risk and shouldn't be shipped to unless we paid cash up front. Meanwhile, Elliot and I were still trying to keep things afloat. We'd exhausted our personal credit cards, and every day we were falling deeper and deeper into debt. We hadn't paid our truck leases, our cell-phone bills, our car leases. And our new landlord, a Syrian bastard, had an eviction order against us and was making us pay double rent until we were current."

I shook my head slowly, still amazed at how deep a financial hole we'd dug for ourselves. Then I said, "It was right around that time, in the winter of '87, when I started hearing rumors about a kid from my neighborhood named Michael Falk. He'd landed a job on Wall Street straight out of college–right around the same time I was starting dental school–and he was supposedly making over a million dollars a year." I paused for effect. "At first I didn't believe it. I mean, growing up, Michael Falk was not a sharp kid. In fact, he was more like the neighborhood loser, someone everyone else made fun of for not taking a shower. He wasn't quick or bright or well spoken or anything else, for that matter. He was just average, nothing more. So I figured it was bullshit, that there was no *way* he could be making that sort of money.

"Then, one day, by sheer coincidence, he came pulling up to my apartment building, driving a convertible Ferrari. Thankfully he was kind enough to condescend to me, and he explained that all the rumors were true–yes, he said matter-of-factly, he was on pace to make over $1.5 million this year, and last year he'd made almost a million. We spoke for a few more minutes, during which time I lied incessantly–explaining how well I was doing in the meat-and-seafood business, pointing to my little red Porsche as proof of that fact. He shrugged his shoulders and mentioned something about chartering a hundred-foot yacht off the Bahamas with a bunch of blond models–ironically, one of whom would become my second wife one day. And then he was off, smoothly, immaculately, and with a puff of expensive Italian exhaust fumes in my face, which at that very moment was a mixture of awe and astonishment."

I let out a few chuckles. "Anyway, I can tell you that I had never been so affected by a single encounter in my entire life. I remember watching his Ferrari pull away and saying to myself: 'If that guy can make a million bucks a year, then I can make fifty million a year!'" I paused, letting those words sink in. "It turned out to be an uncanny prediction, don't you think?" Then I quickly added, "Although I guess I failed to predict the other half of the equation: that I'd be facing a couple of hundred years in jail"–I locked eyes with the Witch–"as well as the eternal damnation of my soul.

"Anyway, I was living with my first wife, Denise, back then, although she wasn't actually my wife yet. We were sharing a tiny apartment in a yuppie-infested apartment building in Bayside called the Bay Club. That's where I first met Danny Porush. He was living upstairs from me, although at the time I hadn't met him yet. I'd seen him around from time to time, but we'd never really spoken." I shrugged. "It's funny, but I remember always thinking how normal he looked, as if he were the perfect yuppie. In fact, he and his wife, Nancy, were the pictures of success and happiness. They even looked alike! But, of course, I didn't know at the time that the two of them were first cousins. And I also had no idea that Nancy's sole mission in life was to torture Danny–to make his life as miserable and as difficult as possible–and that Danny, despite his normal appearance, was completely off his rocker, spending the bulk of his day holed up in a Harlem crack den, smoking his latest business venture into cocaine-induced bankruptcy.

"But I'm jumping ahead here. I still wouldn't meet Danny for another year. Getting back to Michael Falk: It was that same afternoon when I told Denise about my little run-in with this erstwhile loser. When I was done, no words were necessary. Denise just looked at me with her big brown eyes and nodded slowly, and that was that. We both knew right then and there that my destiny was Wall Street. I was the most talented salesman in the world; she knew it and I knew it. My mistake was that I'd picked the wrong product to sell."

"How were you able to get a job as a stockbroker?" asked the Bastard. "Your degree's in biology and you were just coming off a bankruptcy. Why would someone hire you?"

"I was able to get my foot in the door through a friend of my parents, a man named Bob Cohen. He was a mid-level manager at LF Rothschild, and he had enough clout to get me an interview. And from there I sold myself. I went out and bought myself a cheap blue suit, and then two days after that I found myself sitting on the express bus on my way to Manhattan for a job interview. Meanwhile, Denise was sitting at home waiting for a tow truck to come and repossess our Porsche–which it did–right about the same time I was getting myself hired as a stockbroker trainee at LF Rothschild."

Then I smiled sadly and said, "And after that, my next stop was to my meat company, where I dropped the bomb on Elliot." I paused for a moment, thinking back. "I still remember this day like it was yesterday, the bittersweetness of it, the mixed emotions I felt. As happy as I was about my future, I was sad about parting ways with Elliot. He was like a brother to me. We'd been partners since our mid-teens. We'd been through a wall of fire together–digging trucks out of the mud and knocking on doors until our knuckles bled. And now we were going our separate ways.

"The warehouse, of course, was a complete wreck. We were surrounded by broken-down trucks and empty boxes, and the freezer was a total disgrace. The door was wide open, and there wasn't a stitch of food inside. Thick layers of frost were growing out of the freezer, like fungus. It served as a grim reminder of how badly we'd mismanaged things. I remember my self-confidence being shattered.

"With a heavy heart, I said to Elliot: 'I'm sorry I'm leaving, but this is something I gotta do. I gotta give Wall Street a shot. The money that people are making down there is staggering, Elliot. Truly staggering.'

"'I know that,' he answered quickly, 'but I couldn't imagine sitting behind a desk all day. Everything is done over the phone. You'll be cold-calling people you never met before, trying to get them to send money. It doesn't make sense to me....'"

I shook my head slowly. "You know, it might sound funny now, but I remember thinking the exact same thing–that it was inconceivable that someone I'd never met before would send in hundreds of thousands of dollars, based on a phone call. Not to mention the fact that I'd be calling people from all over the country. I mean, what were the chances that a complete stranger from Texas would be insane enough to send me half a million dollars of his hard-earned money without ever laying eyes on me? Yet I still had the image of Michael Falk burning on my brain. The simple fact was that kids were making fortunes on Wall Street. Wall Street was where I belonged."

The Witch chimed in: "So Elliot didn't want to come with you?"

I shook my head. "Believe it or not, he didn't. He wanted to stay in the meat-and-seafood business and give it another shot. He figured he could make money as a one-man show, staying lean and mean." I thought for a moment. "Don't get me wrong–it wasn't like I actually offered him a job or anything; it wasn't in my power to. But I *did* ask him if he'd be interested in coming down for a job interview if I could arrange it. But, again, he said no." I shrugged sadly.

"I arrived home that evening carless, penniless, and personally bankrupt. And you know what? I couldn't have given a shit. I was a Wall Streeter now, and that was all that mattered. And the fact that my pay was only one hundred dollars a week didn't bother me a bit. I had hope–hope for the future, which is the greatest hope of all."

I paused and spent a few moments studying the faces of my captors, wondering what they were thinking about, what they thought of me. And while it was impossible to say, I had a sneaky suspicion that they were more confused than ever. Not about my story but about what made a guy like me tick.

In any event, this morning was just a warm-up. The *juicy stuff*–the hookers, the drugs, the wanton lawlessness–was still a day or two away. With that thought, I looked at OCD and said, "You think we could take lunch now? It's almost one, and I'm getting kind of hungry."

"Absolutely," OCD said warmly. "There're some pretty good places on Reade Street. It's less than a two-minute walk."

The Bastard nodded in agreement. "It's been a very productive morning. You've earned yourself a good lunch."

"Indeed," snapped the Witch. "You've afforded us a rare glimpse into the criminal's mind."

I offered her a dead smile in return. "Well, I'm glad you feel that way, Michele, because I'm eager to please."

CHAPTER 8

STINKOSLOVAKIA

After chirping like a canary for more than seven hours, day one of singing on Court Street had finally come to a close. I had gotten as far as my first day as a licensed stockbroker, which, by sheer coincidence, was October 19, 1987, the day of the Great Stock Market Crash. My four captors, as well as my own attorney, had found great irony in that. After all, between my first day of dental school, my first day in the meat business, and my first day on Wall Street, I seemed to have the Midas touch, in reverse: Everything I touched turned to shit.

Yet, on the flipside of that, there was no denying that I had a certain resilience to me. The way Magnum had put it, if someone were to flush me down a toilet bowl I would come out the other side holding a plumber's license. And while Magnum's words had been greatly appreciated, I was completely certain that there was no plumber's license waiting for me on the other side of *this* toilet bowl.

Right now I was in the limousine again, on my way to Old Brookville, where I would place myself back under house arrest, reduced once more to a prisoner within my own home as well as an emotional piñata for the Duchess to swat around. As always, the babbling Pakistani was behind the wheel, but he hadn't uttered a word since we'd left Sunset Park thirty minutes ago, when I'd threatened to cut his tongue off if he didn't stop talking.

At this moment we were on the Long Island Expressway, somewhere near the Queens–Long Island border. It was the tail end of rush hour, at that hour of dusk where the streetlights come on but make little difference. As we crawled along at a snail's pace, I stared out the window, lost in thought.

The Great Crash of 1987 was the pivotal point of my life, an exceptional happening from which all other happenings would unfold. The Dow had dropped 508 points that Black Monday in a single trading session, sending the longest bull market in modern history to a screeching halt.

In truth, I had been nothing more than a casual observer, not just of the crash but also of the fabulous run-up that preceded it. In the summer of 1982, in the wake of slashed income-tax rates and plummeting interest rates, runaway inflation had finally been tamed, and Reagonomics was the rage of the day. Money had become cheap, causing the stock market to catch fire. Michael Milken had just invented junk bonds, turning Corporate America upside down on its ear. Hostile raiders like Ronald Perelman and Henry Kravis, a new breed of financial celebrity armed with war chests of cash raised by Milken's junk bonds, were becoming household names. One by one, they were bringing America's largest corporations to their knees through hostile takeovers. TWA, Revlon, RJR Nabisco . . . who would be next?

By October of '87 the euphoria had reached its peak, as the Dow crossed the 2,400 mark. The era of the yuppie was in full swing, and there was no end in sight. And as the Michael Falks of the world raked in the dough, people like Bill Gates and Steve Jobs were changing the world. It was the dawn of the Information Age, and it hit with the force of an atomic bomb. Lightning-fast computers were appearing on every desktop; they were powerful, intuitive, and they had shrunk the world to a global village.

For Wall Street, this opened vast possibilities: Faster computers yielded massive increases in trading volume, as well as cutting-edge financial products and novel trading strategies. The financial products, called derivatives, allowed large institutions to hedge their investment portfolios like never before, and the trading strategies, the most exciting of which was called portfolio insurance, began fueling the buying frenzy itself.

In a financial farce of Kafkaesque proportions, portfolio insurance caused advances in the Dow to stimulate computers to spit out massive buy orders for derivatives, which then caused the Dow to advance even further, which stimulated those very same computers to spit out even *more* buy orders for derivatives... and on and on it went. Theoretically, it could have gone on forever.

Actually, it couldn't have, because the two numnuts who'd invented portfolio insurance had programmed a fail-safe mechanism into the software. In other words, after a certain level of price increases the computers said, "Wait a second–there's something rotten in Denmark! We'd better sell all the stock in our portfolios as fast as our silicone wafers will allow!"

That's when the problems started. In a real-life version of *The Terminator,* computers turned on their masters and began spewing out endless waves of sell orders at the speed of light. At first, the market declined sharply; that was bad. But, alas, the computers kept right on selling, and by midday, the volume was so enormous that the computers on the floor of the New York Stock Exchange couldn't keep up. And that was tragic, because *just like that* everything came to a grinding halt.

Meanwhile, stockbrokers, being stockbrokers, stopped answering their phones, thinking: What's the fucking point of listening to my irate clients scream, "Sell, God damn it! Sell!" when there're no buyers around to sell to? So instead of holding their clients' hands and telling them everything would be okay, they leaned back in their seats and put their crocodile shoes up on their desktops and let their telephones ring off the hook. By four p.m., the Dow had plunged twenty-two percent, half a trillion dollars had vanished into thin air, investor confidence had been shattered, and the era of the yuppie had officially come to a close.

Now, more than a decade later, as I'd recounted those events to my captors, I felt strangely detached from them, as if the young man who'd lived through all that–some poor schnook named Jordan Belfort–was a complete stranger to me, someone whose life story I had been narrating in the first person for the sake of simplicity. And odder still was how I had conveniently omitted the personal impact those events had had on me, especially when it came to my marriage to my first wife, Denise, who I'd wed three months prior to the crash. We were both broker than broke. Yet we knew that success was right around the corner. So we had hope and we had faith–until the crash.

And that was where I'd left off: Jordan Belfort had just left the boardroom of LF Rothschild with despair in his heart and his tail between his legs. He was a broken twenty-five-year-old with one personal bankruptcy under his belt and a license to sell stocks that had suddenly become worthless.

Ironically, inside the debriefing room I had grown disturbingly comfortable as the day wore on. Losing myself in the past had allowed me to block out the pain of the present, especially my sense of loss regarding the Duchess. And despite the fact that I knew I was ratting, the information I'd provided was strictly historic–sketching only broad strokes about things marginally illegal. The ninety-seven people on my villains, thieves, and scoundrels list still seemed reasonably safe.

Then the Bastard burst my bubble.

It was a few minutes before five when Joel had said, "We need to put the history lesson on hold for a while. We're fighting a time clock with your cooperation..." and then he went on to explain that there was only so long my esteemed status as a rat could be kept secret. There were telltale signs when someone was cooperating, starting with the court record, which in my case would be conspicuously dull. In other words, there were certain motions filed when a defendant was taking a case to trial, motions that *wouldn't* be filed if he was singing on Court Street.

In practical terms, explained the Bastard, there would be two distinct aspects to my cooperation: historical ratting and proactive ratting. Up until now I had been engaged only in the former. Now, however, the Bastard had asked me to make a recorded phone call to one of the soon-to-be-sorry souls on my villains, thieves, and scoundrels list. And, the Bastard had chosen of all people, my loyal and trusted accountant, Dennis Gaito, aka the Chef.

Dennis Gaito was, indeed, a chef, although not in the traditional sense of the word. It was a nickname born out of love and affection and one that had been earned as a result of his natural propensity to cook the books. He was a man's man, calm, cool, collected. He lived for world-class golf courses, Cuban cigars, fine wines, first-class travel, and enlightened conversation, especially when it had to do with figuring out ways to fuck over the IRS and the Securities and Exchange Commission, which seemed to be his life's foremost mission.

In his mid-fifties now, the Chef had been cooking the books since the early seventies, while I was still in grade school, cutting his teeth under the watchful eye of Bob Brennan, one of the greatest stock jockeys of all time. Bob's nickname was the Blue-eyed Devil—a testament to his steel-blue eyes, devilish trading strategies, and the icy-cool blood that ran through his veins, which was rumored to be two degrees cooler than liquid nitrogen.

The Blue-eyed Devil was the founder of First Jersey Securities, which in the late seventies and early eighties had been a penny-stock operation of unprecedented scope and scale. The Chef had been the Devil's accountant, as well as his chief confidant. As a team, they were legendary, leaving a swarthy trail of unadulterated stock fraud in their wake. And unlike *most* penny-stock guys, the Blue-eyed Devil had walked away with all the marbles, nearly a quarter billion of them.

Therein lay the rub: The Blue-eyed Devil had gotten away with it. He'd outwitted the regulators every step of the way, and there was nothing that the Bastard wanted more than the head of the Blue-eyed Devil on a platter.

Just then the voice of Monsoir snapped me back to the present. "This traffic is brutal!" he declared. "It is a wonder we will ever make it back to Brookville. Don't you think, boss?"

"Monsoir," I said gently, "you happen to be a damn good driver. You never call in sick, you never get lost, and, being a Muslim and all, I don't think you can even drink!" I nodded in admiration. "That's why I have two kind words for you."

"Oh, yeah, boss, what's that?"

"Fuck–off!" I snarled, and I pushed a button on the overhead console and watched the babbling Pakistani's head disappear behind a felt-covered divider. I stared at the rich blue felt for a good few seconds, and my eyes lit on three gold-colored letters–an *N*, a *J*, and a *B*–which stood for Jordan and Nadine Belfort. The letters had been embroidered onto the felt, in 18-karat-gold thread, written in Gothic-style script. *What a fucking mockery!* I thought. Such reckless spending! Such wanton excess! And all so meaningless now....

My mind went roaring back to the Blue-eyed Devil and the Chef. In truth, I hadn't really danced with the Devil, so I couldn't implicate him in any wrongdoing, at least not directly. The Chef, however, was a different story. We had cooked up a thousand nefarious schemes together, too many to even count. Ironically, I had decided to exclude him from my Swiss activities, fearful at the time that his relationship with the Blue-eyed Devil would bring heat to me.

Alas, four years later–which is to say, a few hours ago–the Bastard and OCD had found this exclusion difficult to swallow. It made no sense, the Bastard argued. "Why would you keep the Chef out of this?" he'd asked skeptically. "You include him in everything else and leave him out of this? It doesn't jive–unless, of course, you *did* include him and you're just trying to protect him!" With that, the Bastard had pulled out a stack of old travel records relating to a trip I'd taken to Switzerland back in the summer of 1995, and, by no coincidence, it was a trip the Chef had accompanied me on. Even more incriminating was that after we'd departed Switzerland, rather than flying back to the United States, we made a brief pit stop behind the former Iron Curtain, in Czechoslovakia. According to the Bastard's records, we'd stayed there for less than eighteen hours, literally flying in and out. Something about that didn't sit right with the Bastard; after all, for what possible reason would we do that, other than to drop off cash or open a secret account or cook up a scheme? Whatever we'd done, the Bastard knew I was hiding something, and he wanted to know what it was.

Meanwhile, I could only scratch my head. The Bastard was so far off the mark it was literally mind-boggling. Having no other choice, though, I recounted that excursion in intimate detail, starting with Switzerland, explaining that my sole purpose for being there was to do damage control. I had been trying to wind down the latest in a series of horrific debacles, the sum of which had landed me in the room in which I was now sitting. *This* particular debacle had to do with the untimely death of the Duchess's lovely aunt Patricia, who, unbeknownst to the Duchess, I'd recruited into the heart of my money-laundering scheme.

I had convinced my wife's favorite aunt–a sixty-five-year-old retired British schoolteacher who'd never broken a single law in her entire life–to break more than a thousand of them in one swift swoop, by acting as my Swiss nominee. And the moment she agreed, I began stashing millions of dollars in numbered accounts tied to her name. Then, without warning, she died of a stroke, throwing those millions into limbo.

At first I'd thought her death would cause me great problems, the most obvious of which was that my money would be tied up in the seedy underbelly of the Swiss banking system for all eternity. But I had been wrong, because the Swiss were adept at such matters. To them, the death of a nominee was a huge positive, something to which one cracks open a bottle of champagne. After all, the best nominee is a dead nominee, or so I was told by my blubbery Swiss trustee, Roland Franks,* an affable three-hundred pounder with a voracious appetite for sweets and an unworldly gift for creating forged documents that supported a notion of plausible deniability. And when I had asked my Master Forger why that was so, he shrugged his fat shoulders and said, "Because dead men tell no tales, my young friend, nor do dead aunts!"

Meanwhile, as I had recounted all this sordidness to my captors, I had focused in on the fact that the Chef and I weren't alone on the trip; we'd brought company with us, in the form of Danny

*Name has been changed

Porush, my erstwhile partner-in-crime, and Andy Greene, my loyal and trusted attorney, who was better known as Wigwam.

I had freely admitted that Danny *had* been my partner in all this. "He's as guilty as I am," I'd declared to the Bastard, and then I swore to him that Wigwam and the Chef had had no part in it. They were merely coming along for the ride to Czechoslovakia, I said, which was our next stop on the trip. Neither of them knew that Danny and I had already smuggled money to Switzerland; they just thought we were there to scope things out for future reference.

By this point in the story, the Bastard and OCD seemed to be buying into it, so I plunged into the next leg of our excursion, to Czechoslovakia, explaining how our venture there was part of a failed attempt to corner the market in Czech vouchers, which the new government had recently issued to its citizens as a means of privatizing the economy. Yet, beyond that, I found myself unable to come completely clean with my captors. After all, what had transpired in Czechoslovakia was so utterly decadent that they would never have understood. So, instead, I gave them a calmer, more watered-down version of things, lest they view me as a complete social deviant, who was not worthy of a 5K letter. It was only now, two hours later, that I could fully relish the insanity that had defined that leg of the journey.

It had all started inside the private jet, which was a Gulfstream III. Like all Gulfstreams, this one had a plush, roomy cabin finished in mellow beige tones. The seats were as big as thrones, and the twin Rolls-Royce engines had been fitted with the latest Hushkits, making the ride so quiet that all you could hear was the gentle hum of turbofans as air swept past the fuselage at 550 knots.

It was early evening, and we were high above southern Poland, although I was a good deal higher than that. But I wasn't nearly as high as Danny, who was sitting across from me and had completely lost the power of speech. He was in the latter half of the drool phase, which is to say, he was at that point of his high where he could no longer get the words out without a river of saliva dripping down his chin.

"Iz iz guz zehnzamea!" he exclaimed, with a thick gush of saliva.

Over the last two hours he'd consumed four Quaaludes, nearly a pint of Macallan's single-malt scotch, twenty milligrams of Valium, and a two-gram rock of Bolivian marching powder, which he'd Hoovered up his nostrils through a rolled-up hundred-dollar bill. Then, about ten seconds ago, he'd taken a hit from a thick joint of Northern California sinsemilla, which led me to believe that what he had been trying to say was: "This is good sinsemilla!"

As always, I found it literally mind-boggling how normal Danny looked. What with his short blond hair, average build, and boiling white teeth, he gave off a wonderfully WASPy whiff, the sort of whiff you would expect from a man who could trace his genealogy back to the *Mayflower*. He was dressed casually this evening, in a pair of tan cotton golf pants and matching short-sleeve polo shirt. Over his pale-blue eyes he wore a pair of conservative horn-rimmed glasses that made him look that much more refined, that much WASPier.

Yet, with all this WASPiness, Danny Porush was a purebred Jew who could trace his roots back to a tiny kibbutz near Tel Aviv. Nevertheless, like many a Jew before him, he tried to be mistaken for a blue-blooded WASP—hence, those wonderfully WASPy glasses, which had clear lenses in them.

Meanwhile, the interior of the cabin looked like a flying DEA seizure locker. Between Danny and me, on a mahogany foldout table, a brown leather Louis Vuitton shower bag was overflowing with a fabulous medley of dangerous recreational drugs—a half ounce of sinsemilla, sixty pharmaceutical Quaaludes, some bootleg uppers, some bootleg downers, a sandwich bag full of cocaine, a dozen hits of Ecstasy, and then the safe stuff, from the doctors: a vial of Xanax, a vial of morphine, some Valiums and Restorils and Somas and Vicodins, and some Ambiens and Ativans and Klonopins, as well as a half-consumed pack of Heineken and a mostly consumed bottle of Macallan's to wash things down. Pretty soon, though, all the nonprescription stuff would be gone, shoved up our collective assholes or buried deep beneath our scrotal sacs, as we negotiated our way through Czech Customs.

My trusted attorney, Wigwam, was sitting to Danny's right. He was also dressed casually, although, in his case, he also wore his perpetually glum expression and horrendous-looking toupee. It was mud brown in color, a poor match to his pale complexion, and had the consistency of desiccated straw. In fact, despite the Iron Curtain coming down four years earlier, it was still a safe bet that his horrific hairpiece would draw some second looks from the Czechs.

In any event, Wigwam was buzzed too, although, as our attorney, he was held to a higher standard. He understood that he was not to get *sloppy* until *after* we'd finished dealing with the Czechs. So he'd gone heavy on the coke and light on the Ludes. It was an inspired strategy that made perfect psychotropic sense; after all, taking a Quaalude was like drinking three bottles of grain alcohol on an empty stomach, while snorting cocaine was like consuming eight thousand cups of coffee intravenously. The former made you sleepy and sloppy, while the latter made you pumped up and paranoid. Insofar as business was concerned, it was more effective to be pumped up and paranoid than sleepy and sloppy. But, alas, Wigwam had accidentally snorted himself into a coke-induced paranoia.

"Jesus H. Christ!" Wigwam muttered. "This cabin reeks of skunk weed! Can't you put that shit out, Danny? I mean... we're... we're... we're"–*spit it out, Wigwam*–"we're gonna end up in Czech jail, for Chrissake!" He paused, wiping the beads of sweat that had formed on his pale, paranoid brow. He was actually good-looking, in a boyish sort of way. He was average height, with fine, even features, although he had a bit of a paunch going. "I'm gonna get disbarred," he moaned. "I know it. *Ughhhhhhh...*" It was a paranoid drug groan, and as soon as he'd finished groaning he put his toupee in his hands and shook his egg-shaped skull in despair.

The Chef was sitting to my left, and he was straight as an arrow. In fact, he'd never done a drug in his entire life–being that rare breed of man who could surround himself with world-class drug addicts and be entirely okay with it. The Chef was handsome, in a striking sort of way, like a trimmed-down version of Mr. Clean. He was completely bald on top, with a prominent forehead, a very square jaw, piercing brown eyes, an aquiline nose, and an infectious smile.

The Chef was a born-and-bred New Jerseyite, who could lay his Jersey accent on real thick, especially when the occasion called for it, as it did now. "Whaddaya, whaddaya?" the Chef said to Wigwam. "You godda gedda grip dare, Andy! If you're worried about the smell, then turn on them overhead air vents. The pressure is so low ow dare"–*out there*–"it'll clear the stench out in two seconds flat."

Indeed. The Chef was absolutely right. "You should listen to the Chef," I said to Wigwam. "He has uncanny reasoning skills in these situations." I reached over and placed my left hand on Wigwam's shoulder and offered him a concerned smile. "On a separate note, I strongly advise you to take a couple of Xanax. You need to even yourself out a bit."

He stared at me.

"You look like a train wreck," I said. "Trust me, a couple a Xanax is just what the doctor ordered." I turned to the Chef. "Isn't that right, Chef?"

"Indeed," the Chef agreed.

Wigwam nodded nervously. "I guess I will," he said, "but I need to do some housekeeping first." He rose from his chair and began walking around the cabin and opening air vents. I looked at Danny, who was still smoking a joint. "In spite of our attorney being a cokehead," I said, "he's got a valid point. Why don't you get rid of that joint just to be safe."

Danny held up the half-inch-long joint and cocked his head to the side, as if inspecting it. He turned the corners of his mouth down and shrugged, then threw the joint into his mouth and swallowed it. "Eating *poss* gets you fucked up!" he slurred proudly.

Just then Wigwam sat back down, his jaw still doing a coke addict's version of the Latin hustle. "Here," I said, grabbing the appropriate vial from the LV bag. I unscrewed the cap and poured out a few pills. "The correct dosage is two blues..." I paused, thinking for a moment, "although at this altitude there's no way to be sure. The body might be more susceptible up here." I shrugged.

Wigwam nodded nervously, still trapped in the deep trough of the worry phase. If I plunged into the story of how he'd lost his hair while still in high school and then got caught cheating on his SATs, there was a better than fifty-fifty chance he would make a mad dash for the emergency exit and jump. But I took pity on him and said nothing.

I turned to the Chef and smiled respectfully. "Getting back to business," I said, in hushed tones, "I wasn't all that impressed with the people I met in Switzerland, so I'm not going forward with them. They didn't seem trustworthy enough." I shrugged again. That was a lie, of course, and as much as I hated lying to the Chef, I had my reasons.

Back in the United States, an obsessed FBI agent named Gregory Coleman was hot on my trail, and I needed to set up false trails for him to follow, to divert his attention away from my *real* Swiss accounts. I would have the Chef assist me to that end–opening a Swiss account for me that I would never actually fund but whose existence I would leak to Agent Coleman. And when Coleman petitioned the Swiss government to open my account, I would fight him tooth and nail on it, as if I actually had something to hide. It would keep him occupied for a good two years, I figured, maybe even more. And when he finally *did* get his way and the account was opened, he would find out that I had never actually funded it.

In essence, the joke would be on Coleman, and my *real* business would go on undisturbed. With that in mind, I said to the Chef, "So let's do the stuff you talked about before. What do I gotta do to get things started?"

"You don't gotta do nothing," replied the Jersey Chef, using a double negative to reinforce how little I had to do. "I got the whole thing set up for you–trustees, nominees, and I can be an adviser to the trust. That'll put another buffer between you and the money. And God forbid the boys downtown start snooping around, then I resign as adviser and the money disappears into Liechtenstein and, *you* know . . . *Schhhwiitttt!*"–and he clapped his hands and slung his right arm out toward southern Romania–"we'd be good to go then."

I smiled at the Chef and nodded warmly. He was a man of many talents, the Chef, although his most remarkable was his ability to use an intricate combination of hand gestures and blowing sounds to get his point across. And my favorite was *Schhhwiitttt,* which he elicited by curling his tongue into a reverse C and then forcing out a gust of air. And as he made the *Schhhwiitttt* sound he would clap his hands, sending his right arm flying out into the distance. The Chef used this sound when he was tying up loose ends of a cover story, as if to imply, "Yeah, and with that last phony document we've created, you know... *Schhhwiitttt!*... there's no way the feds will ever be able to figure things out!"

In retrospect, as I now sat on the Gulfstream, I knew I'd made a colossal blunder in not using one of the Chef's many fabulous recipes to satiate my Swiss banking appetite. But his relationship with the Blue-eyed Devil had spooked me. It was common knowledge that they were doing business in Switzerland, and, as hot as I was, the Blue-eyed Devil was that much hotter, and they *still* hadn't been able to catch him! So how did that bode for *my* plight? Rather well, I figured. Like the Devil, I was a careful man, always going to great lengths to cover my tracks.

I held on to that happy thought as I reached into my medicine bag and broke out the Valium, downing three blues. It was a lion's dose, I knew, but given the amount of coke I'd snorted, it was just what I needed to get me safely to Czechoslovakia.

Rather than going through the main terminal at Prague's Ruzyně Airport, the Gulfstream was directed to a small private terminal that, up until a short time ago, had been reserved for communist dignitaries. That suited me just fine, given my current state of intoxication, but as they led us to a room that looked like the inner sanctum of the Kremlin, there was something bothering me, something I couldn't quite place my finger on. Danny was standing beside me, looking disturbed. "You smell something?" I asked, scrunching up my nose.

Danny scrunched up his own nose and took two deep snorts. "Yeah," he replied. "What the fuck is that? It smells like... I don't know, but I don't like it." He took two more snorts.

I turned to Wigwam. "You smell something?" I whispered.

Wigwam darted his eyes around the room like a wild animal. "It's poison gas," he said nervously. "I...I gotta get my passport back. I...please...I'm gonna lose it." He put his index finger to his mouth and began biting his nail.

The worries, I thought. I leaned over to the Chef. "You smell something, Chef?"

He nodded. "Yeah, it's fucking body odor!" he declared. "These commie bastards don't use deodorant!" He scratched his chin, taking a moment to consider. "Or maybe they can't find it in stores. You'd be surprised how commies forgo the normal pleasantries."

Just then a smelly middle-aged Czech, dressed in blue-gray police garb, walked over. He eyed us suspiciously for a moment, then motioned to a series of high-backed leather armchairs that had been arranged around an enormous mahogany conference table. Not too shabby, I thought. We sat down, and a uniformed waiter appeared from out of nowhere, carrying a tray of dessert aperitifs, which he placed before us without saying a word.

I looked up at the waiter, who was sweating bullets. "Excuse me," I said humbly. "Why is it so hot in here?"

He flashed me the look of the disinterested and the lobotomized and then walked away without saying a word. As I reached for my glass, Wigwam warned, "Don't drink the wine!" He began looking around nervously. "That's what they *want.*" He looked back at me, with wild eyes. "You understand?"

Now the Chef leaned over. "I don't think that guy speaks English," he whispered, "but when I was getting off the plane the captain told me they're having their worst heat wave in a hundred years. I think today was the hottest day in the country's history."

Inside the taxi I breathed through my mouth.

"You ever smell anything so vile?" I asked Danny.

Danny shook his head gravely. "Never. The guy needs to be dipped in sulfuric acid." The Chef nodded in agreement, then added more words of wisdom. "Don't worry," he said confidently. "We're staying in the nicest hotel in the country. I'm sure there'll be air-conditioning there. You can count on it."

I shrugged, not entirely believing him. "Is Prague the largest city in Czechoslovakia?" I asked the smelly driver.

Without warning, the driver expelled a giant gob of spit onto his own dashboard. "Slavs are dogs," he snarled. "They are no longer part of country. We are Czech Republic: *Jewel* of East." He rolled his neck, as if trying to regain his composure.

I nodded nervously and looked out the window, trying to take in the beauty of the Jewel of the East, but there were no streetlights and I couldn't see anything. Nevertheless, I was still hopeful; after all, our destination was the fabulous Hotel Ambassador, the only four-star hotel in Prague. And thank God for that! I thought. This leg of our journey seemed to be cursed. A bit of pampering would be just what the doctor ordered!

Alas, what the Chef hadn't been aware of was that the Hotel Ambassador had just been rated one of the worst four-star hotels in Europe. Just *why* I found out the moment we stepped into the lobby and it was two hundred degrees and a thousand percent humidity. In fact, it was so stifling I almost passed out.

The space was vast and grim-looking, like a Cold War–era bomb shelter. There were only three couches in sight, which were a disturbing shade of dog-shit brown.

At the front desk, I smiled at the Czech check-in girl, a pale young blonde with wide shoulders, enormous Czech boobs, a white blouse, and a nametag reading *Lara.** "Why is there no air-conditioning?" I asked the lovely Lara.

Lara smiled sadly, exposing some crooked Czech choppers. "We have problem with air conditioner," Lara replied, in heavily accented English. "It is not at work now."

Out of the corner of my eye I saw Danny sag, but then the Chef offered more words of wisdom. "We'll be fine here," he said, nodding a single time. "I've seen much, much worse."

I recoiled in disbelief. "Really, Chef? Where?"

He smiled knowingly. "You forget I'm from New Jersey."

---

*Name has been changed

Such logic! I thought. The Chef was a true warrior!

Emboldened by his words, I threw down my Am Ex card, smiled at Lara, and said to myself, "How bad could it possibly be? When you're as tired and post-Luded as I am, the tendency is just to pass out from sheer exhaustion."

Two hours later I was lying in bed, staring up at the ceiling, stark naked and contemplating suicide. My hotel room was hotter than the boiler room on the SS *Titanic.* The windows had been bolted shut and the radiator was on. Just why, no one in the hotel could seem to figure out. Nevertheless, there was heat coming from the radiator, nothing was coming from the air conditioner, and I would've paid a million bucks for someone to unleash a swarm of bumblebees to hover over me and flap their tiny wings.

It was a little after two a.m., about eight p.m. New York time. I desperately needed to speak to the Duchess. I needed to hear some kind words from her, for her to tell me that she *loved* me and that everything would be okay. She could always make me feel better, even in my darkest hour. But I'd tried her a half dozen times and kept getting the same fucking recording, saying the overseas lines were busy.

Just then the phone rang. *Ahhh, the luscious Duchess! She always knows!* I reached for the phone and picked it up. Alas, it was Danny. "I can't sleep," he snarled. "We need to drop Ludes and go get hookers; there's no other way."

I sat upright. "You're kidding!" I said. "We're getting picked up in a few hours, Dan! That's insane." I took a moment to think it through, coming to the quick conclusion that his plan was, indeed, insane. "Anyway, where we gonna find hookers this time of night? It's too complicated."

"I already got it worked out with Lara," he said proudly. "There's a place less than ten minutes from here, on the outskirts of Prague. Lara assured me we can find some smelly Czech hookers there, which are the best kind, she said." He paused briefly. "Anyway, we *must* do this, JB. It would be bad karma to let things proceed along their current course. We need to take drastic action. I fear for you if you can't see that."

"No way," I replied. "I gotta take a pass. You're on your own."

Somehow—and I'm *still* not sure how—one hour later I was three Ludes deep, with an enormous Czech hooker with bleached-blond hair and the face of a sheepdog riding me like Seattle Slew. Hardly a word was exchanged, only two hundred U.S. dollars and something that sounded like *"Ta-hank yew!"* right after I came inside her enormous Czech pussy. Whatever. Pussy was pussy, I thought, and despite this one being wide enough to parallel park a Czech taxicab in, I had still felt it my patriotic duty to deposit a red, white, and blue load inside her, if for nothing more than to remind her who won the Cold War.

An hour later I was back in my hotel room, sweating again, plotting my own death, and missing the Duchess terribly. But, above all things, I was wondering why I'd just done that. I loved the Duchess more than anything, yet I couldn't seem to control myself. I was weak, and I was decadent. The Wild Wolf was lurking inside me—just beneath the surface—ready to rise up at the slightest provocation and bare his drug-addicted fangs. Just where all this would end up I hadn't the slightest idea, but the word on Wall Street was that I'd be dead within a few years. Whatever. In more ways than one, I was dead already.

At four in the morning, I broke down and raided the Louis Vuitton bag again. Finally, thirty minutes later, I was fast asleep, with enough Xanax bubbling through my central nervous system to knock out half of Prague.

At 7:30 a.m.—only three hours later—came my wake-up call.

I blinked, then vomited, and then rose out of bed and took an ice-cold shower. Then I snorted a half gram of coke, swallowed a Xanax to quell any future paranoia, and headed downstairs to the lobby. I felt a twinge of guilt about being coked out for my first business meeting in this fine country, but after last night's escapade into the seedy cesspool of Prague's red-light district, there was no other way I could possibly start my day.

Downstairs in the lobby, thirty-year-old Marty Sumichrest, Jr., greeted us warmly. He was tall, thin, pasty-faced, and wore steel-rimmed glasses with very thick lenses. He was living somewhere near Washington, D.C., but was in Prague today because he wanted us to raise $10 million for his company, Czech Industries. At this point, the company was nothing more than a worthless shell, but he assured us that he could use his father's status as a *Czech War Hero* to insinuate himself into the highest echelons of the Czech power structure.

We exchanged morning pleasantries and then crammed ourselves into a horrendous limousine called a Skoda. It was black, boxy, beaten up, and, of course, it had no air-conditioning. The foul stench of body odor was so powerful that it could have incapacitated a platoon full of marines. I looked at my watch: It was 8:15 a.m. Only five minutes had passed, but it felt like an hour. I looked around the limo and all ties were at half-mast; Danny was white as a ghost; the Chef's lips were twisted subversively; and Wigwam's toupee looked like a dead animal.

Sitting in the front seat, Marty turned around to face us. "Prague is one of the only cities in Europe that wasn't destroyed by the Nazis," he said proudly. "Most of the original architecture still remains." He raised his palm toward the window and swept it from left to right in a gentle arc, as if to say, "Behold the wonder and beauty!" Then he said, "Many consider it the most beautiful city in all of Europe, the Paris of the East, so to speak. It's been home to many an artist, and many a poet too. They come here to get inspired, they come here to..."

Holy Christ! I was being bored to death, sweated to death, and smelled to death all at the same time! How could it be? I felt desperately homesick all of a sudden, like a little boy whose parents had sent him off to sleepaway camp and was dying to come home.

"...and the Czechs have always been entrepreneurs. It's the Slavs who gave this country a bad reputation." He shook his head in disgust. "They're morons, lazy drunks with IQs just above the level of an idiot. They were thrust upon us by the Soviet Union, but now they're back where they belong: in Slovakia. And just watch–in ten years from now they'll have the lowest GNP in Eastern Europe and we'll have the highest." He nodded proudly. "You just watch!"

"That's interesting," I said casually, "but if the Czechs are so smart, how come they haven't discovered deodorant yet?"

"What do you mean?" asked Marty, narrowing his eyes.

"Never mind," I answered. "I was just making a joke, Marty. It smells like fucking lilacs in here."

He nodded, seeming to understand. "By the way," he added, "the first company we're seeing this morning is Motokov. They have sole distribution rights to the Skoda"–he slapped his hand on the top of his headrest two times–"so they can flood the world with these bad boys!"

"Hmmm," muttered the Chef. "I bet people all across Western Europe are gonna line up for the Skoda. In fact, the boys at Mercedes better watch their asses or they're gonna find themselves knee-deep in red ink!"

The War Hero's son nodded in agreement. "Like I said, the Czech Republic is brimming with opportunity. Motokov is just one example."

The corporate headquarters of Motokov was a gray concrete office building that rose up twenty-three stories above the streets of Prague. Alas, the company needed only two floors for its operations. But the commies had been strong believers in "bigger is better," viewing concepts like profits and losses as minor trivialities–or at least secondary to the creation of meaningless, low-paying jobs to placate a drunken Czechoslovakian workforce.

We took a linoleum-paneled elevator up to the twentieth floor and walked down a long, silent hallway that seemed low on oxygen. I was about to pass out when we reached a large conference room, where we were offered seats around a cheap wooden conference table large enough for thirty people. But only three representatives of Motokov were in the room, so after we'd taken seats, we were so far apart that you had to raise your voice if you wanted to make yourself heard. Leave it to the commies, I thought.

I was sitting at one head of the table, facing a plate-glass wall that looked out over the city of Prague. At this hour of the morning at this time of June, the sun was shining directly through the plate glass, heating the room to the temperature of the planet Mercury. On the floor were three geraniums in white plastic planters. They were dead.

After a few moments of opening pleasantries, Motokov's president took center stage and began speaking in heavily accented English. The company had suffered greatly due to the breakup of the Soviet Union, he explained. Antimonopoly laws had been passed, basically legislating them out of business. He seemed like an intelligent fellow–an altogether *affable* fellow, in fact–but pretty soon I began to notice something very odd about him. At first I couldn't place it, but then it hit me: He was a blinker. Yes–he was a world-class blinker! For every word escaping his lips, he blinked his eyes, sometimes more than once.

"So you see," explained the Blinker, with three rapid-fire blinks, "under the new law, monopolies are no longer permitted, which puts"–*blink, blink*–"Motokov in a very difficult"–*blink, blink, blink*–"position." *Blink.* "In a way, we have been legislated into near bankruptcy." *Blink, blink.*

Sounds like a hell of an opportunity, I thought, especially if your goal is to flush your money down a Czech toilet bowl!

Still, I played the role of the interested guest, and I nodded in sympathy, to which the Blinker blinked on. "Yes, we are on the edge of bankruptcy," continued the Blinker. "We have the overhead structure"–*blink, blink*–"of a multibillion-dollar company, but we no longer have the sales mandate." The Blinker let out a deep sigh. He looked about forty and had very white skin. He wore the sort of checkered short-sleeve dress shirt and blue cloth necktie that reeked of a mid-level bookkeeper at an Omaha meat-slaughtering house.

Now the Blinker reached into his pants pocket and pulled out a pack of cigarettes and lit one up. Apparently his two underlings took this as a signal to light up too, and next thing I knew, the room was enveloped in an ominous cloud of cheap Czech tobacco smoke. Out of the corner of my eye, I caught a glimpse of Danny, whose right elbow was on the conference table, with his chin cradled in his hand. And he was sleeping. Sleeping? *Sleeping!*

Through exhaled smoke, the Blinker went on: "That's why we are now focusing our attention on Kentucky Fried Chicken franchises"–What the fuck? Kentucky Fried Chicken? Why that?–"which we plan to roll out"–*blink, blink*–"very aggressively over the next five years." The Blinker nodded in agreement with his own thoughts and blinks. "Yes," continued the Blinker, with a rapid-fire double blink, "we will focus our efforts on fried chicken and mashed potatoes; the Kentucky Fried brand, of course, which is quite delicious if–"

SMASH went Danny's head onto the conference table!

There was absolute silence now, as everyone, including the Blinker, stared at Danny, astonished. His right cheek was pressed against the conference table, and a tiny river of drool was slowly making its way down his chin. Then he started snoring one of those deep guttural drug snores from way down in the breadbasket.

"Don't mind him," I said to the Blinker. "He's just jet-lagged from the trip. Please continue. I'm intrigued at Motokov's plans to capitalize on your underserved fried-chicken market." I shrugged. "I wasn't aware that the Czechs were such lovers of fried chicken."

"Oh, yes," blinked the Blinker, "it's one of our staples," and then he started blinking again, and Danny kept snoring some more, and the Chef kept rolling his eyes, and Wigwam's toupee was slowly turning into glue, and every last one of us, including the Blinker himself, was sweating to death.

The rest of the day was no better–lots of smelly Czechs, boiling offices, smoke-filled rooms, and Danny drooling. The War Hero's son shuffled us from company to company, each one in a similar situation to Motokov. Without fail, they had bloated overhead structures, inexperienced management teams, and a limited understanding of the basic tenets of capitalism. What amazed me, though, was the tremendous hope shared by every person we met. They all kept reminding me that Prague was the "Paris of the East," and that the Czech Republic was really part of Western Europe. Slovakia had nothing to do with them, they assured me. In fact, it was populated by a bunch of retarded monkeys.

It was now six p.m., and the four of us were sitting in the hotel lobby on the dog-shit brown couches, in desperate need of salt pills. I said to the group, "I don't know how much more I can take of this: there's no amount of money worth this abuse."

Danny seemed to agree with me. "Please!" he begged, rubbing a golf-ball-size welt that had formed on his right temple. "Let's get the fuck out of here and go to Scotland!" He bit his lower lip, as if on the verge of a breakdown. "I'm telling you, Scotland is beautiful! It's the land of milk and honey!" He nodded his head eagerly. "It's probably in the low seventies there, without a drop of humidity. We can play golf all day... smoke cigars... drink brandy... I bet we can even find young Scottish hookers who smell like Irish Spring soap!" He threw his palms up in the air. "I'm begging you, JB–throw in the towel on this one. Just throw it in."

"As your attorney," added Wigwam, "I strongly advise you to follow Danny's advice. I think you should call Janet right now and get the plane fueled up. I've never been so miserable in my life."

I looked at the Chef. Apparently he wasn't ready to throw the towel in yet; he still had questions. "Can you believe how that bastard from Motokov kept going on and on about Kentucky Fried Chicken? What's so good about Kentucky Fried Chicken?" He shook his head, as if still confused. "I thought they eat mostly pork in this part of the world."

I shrugged. "I'm not really sure," I said, "but did you count how many times that fucker blinked? It was incredible!" I shook my head in awe. "He was like a human adding machine. I've never seen anything like it."

"Yeah, well, I lost count at a thousand," said the Chef. "He must have some kind of disease, probably peculiar to the Czechs." He shrugged too. "Anyway, as your accountant I have to agree with Wigwam: I strongly advise you to hold off making any investments in this country until they start using deodorant." He shrugged again. "But that's only one man's opinion."

Thirty minutes later we were on our way to the airport. The fact that twenty Czechs were waiting for us for a five-hour traditional Czech dinner was merely incidental. At six o'clock tomorrow morning we would be in the land of milk and honey, and I would never see these smelly Czechs again.

Scotland was gorgeous, but its beauty was lost on me.

I had been away from the Duchess far too long. I needed to *see* her—to literally *feel* her in my arms, and I needed to make love to her. Chandler, of course, was also waiting for me. She was almost a year old then, and who could guess what startling intellectual feats she'd accomplished the week I was gone? Not to mention the fact that the Ludes were running out, which meant that we'd be going to work on the narcotics. Then the nausea and vomiting would set in, as well as the intense constipation. And there's nothing worse than being stuck in a foreign country with your head perched over a toilet bowl, while your descending colon is frozen like a glacier.

It was for all those reasons that I nearly collapsed in the Duchess's arms when I walked through the door of our Westhampton Beach house on that Friday morning. It was a little after ten, and all I wanted was to go upstairs, hold Chandler for a moment, and then adjourn to the bedroom and make love to the Duchess. Then I would sleep for a month.

But I never got the chance. I was home for less than thirty seconds when the phone rang. It was Gary Deluca, one of my employees, who happened to bear an odd resemblance to Grover Cleveland, the dead president with the bushy beard and perpetually grim expression. "Sorry to bother you," Grover said grimly, "but I thought you'd want to know that Gary Kaminsky got indicted yesterday. He's sitting in jail, being held without bail."

"Really," I said matter-of-factly. I was in that state of extreme weariness where you can't immediately fathom the consequences of what you're hearing. So the fact that Gary Kaminsky had intimate knowledge of my Swiss dealings wasn't troubling me—at least not yet. "What did he get indicted for?" I asked.

"Money laundering. Does the name Jean Jacques Saurel* ring a bell?"

That one got me! Woke me right the fuck up! Saurel was my Swiss banker, the one man who could *sink* me with Agent Coleman.

---

*Name has been changed

"Not really," I said tentatively, clenching my ass cheeks. "Maybe I met him once, but... I'm not sure–why?"

"Because he got indicted too," said Grover. "He's sitting in jail with Kaminsky as we speak."

To my own surprise, it still took OCD more than three years to secure an indictment against me, despite the fact that Saurel began to cooperate almost immediately. And while some of the delay had to do with the loyalty of my Strattonites, more of it had to do with my recruitment of the Chef to help me devise a cover story. In fact, as my house of cards was collapsing around me, the Chef was busy cooking up one of his legendary recipes. And this particular recipe was *so* tasty and *so* mouthwatering that it kept OCD scratching his head for more than three full years.

And now the Chef was a wanted man. He had a federal bull's-eye on his back, and not just because he'd aided and abetted me, by helping cover up my money-laundering debacle, but also because of his relationship with the Blue-eyed Devil. Jam up Gaito, reasoned the Bastard, and he'll roll over on Brennan, who was the true target.

In truth, I wasn't so sure of that. The Chef was fiercely loyal to the Devil–selling his soul to him, so to speak–and he was the sort of battle-hardened cook who could stand the heat in the kitchen, preferring, in fact, to conjure up his recipes right beside the flames. The Chef loved the action–no, he *lived* for the action–and after all those years of working with the Devil he'd become completely desensitized. Things like fear, self-doubt, and self-preservation were foreign concepts to the Chef. If you were his friend he stood up for you; if you were in trouble he went to *war* for you; and if your back was truly to the wall–and it was either you or him–he would fall on his sword for you.

Perhaps that was why today, this very afternoon, the Chef had defied the conventional wisdom and taken my phone call. After all, the first rule of thumb in *my* world–meaning, the villains', thieves', and scoundrels' world–was that when someone gets indicted, you lose their phone number forever. It was like becoming a leper, and whether a leper actually touches you or not, it doesn't really matter. If you even get close, he infects you just the same.

So tomorrow would be D-Day, the FBI plan simple and devilish: The Chef would come to my house, and I would be wired. After a few minutes of small talk, I would casually bring up the past and get the Chef to incriminate himself. And as sad and despicable as that was, what choice did I have? If I didn't cooperate they would indict the Duchess; and if I didn't cooperate my children would grow up without a father; and if I didn't cooperate I would risk becoming Mr. Gower! All I could hope for was that the Chef would be smart enough not to incriminate himself, that he would dance close to the line but wouldn't actually cross over it.

That was my only hope.

CHAPTER 9

WIRED FOR SOUND

Good Lord—they're defiling my daughter's bedroom!

It was early afternoon, and I was sitting on my gray slate patio, in a $1,200 Smith & Hawken teak armchair, when that horrific thought came bubbling up into my brain. And while I couldn't see them, I knew they were there—*Frick and Frack! Tweedledee and Tweedledum!* OCD and the Mormon were camped out in my daughter's perfect pink bedroom, sneaking peeks at me through the tiny gaps in the perfect pink slats of her Venetian blinds.

What kind of father would allow such a thing to happen? I was supposed to be Chandler's protector! Her guardian! Her savior! It was a daddy's job to keep intruders out; yet now there were two armed intruders defiling her bedroom, as a hundred fifty immaculately dressed Barbie dolls and an equal number of wildly overpriced stuffed animals looked on in utter helplessness, bearing silent witness to Daddy's failure as a protector.

Meanwhile, the Chef was due to arrive any minute, so I needed to grab hold of myself. I needed to rein in all these stray thoughts roaring through my brain–the guilt, the remorse, the panic, the sheer fucking terror! In truth, it wasn't really my fault that the FBI had declared eminent domain over my daughter's perfect pink bedroom; the problem was one of geometry, since Chandler's window happened to be at the perfect angle for OCD and the Mormon to take clandestine snapshots of the Chef as we sat outside on the gray slate patio and I went about destroying his life.

Such shame I felt! Such terrible dishonor! *Me*–the ignoble rat!

Still, it happened to be beautiful outside. It was one of those glorious, uplifting days, where a young man of worth and substance can relish Mother Nature and all she has to offer. And what better place to do it than from the fabulous gray slate patio at Chez Belfort? The scenery, after all, was beautiful; behind me, my ten-thousand-square-foot gray stone mansion rose above the grounds with the grandeur and magnificence of the Palace of Versailles; before me, the crystal-blue waters of my Olympic-size swimming pool sparkled like diamonds; and, beyond that, my breathtaking pond and waterfall system was pumping out thousands of gallons of water per minute, as a jet-powered fountain shot up a thick stream of it twenty feet into the air, in a dazzling display of wealth and excess. Such beauty I'd surrounded myself with! Such opulence!

Then my spirits sank. That lousy pond and waterfall had set me back a million fucking bucks, a million fucking bucks I could really use right now! Just this morning I had had a debilitating attack of money anxiety. I was alone in bed when the cruel reality of having to disgorge most of my assets to the federal government hit me like an iron wrecking ball. Next thing I knew, my heart was beating out of my chest, and I was sweating profusely. I started panicking.

And why was I alone? Because that dirty Duchess hadn't even come *home* last night! Apparently she'd zeroed in on a new gold mine and was now in the process of staking her claim. It was only a matter of time until she became the blond-headed arm candy of another mine owner. Where did that leave me? What woman would want a broke and penniless Wolf who'd ratted out his friends?

I took a deep breath and resisted the urge to sneak a peek up at my daughter's Venetian blinds. I had been up there myself–less than five minutes ago–and the scene was sheer bedlam. The Mormon had been pacing back and forth (while smiling broadly and kindly) with a Minolta camera dangling from his neck, like some grinning Japanese tourist. Meanwhile, OCD had been hunched over on his knees, affixing an ultrasensitive tape recorder just above my loins, using a roll of masking tape he'd purchased at Staples.

For my part, I had mostly been complaining. "Jesus–this is gonna hurt like a bitch when you take it off!" I'd snapped at OCD. I was alluding to the fact that most of my pubic hair would be ripped off when he removed the recorder.

"I know, I know," OCD had replied sympathetically, as he carefully avoided my pubic hair with the back of his hand. "But you gotta trust me on this one; there's no better place to hide a tape recorder." He shrugged as he secured the last piece of masking tape four inches above my scrotal sac. "Even someone as suspicious as the Chef is gonna think twice before he pats down your balls!"

Fair enough, I'd thought, but what about the wire attached to the recorder? It was rising up out of the belt line of my Levi's, then continuing up the midline of my abdomen. At the tip of the wire, a tiny microphone, about the size of a number-two-pencil eraser, was taped between the manly depression of my pectoral muscles. According to OCD, this taping apparatus–called a Nagra–was so sensitive that it would pick up our conversation even if we whispered. And those were his final words of wisdom before I left my daughter's bedroom and headed downstairs to the patio.

So here I was, wired for sound. The Chef, I prayed, would be too smart to incriminate himself.

Just then my longtime maid, Gwynne Latham, emerged from the kitchen's side entrance. She wore white cotton slacks, a loose-fitting white T-shirt, and white tennis sneakers. In fact, dressed the way she was, you might have mistaken her for the Good Humor Lady, if not for the fact that she was carrying a sterling-silver tray with a pitcher of iced tea and two tall glasses on it. Gwynne was in her mid-fifties, although she looked a good ten years younger. She was an ageless, timeless, chubby, light-skinned black woman, with fine Caucasian features and the purest of hearts. Gwynne was a Southerner who, back in the day, had doted on me like I was the child she never had. In the early days of my addiction, she served me iced coffee and Quaaludes in bed, and in the later days, when I was so drugged out that I'd lost most of my motor skills, she changed my clothes and wiped gobs of drool off my chin.

But now, since I'd become sober, she'd redirected that unconditional love toward Chandler and Carter, spending most of her day doting on them. (God save them.) Anyway, Gwynne was like family, and the mere thought of having to let her go one day made me terribly sad. Just how much she knew about what was going on I wasn't quite sure. And then, all at once–*a terrible thought!*

Gwynne was a Southerner, which meant she was genetically predisposed toward idle chatter. And, like everyone, she loved the Chef and would most certainly try to strike up small talk with him. I could only imagine it: "Oh–hi, Chef! Can I fix you something to eat, maybe a turkey sandwich or a bowl of fresh fruit?"... "Well, sure, Gwynne, do you have any strawberries?"... "No, I'm sorry, Chef, the two men in Chandler's bedroom ate the last of the strawberries."... "There are two men in Chandler's bedroom? What do they look like, Gwynne?"... "Well, Chef, one of them smiles a lot; he's wearing headphones and he has a camera around his neck with a telephoto lens; the other one doesn't smile at all, but he has a giant revolver on his hip and a pair of handcuffs dangling from his belt loop."...

Oh, Christ–I needed to say something to Gwynne! I had introduced the occupying forces as old friends, and Gwynne, never one to ask questions, had taken things at face value, smiling warmly at the invaders and then asking them if they wanted something to eat, just like she would with the Chef! I had arranged for the kids to be out this afternoon, and I could probably get by without Gwynne for a few hours, although she might get insulted if I were to just ask her to hightail it off the property without explanation.

"I brought you some iced tea for your business meeting," Gwynne said lovingly, although it came out like, "I brawwght yuh sum ice tea fuh yuh biznez meet'n." She placed the sterling-silver tray on the obscenely expensive round teak table with great care. "Ya sure those men upstairs wud'n care for sumthin'?" she added.

"No, Gwynne, I'm sure they're fine." With great weariness, I said, "Listen, Gwynne, I'd really appreciate it if you didn't mention anything about those two men upstairs while Dennis is around"–I paused, searching for a possible explanation as to why–"because it, uh, has to do with, uh, security issues. It's all about security issues, Gwynne, especially with all that's been going on around here." What the fuck was I talking about?

Gwynne nodded sadly, seeming to understand. Then she began staring at my light-blue polo shirt, twisting her lips. "My oh my, you have a li'l stain on yer shirt. Look," and she began walking toward me with her finger pointed straight at the hidden microphone.

I jumped out of my armchair, as if the teak had suddenly become electrified. Gwynne stopped dead in her tracks, and there she stood, the Good Humor Lady, staring at me with a strange look on her face. *Christ–she knew, didn't she!* It was written all over her face–and all over mine too! I practically shrieked it: *I'm a rat, Gwynnie! I'm a rat! Don't talk to me! I'm wired for sound! I'm wired for sound!*

In fact, her face betrayed nothing save genuine concern that the man she'd worked for for almost a decade had suddenly lost his marbles. In retrospect, there were many things I could have said to Gwynne to explain my irrational behavior. I could have told her a yellow jacket had spooked me, that I'd gotten a cramp in my leg, that it was a delayed reaction to those three torturous days behind bars.

Instead, all I said was, "Jesus, Gwynne, you're right! I better go upstairs and change my shirt before Dennis gets here," and I ran upstairs to my closet and changed into a dark-blue short-sleeve polo shirt. Then I went into the master bathroom–with its $100,000 gray marble floor, oversize Swedish sauna, and glorious whirlpool bathtub that was so large it was better suited for Shamu the Killer Whale than the Wolf of Wall Street–and I flicked on the light and took a good hard look in the mirror.

I didn't like what I saw.

"*Eyyyyyy,*" said a smiling Chef, extending his arms for a welcoming embrace. "Come here and give me a hug, *you*!"

Christ Almighty! The Chef knew too! He had seen it on my face—just like Gwynne had! When he hugged me he was going to pat me down for a wire. I was frozen, panic-stricken. It was precisely 1:05 p.m., and time seemed to be standing still. We were in the mansion's grand marble entryway, separated by only four gleaming squares of black-and-white Italian marble—arranged checkerboard style—and I was trying to conjure up a lame excuse as to why I shouldn't embrace the Chef as I always did.

The calculations began roaring through my brain faster than I could keep track of them. If I *didn't* hug the Chef he would know something was wrong—yet if I *did* hug the Chef he might feel that devilish little recorder taped to my loins or that supersensitive microphone taped to my chest. *Such dishonesty! Such deception! I was a rat!* Yet if I perched my ass out a bit and slumped my shoulders forward, then perhaps I'd be safe.

As I stared at the Chef I became terribly conscious of the devilish wares OCD had affixed to my body—the recorder, the microphone, and the masking tape seemed to be growing larger, heavier, more obvious. The recorder was no bigger than a pack of Marlboros, yet it felt larger than a shoe box, and the pea-size microphone weighed less than an ounce, yet it felt heavier than a bowling bowl. I was sweating profusely, and my heart was going *thump thump thump,* as if a frightened rabbit had taken up residence there. And there stood the Jersey Chef, in his snazzy single-breasted light-gray suit with light-blue overplaid and a crisp white dress shirt with spread British collar. I had no *choice* but to hug him, but then—a brainstorm: *a contagious pathogen!*

With a couple of sniffles, I said, "Jesus, Dennis, you're a sight for sore eyes... *sniff, sniff*... Thanks for coming over." I shot my right hand out and locked my elbow, offering a hearty handshake. "But don't get too close to me; I think I caught something in that jail cell... *sniff, sniff*... A flu bug, I think." I smiled sheepishly and jutted my right hand out an extra inch, as if to say, "Put it there, pal!"

Alas, the Chef was a man's man, and no flu bug on earth was going to scare him away. "Get over here!" he snapped. "Cold or no cold, it's times like these when you find out who your true friends are."

Who your true friends are? Christ–such gut-wrenching guilt! It now had the distinct pleasure of meeting the sheer panic that had already taken up residence in my brain. Then came a lightning-fast fight to the death. The guilt was saying, "How could you rat out someone as loyal as the Chef? Have you no shame?" to which the panic replied, "Fuck the Chef! If you don't rat him out you'll end up like that drooling old bastard Mr. Gower." The guilt countered, "It doesn't matter; the Chef has been loyal and true, and to rat him out would make you lower than pond scum!" and the panic replied, "Who gives a shit! I'd rather be pond scum than sitting in jail the rest of my life! Besides, the Chef will end up ratting out the Blue-eyed Devil to save his own skin, so what's the fucking difference?" The guilt argued, "That's not necessarily true. The Chef isn't a pussy, like you; he's a stand-up guy." Then suddenly–*a fresh wave of panic!*–the Chef had brushed past my hand and was rapidly closing the distance.

Christ! What should I do? *Think, you little rat!* The high road or the low road? Guilt or self-preservation? Alas, when you're a rat, self-preservation outweighs all: Just before the Chef and I embraced, my rat brain unleashed a flood of emergency signals to my musculoskeletal system. Faster than I knew it, my ass popped out like a male hooker advertising his trade, my shoulders slumped forward like Quasimodo ringing a church bell, and that was how we embraced–with the Jersey Chef standing tall and proud, and the Wolf of Wall Street standing hunchbacked and hookerlike.

"Are you all right?" asked the Chef, releasing me from his embrace. He grabbed my shoulders and held me at arms' length. "Did you hurt your back again?"

"No," I answered quickly. "It's just a bit sore from sitting in that jail cell. And also from my cold... *sniff, sniff.*" I rubbed my nose with the back of my hand. "You know, it's amazing, but if I get even the least bit sick it goes straight to my back." Jesus! What the fuck was I talking about? I shrugged, trying to organize my thoughts. "Come on, let's sit outside. I could use a little fresh air."

"You lead, I follow," said the Chef.

A pair of prodigious French doors led out to the stone patio, and the moment we stepped through them I could *feel* the *click click click* of the Mormon's dreaded Minolta. It seemed to be burning holes through me, like a laser beam. When we reached the teak target zone, I offered the Chef the overpriced armchair facing the bedroom window.

I resisted the urge to look up at the Venetian blinds, pouring each of us a glass of iced tea instead. Then I started in with small talk. "I'll tell you," I said wearily. "I can't believe these cocksuckers"—as *cocksuckers* escaped my lips, it occurred to me that OCD and the Bastard might not be appreciative of that characterization of them. I made a mental note to be more considerate in the future—"have me under house arrest. Like I'm really a flight risk with a wife and two kids." I shook my head in disgust. "What a fucking joke."

The Chef nodded in agreement. "Yeah, well, that's the game these bastards play," he said venomously. "They'll do whatever they can to make your life miserable. How's the Duchess holding up?"

I shook my head and let out a great sigh. "Not well," I said. I paused, fighting down the urge to pour my heart out to the Chef. Even rats have pride, after all, and I knew that countless others would be listening to this tape at some point. "She's acting like all this comes as a great shock to her, as if she thought she was married to a doctor or something. I don't know... I don't think we're gonna make it through this, not as a couple."

"Don't say that," the Chef replied quickly. "You two are gonna make it through this thing, but only if *you* stay strong. She's your wife, so she's gonna follow your lead, one way or the other. Show weakness to her and *badabing*"—the Chef clapped his hands a single time—"she'll be out the door in two seconds flat. It's the nature of the female animal; they gravitate toward strength."

I took a moment to consider the Chef's words, and for a brief instant my spirits lifted, but then they sank again. Indeed, the Chef's words were usually full of wisdom, but, in this case, he was completely off the mark. Whether or not I stayed strong had nothing to do with it; the Duchess was strong enough on her own—strong enough to know that under no circumstances would she allow my problems to diminish her quota on ore extraction one iota. She had grown up dirt-poor on the trash-lined streets of Bay Ridge, Brooklyn, and there was no way she would be willing to risk history repeating itself.

Nevertheless, this was a perfect opportunity to make an important point to the Chef, namely, that I had no intention of cooperating. In a dead-serious tone, I said, "Yeah, well, maybe I can't control the Duchess's actions, but I can control my own. You don't have to worry about me staying strong, Dennis. I'm gonna fight this thing to the bitter end, with my last dying breath if I have to. I don't care how much it costs, or how *bloody* it gets, or how many bodies get buried along the way. I don't give a flying fuck about any of it! I'm taking this thing to trial, and I'm gonna get fucking acquitted." I shook my head, liking the way my blustering sounded. It was very Wolflike. Too bad I was such a pussy. "You just fucking wait and see," I added, twitching my nose menacingly.

"Good for you!" the Chef said emphatically. "That's exactly what I wanted to hear. Just keep thinking like that and those bastards downtown are gonna be in for a rude awakening." He shrugged confidently. "They expect you to just roll over and play dead, because that's what everyone else does. But when it comes down to it—they got *their* version of things and we got *our* version of things, and *our* version of things will make just as much sense to a jury as *their* version of things."

"And the burden of proof isn't on us," I added confidently, "it's on *them*."

"Exactly," said the Chef, "and last time *I* checked, you're innocent until proven guilty in this fine country of ours." He flashed me a quick smile and winked. "And even if you *are* guilty, they still gotta *prove* that guilt beyond a reasonable doubt, and that ain't so easy to do when you got two versions of things, understand?"

I nodded slowly. "I do," I said halfheartedly, "but . . . I mean . . . it's a pretty good cover story we have, but it's still not as believable as the truth. You know?"

"Don't kid yourself," snapped the Chef. "The truth is stranger than fiction sometimes." He shrugged. "In fact, I'd take a good cover story over the truth *any* day of the week. Anyway, I think the biggest problem we're facing here is that Danny is still in jail. The longer he sits in there, the more likely he is to flip." The Chef paused, as if searching for the right words. "See, while he's sitting in there, he has no idea what's going on on the outside. He doesn't know that *I'm* with him and that *you're* with him; he might be thinking that he's alone in all this–maybe even that *you're* cooperating. God only knows what the feds are whispering in his ear." The Chef shook his head in consternation, then suddenly his face lit up. "I'll tell you what I *really* need to do: I need to get myself into that cell to speak to Danny, to let him know that everything's gonna be all right." The Chef compressed his lips and nodded slowly. "That would be the best thing for us right now. Maybe I can get myself on the visiting list. Whaddaya think?"

Good Lord–the Chef was as tough as nails! He was prepared to go right into the heart of enemy territory! Did he know no fear? Was he really that much of a warrior? It was all starting to make sense now: The feds had never been able to nab the Chef and the Devil because they didn't think like other men. They were true Scarfaces, white-collar mobsters of a wholly different sort.

Just then Gwynne came walking out of the kitchen.

Oh, Jesus! I thought. *Jabber jabber jabber!*

Would she spill the beans? There was no telling. Her heart was much too pure to fathom all this wickedness going on here, all this deceit. As she approached, I noticed she was holding the cordless phone. She greeted the Chef first, in warm Southern tones: "Well, hi there, Dennis, how are *you*?" which came out like, "*Wail, hi there, Dainess, how'r yew?*"

"I'm fine," answered the Chef, in warm Jersey tones. "Nevuh bedduh. How *you* doing, Gwynne?"

"Oh, ahhhm fahyn, ahhhm fahyn," the Southern belle answered, and there was a very sad smile attached to those two "I'm fines," a smile that so much as said, "As fine as could be expected, considering my boss has one foot in the slammer, his wife has one foot in a new gold mine, and I'm about to be out of a fucking job!"

Then she turned to me and said, "Your lawy'r is on the phone. He said it's important."

Magnum? Why would he call *now*? He knew about this meeting. Why interrupt the flow of things? I held up a finger to the Chef and then rose from my chair and grabbed the cordless from Gwynne. With my back to the Chef, I looked Gwynne in the eye and motioned discreetly toward the kitchen with my chin, as if to say, "All right, why don't you skedaddle on out of here before you spill the beans, jabber-jaw!" to which Gwynne shrugged and headed back to the safety of the kitchen.

I walked a few feet away, to the wrought-iron railing at the edge of the patio, placed my elbows on the railing, and leaned over. I was still within earshot of the Chef when I said into the phone, "Hey, Greg. What's going on?"

"Yeah, it's Greg," said OCD's voice, "but not the Greg you were expecting. Just act natural."

Jesus Christ! Why the fuck was OCD calling? Had he lost his mind? "Yeah," I said casually, "well, that doesn't surprise me. Danny's a stand-up guy; he'll never cooperate." I turned to the Chef and winked, then said into the phone, "Anyway, just tell Danny's lawyer that I'm there for him no matter what. Whatever he needs."

"Good," said OCD, "that was quick thinking. You're doing great so far. But listen to me: Dennis seems very open to talk to you, so I want you to see if you can set up a meeting with Brennan. I think he might go for it."

"I'll try calling her," I said skeptically, knowing full well that the chances of getting a face-to-face with the Blue-eyed Devil were one in a million. Even in the best of times he was one paranoid bastard, but now–in the worst of times–there was no *way* he'd be reckless enough to take a meeting with *me*. "But I haven't spoken to Nancy in almost a year," I said into the phone. "I think she hates Danny more than the government does."

I looked at the Chef, who was staring at me quizzically, the way a person does when they're trying to figure out the other end of a phone conversation. *Christ, if he only knew!* I flashed him a quick smile and rolled my eyes and shook my head quickly, as if to say,

"My lawyer is totally wasting my time here," then I said into the phone, "Yeah, well, you just tell Danny's lawyer to make sure Danny knows I'm with him. That's the"–*beep, beep,* went the call-waiting–"most important thing. Anyway, I gotta go. I got another call coming in." I clicked over to the next line. "Hello?"

An unfamiliar female voice, rather sultry, said, "Hi... is this Jordan?"

"Yeah," I replied, slightly annoyed at the sultry voice. What the fuck did *this voice* want? "This is Jordan, who's this?"

"Maria Elena. I'm Michael Burrico's fiancée." My heart sank to my stomach before my brain even knew the reasons why. Michael Burrico was the Duchess's first love–back from her glorious Brooklyn days–when she was still a Duchess in embryo. Last I'd heard, he was living in Manhattan and he'd struck it rich in the construction business. In the Duchess's mind, I knew, that could translate into only two simple words: precious ore.

In a tone laced with sarcasm, I said to Maria, "Yeah, Maria. Your fiancé was my *loving* second wife's first boyfriend. To what do I owe the pleasure of this phone call?"

Maria let out a tiny grunt before she said, "Well, I know you're going through a bad time right now, but I thought you'd like to know that your wife was knocking on my fiancé's door last night–around midnight. She was..." and Maria kept on talking, but I stopped listening–or, more accurately, I was unable to listen because my head was now filling with steam. I could literally hear the hissing sound, as hurt, anger, embarrassment, and hopelessness flooded my senses all at the same time.

I didn't even know who to be more embarrassed for at this point, her or me. Our life together had come to represent a laughingstock, the ultimate cautionary tale of rich men and trophy wives, of cutting corners in business, of cutting corners in life. We had played the Game of Life hard and fast–careening down the highway at a million miles an hour–and we had ended up losers, the ultimate crash-and-burn story. The only difference between the Duchess and me was that she was trying to walk away from the accident without a scratch, while I had no choice but to accept my fate as a quadriplegic burn victim.

"... and I would really appreciate it," Maria continued, in an edgy tone, "if you would tell your wife to keep her paws away from my fiancé."

Well said, I thought. In fact, I couldn't have agreed with Maria more, which was why I answered her with a big fat *click* in her ear, without saying so much as good-bye. Then I turned to the Chef and froze, bewildered, not knowing what to say. My mind was double-tracking wildly. It had been hard enough to focus before, but now–this was a bit much. Everything was hitting me all at once, from all angles. Every man has his breaking point, and I was now at mine.

As I stared at the Chef, I knew I should be trying to figure out a way to broach the subject of the Blue-eyed Devil, and I knew that OCD and the Mormon were right upstairs, hanging on my every word, making careful notes of my performance–notes that one day would go into my 5K letter and decide how many years I spent in prison.

Yet, with all that was going on, with all that was at stake, with my *freedom* hanging in the balance, the only question my brain was asking itself was: What time is the Duchess coming home tonight? That was all that mattered to me. I wanted to confront her–no, I *needed* to confront her. I couldn't move forward in my life until I had an all-out brawl with her. A rip-roaring fight that could end with only one thing: violence. The Duchess was toast. History. I was not going to let her get away with this, not for one second longer. If this was, indeed, a crash-and-burn story, then it would be one without any survivors, save the children. Let my parents raise them, I figured; they'd certainly do a much better job than the Duchess and me.

"You okay?" the Chef asked warmly. "You look a bit pale."

No response, then–"No... I mean, yeah." I began nodding my head. "It was, uh, just something with Nadine's maternity business. A girl called. She's pregnant. With a baby." I smiled vacantly. "I'm okay. I'm... I'm as right as the mail, Dennis," and the first thing I'm gonna do when the Duchess gets home, I thought, is confront her. But I won't tell her about the phone call, not in the beginning. I'll wait until she denies ringing that bastard's doorbell; then I'll spring it on her. Then we'll see...

I sat back down, my heart beating out of my chest, my mind racing out of control. I placed the phone on the table. My mouth was bone-dry. I looked at the Chef, forcing a smile. It was time to end this meeting. I couldn't sit here anymore. I couldn't muster a single constructive thought until I confronted the Duchess.

With despair in my heart, I threw a Hail Mary pass. "I'll tell you the truth," I muttered, "I don't know which are worse: my problems with the feds or my problems with the Duchess." I shook my head in genuine bewilderment. Then, with a smirk, I added, "Maybe I should go see Bob; maybe *he* can offer me some words of wisdom, because for the life of me I don't have any."

There were a few moments of silence, then the Chef nearly knocked me out of my seat when he said, "I think that's an excellent idea. Bob would love to talk to you. How's Tuesday at the golf course? You think you could work it out with the ankle-bracelet people?"

Yeah, I thought, I'm sure the ankle-bracelet people would be willing to look the other way for a meeting with the Blue-eyed Devil, although, at this particular moment, I couldn't give two shits about that. All that mattered was what time the Duchess was coming home.

Everything else was incidental.

CHAPTER 10

HOW TO CONFRONT A DUCHESS

Step one: Light a raging fire.

The master bedroom's French limestone fireplace was four by six feet wide and had been retrofitted with an electric-starter mechanism. As always, four thick logs of premium-grade ponderosa pine, split lengthwise, sat atop a prodigious heap of white-cedar kindling wood. By this time of September, the fireplace hadn't seen a flame in nearly five months. Fine. Good. At precisely 9:15 p.m. I pushed the stainless button on the wall, igniting the first–but not the last–raging inferno of the evening.

Step two: Burn a piece of overpriced furniture.

Grunting and groaning, I pulled over one of my formerly aspiring decorator's favorite procurements–a $13,000 white silk ottoman that had taken some thieving bastards in High Point, North Carolina, nearly a year to manufacture–to within three feet of the flames. I sat down and stared into the flames. In less than a minute, the kindling wood was crackling away menacingly and the flames were blazing away ominously. Not satisfied, I rose into a crouch, reached behind me, pulled the ottoman closer, and sat back down. Much better. In ten minutes the ottoman and I would be toast.

Step three: Ignite the flames of righteous indignation.

A simple task. Was there a jury that would convict me if I stabbed the Duchess through her ice-cold heart, using that 18-karat-gold letter opener, which was resting comfortably on her $26,000 white lacquer secretary? I would only need to worry about a jury of her peers, which would consist of twelve blond-headed gold diggers who saw no crime in a married woman–*with two children, no less!*–knocking on her ex-boyfriend's door at midnight, while her husband was lying home in bed (under house arrest), contemplating suicide, and dreaming of ways to win her back. I held on to that thought and took some deep, angry breaths. I kept staring into the belly of the flames, letting the fire bake my skin–growing angrier, more righteous, more indignant, with each passing second.

Just then I heard the familiar sounds of the arriving Duchess, the gravel crunching in the driveway, the slamming of the massive mahogany front door, the *clickity clack clack* of her overpriced high heels ascending the sumptuous stairs. And then, finally, the door opened. I turned from the flames and there she was, dressed in black. That was appropriate, I thought, considering she had just arrived at her own funeral.

When she saw me sitting so close to the flames, she stopped dead in her tracks and struck a pose, with her head cocked to one side and her hands on her hips and her shoulders thrown back and her back slightly arched, pushing her glorious breasts forward. She opened her mouth to say something, but no words came out. Then she began chewing on the inside of her cheek.

There were a few moments of silence as we just stared at each other, like two gunfighters waiting to throw down. The Duchess looked good, of course. There was no denying that, even now. The light from the fire set off her entire ensemble: that tiny black dress, those sexy black high heels, those long bare legs, her great mane of shimmering blond hair, those brilliant blue eyes, her high cheekbones, those glistening lips, that perfectly smooth jawline.

Yes, the Duchess was, indeed, a woman of parts, although at this particular moment the only part of her I was interested in was a tiny area just over her left breast implant, right between her second and third ribs. That was where her ice-cold heart was located, and it would be there where I would plunge the golden letter opener. Then I would jerk the letter opener upward and slightly to the left, with a twisting motion–slicing her pulmonary artery, which would cause her to drown in her blood. It would be a ghastly, horrific, painful death, the sort of death a gold-digging Duchess deserved.

"Why the fire?" she asked, giving up her pose and heading toward her white lacquer secretary. "It's a bit early in the season, don't you think?" She flashed me a dead smile as she sat on the edge of the secretary, placing her palms on it and locking her elbows. Then she crossed her legs and wriggled her butt, as if to get comfortable.

I stared back into the flames. "I was cold," I said, *because you sucked every last drop of blood and life force out of me, you conniving, gold-digging cunt,* "so I figured I'd light a fire," *before I slice you to ribbons and rid the earth of you.*

A few moments of silence, then she cocked her head to the side. "Where are the kids?" she asked.

I kept staring into the flames. "At Gwynne's," I answered tonelessly. "They're sleeping there tonight," *so I can murder you without upsetting them.*

Now confusion mixed with trepidation: "Why are they, uh, sleeping at Gwynne's?"

Still staring into the flames: "Because I wanted the house to myself," *without bystanders, witnesses, distractions, or any soul who might try to talk me out of doing what I know I must do to free myself of you,* "that's why."

She chuckled nervously, trying to make light of what she now realized was going to be a very dark encounter. "Yourself?" she answered. "Well, what about me? I'm here too, right?"

I looked up, and she was holding the golden letter opener in her right hand, *tap-tap-tapping* the blade on her left palm. How had she known? Was it that obvious that I was planning to stab her? Or was it just coincidence? No matter. I had once seen Arnold Schwarzenegger stab an Islamic terrorist with the terrorist's own knife, and it had looked rather elementary.

Just then I noticed the Duchess was still wearing her wedding band. What a fucking joke! The philandering Duchess and her wedding band! "You're still wearing your wedding band, I see. Don't you think that's a bit ironic, Nadine?"

She put down the letter opener and extended her left hand in front of her, staring at it quizzically. After a few moments, she looked up and shrugged. "Why?" she said innocently. "We're still married, no?"

I nodded slowly. "Yeah," I said, "I think we are. So what did you do last night?"

A quick answer: "I went to see Earth, Wind and Fire. With my friends." The last three words screamed: *Alibi!*

I compressed my lips and nodded. "Oh, your friends," I said understandingly. "Which friends are those?"

Another quick answer: "Donna and Ophelia."

Donna Schlesinger–*why, that lousy cunt!* She definitely had a hand in this, no doubt about it! She and the Duchess had been friends since high school, and, back in the day, she'd dated one of Michael Burrico's closest friends.

"How was the concert?" I asked casually.

The Duchess shrugged. "It was okay. Nothing special." Then a strategic subject change: "I was hoping the kids would be home tonight."

Why? So you could use them as human shields? Sorry, Duchess, no such luck. It's only you and me tonight–you, me, and the golden letter opener. Prepare to reap the consequences of your infidelity! I said, "Just out of curiosity, where'd you sleep last night?"

"At Ophelia's," she snapped. "Why?"

"You went straight from the concert to Ophelia's?" I asked skeptically. "You didn't stop anywhere along the way, not to eat or anything else?"

She shook her head. "No, I went straight to Ophelia's. No stops."

There were a few moments of silence, during which I found myself desperately wanting to believe her. Just why, I still couldn't explain, although it had something to do with the bizarre nature of the male animal–his vanity, his foolish pride, his desire not be spurned by a beautiful woman. Yes, in spite of everything, my masculine pride was still trying to convince me that my wife was faithful and that this was all some giant misunderstanding.

I took a deep breath and stared into the belly of the fire, relighting the flames of anger, hatred, and righteous indignation. "So how's Michael Burrico?" I asked, and then I looked up from the fire and stared into her eyes.

The Duchess recoiled. "Michael Burrico?" she said incredulously. "How on earth would I know?" She stared at me with a blank expression, and still I wanted to believe her. I really did.

But she was a lying sack of shit; I knew it! "When's the last time you've seen him, Nadine? Tell me! How long ago? Days? Weeks? Hours? Tell me, God damn it!"

The Duchess sagged. "I have no idea what you're talking about." She looked away. "Someone's giving you bad information."

"You're a fucking liar!" I sputtered. "A total fucking liar!"

She kept looking down, saying nothing.

"Look at me!" I screamed, rising from the ottoman. She looked. I plowed on: "Look me in the eye and tell me you weren't at Michael Burrico's apartment last night. Go ahead and tell me!"

She shook her head quickly. "I... I wasn't. I wasn't there." Her tone was just short of panic. "I don't know what you're talking about. Why are you doing this?"

I took an aggressive step toward her. "Swear on the kids' eyes that you weren't there last night." I clenched my fists. "Go ahead and swear to me, Nadine."

"You're fucking sick," she muttered, looking away again. "You're having me followed." Then she looked back at me. "I want you out of this house. I want a divorce." She raised her chin in defiance.

I took another step forward. I was less than three feet from her now. "You... fucking... cunt!" I sputtered. "You no-good, lousy, philandering, gold-digging cunt! I didn't have you followed! Michael Burrico's fiancée called here. That's how I knew where you were, you... lousy–"

She cut me off. "Fuck you!" she screamed. "You're calling *me* a cheat! How many women have you fucked, you fucking hypocrite!" With that she popped off the edge of the desk and took a step toward me, closing the distance. We were less than two feet apart now. "I want you out of my *life*!" she screamed frantically. "I want you out of my *house*! I don't ever wanna speak to you again!"

"Your house?" I sputtered. "Are you fucking kidding me? This is *my* house! I'm not going fucking anywhere."

"I'm hiring a lawyer!" she screamed.

"Yeah, the best my money can buy!" I screamed back.

She clenched her fists. "Fuck you! You're a fucking crook! You stole all your money! I hope you die in jail!" The Duchess took an aggressive step forward, as if she were about to take a swing at me, and then suddenly she did something that I would never forget for the rest of my life. With complete serenity, she dropped her arms to her sides and relaxed her posture and tilted her head back all the way, exposing the most vulnerable part of her long bare neck, and she said, "Go ahead: Kill me." Her voice was soft and mellow, completely resigned. "I know that's what you want, so just go ahead and do it." She tilted her head back even farther. "Kill me right now. I won't fight back. I promise. Just strangle me and put us both out of our misery. You can kill yourself afterward."

I took a step toward her, ready to commit murder, when suddenly my eyes lit on a picture frame affixed to the wall. It was just over the Duchess's left shoulder. The frame was long and narrow, perhaps one by three feet, and inside were three large pictures of our children. Chandler was on top, and she was smiling bashfully. She had on a fancy yellow T-shirt with a buttercup collar and a matching yellow headband. She was three and a half at the time, and she looked like a tiny Duchess. Beneath her was Carter, only eighteen months at the time, and he had on nothing but a snow-white diaper. His eyes were wide open, his expression full of wonder, as he stared at a bubble floating in the air. His blond hair shimmered like polished glass. His regal eyelashes were as lush as butterfly wings. And, again, all I saw was the Duchess. And beneath Carter was a picture of him and his sister. He was sitting in her lap, she had her arms around him, and they were staring into each other's eyes adoringly.

In that very instant the true irony of my plight hit me, like one of Zeus's thunderbolts. It wasn't enough that I couldn't kill my wife because she was the mother of my children; it was much worse than that. The simple fact was that *because* she was the mother of my children I would never be rid of her. She would be in my life forever! Haunting me until the day I died! I would be seeing her at every birthday, graduation, wedding, confirmation, and bar mitzvah. Christ, I would even have to dance with her at my children's weddings!

I would see her in sickness and in health, in good times and in bad, and for better or worse, until death did us part. In essence, I would always be married to her, linked together by the intense love we shared for our two children.

And there she was, standing there, waiting to be choked to death.

"I'll never forgive you for this," I said softly. "With my dying breath, I'll never forgive you." I headed for the door, walking slowly.

Just as I reached the door, I heard her say in a soft, gentle tone, "I'll never forgive you either. Not with my dying breath."

Then I left the room.

BOOK II

CHAPTER II

THE MAKING OF A WOLF

Well, I'm sorry to hear that," said the Bastard sympathetically, and he leaned forward in his cheap black armchair and rested his bony elbows on the conference table. "It's always a shame when kids are involved."

"Yeah," I said sadly–and, *yeah, right!* I thought. This is what you live for, Bastard! You *relish* stripping a man of all his worldly possessions! What else could make a feeble life like yours worth living? "It's sad for all of us, Joel, but I *do* appreciate your concern."

He nodded dutifully. OCD, however, was shaking his head suspiciously. "I don't know," he said. "I really thought you two would stay together; I really did."

"Yeah," I replied glumly, "so did I. But there's just too much water under the bridge. Too many bad memories."

It was a little after ten, and I was singing on Court Street again, albeit to a slightly smaller audience. The Witch, the Mormon, and my towering attorney, Magnum, were all conspicuously absent. The Witch, I was told, was busy with another case today, no doubt destroying some other poor schnook's life; the Mormon was busy attending to personal matters–probably still in bed with one of his Mormon wives, trying to conceive a fresh litter of Mormon babies; Magnum, on the other hand, was busy doing nothing. In fact, the only reason he wasn't here this morning–in the heinous subbasement of 26 Federal Plaza–was that he thought it would be good if I spent some "alone time" with my captors. And while his words seemed somewhat logical, they also seemed suspiciously convenient, considering I had just written him a check for a million dollars last week. (Why show up anymore when he could take the money and run?)

So it was just the three of us this morning: the Bastard, OCD, and myself.

"You're being quiet this morning," said OCD. "If you don't want to talk about your personal life, it's okay."

I shrugged. "What's there to say, other than that my wife must have been sleep-talking during our wedding vows?"

"You think maybe she's having an affair?"

"No, Greg! Not a chance," I said confidently. *Of course she is!* I thought. She's fucking that dimwitted Brooklynite Michael Burrico. A dunce like him was an easy target for a prospecting Duchess. "She's definitely not cheating. What's going on with us cuts much deeper than that."

He smiled warmly. "Don't take offense; I'm just trying to make sense of it all. Usually, when this sort of thing happens, there's another man waiting in the wings. But, hey, what do I know, right?"

Now the Bastard chimed in: "Like Greg, I'm *also* sympathetic to your plight, but the only thing you should be worried about now is your cooperation. Everything else is secondary."

Yeah? What about my kids, asshole?

"Joel's right," said OCD. "It's probably not a good time to be getting divorced. Maybe you and Nadine should wait a bit, until all the commotion dies down."

"All right," snapped the Bastard, "so let's get down to cases, then. Last time we spoke, the market had just crashed and you were out of a job. What happened next?"

What an asshole! I thought. I took a deep breath and said, "Well, I wouldn't actually say I was out of a job, because what I had at LF Rothschild wasn't really a job in the first place. I was a connector, which is the lowest of the low on Wall Street. All I did was dial the phone all day and try to get past the secretaries of wealthy business owners. It was a pride-swallowing siege–but one that I had no choice but to grin and bear. The only thing keeping me going was hope for the future." I paused for effect. "And then came the crash.

"I still remember what it was like coming home that night on the express bus: You could've heard a pin drop. There was a certain *fear* in the air that I'd never experienced before. The media was sensationalizing things to the point of hysteria, predicting bank failures, massive unemployment, people jumping out of windows. It was the start of another Great Depression, they said."

"A depression that never came," added the Bastard, straight-A student of obvious history.

"Exactly," I said. "It never came, although no one had any way of knowing that back then. Remember, the *last* time the market had crashed was in '29, and the depression came right on the heels of that. So it wasn't all that far-fetched to think it would happen again." I paused for a moment. "Now, for people who'd actually *grown up* in the Great Depression–like my parents–the prospect was utterly terrifying, but for people like me, who'd only read about it in history books, it was simply unimaginable. So, whether you worked on Wall Street or Main Street that day, everyone was scared shitless what would happen next." I shrugged my shoulders. "Everyone except Denise; she was as cool as a cucumber!"

"That's pretty impressive," reasoned OCD, "considering how broke you two were."

"Yeah," I said quickly, "and it would have even been *more* impressive if she had the slightest idea the market had crashed." I smiled ruefully.

The Bastard narrowed his eyes. "She hadn't heard it on the news?"

I shook my head slowly. "Denise never watched the news. She was more of a soap-opera girl than a news girl." I paused for a moment, and a profound wave of sadness overtook me. Denise might have had her shortcomings, but she was still a great wife. And she was gorgeous, one of those dark-haired Italian beauties who every teenage boy fantasizes about in high school. She was a great wearer of black leather miniskirts and white cotton sweaters, the latter of which were softer than a baby's bottom.

Thinking back now, the way the two of us had cocooned ourselves in our tiny Bayside apartment had been pure magic. We had sworn eternal love for each other, certain that our love could conquer all. Yet, somehow, we'd managed to destroy that love. We allowed success and money to go to our heads. We allowed it to separate us, to eat away at us. Ultimately, it would turn *her* into a world-class shopaholic and *me* into a rip-roaring drug addict. And then came the Duchess–

"–still with us?" snapped the Bastard. "You need to take a break for a few minutes?" He offered me his sadistic warden's smile.

"No, I'm fine," I said. "Anyway, Denise had no idea the market crashed, so the moment I walked through the door she threw her arms around me, as if I were a conquering hero. 'Oh, my God!' she said. 'You're finally home! How was your first day as a stockbroker? Did you break the company record for the most stock sold?' "

OCD and the Bastard started chuckling.

I chuckled back. "Yeah–it was pretty funny, all right, except by mid-November we were down on our hands and knees, rolling up nickels, dimes, and quarters to pay for shampoo. But it wasn't until a month after the crash that I decided to throw in the towel and leave Wall Street.

"It was a Sunday morning, and Denise and I were sitting in the living room, like two zombies, looking through the help-wanted section. After a few minutes, I came across something that struck me as odd. 'Check this out,' I said to her. 'There's a company advertising for stockbrokers, and they're not on Wall Street; they're on Long Island.'

"She looked at the ad and said, 'What does *PT, FT* mean?'

" 'Part time, full time,' I answered, and I found myself wondering what kind of brokerage firm hired part-time stockbrokers? I'd never heard of that before. Still, given my circumstances it seemed like a reasonable idea. So I said to her, 'Working part-time might not be such a bad thing. Maybe I could earn a few bucks while I'm looking for something else,' to which she nodded in agreement.

"Anyway, neither of us thought much of it at the time, and when I called the next morning, I was completely turned off. A gruff male voice answered the phone and said, 'Investors' Center. How can I helpya?' and I knew right on the spot that it wasn't a switchboard operator. And the company's name sent shivers down my spine. I was used to names like Goldman Sachs and Merrill Lynch, names that resonated with Wall Street.

"I could only imagine myself saying, 'Hi, this is Jordan Belfort, calling from the Investors' Center in Butt-Fuck, Long Island. I'm no closer to Wall Street than you are, so why don't you send me your hard-earned money? You'll probably never see it again!' "

"Very prophetic," snapped the Bastard.

"Yeah," I agreed, "although the Investors' Center wasn't in Butt-Fuck, Long Island; it was in Great Neck, Long Island, which is actually a pretty nice part of town. The company was on the second floor of a three-story office building." I paused for a moment. "You know, I remember pulling up to the building and feeling rather impressed. I was driving Denise's old piece-a-shit Datsun, which was the only car we had at the time, and I was saying to myself, 'Hey, this place doesn't look so bad!' But then the moment I stepped into the boardroom my jaw dropped.

"The space was much smaller than I'd anticipated. It was maybe twenty feet square, and there wasn't a single thing about it that resonated of Wall Street. There were no computer monitors, no sales assistants, no stockbrokers pacing back and forth. There was nothing but twenty old wooden desks—all of them weathered-looking and arranged haphazardly. Only five of the desks had brokers behind them, and there was no pump whatsoever, just a low-level murmur.

"I'd worn a suit and tie to my interview, and I was the only one in the boardroom dressed that way. Everyone else was wearing jeans and sneakers, with the exception of one guy. The only problem was that his suit looked like it came straight out of a Salvation Army box. To this day, in fact, the guy still sticks out in my mind, because of his dim-witted expression. He looked lobotomized. He was in his early thirties, and he had the greasiest black hair imaginable–as if he showered in motor oil and–"

The Bastard began nodding his head again, as if to say, "Move on."

"Well, whatever," I said. "The manager was sitting in a small office at the front of the boardroom, and he seemed oblivious to everything. He was yapping away on his phone, talking to his wife, I recall, and saying something about their dog being sick. When he saw me, he held up an index finger, to which I nodded dutifully. Then he kept on talking.

"His name, as it turned out, was George Grunfeld, and two years prior he'd been a social-studies teacher. He was in his mid-to-late forties, and he happened to be the spitting image of Gabe Kaplan, the teacher from *Welcome Back, Kotter.*" I smiled at OCD. "Remember *Welcome Back, Kotter,* Greg?"

OCD nodded. "Yeah, with Travolta." He looked at the Bastard. "You ever watch *Welcome Back, Kotter*?"

The Bastard flashed OCD a dead smile. "Yeah; up your nose with a rubber hose," he said tonelessly.

"Ah, there you go!" I said warmly. "That's exactly what Travolta used to say to Mr. Kotter." I smiled at my new friend, pleased that I was finally able to find some common ground with him. Alas, he refused to smile back. Instead, he stared at me, stone-faced.

I shrugged. "Well, anyway, he looked just like him, bushy everywhere–his hair, eyebrows, mustache, knuckles. It looked like someone had glued a bunch of tumbleweeds to the guy!"

OCD shook his head, amused, while the Bastard stared ominously.

"Anyway, George finally hung up the phone and came over to greet me. 'Just pick a free desk and start dialing,' he said after a few seconds of small talk.

" 'That's it?' I said. 'You're hiring me?'

" 'Yeah, why not? It's not like I'll be paying you a salary or anything. That's not a problem, is it?' I was about to tell him that it wasn't, when one of the salesmen suddenly popped out of his chair and started pacing back and forth. George motioned toward the guy and said, 'That's Chris Knight; he's our top salesman. He's got a helluva rap. Listen...'

"I nodded and focused my attention on Chris, who was tall and lanky and had a face longer than a thoroughbred's. He was no older than twenty, and he was dressed like he'd just strolled in from a keg party. I remember being appalled at how terrible he sounded. He was mumbling, slurring; I could hardly understand the guy! Then, out of nowhere, he started screaming into his telephone, in short rapid-fire bursts of ludicrous sales hype. 'Jesus Christ–Bill–I *guarantee* it!' he screamed. 'I guarantee this stock is going up! You can't lose here–it's impossible! I have information–it's not even public yet–do you hear me? I don't think you do, because I have inside information!' And then he yanked the phone away from his ear and held it out in front of his own nose and stared at the receiver with contempt. Then, after five seconds of staring, he put the phone back to his ear and started screaming again. I looked at George and said, 'What the hell was that all about?' and George nodded his head knowingly and said, 'He's pretty good, isn't he?' And I just shook my head in disbelief and said nothing. Meanwhile, Chris was still screaming, 'Don't you understand? We can't lose here, Bill! I promise you! The stock is going to the moon! No ifs, ands, or buts! You gotta buy it now–right now!'"

I shrugged and said, "During my six months at LF Rothschild, I never heard anything so ridiculous, and I'm not just talking about all the securities laws he was violating but also his complete lack of professionalism. All this screaming and shouting and ridiculous sales hype was so Mickey Mouse–ish that no one with even the *slightest bit* of financial sophistication would give this guy the time of day."

The Bastard held up his hand. "Let me get this straight," he said skeptically. "You're saying you're *not* a proponent of sales hype?"

I turned the corners of my mouth down and shook my head. "No, I'm not, actually. Selling through hype is a complete waste of time. In military terms, it's like carpet bombing. It's very loud and menacing, but it's only marginally effective. At Stratton, I taught a different style of selling, which was the equivalent of dropping laser-guided smart bombs on high-priority targets." I shrugged. "Let me take things in order and you'll see exactly what I'm talking about."

The Bastard nodded slowly.

"All right," I said. "So as awful a salesman as Chris Knight was—or, should I say, as untrained a salesman as he was—it was what came out of his mouth next that truly shocked me. 'Oh—come on!' he screamed at his client. 'The stock's only thirty cents a share. Pick up a thousand shares, that's all I'm asking! It's only a three-hundred-dollar investment; how could you go wrong?'

"With that, I turned to George and said, 'Did he just say thirty cents a share?' And George said, 'Yeah. Why?'

" 'Well, it's just that I've never heard of stocks that *cheap.* I was trained at a Big Board firm—meaning we sold mostly New York Stock Exchange stocks. And even *then,* the stuff we did on NASDAQ was in the fifteen-to-twenty-dollar range.'

"Meanwhile, Chris was busy slamming down his phone in anger. Then he started muttering: 'That motherfucker hung up on me! What a rat bastard!' So George looks at me and says, 'No worries, he'll get the next one. But either way, you should sit next to him for a few days, so he can show you the ropes.'

"Well, I was about to break out into outright laughter, but then George added, 'He *did* make over ten grand last month. How much did you make?'

"I looked at George in disbelief, wondering how a moron like Chris Knight could make ten thousand dollars in a month; then something very odd occurred to me. 'Wait a second,' I said to him. 'How the hell did he make ten thousand dollars working on three-hundred-dollar trades?' Then I explained to George how a three-hundred-dollar trade at LF Rothschild would yield a commission of between three and six dollars—depending on how aggressive you wanted to get with the client. And sometimes the commissions were even lower than that, I added, especially on tickets of a half million or more.

"So George waved me into his office to offer me a visual explanation. He grabbed a sheet of paper off his desk and said, 'These are the only stocks you'll be recommending here. There are six of them.' He handed me the sheet of paper, and I took a moment to study it. 'KBF Pollution Control?' I muttered to myself. 'Arncliffe National?' I was about to say, 'I've never heard of any of these stocks,' when George pointed to a column of numbers and said, 'These are the bids for the stocks,' and I saw that they were all under a dollar. I was about to say, 'These must be real pieces of shit if they're all under a dollar,' when he pointed to another column of numbers and said, 'And these are the offers. Everything in between is your commission.'"

I paused for a moment to let my words sink in. Then I smiled and said, "You might find this hard to believe, given my current level of sophistication, but back then I didn't understand the difference between the bid and the offer. I mean, I knew you sold at the bid and bought at the offer, but I'd never really considered what happened to the money in between.

"You see, with big stocks the difference between the two is small, maybe half a percent, and only *occasionally* do the brokers get a sliver of it; usually it's glommed up by traders. In fact, at Rothschild, the brokers would go absolutely wild when a block of stock came with a spread in it. They would call their clients and bang them over the head, because they were making double commission.

"But at the Investors' Center, I couldn't believe my eyes. The spreads were enormous—at least fifty percent or better. I said to George, 'How could the bid for Arncliffe National be twenty-five cents and the offer be fifty cents? My commission can't *really* be a quarter a share, *can it*?' to which he replied, 'Sure, why not?'

"I said, 'Well, let's just suppose a client purchases a quarter million dollars of Arncliffe National'—that was an average trade at LF Rothschild—'Would my commission really be $125,000?' I asked.

"'Yeah, in theory,' he answered, 'but it doesn't really work that way, because no one puts that kind of money into penny stocks.'

"'Why not?' I asked.

"'Well...' he replied, not that confidently, 'we...uh...we don't *call* people who have that kind of money. We call working-class people.'

"'Really?' I said. 'Why call people who don't have money to invest in the stock market? It seems illogical.'

" 'Yeah, maybe so,' he replied, 'but rich people don't buy penny stocks.'

" 'Why not?' I asked for the second time, to which he started hemming and hawing. He really *had* no answer other than telling me just to trust him, which I did. In retrospect, I think I was too beaten down to argue, because under normal circumstances I would have debated him until I was blue in the face. In any case, I decided to take his words as gospel and go along with the program. I took a seat next to Chris Knight and then wrote a script for a cosmetics company called Arncliffe International."

"Why'd you choose that one?" asked OCD.

I shrugged. "It seemed like the dog with the least fleas. I mean, they had no real sales to speak of and there were something like fifty million shares outstanding. But, on the positive side, they'd just landed Macy's as a customer, which I knew would sound good in a sales pitch. That, and the president of the company had once been a vice president at Revlon, and I knew that would sound good too.

"Anyway, when I finally was done with the script, I remember feeling very impressed with it. I'd made Arncliffe National sound like IBM or at least the next Revlon, and I hadn't even lied that much. Of course, I'd omitted some material facts–meaning, information that the client really deserved to know to make a decision–but all in all I hadn't really violated any securities laws."

The Bastard shook his head gravely. "Material omissions *are* violations of securities laws," he snapped.

"Yeah, I'm aware of that now. In fact, I was aware of it then too, although I knew it would be difficult to prove. See, what's material and what's *not* material is somewhat subjective. Don't kid yourself–on Wall Street, material omissions are the rule rather than the exception. And that's at big firms as well as small ones."

A few moments of silence passed.

"In any event, as fabulous as my Arncliffe script was, Chris Knight hadn't grasped the true beauty of it. 'You're wasting your time with that,' he said, pointing to my script. 'You don't need a script to sell stock. You just swear to the clients that the stock is going up and they buy from you.'

" 'Yeah, well, thanks for sharing,' I said, and then I picked up the phone and started dialing. I was using leads George had given me, which were actually return postcards from people who'd responded to a mass mailing. On the front of the cards was some cheesy sales hype along the lines of *Make a Fortune in Penny Stocks,* and on the back there were people's names and phone numbers. They seemed like total dunk shots, these leads. I mean, what better lead was there than someone who'd filled out a postcard and dropped it in the mailbox?

"So when I got my first prospect on the phone–some friendly Southerner named Jim Campbell*–I had reasonably high hopes. In a totally upbeat tone, I said, 'Hey, Jim! Jordan Belfort calling from the Investors' Center! How are you today?'

" 'Uh, I'm awe right!' he answered. 'How *you* doin'?'

" 'Oh, I'm great. Thanks for asking. Now, Jim, if you recall, about a week ago you mailed me a three-by-five postcard, saying you were interested in investing in penny stocks. Does that ring a bell?' And after a few seconds of silence, Jim finally said, 'Uh, yeah, I guess I *did* that. I mean, it sounds like sumthin' I'd do!'

"I remember thinking, *Good God!* He was so eager! So incredibly receptive! It was mind-boggling. I maintained my composure and said, 'Great, Jim. Now the reason for the call today is that something just came across my desk, and it's the best thing I've seen in the last six months. If you have sixty seconds, I'd like to share the idea with you. You got a minute?' And Jim said, 'Sure! Fire away!' With that I rose from my chair and prepared to give Jim my *shpil.* I remember catching a glimpse of Chris, who was sitting in his chair, watching me, and sipping a bottle of Evian.

"Into the phone, I said, 'Okay, Jim, now, the name of the company is Arncliffe National, and it's one of the fastest-growing companies in the cosmetics industry. All told, it's more than a thirty-billion-dollar industry, cosmetics, growing at twenty percent a year. And it's virtually recession-proof–yielding consistent growth in good times and bad. You follow me so far?'

" 'Yeah!' said an impressed Jim. 'I follow you.'

---

*Name has been changed

" 'Great,' I said, and I went on about giving him some very loose facts about Arncliffe–the names of some of the products they sold, where the company was headquartered, and then, finally, I touched on the contract they'd just signed with Macy's. Then I said, 'But as good as all that sounds, the most important thing in any company is management. Wouldn't you agree?'

" 'Yeah,' answered Jim, 'of course.'

" 'Good,' I said shrewdly, 'and in the case of Arncliffe National, management is blue chip all the way. The chairman of the board, a man named Clifford Seales,* is one of the most astute minds in the cosmetics industry. He was a former VP of Revlon, a *key* player over there. And, with *him* at the helm, Arncliffe can't go wrong.

" 'But the reason for the call today, Jim, is very specific: Clifford Seales is about to go down to Wall Street to tout his stock, and he's going on the heels of staggering sales growth and a major contract announcement. He'll be going to banks, insurance companies, pension funds–the *institutional* players. And you know what they say, Jim: Institutional money is usually *smart* money, and even when it's not, it's not enough to fuel the market anyway. You follow me?'

" 'Oh, yeah!' said Jim, 'I sure as hell do!'

" 'Good, Jim. Now, the stock is trading at only fifty cents a share right now, which is ridiculously cheap, considering the company's future. And the key to making money here is to position yourself now, *before* Seales goes to Wall Street and meets with all the fund managers and pension managers, because once he does that, it's too late.' I paused for effect. 'So what I'd like you to do is this, Jim: Pick up a block of one million shares of Arncliffe National'–and *splat* went a mouthful of water from Chris Knight's mouth. Then he started choking, and then he popped out of his chair–Evian in hand–and ran toward George's office. I shook my head in disbelief and continued with my sale, noticing for the first time that the other brokers were gathered around me. 'It's a cash outlay of only half a million dollars,' I said casually, 'and it's not a question of funds today or tomorrow, Jim; you have a week to pay for the

---

*Name has been changed

trade. But, believe me,' I said, lowering my voice to just above a whisper, 'if you position yourself now, *before* Seales comes down to Wall Street, the only problem you'll have is you didn't buy more. Sound fair enough?' "

"You asked the guy for half a million dollars?" asked OCD, chuckling.

"Yeah, I did. That's what they used to do at Rothschild, so it just sort of slipped out. But, meanwhile, as I was waiting for Jim to respond to my half-million-dollar request, George came running out of his office, with Chris Knight in tow. I heard George muttering, 'Someone go get a tape recorder! Hurry up! Who's got a tape recorder?' And then Jim said, 'Uh, I'm sorry, Jordan, but I think you got the wrong guy. I work in a hat factory. I'm a machine operator. I only make thirty thousand a year.' " I paused for a moment. "Anyway, not to belabor the point, I ended up closing Jim for ten thousand shares, which was a five-thousand-dollar trade, which was one of the biggest trades in Investors' Center history. I was about to learn that Investors' Center was no small-time operation. They employed over three hundred brokers and had over thirty offices–all of them small, and all of them just as mismanaged as this one.

"But getting back to Jim Campbell for a second, I'd convinced him to buy the stock with the money in his IRA, which was the only real savings he had." I paused and let out a troubled sigh. "And if you're wondering if I felt guilty about that, the answer is yes: I felt absolutely horrendous. Despicable. I knew he shouldn't be investing his IRA in a penny stock. It was much too risky. But I was so utterly *broke* at the time that the words *rent money, rent money* were playing in my head like a broken record. In the end, they drowned everything else out, including my conscience.

"Then, the moment I hung up the phone, I was instantly awash in the admiration of my peers–quashing any residual doubts. I remember George saying to me: 'Where did you learn to sell like that, Jordan? I've never heard anything even remotely like it! It was amazing!' Of course, I won't deny that I relished every last drop of his admiration. And, not surprisingly, the rest of the brokers were equally taken with me. They were all staring at me wide-eyed, as if I were a god. I *felt* like a god at that moment. The dark cloud that had followed me around since the meat business had finally evaporated. I felt like a new man, or, better yet, I felt like myself again.

"Right then and there, I knew that my financial problems were finally over, and I knew that Denise would finally have the things we'd talked about and dreamed about during the dark days. A world of *infinite* possibility had suddenly opened, a world filled with a thousand opportunities. And from there things moved very quickly, starting when George approached me a few weeks later, asking me to train the salesmen.

"It was almost identical to what had happened in the meat business, when the manager asked me to train the salesmen. And again, just like in the meat business, my training sessions quickly turned into motivational meetings, and the room began to pump. In addition, I went about reorganizing the office, setting up the desks classroom style and instituting a dress code, and I put an end to all this nonsense of part-time stockbrokers.

"What I was trying to do, in essence, was to make the place feel like Wall Street, to make the brokers feel like *true* stockbrokers. And I got resistance from no one; they all followed me blindly—both George *and* the salesmen—and everyone's commissions soared, especially mine. My first month, in fact, I took home a check for forty-two thousand dollars." I paused for a moment, letting the number sink in. "And let me tell you something: It was more money than I'd had in my entire life. Straightaway, Denise and I paid off all our bills, and then we went out and bought a brand-new Jeep, a Wrangler, for thirteen thousand dollars. Then we both bought new wardrobes. I bought her her first gold watch, then a diamond tennis bracelet. And at the end of the month we *still* had ten thousand left over!

"The next month I made sixty thousand dollars, and I went out and bought the car of my dreams: a brand-new pearl-white Jaguar XJS." I smiled at the memory. "It was the two-door model, the one with twelve cylinders and three hundred horsepower. The thing was a total beast. And while Denise refurnished our apartment, I was paying back all my old creditors from the meat business. And the next month I made another sixty thousand, and that was it; that was when Denise and I looked at each other in awe. We simply didn't know what to do with all the money. We had everything we needed, and money was pouring in faster than we could spend it. I remember one day in particular, when we were sitting at the edge of a long wooden dock in Douglaston, not far from where Investors' Center was. It was the middle of March, and it was one of those warm winter days where you feel the first hints of spring in the air.

"I think I remember this day so vividly because it was one of the few times in my life when I'd been truly happy, truly at peace. It was late afternoon, we were sitting on two fold-up lounge chairs that we'd carried down with us, and we were holding hands, watching the sun set. I remember thinking that I'd never loved a person as much as I loved this woman, that I'd never thought it was even *possible* to love someone so purely, so completely. I didn't have a single misgiving about her, not a single second thought.

"On the other side of Little Neck Bay, I could see the edge of Bayside, where Denise and I lived, where I grew up, and just behind me was the North Shore of Long Island, where I would be moving in a few years and raising a family." I shook my head sadly. "In a million years I would have never guessed that home wouldn't include Denise and that the mother of my children would be another woman. It would seem utterly impossible at the time.

"But what I had no way of knowing back then was that the *insanity*—as I'd come to call it—was right around the corner, slowly creeping up on me, without me knowing it." I shook my head once more. "In the end, it spared no one. Not me, not Denise, not my family. Almost everyone I knew and everyone I grew up with would come to work for me soon, or at least become financially dependent on me. You understand what I'm saying?"

They both nodded, then the Bastard said, "How long after this did you meet Danny?"

I thought for a moment. "Not long; maybe three or four months. I'd seen him around the building a few times, but I'd never said more than a few words to him. Kenny, however, was about to reenter my life almost immediately. It was that very weekend, in fact, or the weekend after, when he called me out of the blue and asked if I'd train him to be a stockbroker."

"How did he know you'd gotten in the market?" asked OCD.

"From his cousin Jeff. He was one of the few people I still kept in touch with from college. Jeff had told Kenny how well I was doing. But I was totally turned off by Kenny's call at first. I mean, the last time we'd crossed paths, the guy had crashed one of my meat trucks, then left me with a three-hundred-dollar food bill. And what vague memories I *did* have of him were entirely negative. There was something a bit off about him, something I couldn't put my finger on. And that was even *before* I met Victor Wang. Together, though, the two of them were like a complete freak show: the budding Blockhead and the Talking Panda." I rolled my eyes. "Anyway, let's just say my memories of Kenny were less than fond. I had him pegged as someone who loved to talk about rolling up his sleeves and working hard but hadn't the vaguest idea what the concept meant."

"Why'd you hire him, then?" asked OCD, smiling.

I smiled back. "That's a damn good question, Greg... but let's just say the *Kenny Greene* I met in the meat-and-seafood business and the *Kenny Greene* I met the second time around were two different people. I mean, he was still a budding Blockhead and everything, but now, at least, he was a *humble* budding Blockhead. He seemed to know his place in the world. In fact, one of the first things he said on the phone was that he wanted to meet me for a cup of coffee so he could pay back the money he owed me.

"The only problem was that I didn't need the money anymore. So I was tempted just to say to him, 'Fuck you, pal! Where were you and your damn checkbook when I needed you?' But, of course, I didn't. Truth is, there was something about the Blockhead that I liked. I mean, even to this day I still feel a certain warmth toward him, although I have no idea why. He's like having a giant lapdog that pisses and shits all over your house, but you know he doesn't mean anything by it; he just can't control himself. Yet every morning you can be *damn* certain he'll be out on your front lawn, fetching your newspaper.

"Anyway, the two of us met at a little Greek diner, just down the road from Investors' Center, and the moment we sat down Kenny handed me a check for three hundred dollars, along with an apology for having crashed my meat truck. Then he told me how his cousin Jeff was always telling him that I was the sharpest guy around and how there was nothing more in the world he wanted than to work by my side, as my right-hand man." I shook my head and chuckled. "It's rather ironic that Kenny had more foresight in this department than I did. He was convinced I would be the next great thing on Wall Street, while I had zero aspiration in this area. I think I was just too shell-shocked from the meat business still; that, and I was so in love with Denise that I didn't want anything to change."

OCD narrowed his eyes. "What made Kenny believe in you so much? I mean, I understand that he heard you give a sales meeting at your meat company, but it still seems like a bit of a leap of faith on his part."

"Yeah..." I said open-endedly, "well, I actually missed one important thing. You see, I wasn't really sure if Kenny was cut out for the stock market, so rather than agreeing to train him on the spot, I told him after the meeting to come to the Investors' Center that night, so I could give him a firsthand demonstration of being a stockbroker. And it was after hearing me on the phone for the first time that he swore loyalty to me. Does that make more sense?"

OCD nodded. I nodded back and took a moment to think back to that night. Then I started chuckling. "What's so funny?" snapped the Bastard.

I shook my head quickly. "You don't want to know," I replied.

"Actually, I do," he shot back.

"Well, if you insist," I said with a smile, and I gave my neck a nice, slow roll. "Okay...so rather than just meeting me at the Investors' Center, Kenny offered to pick me up at my apartment. When he pulled up to my building, he wasn't alone; he'd brought his girlfriend along for the ride with him." I paused for a moment, twisting my lips at the thought of her. "Let's just say she had tits the size of NFL footballs and the lips of a goldfish. She wasn't gorgeous or anything, but she was one of the sexiest little numbers I'd ever laid eyes on.

"In any event, the two of them sat in the boardroom and watched me do my thing on the phone—and, of course, I couldn't help but ham it up a bit for the Goldfish, who was busy undressing me with her eyes as I pitched into the phone. I ended up having a pretty decent night—making around three grand—and I remember her whispering to Kenny how wet she was getting, just from listening to me. But it wasn't until the ride home that I got my first pure dose of the Goldfish and, for that matter, Kenny Greene.

"We were in Kenny's red Mustang: He was behind the wheel, I was in the passenger seat, and the Goldfish was sitting between us, on the armrest, wearing a tiny midriff T-shirt and some wildly sexy perfume. We were on the Cross Island Parkway near the exit for Bayside, when Kenny said to her: 'Go ahead, sweetie, tell him!'

" 'No,' she whined, 'I'm too embarrassed, Kenny!'

"So Kenny said, 'Fine, I'll tell him, then,' and he looked at me and said, 'She got really turned on watching you sell tonight, so she'd like to blow you. And trust me: The girl can suck the chrome off a trailer hitch! Just look at her mouth. Pucker up for him, sweetie.'

"I looked at the Goldfish, astonished, as she stared back at me with her fabulous goldfish lips puckered up into a sensuous pout. Then she started nodding her head bashfully, as if to say, 'I'd really like to blow you, sir!' "

I paused for a moment, searching for the right words. "Now, I want you to know that I had every intention of resisting the Goldfish's charms; I mean, I loved Denise with all my heart and soul and I had never cheated on her before. But then the Goldfish began rubbing me over my jeans and sticking her NFL footballs in my face. While she had me still stunned by that, she crawled down to the little foot area in front of me and slowly unzipped my fly." I paused and shook my head gravely. "Well, needless to say, the Goldfish overpowered me, and next thing I knew she was giving a world-class blow job as we cruised down the Cross Island Parkway.

"And as I groaned in ecstasy, Kenny the Pervert kept one eye on the road and one hand on the steering wheel, and his other eye on the Goldfish's mouth and his other hand holding back her brown hair, so it wouldn't disturb his view." I shrugged. "I shot my load, if I recall correctly, right in front of P.S. One Sixty-nine, where I'd attended public school.

"Anyway, I want you both to know that I felt absolutely *terrible* when I walked in the door that evening. I felt dirty and disgusting, and I swore to myself that I'd never cheat on Denise again. And I continued to feel guilty long after that, especially when the four of us were together." I paused and shook my head gravely. "I think that was the most difficult part of all–that Denise and the Goldfish became good friends. But that was the way it went down; Kenny got his wish and became my right-hand man, and the four of us became inseparable."

Just then the door swung open and in walked the Witch, dressed in black. The three of us looked at her, speechless. She sat down next to OCD and said, "What did I miss?"

Nothing but silence.

Finally OCD said, with mock formality, "Well, Jordan was just giving us some valuable insight into his relationship with Kenny Greene and the Gold–"

"And I think this is a good time to break for lunch," reasoned the Bastard.

"Yeah, I'm famished," I agreed.

"Hmmm," muttered the Witch. "You'll have to fill me in, then, Joel."

Indeed, I thought, and maybe you can convince her to blow you while you're at it–although, on second thought, she looks like a biter!

We broke for lunch.

CHAPTER 12

LEAPS OF LOGIC

Precisely one hour later, I was back in the Bastard's dungeon, with two slices of pizza digesting in my stomach and my three captors staring at me intently. I had spent the last fifteen minutes talking about the Blockhead–explaining how he'd insinuated himself into every aspect of my life, both business and personal. He did everything for me, I told them, almost like a second wife. And although I maintained no official rank at the Investors' Center, anyone who saw us together knew I was the boss. And Kenny was fine with that; in fact, he relished it.

There are kings and there are kingmakers, I said to my captors, and the Blockhead was definitely the latter. I explained how Kenny began spending the bulk of his day running the operations of what had now become our office within an office. We had our own section at the back of the boardroom where our staff sat. At the time, we had four connectors, three stockbrokers, and one female sales assistant, all of whom had sworn loyalty to me (at Kenny's urging).

And I was now saying, "What impressed me most about Kenny–

or should I say, what baffled me most—was the never-ending stream of friends he paraded into the office. And they were all cut from exactly the same mold: in their late teens or early twenties, from reasonably good families, and reasonably well educated."

"Interesting," said the Bastard. "And these were his former drug clients?"

I shrugged. "For the most part, yes, although I wouldn't place too much emphasis on that. These were good kids, not derelicts. It was like the movie *Risky Business,* where Tom Cruise becomes 'pimp-for-a-night' and hooks up his high school buddies with a happy hit squad of high-class hookers. That's what Kenny did, and his friends kept right on coming."

"And where did Victor Wang stand in all this?" asked the Witch.

Uh-oh! I thought. Victor's goose was cooked now! "Well, the Chinaman—I mean Victor—stayed out of the mix for a while. He was too busy waiting on the sidelines, observing. See, he and Kenny had this completely bizarre friendship at the time. It was a mixture of love, hate, and mutual contempt, and, depending on the moment, how they felt about each other was a complete crapshoot. They could be best friends, mortal enemies, or anywhere in between.

"In the spring of 1988, when all this was happening, Kenny and Victor were on the outs. I would only find out later that it was because of me."

"Why is that?" asked OCD.

"Because Victor had taken Kenny's swearing loyalty to me as a personal affront. Since they were kids, they'd always planned on going into business together, and since Victor was the brighter of the two, he was their undeclared leader. Even when Kenny had brought Victor to my meat company, it was only for him to scope things out, to see if the idea was worth stealing for him and the Blockhead—which, of course, it wasn't. But flash forward eighteen months later, and the same forces were at work when Kenny called me out of the blue wanting to be a stockbroker.

"In the beginning, he had every intention of learning what he could and then going off with Victor. But what Kenny hadn't counted on was being blown away when he heard me on the phone. Suddenly he realized that there were other people out there even sharper than his beloved Victor Wang. So he shifted loyalties; rather than trying to tap my brain for knowledge and wisdom, he took the opposite approach, throwing every last drop of himself into promoting me–and trying to turn me into a king."

"What a sordid tale," muttered OCD.

"Yeah, it certainly is. But, anyway, to sum up all this Victor Wang business, Kenny had tried to get him into the picture while we were still at the Investors' Center. He'd *begged* Victor to swear loyalty to me, but Victor refused; he was too proud. So he pooh-poohed the whole stock-market idea and continued dealing coke." I shrugged. "And as the months passed, I quickly grew in power, and the window slammed shut in Victor's face. In less than a year, Stratton would be Stratton, and most of Victor's friends would be working for me. The dullest would go on to make hundreds of thousands a year, the sharpest would make millions, and a select few would make tens of millions. The latter were the ones I backed in their own firms, which I used to expand my nefarious empire and keep the regulators off balance. Ultimately, Victor would come to own one of those firms–namely, Duke Securities–and the only reason I agreed to finance him was to placate the Blockhead.

"I had been entirely against it at the time, because I knew Victor for what he was: a man of perceived insults and silent grudges. He could never stay loyal to me, nor anyone else, for that matter." I looked into the Witch's black eyes. "Make no mistake about it, Michele: Victor is, was, and always will be an insane character. He's two hundred pounds of indestructible muscle surrounded by fifty pounds of lavish fat, and he's not scared to go to fisticuffs if the need arises. In fact, he once hung my gay butler out the fifty-third-story window of my apartment–and that was *after* pounding the guy's face into chopped meat!"

My captors stared at me, astonished. "Yeah, it's a little-known story. My gay butler stole fifty thousand dollars from me, *after* Nadine walked in on him having a gay orgy in our apartment." I shrugged. "I can give you all the dirty details if you want, although violence, I assure you, played no role at Stratton. What happened with my butler was a single aberration, as well as a testament to

Victor's savagery. Danny, on the other hand, is *not* a savage. The moment he saw Patrick bleeding, he ran into the bathroom and started vomiting."

The Bastard held up an index finger and said, "Excuse me," and he leaned over and whispered something in OCD's ear. Now the Witch leaned over and added her own two cents.

I made no effort to eavesdrop. After all, I was too busy lost in thought, wondering how my life had spiraled so far out of control. Perhaps if I'd followed my mother's advice and gone to medical school, maybe I would have become a cardiac surgeon like my first cousin; or maybe I would have become an orthopedist, like my other cousin; or perhaps I'd be a lawyer now, like my sainted brother, Bob. Who knew anymore? It was all so complicated.

Just then my captors broke from their huddle. "Okay," said the Bastard, "let's move on to Danny now. When did you two finally meet?"

I thought for a moment. "In June of '88," I said, "which was right around the time I decided to leave Investors' Center. I knew the place was a total scam by then, and if I didn't leave soon my clients would get slaughtered." I paused for a moment, considering my words. "*Scam* is probably too strong a word, though. I didn't think what I was doing was actually illegal."

"You don't really expect us to believe that?" sputtered the Witch, with a disturbing twitch of her nose. I flashed her a dead smile. "Yeah, Michele, I really do, and, frankly, it shouldn't come as much of a shock to you. The Investors' Center was a licensed brokerage firm with a compliance department, a trading department, and all the other bells and whistles. They were even members of the NASD! It wasn't like they were operating in the shadows!

"Every other month they'd take a company public, and right there on the front page of the prospectus it would say: *This deal had been reviewed by the SEC.*" I shrugged. "And, also, you keep forgetting how broke I was at the time. When I walked into the Investors' Center, the only thing I was thinking about was rent money. It was driving all my decisions." I let out an obvious sigh. "I can't explain it any better than that, although I *will* admit that once rent money was no longer an issue, I began to notice a few things. At first I tried to rationalize them, but with each passing month it became more and more difficult. And I felt more and more terrible inside."

The Witch: "So why not quit if you felt so bad?"

"Well, believe it or not, Michele, that's exactly what I had in mind when I met Danny. That was actually how I met him in the first place: I was hanging out on my terrace, playing hooky from work. I was dressed in my usual garb–a white terry-cloth bathrobe–and I was pondering the direction of my life. I had a pretty decent nest egg by then, so I wasn't under any pressure. All options were open to me–all options except opening a brokerage firm, which I had already ruled out.

"It was mid-June now, and George had broached the subject with me. He'd called me into his office and said, 'The owners of Investors' Center are making a fortune. It's a shame to leave so much money on the table, don't you think?'

"And my answer to George was: No, I didn't think! I wanted no part of owning a brokerage firm, especially one like the Investors' Center. My meat-and-seafood debacle was still fresh in my mind, and I knew that every business appeared lucrative from the outside looking in; it was only when you were on the inside looking out that you got the true picture. Of course, George had no idea of that, because he'd never been in business before. All he saw were dollar signs, not a single liability."

"So you met Danny while you were on your terrace?" asked the Bastard.

"Yes, I was living on the fourth floor, and Danny was playing with his son, Jonathon, in the playground. Jonathon was two at the time, and he always stuck out to me, because he had this terrific head of platinum-blond hair. He was incredibly cute. Anyway, after a few minutes of playing the good father, Danny appeared to be getting bored, and he drifted off to the side and lit up a cigarette. Eventually we locked eyes, and I flashed him a warm, neighborly smile.

"I think what shocks me most about this day is how normal Danny looked. He had on powder-blue golf shorts and a matching short-sleeve polo shirt. It was a golfer's ensemble, I thought, or maybe it was a yachter's ensemble. It was difficult to tell. Either way, I would've never guessed he was a Jew."

The Bastard stared at me, confused. I continued: "Anyway, as Danny and I exchanged hellos, I noticed that Jonathon had made his way to the top of the sliding pond. At first I was impressed, because it seemed like a mighty feat for a two-year-old, but then it occurred to me that I should probably say something to Danny.

"And then, suddenly, Jonathon lost his balance and I screamed, 'Holy shit! Watch out, Danny! Your son!' And Danny spun around just in time to watch Jonathon take this wild tumble off the sliding pond and hit the pavement like a lead balloon." I paused and shook my head gravely. "I'll tell you the truth: At first I thought the poor kid was dead. I mean, he was just lying there, motionless, and Danny was also motionless, too astonished to move.

"Finally, though, after a few painfully long seconds, Jonathon lifted his head and started looking around, but he wasn't crying yet. That came a second later, when he locked eyes with Danny. Then he went absolutely wild–screaming at the top of his lungs and flailing his arms about and kicking his legs wildly. So I figured I'd run downstairs and give Danny a hand. It seemed like the neighborly thing to do.

"But when I reached the playground, Jonathon was crying even louder. He was in Danny's arms and literally going ballistic! I said to Danny, 'You want me to go find your wife for you?' And Danny recoiled in horror and said, 'Good *God*! Find anybody but her! Please! You can call the cops, for all I care, and have me arrested for being a bad father, just don't call my wife, *please*!' "

"Of course I thought he was kidding at the time, so I nodded my head and smiled. But he didn't smile back, and that was because he wasn't joking. I wouldn't find out why, though, for a few more days, until Denise and I had the pleasure of going out for dinner with them and watching Nancy pull a lit cigarette out of his mouth and throw it in his face. But, not to jump ahead here: Jonathon *did* finally calm down, at which point Danny said to me,

'My wife tells me she sees you hanging out on your terrace all week in a bathrobe. What do you do for a living?'

" 'I'm a stockbroker,' I replied casually.

" 'Really?' he said. 'I thought you needed to work on Wall Street to be a stockbroker.'

"I shook my head no. 'That's a total misconception. Everything is done over the phone now. You could be anywhere. I, for one, work in Great Neck, and I made over fifty grand last month.'

" 'Fifty grand!' he said. 'I don't believe it! I have a bunch of friends who are stockbrokers, and they're all sucking wind since the crash!'

" 'I only deal in small stocks,' I said. 'They weren't hit as hard by the crash. What kind of work do you do?'

" 'I'm in the ambulette business,' he answered quickly, 'and it's a total fucking nightmare. I have seven vans that constantly break down and seven Haitian drivers who barely show up for work. I'd torch the place, if I thought I could get away with it.'

"I nodded in understanding. Without even thinking, I said, 'Well, if you want to make a change, I'm sure I can get you a job at my company. I'll train you myself,' to which Danny looked me in the eye and said, 'Pal, if you prove to me you're making fifty thousand a month, I'll be at your doorstep, six a.m. tomorrow morning, ready to shovel shit for you!' "

"When did he actually come to work for you?" asked the Bastard.

"The next morning," I said. "True to his word, he was waiting at my door, holding a copy of *The Wall Street Journal.*"

"What about his ambulette business?"

I shrugged. "He never went back. He had a fifty-fifty partner, and he just handed the guy the keys and said, 'See ya later, pal. Nice knowing you!' and that was it. He cold-called for me for the rest of the summer and then passed his broker's test the first week of September. George, meanwhile, was becoming more and more aggressive with me about opening up our own brokerage firm. The SEC had started investigating the Investors' Center. If word leaked out, he said, the firm would quickly collapse.

"What worried me most was that I had just convinced Lipsky and the Penguin to come work for me. The Penguin had finally thrown in the towel on the meat-and-seafood business, and Lipsky's furniture business was on the verge of bankruptcy. So, in a way, I was responsible for them now too. That was why I finally agreed to go with George to see a lawyer, because I wanted to gather intelligence."

"Which lawyer did you see?" asked the Bastard.

"His name was Lester Morse, although Danny and I used to call him Lester *Re*-Morse, because everything about the guy was remorseful, or, better yet, *moroseful.* He was the ultimate doom-and-gloomer, almost difficult to fathom.

"I mean, every person he knew was either rotting away in jail or had lost their last dime to the SEC. And the way the Moroser told a story made you want to slit your own wrists. He would start off by saying what a great guy someone was and how he'd made a fortune in his heyday, but the story would quickly degenerate into a cautionary tale, and he would end by saying, '... and what the government did to him was a real travesty. He's in Allenwood now, and he won't be getting out for ten more years.' Then he'd shake his head and move on to the next victim."

"Interesting," mumbled the Bastard.

"Yeah," I said, "what's even *more* interesting is that one of the names he brought up was Bob Brennan, the Blue-eyed Devil himself."

The Bastard perked up. "Oh, really! What did he say about him?"

I shrugged. "He said he was the only person to ever walk away with all the marbles—two hundred million, by Lester's account."

"Hmmm," muttered the Bastard. "Did he say anything else?"

"Yeah, he said that Bob was too smart to get caught. He said that he was always two steps ahead of the regulators and that he covered his tracks like an Indian. I remember being very intrigued at the time—swearing to myself that if I ever decided to go into the brokerage business, I would want to be just like Bob Brennan.

"You see, Lester didn't paint out Bob to be an archcriminal—in fact, quite the contrary. According to Lester, it was the fault of overzealous regulators, along with a two-tiered justice system that was biased against penny-stock firms. WASP firms, on the other hand, got away with murder."

"Did you believe him?" asked the Bastard.

"For the most part, yes, although I won't deny that his words seemed a bit self-serving. I knew enough at this point to realize that penny stocks stacked the deck against the clients, although a stacked deck and blatant illegality are two different things. Meanwhile, Lester's office reminded me of the Investors' Center. It was small and dingy and didn't reek of success. And Lester reminded me of an aging leprechaun. He was a squat five foot four, and he was completely bald on top, with thick swaths of curly gray hair over his ears."

"So it was just the three of you at the meeting?" asked the Bastard.

"No, there were four of us. Mike Valenoti was there too." I looked at OCD. "Mike, I'm sure, you're familiar with."

OCD nodded. "I have a bunch of questions about Valenoti."

"I'm not surprised," I said. "If there was a single person who helped me turn Stratton into Stratton, it was Mike Valenoti. He was the operational brain behind everything, the one who kept the place cranking away on all twelve cylinders. He was my first mentor–even before Al Abrams–and he was also the first Wall Street wizard I'd ever met. I mean, his breadth of knowledge was absolutely staggering!"

I shrugged. "But to save you time, I'll tell you that Mike Valenoti is completely innocent in this. He was always trying to keep me on the straight and narrow, and I was constantly swearing to him that I was doing things right. In the end, though, he became so overwhelmed with the influx of business that he couldn't see the big picture anymore. He had no idea I was breaking the law."

OCD twisted his lips for a moment. "I appreciate your loyalty to Mike," he said, "but it seems just a *tiny* bit implausible that someone as sophisticated as Mike wouldn't know what was going on." He flashed me a quick, disbelieving smile. "You see what I'm saying?"

I nodded slowly. "Yeah, what you're saying makes total sense,

Greg. But it also happens to be totally wrong." I paused for effect. "Understand that ninty percent of Stratton's business was completely legitimate: We didn't steal money from clients' accounts, we didn't take fraudulent companies public, and, contrary to what the press might say, our clients could always sell if they wanted to." I shrugged. "Of course, our sales practices left a lot to be desired, but whose didn't? Prudential-Bache's? Lehman Brothers?

"Pru-Bache was busy ripping off grandmas and grandpas, and Lehman Brothers made them look like choirboys. In fact, it was the Lehman Brothers' scripts that served as the blueprint for Stratton's!" I shook my head slowly. "The fraudulent side of Stratton occurred in tiny blips, and unless you were privy to those blips, everything seemed normal. But let me get back to Lester's office for a second.

"First, I quickly realized that George Grunfeld was completely worthless. He knew even less about the brokerage business than I did, and every word that came out of his mouth was utter nonsense. Lester, however, was a different story. He was knowledgeable enough, but he was completely devoid of charisma. He spoke in a low, squeaky drawl, and his words came out slowly, *painfully,* as if a turtle were speaking.

"I found it hard to keep my mind in one spot, so I just sat there, pretending to listen, sneaking peaks at Mike out of the corner of my eye. Lester had painted him out to be some kind of operations guru, but up until now he'd said only a few words. From a physical perspective, I was entirely unimpressed. He was dressed in a cheap blue suit and an even cheaper rayon shirt, and his hair was askew"—*kind of like yours, Bastard, although Mike's hair was salt-and-pepper, while yours is a plebian shade of mud brown*—"although, in retrospect, I should have known an old Wall Street war dog when I saw one."

"What's an old Wall Street war dog?" asked the Bastard.

"It's someone who's worked on Wall Street for far too long and who's been through bull markets and bear markets, someone who's seen the dizzying excesses and the crash-and-burn stories. It's someone who's seen countless men go from rags to riches and then back to rags again, and then back to riches once more. He's seen the hookers and the drugs and the ludicrous gambling, and he's seen Wall Street go from the dark ages of fixed commissions and physical stock delivery to the modern era, where discount brokerage firms compete with Merrill Lynch and stock trades settle electronically." I shrugged. "There are only a few true old Wall Street war dogs left in the world, because most of them have already died of either a heart attack or cirrhosis of the liver. But if you're lucky enough to actually find one, they're worth their weight in gold.

"And Mike Valenoti was one of this dying breed. Perhaps I should have known it the moment I laid eyes on him. I should have noticed the battle-ravaged look in his eye as he sat there listening to George's and Lester's inanities. He kept his chin tucked between his collarbones and his shoulders slumped over, as if he were about to fall asleep. And then there was Mike's nose, which was a real showstopper! It was coated with red spidery veins and was the size of a sweet potato! Yet, on the flipside of that, Mike had the most intelligent brown eyes I'd ever seen. They were utterly piercing, and you could tell just by *looking* at them that he wasn't missing a trick.

"Anyway, not to belabor the point, the simple fact was that Mike and I hit it off fabulously that day. We spoke exactly the same language, and it was the language of Wall Street. When he started a sentence, I finished it, and vice versa. In fact, by the time the meeting was over, I'd given Mike a full-blown sales pitch, pretending he was a customer. And, of course, it completely blew him away, as it did Lester.

"But I think what's even more important about this day is the effect Mike had on me. Suddenly, I felt like the old Jordan again." I shrugged. "Whatever the case, I knew I'd sounded sharper than sharp that afternoon, so it came as no surprise to me when Lester called me at home that night and told me that I should consider opening my own brokerage firm. Apparently Mike had pulled him aside after the meeting and said that he'd work for me for free—meaning for no up-front salary. All he wanted was a small percentage of the profits. In return, he would build me a first-class operations department to rival any firm on Wall Street.

"Lester, too, was willing to work for free. He would file all the necessary forms with the NASD and then accompany me to my membership interview. In return, all he wanted was a shot at representing the companies I took public. Whether or not they decided to use him wasn't my responsibility. I just needed to make the introduction; he would do the rest."

"What about Grunfeld?" asked OCD.

I shook my head. "George was out. In fact, it was the first thing Lester brought up. He served no useful purpose, squeaked Lester. He was a helluva nice guy, but he was deadweight. Between Mike and me we had everything we needed to run a firm.

"Anyway, I told Lester I would think about it, although, deep down, I really didn't have any intention of going through with it. I was still gun-shy from the meat-and-seafood debacle, and I figured I'd just wait and see for a while."

"Where are we now on the time line?" asked the Bastard.

"Early September," I replied, "which is when things start to really heat up. First, Danny passed his broker's test, and I called him up to my apartment for a training session. Sitting on my living-room couch, I began.

" 'Okay,' I said to him, 'here's the deal: The first key to selling stock is to learn to read from a script without sounding like you're reading from a script. You follow me?'

" 'Yeah,' he said confidently, 'and it's no problem whatsoever.'

" 'Good,' I shot back. 'Just pretend you're an actor on a stage: You raise your voice and lower your voice; you speed up and then slow down. You keep your clients interested, hanging on your every word. And don't even *think* of picking up the phone until you know the answers to all potential objections. You can never sound stumped, Danny—ever!'

"He nodded confidently. 'I got it, buddy. You don't have to worry about Danny Porush. He can sell ice to an Eskimo and oil to an Arab!'

" 'I'm sure he can,' I agreed. 'But, remember, you have to know this script like the back of your hand. You can't stutter; it's the first sign of a rookie salesman, and a client will smell it right over the phone.' I smiled at him, while Denise looked on with anticipation.

I had told her what a great salesman Danny was, in spite of never actually hearing him sell before. But he had a very cocky demeanor about him, so I just *knew* he'd be great.

"With coffeepot in hand, Denise smiled at Danny and said, 'You want me to go into the kitchen, so I don't make you nervous?'

"And Danny waved her off. 'Please, Denise, this is like shooting fish in a barrel for a guy like me!' And Denise shrugged and said, 'Okay, well, I'll just stand here and listen, then.' And Danny nodded, and I handed him a script for Arncliffe National.

" 'Okay,' I said, 'just pretend you're pitching me over the phone, and we'll role-play back and forth.'

"He nodded and took the script from me, then cleared his throat with a couple *uhums* and *uhus.* Finally, with great confidence, he said, 'Hi, is Jordan there?'

" 'Yeah,' I replied quickly, 'right here. How can I help you?'

"Danny rolled his neck, like a prizefighter stepping into the ring. 'Hi, Jordan, this is Danny Porush calling from... calling from... calling from, uh, the–uh–the–uh... the In... Investors' Center. How... are you today?' and then he paused and started sweating.

"Denise said, 'I think I'll go into the kitchen and leave you two boys alone.' And a suddenly humble Danny replied, 'Yeah, I, uh, think that's a good idea, Denise. This is a bit harder than it looks,' and then he wiped a bead of sweat off his brow."

"Come on!" said OCD. "You're exaggerating; he couldn't have been *that* bad!"

I started laughing. "He was, Greg! In fact, he was so bad that, when he left the apartment that night, Denise said, 'There's no way he's gonna make it, honey. He sounds retarded. I mean, why was he mumbling all night? Why couldn't he just speak up like a normal person?'

" 'I'm not really sure,' I answered. 'Maybe he's got a rare form of Tourette's that only comes out when he sells,' and Denise nodded in agreement.

"Anyway, I made it a point to go to work the next morning, because I wanted to witness the carnage firsthand, and that's when something *odd* happened, something very unexpected. I was sitting a few feet from Danny, trying to contain my laughter. He was doing the old, 'Hi–uh, this is, uh, Da-anny Por-ush. How, uh, are you?' But then, after about five seconds, suddenly–*snap!*–he completely stopped stuttering and he started sounding totally unbelievable. Almost as good as me, in fact, but not quite." I winked at my captors.

"He started closing accounts left and right, and two weeks later, as a sign of friendship, I asked him to take a ride into the city with me to see my accountant. October fifteenth was right around the corner, and I was still on extension for my '87 taxes. Of course, Danny happily agreed, and off we went. We hopped into my pearl-white Jaguar and we headed into Manhattan on a Wednesday afternoon.

"Now, mind you, up until then I thought Danny was completely normal. He dressed conservatively, he acted conservatively, and he came from a very good family. He'd grown up on the South Shore of Long Island, in the town of Lawrence, which is a very wealthy area, and his father was a big-time nephrologist. Danny referred to him as the Kidney King of Brookdale Hospital.

"However, on the home front, Denise had been hearing some very strange rumors about Danny: namely, that he and his wife, Nancy, were first cousins. Of course, I told Denise she was crazy, because there was no way Danny would withhold such a fact from me. Most of the time we spent together he was bitching about his wife, explaining how her sole mission in life was to make him as miserable as possible.

"So, I figured, why wouldn't he confide in me that he and Nancy were first cousins? It made no sense. I mean, if it was true, it would definitely be playing a role in things. But I could never figure out a way to broach the subject with him, so I just kind of brushed the whole thing off, dismissing it as a vicious rumor.

"In any event, after I finished with my accountant, the two of us hopped back in my Jaguar and headed out of the city. We were somewhere around Ninety-fifth Street on the edge of Harlem when the insanity started. I remember Danny saying 'Jesus Christ! Pull over! You gotta pull over.' I pulled over and Danny jumped out of the car and went running into a dilapidated bodega with a cheap yellow sign *Groceteria.* He came running back out a minute later, holding a brown paper bag. He jumped back in the car with this insane smile on his face, and he said, 'Drive! Hurry up! Head north, to One Hundred Twenty-fifth Street.'

" 'What the fuck is wrong with you?' I muttered. 'That's Harlem, Danny!'

" 'It's all good,' he said knowingly, and he reached into the bag and pulled out a glass crack pipe and a dozen crack vials. 'This stuff will make you into Superman. It's my gift to you, for all you've done for me.'

"I shook my head and started driving. 'You're fucking crazy!' I snarled. 'I'm not smoking that shit! It's pure evil.'

"But he waved me off. 'You're exaggerating,' he said. 'It's only evil if you have constant access to it, and they don't sell it in Bayside, so we're in the clear.'

" 'You know, you're a real fucking retard!' I sputtered. 'The chances of me smoking crack right now are less than zero. You got that, pal?'

" 'Yeah,' he replied, 'I got it. Now, make a left up here and head toward Central Park.'

" 'This fucking guy,' I muttered to myself, and I shook my head in disgust and made a left turn. Fifteen minutes later I was in the subbasement of a falling-apart Harlem crack den favored by toothless hookers and Haitian winos, and I was putting the glass pipe to my lips while Danny held a torch to the bowl. And as the crack sizzled like a strip of bacon, I took an enormous hit and held it in for as long as I could. An indescribable wave of euphoria overtook me. It started in the base of my aorta and shot up my spinal column and bubbled around the pleasure center of my brain with a billion synaptic explosions.

" 'Oh, Jesus,' I muttered, 'you–are–the–best–friend–I–ever–had, Danny!' and I passed him the pipe.

" 'Thanks,' he said. 'You are too; we're brothers to the end,' and he reloaded the pipe with more crack."

OCD shook his head in disbelief. "What the fuck is wrong with you? Why would you do that?"

The Witch said, "Because they're drug addicts, Greg; they have no shame."

"How long did you stay there for?" asked the Bastard, in the tone of the morbidly curious.

"For a very long time," I said, nodding. "You see, the thing about crack is that once you get started, there are only two ways to stop: The first is to run out of money, and the second is to die of a heart attack. Fortunately, our binge ended with the former, not the latter. I only had about seven hundred dollars in my pocket and Danny had about five, so we pooled our money, like good socialists, and were able to keep our binge going well past midnight."

I shrugged. "On the brighter side, though, I was able to gather some very valuable intelligence during our binge. You see, like all drugs, there are various phases of the high, and with crack they're particularly acute. If you'd like, I'll share them with you."

OCD shook his head gravely. "You know, it's a mystery to me why I'm interested in hearing about this, but since you've let the genie out of the bottle, you might as well get on with it."

I flashed OCD a knowing smile. "It would be my pleasure, Greg. The first phase of a crack high is the euphoria phase. This is when you feel *so* incredibly wonderful that you want to just scream from the fucking hilltops: 'I love crack! I love crack! And all of you out there who ain't smoking this shit don't know what you're missing!'" I shrugged. "And if you think I'm kidding, just take a hit of it yourself and you'll see what I mean."

"How long does that phase last?" asked the Bastard.

I shook my head sadly. "Not long enough," I replied. "Maybe fifteen or twenty minutes; then it's over and you slide into phase two, which is *almost* as good, but not quite. It's called the diarrhea-of-the-mouth phase, which is somewhat self-explanatory. In this case, however, the sort of drug-induced oral diarrhea spewed out differs from your garden-variety oral diarrhea that the typical sober bullshit artist slings at you."

"What's the difference?" asked the Witch, searching for a way to peg a bullshit artist when she saw one.

I narrowed my eyes sagely. "Well, it's very difficult to describe meaningless drug talk to those who've never immersed themselves in it, but let's just say that it consists of an endless stream of inane ramblings, which other people in the phase think are brilliant. Yet, to all those outside the phase, they sound like complete nonsense."

OCD seemed to understand: "So it was during *this* phase that you did the bulk of your intelligence gathering, I assume."

"Indeed, Greg; that's a very logical assumption. Danny and I were sitting on a concrete floor, beneath an asbestos-laden ceiling, with our backs against a cheap plasterboard wall, which was in the process of shedding two coats of lead-based paint, while three toothless crack whores looked on in admiration, and I said to him, 'I can't think of a better place to ride out a crack high than this, buddy. Right?'

" 'No way,' he mumbled. 'Think I'd steer you wrong?' And he put the pipe to his lips and took another hit.

" 'Let me ask you a question,' I said. 'You know, there are some pretty crazy rumors floating around the building about you and Nancy being first cousins. Of course, I know they're not true and everything, but I just figured I'd let you know, so that you'd be aware that people were spreading rumors about you.'

"Suddenly he started coughing violently. '*Ho-bee Jesus*...' he muttered, '*ho-bee Jesus,*' and he shook his head quickly, as if trying to gain control of the rush. After a few seconds he said, 'It's not a rumor, buddy, it's true. Nancy and I *are* first cousins. Her father and my mother are brother and sister.' He shrugged.

" 'Aren't you worried about inbreeding?' I asked him. 'I mean, Jonathon seems pretty normal so far, but what about your next kid? What if he comes out deformed?'

"Danny shook his head. 'The risk is low,' he said confidently. 'My father's a doctor and he checked it out. But if I do get dealt a shitty hand, I'll just leave the mutant on the institution steps. Either that, or I'll lock it in the basement and lower down a bucket of chopped meat once a month.'

"Remember, *I'm* not the one who said this–Danny was! Besides, we were in the middle of the diarrhea-of-the-mouth phase, and even the most absurd things make sense then!"

OCD and the Bastard started chuckling. "So what other intelligence did you gather?" asked the Bastard.

I nodded, eager to change the subject. "Well, I also found out that he'd snorted his last two businesses right up his nose. See, *before* the ambulette service there was a messenger service in Manhattan, and that's when he started smoking crack: with the bike messengers. That was the start of Danny's financial demise. Before that, he'd always been successful; now, however, he was a shell of his former self. His confidence was shattered; his bank account depleted; and his wife, never a bowl of cherries to begin with, was determined to turn his life into a living hell.

"Anyway, we didn't leave the city that night until after midnight, and it was only *then* that I realized that I'd forgotten to call Denise. And it was also then when I started falling off an emotional cliff, hitting bottom just as we got off the exit ramp for Bayside, and I landed right smack in the heart of the worry phase." I paused for a moment, feeling worried just *thinking* about the worry phase.

I took a deep breath and said, "This is phase three: a vicious onslaught of negative thoughts washing over you like a killer tsunami. You worry about everything: mistakes of the past, problems of the present, and anything that might pop up in the future. In Danny's case, his worries had to do with money, and I knew this because, just as we pulled off the exit ramp, he said, 'Citibank is about to foreclose on my condo and throw my family into the street. You think you can lend me ten thousand dollars? I have nowhere else to turn.'

"I took a deep breath, trying to draw power from Danny's worries, figuring that if Danny's life was in worse shape than mine, then how much did I really have to worry about? 'Yeah,' I said. 'Do you have any Valium or Xanax to take the edge off? I'm not feeling so well.'

"He shook his head no. 'I don't have any. But why don't you smoke the screen? There should be a little crack resin on it. It'll make you feel better.'

"I nodded and grabbed the pipe. 'Thanks; hold the wheel while

I light up. I don't wanna burn myself.' And Danny grabbed the wheel, and that's how we made our way through Bayside: with me smoking the screen and Danny steering the car.

"On our way up in the elevator we didn't say a single word to each other. We didn't even lock eyes. We were both too embarrassed. And I remember swearing to myself that I would never speak to him again. I knew someone like Danny could not be good for me. Someone who talked about his family the way he did, someone who consumed drugs the way he did, and someone who had the fucking *audacity* to lead me into the depth and despair of a Harlem crack den–I knew he would only bring out the worst in me.

"Anyway, the moment I stuck my key in the lock, the door swung open and there was Denise, crying. I looked at her with panic in my eyes. My heart was literally beating out of my chest. I threw my palms up in the air and opened my mouth to say something, but no words came out. That's when I entered phase four, the suicide-contemplation phase.

"There are only two known antidotes to it: The first is the massive consumption of benzodiazepines–preferably Xanax or Valium and Klonopin. The second is massive quantities of sleep, on the order of two or three days. Anything less and you still might attempt suicide. And as I stood before Denise, reeking of urine and hookers and crack and funk, she took pity on me, and she loaded me up with enough Xanax to knock out a blue whale. Then she undressed me and tucked me in. And then I passed out."

"Jesus," muttered OCD.

I nodded in agreement. "Yeah," I agreed, "Jesus is right. In fact, it would take me three days to recover, which takes us to Sunday morning. That's when I entered the resurrection phase, which is the most productive phase of all. Your brain's dopamine stores have fully replenished themselves, and you're promising yourself that you've officially learned your lesson this time. You know what you did was completely foolish, and only a crazy person would do it again; and you're definitely not a crazy person!

"What makes this phase so productive is that you can look at all your worries now with an icy detachment, dismissing the imagined ones and devising strategies to deal with the real ones. It's a time of tremendous clarity, a time when a man takes stock of his life. And as long as you're not a full-blown crack addict, thinking about heading back to the crack den again, you emerge from this experience a much better man, a more *focused* man, and–"

"Oh, please!" sputtered the Bastard. "Save your rationalizations for the less informed! Crack doesn't make you better or more focused; it's pure evil, nothing more."

OCD let out a single chuckle. The Witch raised an eyebrow. I said to the Bastard, "You have an excellent point there, Joel, although, in this particular case, the resurrection phase happened to be unusually productive, because I quickly realized that I had only one thing to worry about, and that was the Investors' Center. If George was right, then I needed to make a move now, before the shit hit the fan. To sit and wait would be like an ostrich sticking its head in the sand.

"So the next day I pulled Kenny aside and told him that I was ready to make a move. The Investors' Center was on the way out, I explained to him, and we needed to start setting things up now, in anticipation."

"What about your future partner-in-crime?" asked the Witch. "Did you lend Danny the money?"

God–how I would have loved to just smack her in that mousy little head of hers! I smiled warmly at the Witch and said, "Yes, Michele, I did, and if you want to know why, the answer is, I'm not really sure. On my way to the office I had every intention of firing him. I really did. But when I saw him sitting at his desk, I just couldn't bring myself to do it. He looked nervous and embarrassed. And when we finally locked eyes, he flashed me the saddest of smiles, then he put his head back down and started dialing again. I remember staring at him–watching him bang away at the phone–and feeling utterly confused inside.

"I really *wanted* to fire him, but I just couldn't bring myself to do it. He had a wife and kid, both of whom I knew and both of whom I cared about. And I knew how talented he was, so greed was gnawing at me too. So I decided to lend him the money and keep him in the fold. I would just keep my guard up and make sure I controlled him.

"But a few days later, on my way into the building, the doorman stopped me and handed me a certified letter. I looked at the envelope and froze: It was from the SEC. Without even opening it, I knew it was a subpoena."

"What was it for?" asked the Bastard.

"For records," I answered, "as well as a personal appearance. And while it didn't give a specific date, the next morning Lester Re-Morse called bright and early and said, 'I think the Investors' Center is going to shut its doors this week. In fact, it'll be a miracle if they make it past Wednesday.'

" 'What the fuck are you talking about?' I snapped. 'How can the SEC shut them down before they even investigate them?'

" 'The SEC's not shutting them down,' he replied. 'They're shutting themselves down. They're out of money.'

"Out of money! I thought. How the fuck could that be! 'How on earth could they be out of money, Lester? They were making a fortune!'

" 'No, no,' Lester squeaked. 'They were making a couple a million a year at most, and they sucked it all out of the firm. The rest of Wall Street has been shorting their stocks since Wednesday, when word of the investigation leaked out. So it's only a matter of time now.' "

I looked at my captors and shrugged. "And those were the famous last words from Lester Re-Morse. Brokerage firms all over Wall Street were shorting their stocks, figuring the investigation would put them out of business. So now the whole thing was becoming a self-fulfilling prophecy.

" 'How long will it take to get my own firm started?' I asked him.

" 'It'll take you anywhere between six and ninth months.'

" 'Six to nine months! I don't have six to nine months! I'll lose everything if it takes that long.' Then something *else* occurred to me. 'Oh, Jesus! What about our paychecks, Lester? Monday is payday!' to which he mumbled, 'Yeah, well, you know... let's just say that if I were you I wouldn't hold my breath. Brokers never end up getting paid when this sort of thing happens. I would just write the whole thing off.'

"I started laughing at Lester's words, because Danny was supposed to get his first paycheck on Monday. It was close to forty grand, and it would be the ultimate crushing blow for him. I knew right then that if I wanted to keep Danny in the fold I would have to carry him until I set things up. Yet Danny was only *one* of my problems. I had seven other people in my crew, and, as loyal as they were, they wouldn't wait six to nine months. 'There's gotta be a quicker way, Lester. Six to nine months is a death sentence for me. I need to speak to Mike Valenoti; maybe he knows a way.'

" 'I already spoke to Mike,' said Lester, 'and he's with you. He said he'd come to my office today and sit down with you if you'd like. We can meet at twelve.'

" 'All right,' I said. 'I'll be there at twelve.'

" 'You know, come to think of it,' said Lester, 'you could start off as a branch of another brokerage firm. It's called an OSJ, which stands for Office of Supervisory Jurisdiction, and–'

"I cut him off. 'Yeah, I know what an OSJ is, and they're a total nightmare. The owner constantly tries to fuck over the branch manager. I don't want to start something that's going to blow up in six months.'

" 'What you're saying is true,' replied Lester, 'and normally I wouldn't recommend one to you. But I happen to know a little firm that's a diamond in the rough; they have no operations to speak of, just a tiny office on Maiden Lane, a block off Wall Street. You could open a small office on Long Island and pay them a percentage. The owner happens to be a very honest guy–an altogether lovely guy, in fact. But he lost all his money in the crash, and he's on the verge of going bankrupt.'

" 'What's his name?'

" 'Jim Taormina. And the firm is Stratton Securities.' "

"And there we go," said OCD, with a smile.

The Bastard said, "Okay, so there we have it. We're finally at the beginning–one day and five hours of cooperation later."

"Yeah," I agreed, "well, no one will ever accuse me of not being able to tell a good story, right?" I smiled warmly at my captors. I was at the guts of the story now, and it was a milestone of sorts. The four of us had bonded in a strange yet altogether pleasant way, and I couldn't help but marvel at Magnum's wisdom. In his absence, the walls of formality had come tumbling down, replaced by a hearty familiarity and esprit de corps. In fact, I finally felt like part of Team USA!

Alas, the Witch was quick to burst my bubble. "So this is when you embarked on your life of crime," she said. "Everything before this was simply a warm-up."

"So what happened next?" asked the Bastard.

I shrugged and let out a great sigh. "Well, the rest of the day was utter insanity. Before I went to Lester's, I called George Grunfeld's house, but his wife told me he wasn't home. 'He's at the office taking care of *paperwork*,' she said, and by the tone of her voice I could literally *hear* the paper shredder whirring in the background.

"Then I called the Blockhead and told him what was going on and that he better get down to the office to take care of *our* 'paperwork' before the *federales* raided the place. And then I called Danny and told him the bad news, that he wouldn't be getting paid on Monday. Of course, Danny being Danny, he took the bad news in stride.

" 'I got bigger problems than that,' he snarled.

" 'Oh, really?' I said. 'Like what?'

" 'Well, I'm still married to Nancy,' he replied. 'Isn't that enough?'

"As usual, I resisted the urge to ask him why the fuck he'd married his first cousin in the first place. But I told him not to worry, that I would cover his mortgage and expenses and whatever else he needed until I sorted things out. To that, he thanked me graciously and told me that he was with me to the bitter end. Then I hung up the phone and headed for Lester's."

"I'm curious," remarked the Bastard. "What kind of documents were you looking to destroy?"

"Scripts, mostly, and maybe some buy tickets and sell tickets. But, in truth, there wasn't much I could destroy that wasn't stored in two or three other places. Nevertheless, on my way to Lester's there was a plan forming in my mind. Things were becoming very clear to me. In fact, this would mark the beginning of what I would come to think of as my Great Window of Clarity. It started on the car ride to Lester's and lasted through the beginning of 1993, when I settled my case with the SEC and sold the firm to Danny for $180 million. It was a remarkable time in my life, a four-and-a-half-year period during which there was no problem too complicated for me to work through. My brain was in overdrive, it seemed. I could be going in twenty directions at the same time yet find each destination without making a single wrong turn." I paused for a moment, considering my words.

"I'm not trying to sound cocky here; believe me, that's the last way I feel right now. I've been humbled by my own life: by my drug addiction, by my indictment, and by my"–*backstabbing*–"wife leaving me on the courthouse steps. But I'm just trying to paint a picture for you, a picture of what I was like back then, so you can see why everyone followed me blindly: people like Mike Valenoti and my father, and Danny and Kenny and Jim Taormina, and, ultimately, thousands of other people who would come to work at Stratton.

"It was a time when I had all the answers, when I was able to master the brokerage business in a matter of days–both the operational side *and* the trading side. Mike would come to call me the world's most able pupil, and many others would eventually call me just the same. And, alas, many of them belonged on a who's who list of securities felons." I shook my head sadly. "Anyway, I would look back at this time with mixed emotions, and with a healthy dose of wonder.

"In some ways, I think it was the very clarity that led me to drugs and hookers and to everything else. I'd always suffered from insomnia, but suddenly I found it impossible to sleep more than a couple hours each night. I couldn't quiet down the thoughts that were roaring through my head. In the early nineties, I was managing the trading accounts of four different brokerage firms–Stratton, Monroe Parker, Biltmore, and a secret account I held at M. H. Meyerson, which I used to balance out the others–and I knew what each firm had in its account, right down to the share." I paused for a moment, letting my words sink in.

"When the clarity finally faded, I found myself desperately trying to recapture it. I tried a dozen different businesses: I made movies, started a vitamin company, worked with Steve Madden Shoes; I even tried short-selling stocks–figuring I could make money attacking the industry I'd created.

"But, in the end, I couldn't recapture it. I never got back to the point where I felt like my brain was firing on all cylinders." I shook my head sadly. "Sometimes I wonder if I ever will. I mean, I know I have a long road ahead of me and that I'll probably end up spending a considerable amount of time in jail, but after it's all said and done–after I've done my time and *paid my debt to society,* so to speak–I wonder if I'll ever accomplish anything extraordinary again. I wonder if I'll ever have another window of clarity." I let out a genuinely heartfelt sigh.

After a few moments of silence, OCD finally said, "I have a sneaky suspicion you will, but I hope for *your* sake–and for the sake of the public at large–that you do something more *positive* with your next window of clarity."

"I couldn't agree more," said the Witch, and she narrowed her eyes at me and cocked her head to the side at a very knowing angle, as if she were studying a tiny lab specimen. "I think what bothers me most about you is how you took a God-given gift and misused it. A common thief or even a thug, for that matter, is much easier for me to stomach. But you–well, it was nothing more than greed that motivated you, greed in all its forms, for all things carnal, and for all things *self-serving.* It was *that* and an unbridled lust for power."

There was more silence, as the Witch's words hung in the air like nerve gas. Finally the Bastard said, in the tone of the peacemaker: "Well, I think we all agree that the final chapter of your life is yet to be written, but for now we need to stay focused on the present–or the past, I should say, and, more specifically, on your meeting at Lester's office."

Yes, I thought, you are my savior and protector, Bastard, and that speaks volumes as to the horrific status of my life. After all, you would like nothing more than to see me rotting away in a jail cell, yet there's another human being in the room who wishes me even greater harm than you do.

I nodded and said, "Right... well, by the time I reached Lester's office, my window of clarity was fully open, and I had worked things out in my mind. There were three things I needed to accomplish: First and foremost, I needed to cut a deal with Mike; second, I needed to cut a deal with Jim Taormina; and, third, I needed temporary office space to interview salesmen until my permanent space was set up.

"So when I got to Lester's office, I didn't waste a second. It was just the three of us this time–Lester, Mike, and myself–and I went right to work. 'Just name your price and I'll pay it,' I said to Mike. 'All I ask is that you take the bulk of your pay as a percentage of profits, or, better yet, as a percentage of revenue. This way you'll never have to worry about me trying to fuck you over by running personal expenses through the company.' I smiled at him, trying my best to ignore that world-class schnozolla of his. 'I know how valuable you are, Mike, and I can't do this without you. You've forgotten more about this business than I'll ever learn. You're my linchpin, my secret weapon.'

"Mike, of course, loved that, and I knew he would. See, on Wall Street, the back-office people are the unsung heroes, the ones who keep the machinery humming, while the brokers and bankers make a fortune. They're dramatically underpaid, in my opinion, and they're wildly underappreciated. So it came as no surprise to me when Mike said, 'I don't need a salary. Just pay me whatever you think is fair, and I'll be fine with it.'

"I had already checked this with Lester, and a first-class operations guy was worth one hundred fifty thousand dollars a year, he said. So I said to Mike, 'How's ten percent of revenue up to half a million a year?' And that was it. Mike was mine. Then I turned to Lester and said, 'Call Jim Taormina and get him down here. I want to cut a deal with him before the day is out. What's standard for an OSJ?'

"Lester mumbled, 'Well... uh–'

"'Ten percent of revenue,' snapped Mike, 'plus a ten-dollar

ticket charge, only on the buy side, though. Sell tickets are free. But the most important thing is that I don't want him holding our money. We get to sweep the trading account once a week. He can hold a small deposit, maybe twenty-five thousand; that's it.'

"I nodded. 'All right,' I said to Lester. 'Call Jim, and tell him that I'll pay fifteen percent of revenue, but with a cap of thirty thousand dollars a month; that's the most he can make off me. After that, I keep everything. You think he'll go for that?'

" 'Uh, of course he will,' mumbled Lester. 'He's on the verge of bankruptcy. But he's, uh, sort of a low-energy guy, Jim. I'm concerned you might scare him off.'

" 'Don't worry,' I said. 'I know exactly how to speak to a guy like Jim. Just get him down here and I'll do the rest,' and, of course, I was right. And Stratton got started just like that. Lester excused himself from the conference room, and Mike spent the next few hours giving me a crash course in the brokerage business. And when Jim finally showed up, he was a complete lay-down. I cut a deal with him in less than a minute."

"And what about your SEC subpoena?" asked the Bastard.

I chuckled. "Yeah, well, that turned out to be the biggest joke of all. In fact, by the time they got around to deposing me, Stratton had already been in business for a year! And when they *did* actually sue Stratton, they never tried to use what happened at the Investors' Center as a knockout punch." I shrugged my shoulders. "But that's the SEC for you: The right hand never knows what the left hand is doing."

After a few moments of silence, the Bastard asked, "How much longer did the Investors' Center stay in business?"

"About five or six minutes," I said casually. "In fact, after I left Lester's office, I swung by the Investors' Center, which bore an odd resemblance to what I imagined the headquarters of the Third Reich looked like as the Russians were closing in on Berlin. There were papers everywhere, and brokers were running around carrying boxes, but that was nothing compared to the next week, when our paychecks bounced. Then brokers started tearing things off the walls."

I shrugged. "Not surprisingly, the Blockhead turned out to be very adept at this sort of thing. First, he wheeled out an industrial-size Canon copier for our future brokerage firm, and then he used a crowbar to break into the office's safe and steal all the new-account forms. There were literally thousands of them, a veritable gold mine of people who'd shown a propensity to invest in penny stocks. It was those new-account forms that served as our first lead source, when we started cold-calling two weeks later. That was how long it took to get our space together."

"What did you use in the meantime?" asked OCD.

"I used my friend's car dealership. It was just down the road from the Investors' Center. I stayed there for about two weeks, until I found the right space, in the town of Lake Success, Long Island. It was just east of the Queens–Long Island border, and in spite of being small, the building was clean and upscale. With a bit of cramming, I figured we could fit twenty brokers in the boardroom. That would be perfect, I thought. With twenty brokers I could make a fortune."

OCD, with a chuckle: "Twenty brokers?"

I nodded slowly. "Yeah; I guess I set my sights a bit low."

"What was the breakdown of ownership?" asked the Bastard.

"Seventy–thirty," I replied. "Seventy percent me, thirty percent Kenny."

"Danny wasn't a partner?" asked the Witch.

"No, it was just the Blockhead and me. Danny bought in later, over time."

The Witch again: "How much start-up capital did you put in?"

"About eighty thousand," I replied quickly. "And despite my owning twice as much as Kenny, we split the investment equally: forty thousand each. That was because I was the lead horse," I said respectfully. "So splitting the investment seemed fair. The only casualty in all this was Elliot Loewenstern, the budding Penguin. What happened at the Investors' Center had spooked him, and he took a job in Manhattan, at Bear Stearns. He *did* come back, of course, right *after* I hit on my idea of selling five-dollar stocks to the rich."

"And when was that?" asked the Bastard.

"About a month later," I replied casually. "In early November."

"What made you think of it?" asked OCD.

I cocked my head to the side and smiled. "Do you mean was there a eureka moment?"

"Yeah," he shot back, "a eureka moment. As in, *Eureka!* I just figured out a way to steal a quarter billion dollars and fuck over the SEC in the process!"

Hmmm, I thought, very clever and cynical this OCD was. Alas, he also happened to be right, although I would dispute the amount of money I stole. I mean, it couldn't have possibly been a quarter billion dollars! Or could it? With a sinking heart, I said, "Yeah, well, whatever the amount was, I tell you the God's honest truth that I didn't *start* Stratton with bad intentions. But, like they say, the road to hell is paved with good intentions."

"Fair enough," snapped the Bastard. "You can tell that to the judge at the appropriate time." He flashed me his warden's smile. "But for now let's just stick to the facts."

I nodded in resignation. "Well, it started with George Grunfeld and what he'd said to me my first day at the Investors' Center. This whole notion about rich people not buying penny stocks had never made sense to me, so I had Danny do a little experiment for me–trying to sell penny stocks to rich people. But rich people weren't interested. So I figured maybe they were turned off because the stock was less than a dollar, so I found a six-dollar stock and had him try that. But that didn't work either, and I have to say it surprised me.

"I mean, I *really* thought rich people would go for that, but when I called Danny into my office, he completely disagreed. 'Maybe if I were calling from Merrill Lynch,' he said. 'But not when I'm calling from Stratton Securities; there are just too many things working against me. They haven't heard of me, they haven't heard of the firm, and they haven't heard of the *stock.* You see what I'm saying?'

" 'Yeah,' I said, 'I see exactly what you're saying,' and–*boom!*– just like that it hit me. I had my eureka moment. 'Come back in here in fifteen minutes,' I said to him, and before he was even out the door I had already picked up my pen and started writing a new cold-calling script. Fifteen minutes later, he was back in my office and I was explaining my new system. 'Okay,' I said, 'when we call someone for the first time, we're not gonna try to sell them anything; we're just going to introduce the firm and ask them if they'd be interested in hearing from us down the road.' I handed him my new script. 'Read this to me and tell me what you think.'

"He looked at the script for a second, and then started reading: 'Hi, this is Danny Porush, calling from Stratton Securities. I know you're busy, so I'll get right to the point. You probably haven't heard of us before, because for the last ten years we've been strictly an institutional block-trading firm, dealing with banks, insurance companies, pension funds.' Danny started laughing. 'This is classic . . .'

" 'Just shut up and keep reading,' I said.

"He nodded and continued on: 'However, we've recently opened up our doors to the more substantial private investor, and what I'd like to do, sir, with your permission, is send you out some information on our firm, Stratton Securities, and then get back to you down the road, next time we're making a recommendation to one of our institutional clients. Sound fair enough?' Danny stopped and flashed me one of his famous smiles.

"Ironically, Stratton really *had* been in business for ten years, and the only business they *had* done was trading with other brokerage firms, and since brokerage firms are considered institutions, I wasn't really lying about Stratton's business being strictly institutional." I smiled at my own twisted logic. Then I gave up my smile and said, "I won't deny that the script was a bit misleading, but that's besides the point.

"Anyway, Danny was getting about ten leads a day, and after a week it was time to execute step two of my plan, which was to start off by selling a big stock, meaning a New York Stock Exchange stock they were familiar with. That's why I chose Eastman Kodak: because of the name recognition and also because it was a very sexy story. They were in litigation with Polaroid at the time over patent infringement, and my script focused on how Kodak was sure to trade higher once the litigation settled.

"Yet, as good as my script was, Danny wasn't all that impressed.

He said, 'Even if someone buys ten thousand dollars of Kodak, my commission is only a hundred bucks. So what's the fucking point?'

" 'Think of it as a means to an end,' I replied. 'Next week, after they've paid for their trade, we'll call them back for step two.' And, with that, Danny shrugged and walked off, spending the next ten days opening accounts on Kodak, twelve of them in all, and each for around five thousand dollars, which was a hundred shares.

"Then I called him back into my office and explained step two, which wasn't quite what he thought it'd be. 'You mean you don't want me to get them to dump their Kodak and buy a house stock?' he asked.

" 'No,' I said. 'I want you to tell them that everything looks great with Kodak and that they should hold it for the long term.' I handed him a script I'd written for a company called Ventura Entertainment." I paused, offering my captors a wry smile. "I'm sure you're all familiar with Ventura; it was the first stock we ever recommended."

"Yeah," said a cynical OCD. "And it was also the most overvalued entertainment stock in the history of entertainment stocks."

I nodded sheepishly. "Yeah, but it wasn't intentional. I just couldn't keep up with the demand." I shrugged. "But, that aside, Ventura was only a six-dollar stock back then, a tiny start-up not even listed on NASDAQ yet. It was still trading on the Pink Sheets. In truth, it could have just as easily been a penny stock, but by sheer coincidence the company's president, a man by the name of Harvey Bibicoff, had been thinking the same thing as me—namely, that a six-dollar stock sounded more valuable than a twenty-cent stock. So when he took Ventura public, he structured it with only a million shares outstanding, as opposed to the twenty million shares a typical penny stock would have." I looked at OCD. "You follow me, I assume."

He nodded. "Yeah; a million shares at six dollars is the same as twenty million shares at thirty cents."

"Exactly," I said. "On a mathematical level they're one and the same; however, on an *emotional* level they're entirely different. And as Danny stood in my office, studying the script, I knew it was perfect, especially the opening, where I transitioned from big stocks to small stocks.

" 'Read it to me,' I said to him. And he nodded and started reading: 'Mr. Jones, two reasons for the call today. First, I wanted to give you a quick update on Kodak. Everything looks great there; the stock is right where we bought it, and it looks to trade higher over the short term. There's been heavy institutional interest over the last few days, so for right now we'll just sit tight.

" 'And the second reason for the call is that something just came across my desk this morning, and it's perhaps the best thing I've seen in the last six months. It's one of our own investment-bank deals–a company we're *intimately* familiar with–and the upside is much greater than Kodak. If you have sixty seconds, I'd like to share the idea with you.' Danny looked up and said. 'This is fucking great! Let me give it a whirl!'

"I nodded in agreement. 'Okay, but remember: These people are rich and sophisticated, so they're not going to fall for hype and bullshit. You use logic and reason, and massive pressure. Never forget, Danny: We–do–not–work–on–callbacks! You have only one shot with these people. So stick to the script like glue.' With that, Danny reminded me once more that he was Danny-fucking-Porush and that he could sell oil to an Arab and ice to an Eskimo! Then he nodded and walked off."

I shrugged. "In retrospect, it's rather ironic that I was only hoping to get a slightly bigger trade from my new system–maybe a thousand shares of Ventura, versus two hundred shares–but that was what I had in mind at the time.

"But five minutes later Danny came running back in my office, literally out of breath. 'Jesus Christ!' he snapped. 'The first guy bought twenty thousand shares from me! Twenty–thousand–fucking–shares! Then he apologized to me for not buying more! He said that he wasn't liquid right now, but as soon as he was, he'd buy more. Can you imagine?'

"And that was it. In that very instant, I knew. I knew that Danny's client hadn't made a distinction between sending a hundred twenty thousand dollars to Stratton Securities and sending a hundred twenty thousand to Merrill Lynch. And it was all because we'd recommended a blue-chip stock first. Meanwhile, Danny was happier than a pig in shit, because he'd just made twenty thousand in commission. But what he didn't know was that I'd just made an additional sixty thousand dollars below the bid. And that was where the *real* juice was!"

"Explain that," said the Bastard.

"Okay, follow me for a second: Ventura was five bid, six offer—meaning that if a client wanted to buy it he had to pay six dollars, but if he wanted to sell it he could only get five dollars. That's why Danny's commission was a buck a share, or twenty thousand dollars. But Harvey was giving Ventura warrants that had an exercise price of two. In other words, Ventura was costing me only two dollars a share. All told, on Danny's twenty-thousand share block, I made sixty thousand below the bid, plus ten thousand above the bid, which was my half of Danny's commission. And all of that was from a single phone call, from a single lead. But that was only the beginning.

"I knew right then and there that if Ventura went up, and there were thousands of clients in the system, they would send in millions more." I paused for a moment, considering my words. "Of course, it would turn out to be hundreds of millions more, but at the time I wasn't thinking that far ahead. I still had serious obstacles to overcome, not the least of which was that Harvey had only a million warrants to sell, and with my new system, I would eat through those in a matter of weeks. Then I would have to buy stock in the open market.

"But first things first, I thought; I had to shut down the 'Old Stratton' and retrain everyone. But I went to Mike first to tell him my plan. It sounded good, he thought, but I could tell that he definitely wasn't bowled over. 'Give it a shot,' he said casually. 'However much business you bring in I can handle with no problem.' And those were the famous last words of Mike Valenoti.

"A minute later I was standing in front of the boardroom, ready to give the meeting of a lifetime. I still remember this day like it was yesterday. 'Everyone, hang up your phones!' I said to the brokers. 'Hang up your phones right now! I have something to say.'

"Most of them were right in the middle of calls, and they didn't hang up the phones at first. So I winked at Lipsky, and he rose from his chair and began disconnecting their calls in mid-pitch. Then Danny joined in the act, and a few seconds later the room was quiet.

"'Okay,' I said. 'Now that I have your attention, I want you to gather up your leads, your pitches, your rebuttals, your client books, and anything else on your desk that relates to being a stockbroker. I want you to gather it all up and throw it right in the fucking garbage can!'

"Of course, no one did anything at first; they were too dumbfounded to move. So Lipsky started snarling at everyone. 'Let's go! Chop chop! It's time to clean house, like the boss says!' And next thing I knew, Danny and the Blockhead were walking around holding trash bags, and the last vestiges of the old system were disappearing before my eyes. Within minutes, there were only twelve wooden desks, twelve old telephones, and twelve obscenely young stockbrokers, dressed in varying degrees of cheap, off-the-rack suits. And they were all staring at me wide-eyed, waiting to hear what I'd say next.

"'I want everyone to listen up,' I said, 'because what I'm about to say is going to change your lives forever. The simple fact is that all of you are going to be rich beyond your wildest dreams.' And I went on to explain my new system to them, pointing to Danny as proof that it worked.

"'How much commission did you just gross in one trade?' I asked him.

"'Twenty grand!' he shot back. 'Twenty–fucking–grand!'

"'Twenty fucking grand,' I repeated, and I began pacing back and forth, like a preacher, letting my words hang in the air. Then I stopped. 'And using my new system, Danny, how much do you think you can gross in a single month? Just a ballpark...'

"He pretended to think for a moment, playing the part perfectly. 'At least a quarter million,' he said confidently. 'Anything less and I'll fall on my sword!' And with that, the room broke out into complete pandemonium."

I shrugged. "The rest was easy. I retrained my Strattonites, using the straight-line theory. It was something that I'd come up with at the Investors' Center but hadn't considered crucial then, because when you're speaking to poor people it's more a question of whether or not they have money to invest; if they do, convincing them is easy. But with rich people, the rules are entirely different: They *do* have money to invest; it's just a question of convincing them that you're the one to invest it with. Are you smart enough? Are you sharp enough? Do you know things their local broker doesn't? Are you a Wall Street wizard, worthy of managing a rich man's money?

"That's exactly what the straight line did: It allowed a twenty-year-old kid, with a high school diploma and an IQ just above the level of Forrest Gump, to sound like a Wall Street wizard." I paused for a moment, thinking of a way to explain the theory. "In essence, it was a system of scripts and rebuttals that allowed even the most dim-witted of stockbrokers to control a sale. It kept things moving forward, from point A to point B–from the open to the close–until a client finally said, 'All right, for Chrissake! Pick me up ten thousand shares! Just leave me alone!' I know it sounds simple, but no one else had ever done this before. There were hundreds of scripts floating around Wall Street, but no one had ever organized them into a cohesive system.

"Anyway, for ten solid days I taught it to them–going back and forth, role-playing, like I'd done with Danny that night–until they knew it so well that they could recite the fucking lines in their sleep. Actually, I only spent half of each day teaching them; the other half they spent cold-calling, building a massive war chest of leads to call.

"And finally, on day ten when the leads came due, they started opening accounts on Kodak with such ease that it was literally mind-boggling. It was as if the straight line could turn even the weakest salesman into a total killer. And that emboldened me even further, and I began pounding at them even *more* mercilessly, promising them riches beyond their wildest dreams.

" 'I want you to start spending money now,' I preached to them.

'I want you to leverage yourselves! To back yourselves into a corner! To give yourselves no *choice* but to succeed! Let the consequences of failure become so dire and so unthinkable that you won't be able to stomach the thought of it.

"'Understand this,' I said. 'When Pizarro came to the New World, the first thing he did was burn his fucking ships, so his crew would have no choice but to hack out an existence in the New World. And that's what I want you to do! I want you to cut off all exit ramps, all escape routes!

"'After all, you owe it to the person sitting next to you to dial the phone. You owe it to every other Strattonite sitting in this room to dial the phone. That's where our power comes from: from one another, from a collective effort, from the combined energy of a room full of the most motivated people to ever hit Wall Street, a room full of winners!'"

I paused and took a moment to catch my breath. "Anyway, you all know what happened next: Seven days later they began pitching Ventura, and all hell broke loose. Blocks of tens and twenties began slinging around the boardroom like water, and money began falling out of the sky." I shook my head slowly. "And I can't even begin to describe how quickly we grew from this point. It was as if gold had been struck, and young prospectors began showing up in Lake Success to stake their claims. At first they trickled in, then they poured in. It started from towns in Queens and Long Island and quickly spread across the country. And just like that, Stratton was born.

"Anyway, it was only a few weeks after this when I walked into my office one morning and found Jim Taormina waiting for me. 'Here,' he said. 'Stratton is yours,' and he handed me a set of keys he was holding. 'I'll sell you the place for a dollar and be your head trader. Just *please* take my name off the license!'

"And then Mike came in, the old Wall Street war dog, who'd thought he'd seen everything. 'You have to stop them!' he begged. 'We can't handle any more business right now. We're on the verge of blowing up our clearing agent.' He shook his head in disbelief. 'I've never seen anything like this, Jordan. It's absolutely incredible. . . .' The funny thing was that our clearing agent–meaning the company that processed our trades–couldn't handle the influx of volume and was threatening to pull the plug on us unless we slowed things down.

"And then came the Blockhead. 'I'm underwater with commissions,' he said, panic-stricken. 'I can't keep track of them. Millions are pouring in, and the bank keeps calling me.' I had put the Blockhead in charge of our finances, and he was underwater now–drowning beneath a sea of money and paperwork.

"In any event, these were all good problems, problems that were easy to handle. With Jim Taormina, I did as he asked: I bought the firm from him for a dollar and made him my head trader. With Mike, I did as he asked too: I stood before the boardroom and gave a sales meeting that turned the whole thing into a positive.

"With piss and vinegar, I said, 'What we have here is so powerful and so effective that the rest of Wall Street can't even keep up with us!' And, with that, my Strattonites clapped and cheered and hooted and howled. Then we spent the next two weeks just getting leads, which ultimately fueled our growth even further.

"And to help the Blockhead, I turned to my father, who was still unemployed. He was a brilliant man, a licensed CPA who'd spent the better part of his life as the CFO of various private companies. But he was in his mid-fifties now–a bit too old and way too overqualified to land a good job.

"So I recruited him–reluctantly at first, but I recruited him nonetheless. And he moved into the Blockhead's office, where the two of them had the pleasure of driving each other crazy. Mad Max quickly bared his fangs–calling the Blockhead a fucking twerp and a fucking moron and a thousand other fucking things, including, of course, a fucking blockhead. And the fact that the Blockhead was allergic to cigarette smoke was something Mad Max relished beyond belief–consuming four packs a day and exhaling thick jets of smoke right in the Blockhead's face, with the force of a Civil War cannon.

"But, that aside, you can see how I had the whole thing wired now. Between Mike and my father I had my rear flank covered, and between Danny and Kenny I had a tip of a sword that rivaled the Mossad. And *I*... well, let's just say that I had all the time I needed to sit back and give meetings and focus on the big picture—and to resolve the last missing piece of the puzzle, which was where to find more warrants that would provide me with cheap stock, like Ventura warrants did."

I looked at OCD and smiled. "Care to guess who I turned to for that?"

OCD cringed. "Al Abrams," he muttered.

"Indeed," I said. "Mr. Al Abrams, the maddest of all Wall Streeters." I cocked my head to the side and stared down OCD. "Correct me if I'm wrong, Greg, but I once heard a rumor that Al was writing letters to Bill Clinton about you, saying you were a rogue agent."

OCD shook his head wearily. "He's one crazy old bird, that guy. When I arrested him, he had a hundred documents on him, some more than thirty years old!"

"Well, that sounds like Al," I said casually. "He never liked to throw things out. He's what you call a *careful criminal*."

"Not careful enough," said the Witch. "Last time I checked, he was still behind bars." She flashed me a devilish smile.

Yeah, I thought, but not because of you, Cruella; it was OCD who'd caught him. But I kept that thought to myself and said, "Actually, I think he's out now, probably back in Connecticut, driving his poor wife insane." I looked at OCD. "Just out of curiosity: When you arrested him, did he have any food in his pockets? Any half-eaten Linzer tortes? He loved those."

"Just a few crumbs," answered OCD.

I nodded in understanding. "Yeah, he was probably saving those in case of a famine..." and I spent the next few hours explaining how Al Abrams had taught me the dark art of stock manipulation. Thrice weekly we'd meet for breakfast at the local Greek diner, where I had the pleasure of watching Al consume countless Linzer tortes, with half the torte making its way into his mouth and the other half making its way onto his cheeks and forehead; meanwhile, he would be drinking cup after cup of overcaffeinated coffee, until his hands shook.

Through it all—through all the slobbering and shaking and

squeaking and squawking–he gave me the education of a lifetime. But, alas, unlike my education from Mike, this one concerned the dark side of things, the seedy underbelly of Wall Street's over-the-counter market–which was the precursor to the NASDAQ–where stocks traded by appointment, and prices were set at the self-serving whims of dark-intentioned men like Al and me.

Most troubling, I admitted, was that it wasn't long before I was teaching *Al* a thing or two. Within weeks, in fact, I was modernizing his rather dated stock scams–bringing my own flair and panache to them, along with the sort of brazenness that would come to characterize the Wolf of Wall Street.

By now it was a little after five, and I was finally done singing on Court Street for the day, a day that my captors considered a great success. After all, they now knew exactly how Stratton Oakmont came into existence and how–through a series of tiny coincidences and happenstances–it wound up on, of all places, Long Island.

Before I left the debriefing room, the last thing I asked the Bastard was how long he thought it would be until I actually got sentenced. Would it be three years? Four years? Perhaps even five years? The longer the better, I thought.

"Probably four or five years," he answered. "These things have a way of dragging on sometimes."

"That's true," added the Witch, "and they won't be easy years. Your cooperation will be made public sometime next year, and we'll be seizing your assets accordingly."

Now OCD chimed in, offering me a thin ray of hope: "Yeah, but you'll have a chance to start a new life. You're a young guy, and next time you'll do things right, hopefully."

I nodded in agreement, hanging on to the words of OCD and the Bastard while ignoring those of the Witch. Unfortunately, they would all be wrong, and I would be seeing the inside of a jail cell long before that.

And I would lose everything.

CHAPTER 13

THE REVOLVING DOOR

Two Months Later

Southampton Beach! For better or worse, there was no denying that Meadow Lane was a fabulous place to watch the walls of reality come crashing down on me. The blue waters of the Atlantic were just behind me; the gray waters of Shinnecock Bay were just before me; and on either side of me, stately mansions–like mine–rose up from out of the dunes, like Greek temples bearing silent witness to how wonderful it was to be a wealthy WASP or a nouveau riche Jew.

My particular mansion, which would soon be owned by OCD and the Bastard, was a sprawling gray and white affair, built in the Cape Cod style. On the rear deck, a pool and Jacuzzi looked out over the Atlantic; on the front lawn, an all-weather tennis court looked out over the Shinnecock; and out in front, a row of immaculately trimmed box hedges rose up twelve feet in the air, concealing the property from view.

At this particular moment, I was sitting on a shabby-chic couch in the mansion's shabby-chic living room, staring into the doelike eyes of Sarah Weissman,* self-proclaimed Jewish blow-job queen. She was sitting less than two feet away, wearing a black cotton turtleneck and black knit leggings, accentuating a tight little body that reeked of past beauty and present-day bulimia.

Nevertheless, the Blow-Job Queen was still a looker. Only twenty-two, she had a pleasantly narrow face, gleaming black hair, jet-black eyes, olive skin, a first-class nose job, ortho-perfect teeth, and a lower lip lusher than the Nile. And despite knowing her only fifteen minutes, I thought she seemed like a reasonably good egg. We'd met this evening at a local AA meeting and had hit it off instantly. She was newly sober (less than a week, actually), battling a triple addiction to crack, booze, and self-induced vomiting, the latter of which I found rather disgusting. But she was on the rebound now, fresh out of detox and back in the Hamptons, ready to resume her life.

Up until now we had made mostly small talk–trading war stories about our drug addictions–but apparently she was ready to get down to business, because she was in the middle of saying, "...that it's Jewish girls who give the best blow jobs in the world. Did you know that?"

"Uh...no," I answered. "I've never dated a Jewish girl before."

"Well, they do," she said proudly, "and if you want, I'll prove it to you."

"Yeah, that would be great!" I answered, and the Jewish Blow-Job Queen quickly went to work–rising into a crouch and kneeing her way toward me with a lubricious smile on her face. Instinctively, I leaned back and rested my head on a soft, circular throw pillow, as the Blow-Job Queen reached forward with her tiny hands and unzipped my fly. Then, with remarkable efficiency, she pulled down my jeans to my ankles, climbed between my legs, and twisted her long black hair into a ponytail.

Suddenly she paused.

"What's wrong?" I asked.

"Nothing, silly," she said, as she removed her gold necklace, on the end of which dangled a diamond-studded Jewish star. She put it in her pocket. "I don't want it to get in my way."

---

*Name has been changed

I nodded in understanding, and I closed my eyes, hiked up my legs, and prepared for the blow job of a lifetime. It would be just what the doctor ordered, I thought. One hummer from the Blow-Job Queen and I would forget about the Duchess forever!

"Oww!" snapped the Blow-Job Queen. "There's something jabbing me in my butt!" I looked down and–*Christ!* My ankle bracelet was jabbing the Blow-Job Queen in her bony butt.

I lowered my legs with the speed of a jackrabbit. "It's nothing," I said. "Just a beeper I wear for work. It's okay; keep going."

The Blow-Job Queen narrowed her eyes suspiciously. "A beeper, huh?"

"Yeah," I said, "a beeper."

A few moments passed as she continued to stare. "All right," she finally said. "I'll take your word for it," and she slowly leaned over and started blowing me... and it was one of those long, sumptuous blow jobs, the sort a man only gets from his wife during the courting period.

I started moaning in appreciation: "*Oh, God,* Sarah! It feels *sooo* good. You were right: Jewish girls *do* give the best blow jobs!"

"Uhm-hum," she mumbled, unable to speak.

"Ahhhh..." I moaned, and I closed my eyes and let my nervous system dissolve... letting my problems drift further and further away... until nothing mattered anymore... just the Blow-Job Queen and her blow job... and my mind started to wander... wander to the Duchess.... What was she doing right now? Was she at home with the kids, or was she out with another man? It was a weeknight, so she would probably be home with the kids... although I was hearing rumors that she was having an affair with her personal trainer, some Romanian dirtbag named Alex... although that was unimportant now.... It was the kids who were important... they were everything to me....

Just then–*a cool sensation!* I opened my eyes and the Blow-Job Queen's head was popping up, a concerned expression on her face. "What's wrong?" she said. "It doesn't feel good?"

I looked down–*oh, Christ!* My penis looked like a strand of overcooked spaghetti! How very fucking embarrassing! "Oh... uh... no," I mumbled, "everything's fine. I mean, it's the best blow job I ever got. It's just that"–desperately I searched for the proper words–"uh, it's just that you're the, uh, the first girl I've been with in like, uh, ten years. I mean, not including my wife, of course–I mean, my ex-wife, or my soon-to-be ex-wife is more like it." I paused for a second, asking myself if the fact that I'd slept with close to a thousand hookers while I was married to the Duchess meant I was now lying to the Blow-Job Queen.

I sat up straight and took a deep, troubled breath and let it out slow. "I'm really sorry," I said softly. "Maybe it's too soon for me. I'm not sure." I shook my head sadly.

The Blow-Job Queen took no offense; instead, she offered me the warmest of smiles, an altogether *maternal* smile. "That's okay," she said. "I think it's *sweet* that you're nervous. It makes me want you even more." She smiled again, and I noticed that her teeth were very white. That's good, I thought. The Blow-Job Queen has very white teeth.

"Now, lie back down and relax," she said warmly. "And stop worrying! Everything's gonna be fine." And, with that, the Blow-Job Queen placed her tiny hand on my shoulder and gently pushed me back down. "Just relax your mind..." she said, in a tone normally used by a hypnotist, "relax your body...relax everything...it's all gonna be okay...."

I nodded dutifully and closed my eyes, thinking–Jesus H. Christ! The Blow-Job Queen really has her shit together! I mean, here she is, three days sober, a crack addict, a bulimic, an alcoholic, most certainly a pill-popper, and probably an anorexic too, yet she's completely taken control of the situation. I felt lucky to have her.

And indeed I was. In no time flat, the Blow-Job Queen was humming away, with the sort of unbridled relish you usually see in porn videos. A few minutes later, I screamed, "Oh, my God! I"–I held back the words *love you,* which was what I truly felt like screaming, and screamed–"can't take it anymore!" And a split second later I was done. True to her word, the Jewish Blow-Job Queen had gotten the best of me, and my body was now limp.

Just then she popped up her head and wiped her chin with

the back of her hand. "So how do you feel *now?*" she asked provocatively.

"Amazing, Sarah. I feel truly amazing."

She smiled broadly and kindly. "I'm glad," she said happily. "I'm really glad," and she started looking around the living room at the towering sandstone fireplace behind her, at the dozen pieces of shabby-chic furniture surrounding her–all the couches and armchairs and ottomans and coffee tables and end tables and the throw pillows and flowers and vases and paintings on the walls and, just off the living room, the shabby-chic dining-room table, which was larger than a horseshoe pit. Then she looked up at the thirty-foot ceiling, and then, finally, she looked at the plate-glass wall that ran the entire length of the back of the house and looked out over the Atlantic.

"You know," she said, "this place is really beautiful. I mean, I've been around money before, but this place *reeks* of old money! You know what I mean?"

Old money? Jesus! If there were newer money anywhere in the Hamptons, I was yet to find it. Perhaps she meant evaporating money? That would be more accurate. "Thanks," I said, "but it's not old money, Sarah. It's as new as it gets." I smiled, eager to change the subject. "Anyway, you want to take a walk on the beach? It's a beautiful night tonight."

"I can't," she said sadly. "I gotta get home; my boyfriend's waiting for me."

I popped upright. "Your boyfriend! You have a boyfriend?"

She shrugged. "Yeah, I live with someone. I probably shouldn't be here. You know what I mean?"

I took a moment to run that through my mind and decided she was right: She probably shouldn't be here. But, then again, at this time of year there weren't many girls in the Hamptons, so if I let the Blow-Job Queen go I would be alone again. I took a moment to study her features. Was she beautiful enough? Could she stand up to the Duchess? She had a very nice nose, the Blow-Job Queen, and perhaps I could find peace through her blow jobs. In fact, maybe I could even turn her into another Duchess! I could take her shopping and buy her clothes and jewelry, and then take her out for fancy dinners; maybe I would even introduce her to my kids. After all, she was sober for three whole days now and was definitely on the rebound. All in all, I would say, she was a very good catch!

And so it was that five days later I convinced the Jewish Blow-Job Queen to break up with her boyfriend, and I moved her into my mansion on Meadow Lane, where twice a day she gave me world-class blow jobs and occasionally made love to me. And it was perfect. We exchanged our first "I love yous" on day seven and started talking marriage on day ten. She shrugged off my ankle bracelet as if it were no big deal–in fact, the Bastard, in a rare moment of humanity, had eased my restrictions, changing them from a twenty-four-hour lockdown to a midnight curfew–and I shrugged off her excusing herself from the dinner table and vomiting up her food with the same kindness and understanding.

Meanwhile, my cooperation was going fabulously. I hadn't heard from OCD in weeks, which, according to Magnum, was par for the course. After all, I had spent a solid month singing on Court Street, going through all of Stratton's deals while giving OCD and the Bastard the education of a lifetime. Now they needed to do their homework–to subpoena records, interview witnesses, follow paper trails.

On a down note, my meeting with the Blue-eyed Devil had turned out to be a complete waste of time. He was far too cagey to get caught speaking on tape, especially to someone under indictment. Nevertheless, my captors had taken my failure in stride, assuring me that it wasn't my fault. As long as I tried my best, said OCD, I would receive my 5K letter. It was all about honesty; just remember that, he'd urged, and I'd emerge from jail still a young man.

And that was the last time we'd spoken, with the exception of a brief heads-up call, during which he told me that Danny had made bail and that Victor Wang had finally been indicted. And without saying it, the message was clear: Danny was cooperating, and Victor had become the Witch's captive, her personal trophy to be put on display.

Whatever the case, it was sometime around Thanksgiving when I finally introduced the kids to the Blow-Job Queen. And she was wonderful with them; in fact, with the exception of one hiccup—she suffered a panic attack, accompanied by violent body shakes, while the four of us were having lunch in East Hampton—I began to view her as a suitable stepmother for the children. And while we hadn't actually set a wedding date, it was only a matter of time. We were perfect together, two damaged souls who had somehow managed to fix each other.

And then disaster struck. It was the week before Christmas, and we were lying in bed together, happy as clams. It was a Saturday afternoon, and I was watching TV and she was reading a book. I glanced over and noticed that she was wearing granny glasses. I also noticed a tiny scar beneath her chin. I stared at the scar. *Not very attractive!* I thought. Then I stared at the granny glasses. *Even less attractive!* I thought. Then I lowered my gaze to her tiny chest and her reed-thin arms. *Downright ugly!* I thought.

We were lying beneath the white silk comforter, so I couldn't take in her whole body, but, in spite of that, there was no denying that I'd caught her at a very bad angle. And that was it: I no longer loved the Blow-Job Queen.

I took a deep breath and tried to steel myself, but it was no use. I couldn't have her in my house anymore. I needed to be alone, or with the Duchess. Perhaps I could convince the Duchess to get back together for the sake of the kids. Alas, I had already tried that angle, to no avail. The latest rumor was that she was banging Michael Bolton, that ponytailed bastard of a singer!

In any event, the next day I threw the Blow-Job Queen out—or at least *tried* to, at which point she had a nervous breakdown in my living room, threatening suicide. So I told her that I was only kidding, that I didn't *really* want to end things. I was just getting cold feet as a result of all the turmoil in my life.

To that she smiled sadly and asked me if I would like a blow job. I pondered that for a moment, knowing that this would most certainly be the best blow job of all, considering the Blow-Job Queen would now be blowing me to maintain her position on Meadow Lane.

But in the end I told her that I wouldn't, although perhaps I would later. She seemed relieved by that, so I quickly excused myself, saying I needed to take a quick ride to see my sponsor, George, who lived just down the road.

"Can't you just come over with a straitjacket and take her away?" I asked George. "I don't see any other solution."

Those weren't the *first* words I'd uttered to George that afternoon, but they were close to the first. The first were: "I'm in deep shit, George. The Blow-Job Queen is threatening to commit suicide, and my dick is so sore from all the blow jobs that it's ready to fall off!"

George and I were sitting in his French country kitchen on opposite sides of his bleached-wood table, while his wife, Annette, a five-foot-tall, beautiful Brooklyn firecracker with strawberry-blond hair, perfect Irish Spring skin, and a ferocious Brooklyn accent fixed us coffee. Actually, it was more than coffee (it was donuts, muffins, coffee, and freshly cut fruit), because Annette never did anything half-assed, especially when it came to achieving her life's primary mission, which was to make George's life as comfortable and wonderful as possible. And, in truth, George deserved it.

At sixty-two, he was twelve years older than Annette and served as living proof that a leopard *can* change its spots. Those who hadn't heard from George in the last twenty-two years would warn you: "If you see this guy walking down the street, cross it and don't make eye contact. He's angry and dangerous, especially when he's drunk, which is always. And if he *does* happen to beat you up or simply hold you upside down by your ankle and shake you for a while, don't bother calling the cops, unless you tell them that it was some six-foot-tall, two-hundred-fifty-pound guy named George who assaulted you. This way they'll know to bring *tranq-darts*!"

Whatever the case, George eventually got sober, and spent the next twenty-two years of his life redeeming himself. He made his first fortune in real estate, his second fortune in drug rehabs, and, along the way, helped more recovering Hamptons alcoholics than any other ten men combined.

Ironically, the first time I met George was on TV, when his menacingly handsome face popped onto my screen at three in the morning, while I was in the midst of a cocaine binge. George was doing an advertisement for his rehab facility, Seafield, and he was saying things like, "Are you stoned . . . drunk . . . high? Where is your family right now? You need help; Seafield has the answers. . . ." My response to that was to throw a bronze sculpture through my TV screen, putting a premature end to George's commercial.

Yet I remember thinking at the time that the face on my TV was the sort I would never forget—those gruffly handsome features, those piercing brown eyes, that perfectly coiffed salt-and-pepper hair—which was why it didn't take long to recognize him when I ran into him six weeks later in Southampton, in the rooms of Alcoholics Anonymous. And now, eighteen months after that, he was much more to me than just a sponsor. In point of fact, he was like a father.

"I can't just come over with a straitjacket," said George, with a few shakes of his enormous head. "You know, I warned you about this: Two alcoholics dating are like two dump trucks running into each other." He shrugged his enormous shoulders. "Anyway, like I said before: You–are–not–done–with–your–wife–yet. It's too soon."

Just then Annette chimed in, with her wonderful Brooklyn accent: "Oh, what's the harm, *Gawge*? A few BJs *ain't* gonna kill anyone! Jordan's lonely; he needs to have a little fun!" With that, she padded her way across the gleaming terra-cotta floor and placed the coffee and consumables on the kitchen table.

"Annette," said George, staring at her for a second too long, "he does *not* need to be encouraged in this department." Then he looked at me and said, "I'll see if I can convince Sarah to check into Seafield, but only because I think it would be good for her. In the meantime, I suggest that you don't date for a while. You should stay alone for a year and learn to be by yourself. And keep going to the high schools, giving antidrug lectures; that's the best way to spend your free time right now, being productive and not getting laid."

I promised George that I would, and for the next four weeks I followed his advice to the letter–almost. The "almost" had to do with an occasional tryst with a young Russian gold digger–or a *Natasha,* as the newspapers referred to them–courtesy of a casual acquaintance of mine in the Hamptons, a local playboy type who could send a posse of naughty Natashas to all four corners of the earth at the drop of a dime.

Pretty soon, though, that got old too. In fact, by the beginning of April, I decided to close the revolving door for good, or at least for a while, and I settled into a daily regimen of boringness and tediousness, punctuated by weekend visits from the kids and nightly dinners with George and Annette.

Yes, it was boring and tedious, all right, but it also gave me a chance to find myself, to try to figure out *who* Jordan Belfort really was. The last decade of my life had been unspeakably complicated, and the child my parents had sent out into the world bore little resemblance to the Jordan Belfort of today. So who was I now? Was I a good man or a bad man? Was I a battle-hardened career criminal or an upstanding citizen who'd simply lost his way? Was I capable of being a loyal and loving husband, or was I a habitual whoremonger who would refuse to wear a condom until his dick fell off? And what of my drug addiction? Was the beast merely sleeping or had I kicked the habit for good?

All these questions and many more like them had been ricocheting around my skull as I passed the rest of my winter in exile. The *insanity,* as I had come to think of it, had penetrated every aspect of my life and had destroyed everything in its path. So this was my chance to finally sort things out, to get to the *bottom* of things. The only question was, how long would I have?

Not long, as it turned out, because OCD quickly broke the boredom.

It was a Monday evening when he called, and it was a disturbing call to say the least. I was sitting in my living room, on an armchair, when the cordless phone rang. I put down my AA handbook and picked it up. "Hello?"

"Hey–it's me," said OCD. "Are you alone?"

Given the fact that it was the FBI calling, I actually looked around my own living room to make sure that I was alone. "Yeah," I said, "I'm alone." And I stood up and started pacing around nervously. "What's going on? How've you been?"

"Busy," he replied. "Following up on things. Anyway, how ya holding up out there? Slept with any Ruskies lately?"

"Very funny," I replied, with a healthy dose of nervous laughter. "I'm done with the Natashas for now. I can't take their accents. You know, *da, da, da... blah, blah, blah.* It gets annoying after a while." On the advice of Magnum, I had told OCD about the naughty Natashas, lest it come out on the witness stand under cross-examination. So OCD did his own investigation, and, not surprisingly, came to the legal conclusion that there was nothing inherently against the law about getting raked over the coals by gold-digging Russians. "Anyway, what's going on?" I asked. "I haven't heard from you in a while."

No response at first, just a few moments of sickly silence, the sort you hear when a time bomb ticks down to zero and there's a seemingly *endless* delay before the explosion. Finally he said, "Not much, really, but I need you to wire up against Dave Beall." More silence. "I know this isn't pleasant for you, but you need to do this."

"Why?" I snapped. "He's nobody!" And even as the words escaped my lips, I knew how ridiculous they sounded. It had nothing to do with whether or not I had committed crimes with Dave Beall (of course I had, simply because I'd committed crimes with all my friends), and it had everything to do with whom Dave Beall could lead them to.

OCD, calmly: "Who he is isn't what's important; what is important is that I know he's one of your closest friends." He paused for a moment, as if searching for the right words. "Listen–I don't take any great pleasure in this, and, believe it or not, neither does Joel. But this is something you have to do. I want you to try to set a dinner meeting with him, okay?"

With a sinking heart: "Yeah. I mean, what fucking choice do I have, right?" I let out an obvious sigh. "When do you want me to call him?"

"There's no time like the present," said OCD. "Can I make the call?"

I shook my head sadly. "Yeah, what's the fucking difference anymore? Where do you want me to set the meeting?"

"In a restaurant, a quiet one, somewhere on Long Island, but not in the Hamptons. It's too far for me."

I thought for a moment. "How about Caracalla, in Syosset? It's Italian, small, quiet, good food." I shook my head in despair. "It's as good a place as any to betray my best friend, you know?"

"Don't be so hard on yourself," said OCD. "If the shoe were on the other foot, he would do the same thing. Trust me."

"I do trust you," I said, but what I didn't say was that I knew he was wrong. Dave would never betray me. "Go ahead, make the call. Let's get it over with."

"All right, hold on a second..." Silence for a moment, then two clicks, then: "This is Special Agent Gregory Coleman of the Federal Bureau of Investigation. The date is April third, 1999, and the time is eight p.m. This is a consensually recorded phone conversation between Jordan Belfort, a cooperating witness with the federal government, and David Beall." Another moment of silence, then I heard the dull-thudded ringing of Dave's home telephone, and with each ring my spirits sank lower. The moment Dave picked it up, it occurred to me that I was no longer lower than pond scum.

Now I was lower than the mucus that *feeds* off pond scum.

CHAPTER 14

A CRISIS OF CONSCIENCE

In a way, David Michael Beall came to represent everything that could have been righteous and pure about Stratton Oakmont. Born in the ultrahick town of Burtonsville, Maryland, where sports like horseshoes and cow-tipping were the favorite pastimes, he had grown up dirt-poor and without the benefit of a father. It was the sort of do-it-yourself childhood in which a deep cut was stitched up by your own mother, using a heated sewing needle and thread.

Intellectually, Dave was neither overly bright nor overly dumb; he was average. And he wasn't much of a salesman; he was too honest and forthright, speaking with the sort of slow Southern drawl that couldn't convince anybody to do something they didn't want to do in the first place.

Like most kids from Burtonsville, he didn't grow up with a burning desire to be rich–that would come later–but what he did grow up with was a clear understanding that the world was filled with few chiefs and many Indians and that he was an Indian, and there was nothing wrong with that.

Normally, a six-foot-two-inch country bumpkin like Dave Beall would never go to college; instead, he would take a job at the local garage, doing oil changes and tune-ups, and then pass his weekends trying to get into the skintight jeans of the local Mary Joe Something-or-other. But as luck would have it, Dave was blessed with two wonderful things–speed and strength–which together earned him a full ride to the University of Maryland on a wrestling scholarship.

Along the way, he met a beautiful blond Jewess named Laurie Elovitch, who was half his size and his complete opposite. Laurie was from Long Island, and she came from a very wealthy and politically connected family, so after she and Dave graduated, they moved up to Long Island to be near them. It was understood that a guy like Dave–whom you would normally find sitting on a bale of hay, wearing denim overalls and no shirt–would be a fish out of water in cutthroat Long Island. Everyone assumed that Laurie's father, Larry, would help Dave find his way, that he would use his political connections to get Dave a decent job (perhaps in the parks department or in sanitation).

But again, fate would intervene in the life of Dave Beall–when, in November of 1988, Laurie stumbled upon a help-wanted ad in the *New York Times* and Dave became one of the first young Americans to answer the Stratton call-to-arms. Like many young bucks who came after him, he drove to his interview in a piece-a-shit car, wearing a piece-a-shit suit, which, in his case, was so tattered that his future mother-in-law had to use masking tape to stop it from coming apart at the seams.

Nevertheless, he passed the mirror test without incident and then went through the training program and learned how to sell–or, in Stratton terms, he learned to become a killer. Twice a day, as I stood before the boardroom and did my thing, he also came to believe that greed was good, that clients should either buy or die, and that a life of wealth and ostentation was the only true path to happiness.

And–*voilà!*–six months later, Dave Beall was driving a convertible Porsche, dressing in $2,000 suits, and speaking with the unbridled cocksureness of a world-class stockbroker.

However, it was through his marriage to Laurie that his fate would ultimately be sealed; Laurie would strike up the closest of friendships with the Duchess–thereby thrusting Dave and I into a very unlikely one. We were an odd couple, for sure, yet, as my drug addiction spiraled out of control, Dave became the perfect companion for me. After all, he never had much to say in the first place, and now I was too stoned most of the time to understand him anyway. So we watched movies together, the same ones over and over again–James Bond, mostly, and original episodes of *Star Trek*–while we holed up in my basement, with the shades drawn and the lights dimmed, and I consumed enough drugs to knock out a family of grizzly bears.

Of course, Dave loved his drugs too, but not nearly as much. (Who did, save Keith Richards of the Rolling Stones?) Either way, he was always sober enough to keep an eye on me, which was the Duchess's order. Her own patience had already run out, so she put Dave in charge of making sure I didn't kill myself before she figured out a way to get me into rehab.

Eventually, she did, but not before I *did* try to kill myself.

And as I had stood in Dave's kitchen two years ago, distraught and desperate, chewing on a hundred tablets of morphine, he wrestled me to the ground and stuck his fingers in my mouth and scooped the pills out. Then he called an ambulance and saved my life.

Four weeks later, when I emerged from rehab and arrived in Southampton with my marriage in tatters, it was Dave and Laurie who came out to the beach and did what they could to help us pick up the pieces. While I was well aware that that was something only the Duchess and I could do, it was a gesture I would never forget.

Yet even more telling was how Dave and Laurie acted after my indictment: While most of my friends ran for cover, Dave stood by me, and while most of the Duchess's friends jumped on the *dump-your-husband* bandwagon, Laurie tried to convince her to stay.

It was for all those reasons that, as I now sat with Dave in Caracalla restaurant, I felt like the world's biggest louse. I wore dark-blue Levi's, which concealed OCD's devilish little Nagra, and beneath my black cotton sweater was OCD's ultrasensitive microphone, which was rising up my sternum and coming to rest just to the right of my breaking heart.

Although it would be just the two of us this evening, we were sitting at a table for four, set for four, with a starchy-white tablecloth, bone-white china, and gleaming silverware. Dave was sitting just to my left, less than two feet away–so close, I thought, that OCD's microphone would pick up the sound of his breathing. He wore a navy sport jacket over a white T-shirt–typical dress for Dave Beall–and on his large, handsome face he wore the most innocent of expressions: a lamb waiting to be slaughtered.

After a few minutes of small talk, he handed me a stack of papers. "You mind taking a look at these?" he asked. "I'm thinking about going into the currency-trading business. People are making a fortune in it."

"Sure," I replied–and *Jesus Christ!* I thought. How terribly simple this is going to be! This so-called currency-trading business was the latest scam floating around, and I had no doubt that I could get Dave to incriminate himself in under a minute. Still, this had nothing to do with what OCD and the Bastard were interested in; rather, they wanted to know about the brokerage firm Dave had worked for after Stratton closed. Whatever the case, it would be just as easy to get Dave to spill the beans about that.

So I spent a few moments pretending to look at his papers, which had words like *yen* and *deutsche mark* plastered on them as I snuck peeks around the restaurant out of the corner of my eye. Caracalla was a small place, with maybe fifteen or twenty tables. At eight p.m. on a Wednesday, only a few of them were occupied. It was mostly middle-aged couples, none of whom had any idea of the utter deceit that was transpiring just a few yards away. OCD and the Mormon were waiting for me in the parking lot of a local movie theater, so it was just Dave and me . . . *the man who'd saved my life . . . the only friend who'd stood by me. . . . Our children were friends . . . our wives were friends . . . we were friends! . . . How could I do this?*

I couldn't.

Without even thinking, I put down the papers, excused myself from the table, and headed for the bathroom. On the way, I stopped at a waiters' station and snatched a pen. Inside the bathroom, concealed by a stall, I grabbed a paper towel out of a dispenser, leaned it on the wall, and in big block letters I wrote: *DON'T INCRIMINATE YOURSELF! I'M WIRED!*

I looked at the note for a second, my heart beating out of my chest. If OCD and the Bastard found out about this, I would be dead meat. They would break my cooperation right on the spot, and I'd be sentenced without a 5K letter. *Thirty fucking years!* I thought. I did the calculations: I would be sixty-six years old! I took a deep breath and tried to steel myself. There was no way OCD could ever find out. I was certain of it.

Emboldened by that thought, I exited the bathroom and headed back to the table, my eyes darting around the restaurant, like a jackrabbit's. No one looked suspicious. The coast was clear; there were no government agents.

The moment I reached the table, I placed my left hand on Dave's shoulder and put my right forefinger to my lips, in the sign that says: "Shhh!" In my left hand was the note, folded in half. I removed my hand from his shoulder, unfolded the note with my fingers, and then placed it on the table in front of him.

As I sat down, I watched his blue eyes literally pop out of his beefy skull, like hat pegs, as he read the note to himself. Then he looked at me, dumbfounded. I looked back, stone-faced. Then I nodded slowly. He nodded back.

"Anyway," I said, "as far as the currency-trading business goes, I think it's a good thing, but you need to be careful. There's a lot of cash floating around there–at least that's what I hear; everyone's taking kickbacks. I mean, it was one thing when you and I did it, but it's different when there're strangers involved." I lowered my voice for effect. "Let me ask you a question," I whispered. "You never deposited any of the cash I gave you, did you?"

He looked at me wide-eyed. "I don't know what you're talking about. I'm broke right now."

"I understand that," I whispered, "but I'm not talking about *right now.* I'm talking about *two years ago.* I'm worried about the quarter million I gave you. What did you do with the cash?"

A bead of sweat began running down his thick brow. "I think you were stoned back then, big guy! I'm broke right now. . . ."

And that was how the evening went down.

An hour later, when I handed OCD the tape, I felt a slight twinge of guilt, but only a slight twinge. After all, if OCD were to find out about this, he would understand. Ohhh, he would still have no choice but to throw me in jail for the next thirty years; but he wouldn't take my betrayal personally. He would agree that there's only so low a man can stoop before he's no longer a man, and, tonight I had reached that point, and, yes, tonight I had acted like a man.

On my way back to Southampton, I realized that I had found something very important this evening, something that I had lost many years ago, on that very first day I had walked into the Investors' Center and saw the spreads.

My self-respect.

CHAPTER 15

THE WONDERFUL WORLD OF KARMA

It was *karma,* I thought.

After all, what other explanation could there possibly be that, within three days of slipping Dave Beall the note, the Duchess called me to reconcile? Actually, it wasn't a *full* reconciliation, but it was a major step in the right direction.

"So," said my luscious Duchess, walking arm in arm with me along the water's edge, "if you buy me a house in the Hamptons, I think it'll be really good for us. We'd get rid of the Old Brookville house and see each other all the time again. Who *knows* what'll happen from there, right?"

I nodded and smiled warmly as we walked in silence for a few moments. We were walking west, toward the setting sun, and in spite of it being April, it was still warm enough at five o'clock that our matching blue windbreakers were all we needed to protect us against the salty breeze.

"Anyway," continued the Duchess, "I was really mad at you for a while. I never really got over what happened on the stairs. I mean, I *thought* I did, but I just kind of buried it under the rug, along with a lot of other things." She paused for a moment, squeezing my arm tighter. "But I'm as much to blame as you for that. You see, all those years I thought I was helping you, I was actually killing you." She shook her head sadly. "But how was I to know? I was so codependent at the time, I didn't know which way was up anymore."

"Yeah," I said softly, "you're right; but only about the last part. What happened with the drugs wasn't your fault; it wasn't really anyone's fault; it just kind of happened. It slowly, insidiously crept up on us."

She nodded but said nothing. I soldiered on, in an upbeat tone: "Anyway, I was a drug addict and you were a codependent, and together we made a mess of things. But at least we made it out alive, right?"

"Yeah–*barely*," she said. "I've had to work really hard on myself over the last six months. You know, codependency is a terrible disease, Jordan"–she shook her head gravely–"a *terrible, terrible* disease, and I was about as classically codependent as you can get."

"Yeah," I said solemnly–and what a fucking joke! I thought. Codependency, shmodependency... blah, blah, blah! The whole thing was fucking laughable. Yes, the Duchess had been codependent, but to actually seek out a self-help group that had the audacity to call itself *Codependents Anonymous*? Still, when the Duchess had first started talking about it, I wanted to have an open mind. In fact, I even asked George if he'd ever heard of such a group, and, surprisingly, he told me he had. Yes, they existed, he said, but no one took them seriously. It was a man-haters club more than anything, a place where they turned meek women into pit bulls. In short, he concluded, they were dangerous.

But that was the Duchess: always aspiring to be perfect at *something*, and this was her latest gig–to be perfectly codependent. So I had no choice but to go along with it, to pretend that codependency was the latest rage. On the plus side, though, anything that motivated her to put away her prospecting shovel was fine with me.

Just then I felt a playful nudge. "What are you thinking about? I see those wheels of yours turning."

"Nothing," I replied. "I was just thinking how much I still love you."

"Well, I love you too," she said. "I'll *always* love you."

Shit! The second half of her statement was not encouraging! After all, by saying that she would *always* love me, she was inferring that her love was not of a wifely nature, which is to say of a spread-your-legs nature. Instead, it was of a you're-the-father-of-my-children nature or a we-share-history-together nature, both of which were unacceptable to me. I wanted *wifely* love. I wanted *lusty* love. I wanted the sort of love that we used to share–before I'd been dumb enough to get myself indicted! Still, this was a beginning, a starting point from which I could maneuver her accordingly. "Well," I said confidently, "as long as we still love each other we can work the rest out, right?"

She nodded slowly. "Over time, yeah, but we need to become friends first. We were never really friends, Jordan. In the beginning, all we did was have sex; I mean, we hardly came up for air, you know?"

"Yeah," I said gravely–and what the fuck was wrong with that? I thought. Those were the best times of my life, for Chrissake! All those lazy afternoons we made love in the closet, all those nights on the beach, the way we did it doggie-style in the back of the limousine, that time in the movie theater, during *Interview with the Vampire,* while that old couple one row up rolled their eyes. Who could ask for anything more?

"Yeah is right," added the Duchess. "We were like two sex maniacs!" Suddenly she stopped and turned to me. Her back was to the ocean now, her blond hair shimmering brilliantly in the afternoon sunlight. She looked like an angel, *my* angel! "So what do you think, honey? Will you buy me the house?" She puckered up her lips into an irresistible pout.

"I'm not against it," I replied quickly, debating whether or not to nail her with a kiss, "but with everything that's going on right now, don't you think it would make more sense for you to move in here?" I motioned toward the dunes. "Let's give it a shot and see what happens, Nae! If it doesn't work, I'll buy you the house in two seconds flat."

She shook her head sadly. "I can't do that yet; I'm not ready." Then, nervously, she added, "Is it the money? Is the government hassling you?"

I shook my head. "No, I can still spend what I want, as long as it's reasonable."

"Well, what does Greg say?"

I smiled. "Greg who? Greg my lawyer or the *other* Greg?"

"Greg your lawyer!"

I smiled again. "He doesn't say much, Nae. He's trying to negotiate the best deal he can, that's about it. But the good news is that he thinks"–*thinks!*–"we can keep the houses for a while, at least until I get sentenced, and that won't be for another four years or so. So we have some time."

Not letting go: "Where does that leave me? Will you buy me the house or not? It's only a million dollars, Jordan. It's a lot less than Old Brookville, so I'm sure the government will be happy with that, no?"

I shrugged. "One would think, although I would still have to get it approved." Just then something odd occurred to me. "You already found a house, Nae?"

She shrugged innocently. "No, well . . . not really. I mean, I *did* see something that would be perfect for the kids and me"–then, as an afterthought–"and maybe perfect for you too one day!" She smiled eagerly. "So what do you think, honey? Will you buy it for me?"

I smiled back, thinking how wonderful it would be to live with the Duchess and with the *kids* again! No more Jewish blow-job queens and Russian Natashas; how wonderful that would be! "I think we should go look at the house right now," I said, smiling, but what I *didn't* say was: "Before I actually buy it for you, Duchess, I'm gonna make damn sure you're not playing me like a fiddle!"

"She's playing you like a fiddle," snapped my longtime private investigator, Richard "Bo" Dietl, sitting across from me at a table for two at Caracalla. "I'm certain of it, Bo."

"Maybe so," I replied, "but I need to know for sure. You know, I was just starting to get over her when she called, and now she's got me back on the hook again." I paused, and shook my head angrily. "But this is it, Bo; if she fucks me over *this* time, I'm done for good."

"That's fair enough," Bo said skeptically, "but I still think it's bad karma, this *planatation* of yours. And it ain't so legal either."

I shrugged noncommittally, amazed at how well I understood Bo-speak, which required that you not only disregard Bo's odd habit of calling everyone around him Bo (in spite of his own nickname being Bo) but that you also disregard the ending *atation,* when he chose to add it onto an unsuspecting noun. So a *plan* could be a *planatation,* and *lunch* would be *lunchatation.* Still, Bo was smarter than a whip, and he happened to be the best private investigator in the business.

"I'm not too worried about the bad-karma part," I replied casually, "because I've done some *damn* good things lately." I smiled knowingly, resisting the urge to explain to Bo that the reason I'd chosen Caracalla was because I'd created so much good karma last time I was here (by slipping Dave Beall the note) that I was certain it would offset any bad karma I might create with my latest plan, which was: to bug the Duchess's Codependents Anonymous meeting. "So I'm pretty much bursting at the seams with good karma, Bo."

"That's fair enough," he said, "but I still can't bug the *roomatation* for you. If we get caught, they'll throw us both in jail for that."

I shrugged again and then took a moment to regard Bo.

As always, he was dressed impeccably, with his two-hundred-pound, five-foot-ten-inch frame swathed in a $2,000 gray pinstripe suit with a size-fifty chest, a crisp white dress shirt with an eighteen-inch neck, and a solid gray crepe de chine necktie, knotted flawlessly in the Windsor style. On his left hand he wore a diamond pinky ring that looked heavy enough to do wrist curls with, and, along with the rest of him—that gorilla-size neck, those broadly handsome features, his perfectly coiffed grayish beard, that slightly thinning head of hair—it gave off the regal whiff of a *classy mobster.*

Of course, Bo was not a mobster; he had simply grown up around them, raised in that section of Ozone Park, Queens, where an Irish-Italian kid like Bo had only two possible career paths: to become a cop or a mobster. So Bo became a cop–rising quickly through the ranks of the NYPD and earning his gold shield at a remarkably young age. He then retired young and used his connections, on both sides of the law, to build his company, Bo Dietl and Associates, into America's most well-respected private-security firm.

Over the years, Bo had been a tremendous asset to me–doing everything from protecting my family to investigating the companies I took public to scaring away the occasional low-level mobster who'd made the mistake of trying to muscle his way into Stratton's business. Right now, however, Bo had no idea that I was cooperating; perhaps he suspected it, I thought, but he was too professional to ask. Besides, when it came down to it, Bo was my friend, and, like any friend, he didn't want to put me in a position where I had to lie to him.

"I understand what you're saying," I said to Bo, "but I'm not asking you to bug the room."

He shrugged. "So what are you asking me to do, then: hide in the fucking closet?"

I smiled warmly. "No, no, no; I would never ask you to do anything so sneaky and underhanded. What I want you to do is wire up one of your female operatives and have her infiltrate the meeting." I winked. "As long as the bug is on her, it's legal in this state, right?"

Bo stared at me, astonished. I continued: "Anyway, I'm pretty sure that a recorded conversation with one side consenting is perfectly legal." I chose not to tell him why I was so sure. "So as long as we keep the bug on her, we're in the clear!" I gave my eyebrows two quick up and downs. "It's a pretty good plan, don't you think, Bo?"

"Jesus," muttered Bo. "You–are–one–twisted–fuck, my friend!"

I shrugged. "I'll take that as a compliment from a guy like you. Anyway, I can only imagine what these women say in these meetings. I mean, think about it: We'll be like two flies on the wall. If nothing else, it'll be the laugh of the century!"

Bo, the caveman: "What the fuck does this codependent shit

mean anyway? It sounds like a boatload of crap to me." He shook his head in disbelief. "I bet you some of those women could benefit from some time in a mental ward. You know what I'm saying, Bo?"

I nodded in agreement. "Yeah, I know exactly what you're saying, but this is the Duchess's latest trip: She's an aspiring codependent, and there's nothing I can do about it. Anyway, will you do this for me, Bo? Will you ride this out with me to the bitter end?"

"Yeah," he answered unenthusiastically. "I'll ride it out with you, Bo. But if your *wifeatation* ever finds out about this, she's gonna crucify you!"

I dismissed his concern with a flap of the back of my hand in the air. "Don't even worry about that, Bo. *I'm* not gonna tell her and *you're* not gonna tell her, so how the hell is she ever gonna find out?"

Just then a tall, thin waiter came over with our drinks. He wore a red waiter's bolero, a black bow tie, and no expression. He handed Bo a snifter of Jack Daniel's, and me a Coke. Bo looked up at the waiter and said, "Bring me another one of these *drinkatations,* Bo, will ya?"

The waiter stared at Bo, confused. Bo pressed on: "What's wrong, Bo?"

I said to the waiter, "He'd like another one, please."

The waiter nodded and walked off.

Bo shook his head in disgust. "Fucking guy," he muttered. "He don't barely speak English and they got him serving us *lunchatation.* It's a fucking travesty." With that, Bo lifted his glass. "Anyways, I hope you get the answer you're looking for, Bo, because my experience with these things is that a woman's secret thoughts are never pretty."

"What a crazy bunch of women!" muttered Debbie Starling.*

It was two nights later when one of Bo's favorite operatives, Debbie Starling, muttered those very words into a Long Island pay

---

*Name has been changed

phone, just a few blocks from the Duchess's Codependents Anonymous meeting. Bo and I were on the conference call. "I've never heard anything like it!" she added. "I mean, I don't know how to even describe it to you guys. It was like, uh . . ." There were a few moments of silence, as I sat on the edge of my seat, and Bo, I assumed, sat on the edge of his own seat. He was working late this Wednesday evening, still in his office, waiting for Debbie's postmeeting debriefing.

I had never met Debbie, but, according to Bo, she was perfect for the job. In her mid-forties now, she had spent most of her career camped out on a park bench, looking sexy and vulnerable, waiting for a would-be mugger to approach. When he did, she would lure him close and then slap the cuffs on him. Then she would blow a whistle–at which point half a dozen of New York's finest would emerge from the shadows and beat the shit out of the guy. Then they would arrest him.

Still, this wasn't what impressed Bo about Debbie, especially when it came to this operation. In fact, it had more to do with Debbie being in the drama club back in her college days, where she'd earned rave reviews from the critics. She was perfect, Bo had said. She was a born actress, who could infiltrate the man-haters club faster than the Duchess could say *codependency*! So he wired her up and sent her behind enemy lines.

Finally, the aspiring actress spoke: "You know, maybe I could explain it to you guys this way: You ever see the movie *Jerry Maguire*?"

"Yeah," we replied in unison.

"Okay, well, remember that scene in Renee Zellweger's living room, where all the divorced women are sitting around, bitching and moaning, calling men *the enemy*?"

"Yeah," we said again.

"Well, it was like that–but on steroids!"

We all broke up over that one, but after a few seconds I found myself wanting to jump through the phone. Bo regained his composure and said, "All right, Debbie, so what went down in Fantasyland tonight?"

"Well," said Debbie, "it seems like Jordan's wife is the ringleader over there. Does that surprise you, Jordan?"

"No, not at all," I said. "That's how she is. Whatever she's hot for at the moment, she plunges into headfirst. Today she's an aspiring codependent; tomorrow she could be an aspiring astronaut; there's no rhyme or reason, no telling. But I love her anyway."

"Well, she's very beautiful," noted Debbie.

No shit! I thought. Why else do you think I'm in love with her—because of her fucking personality? Christ, she's enough to drive any five men crazy! "Thanks," I said, "but that's not why I love her, Debbie. Beauty is only skin-deep"—while ugliness cuts straight to the bone, I thought. "It's her personality I love: her feistiness, her quick wit, the way she gives me a run for my money," and the way she used to blow me while I was driving my Ferrari on the LIE during rush hour, as truckers honked in appreciation. "Looks have nothing to do with it, nothing at all."

There were a few moments of silence, while my bullshit hung in the air like Los Angeles smog. Finally Bo said, "All right, so what's the verdict, Debbie: Does she love him or not?"

"Yes, she loves him," said Debbie—*my spirits soared!*—"but she also hates him"—*my spirits plunged!* Debbie paused for a moment. "More than anything, I think she's just confused."

"Confused about what?" I asked.

"Yeah," added Bo. "What the fuck does *she* have to be so confused about? She ain't the one who got indicted! It's un-fucking-believable, these women."

Debbie, with patience: "Are you finished, Bo?"

"Yeah, I'm finished," he muttered. "So what's the story with the house?"

I immediately perked up. "Yeah, did she bring up East Hampton?"

"Not directly," said Debbie—*shit!* I thought—"although she did say that she wanted to move out of Old Brookville."

I perked up again. "Oh, really? Did she say why?"

"Yes; she said your name is in the paper all the time, and she's embarrassed"—*my spirits plunged!* "She says people are looking at her funny, especially at your daughter's school. She just wants to get away from it all and take the kids with her."

"Well, that doesn't sound too promising," I said softly.

"No it doesn't," agreed Bo. "I think it's time you stop this *housitation* hunt. You know, Bo?"

"I wouldn't jump the gun," countered Debbie. "See, right after she said that, then she started saying that she still loved you. She even said that she missed being with you."

"Well, that's great!" I said.

"Well, don't jump the gun there either," warned Debbie. "A second later she said she hoped you'd die in a fire, or something along those lines. That way she'd be rid of you for good."

"Can you imagine?" snapped Bo. "You can't trust these females for a second! You turn your back and they stick the knife in!"

Debbie, losing patience: "You're not being constructive here, Bo." A short pause, then, "Listen, Jordan: Like I said, she's very confused right now. Maybe you should give her some space for a while, just give her some time to sort things out. Then maybe she'll come back to you. Either way, you have one thing going for you, Jordan."

"What's that?" I asked.

"She hates her father even more than she hates you."

"Well, that's comforting," I said. "He abandoned her when she was three."

"So where does this leave us?" Bo asked Debbie. "Can you give us an opinion on this thing?"

"I'm not really comfortable doing that," Debbie said. "Maybe if I go back next week I can find out more. I'm sure she doesn't suspect anything. I was welcomed into the group with open arms. I think they were just happy to drag someone else into their misery."

"This might take a long time, Bo," said Bo.

"I don't *have* a long time," I shot back. "My wife is not gonna stop pressuring me with this; I know her." And I was running out of time for other reasons as well, reasons that I couldn't share with Bo and Debbie. Next month I would be going before the judge to enter my guilty plea, and, as part of that, I would have to put together a detailed financial statement. Of course, all this would be done in secret; nothing would be announced until next year, *after* my cooperation became public. But, still, the best time to sell the

Old Brookville house would be now, *before* I completed a financial statement.

Bo said, "There's gotta be a way to get her to spill the beans quicker."

The former actress: "Maybe I could strike up a friendship with her. I mean, what if I walked into next week's meeting, hysterically crying, saying that my husband just beat me or something?" The actress paused for a moment. "From what little I know about your wife, Jordan, I think she would come running to my side to help me."

Oh, good Lord! I thought. I was going straight to hell with this one. There was no way I could ever let this happen. Never! Not in a million years! "That's an amazing idea, Debbie! You could invite her out for a drink even, and then get her sloshed. You should see what she's like with a couple of drinks in her. It's like truth serum!" Good God–what was I saying? "And I know the perfect place for you to bring her: It's called Buckram Stables. It's some old WASP hangout in Locust Valley; it's nice and quiet there, so you can make a clear tape."

"This is terrible," said Bo. "I can't allow this to happen"–a pause–"without giving Debbie some sort of small bonus, if she pulls it off."

"Well, thank you," said Debbie, "but have no fear: I'll pull it off. I'll just bring an onion with me and peel it in the car before I go into the meeting. I'll walk into that church with tears streaming down my cheeks!"

There were a few moments of silence.

"Christ!" said Bo. "This is bad, really bad. Let's do it!"

"I cannot allow this to happen!" I said forcefully. And then I said, "The only problem is that it's out of my control. It's already been decided. So what can I do?"

"Nothing," answered Bo. "We've passed the point of no return."

"Great," said Debbie. "I'll go buy the onion!"

The man-haters club met once a week, on Wednesdays, and the meeting lasted for an hour, ending at eight p.m. Right now it was close to eleven, and I still hadn't heard from Bo. So I was pacing back and forth in my living room, trying to remain calm and doing my final calculations as to how much good karma I had left in my karma tank.

In a way, though, the Duchess had brought this upon herself, hadn't she? I mean, what man *wouldn't* want to know his estranged wife's secret thoughts? I was no worse than any other obsessed husband! The only difference was that I had the resources to take things a bit further than most men. Besides, if she were willing to share her secret thoughts with the first stranger who came along...well, that made her secret thoughts fair game for public consumption.

In truth, I was pretty confident that I would be getting good news tonight. After all, I had gone through everything Debbie had said last week and, all in all, I had distilled the Duchess's inner thoughts down to two simple truths. Truth one: She still loved me, but she was confused. Truth two: In time, she would miss making love to me *so* much that she would have no choice but to come back. Yes, even that day on the beach she had specifically raised the issue of sex two times: once referring to us as plain old sex maniacs (which was certainly a good thing), and also commenting on how we never came up for air (which was an even better thing!). Of course, I had heard the past disturbing rumblings about Michael Bolton and her dirt-bag personal trainer, Alex the Douche, but in the end they were probably just that: rumblings.

Emboldened by those truths, I had called Magnum last week and told him what was going on with the Duchess. "Would the Bastard object to me selling my Old Brookville house and buying a much cheaper house in the Hamptons?" Magnum had responded with cautious optimism. He was knee-deep in negotiations with the Bastard, he said, and the Bastard was being his usual difficult self. However, he thought he would look positively on anything I did to cut my expenses. Either way, he hoped to have a deal hammered out by the beginning of May, at which point I would go before Judge Gleeson and enter my guilty plea.

Just then I heard the phone ringing. *It was Bo!* I made a beeline for the kitchen. When I reached the phone, I froze dead in my tracks. It wasn't the phone; it was the intercom system that *interfaced* with the phone. Someone was at the front gate! Who the hell? Cautiously, I picked up the phone. "Hello?"

"Yo–Bo!" said Bo. "It's me, Bo!"

"Bo!" I said to Bo. "What are you doing here?"

"Let me in. I'm making a personal delivery, Bo."

I took a deep breath, trying to remain calm and trying to keep track of all the Bo-Bos. It could only be good news, I thought. Why else would Bo drive all the way out to Southampton? If it was bad news he would've just called me on the phone–unless, of course, he was one of those people who took joy in seeing another's misery up close and personal. No, Bo was not like that! How could I even think such a thing? He was a true friend, Bo, and he'd proved his loyalty to me a thousand times over. He just wanted to bring me the good news in person.

"Yo–Bo!" snapped Bo. "Are you gonna open the *gate-atation* or what?"

"Yeah, yeah," I said. "I'm sorry, Bo." I punched in the gate code and headed for the door.

A few minutes later we were sitting at my dining-room table, beneath a wrought-iron chandelier that cost a bloody fortune. Resting on the bleached-wood table was a small tape recorder. Bo was yet to reveal the contents of the tape; he was still in the process of explaining how former actress Debbie Starling had given an Academy Award–winning performance, quickly worming her way into the Duchess's confidence.

". . . .and the *onionatation* trick worked like a fucking charm," Bo was saying. "So, Debbie's sneezing and wheezing her little head off, and the tears are streaming down her *face-atation,* as she's telling your wife about how her husband called her this and that and everything else. And, of course, the uh . . . *the Duchess* was very sympathetic to that, because that's how she is with everything." Bo shrugged. "So the two of them bonded before the meeting even got started."

I nodded and scratched my chin thoughtfully. "Huh," I muttered. "That sounds pretty good so far. So what did she say during the meeting?"

Bo shook his head slowly. "It's not what she said *during* the meeting; it's what she said *after* the meeting."

I perked up. "Oh, really? They went for dinner?"

Bo began rubbing his beard. "Drinks," he answered. "You know, like *in vino veritas.*"

"Interesting," I said. "So what *truths* did the *vino* draw out?"

Bo twisted his lips and nodded in resignation. "Well, I think you could stop your house-hunting, Bo. It's not recommended given the, uh, current circumstances."

All at once I felt my heart drop to my stomach. *The Duchess had been deceiving me!* Such underhandedness! Was there no level she wouldn't stoop to? To play me for a house showed a complete lack of ethics on her part.

Bo continued: "You know, I came out here tonight because I look at you as more of a friend than a client, Bo." With that he paused and looked down at the tape recorder, which was no bigger than a deck of playing cards, and then he looked back up. "So I'll make you a deal, Bo: This whole *bugatation* exercise has run about five Gs so far, but if you let me destroy the tape before you listen to it, we'll call it even. I'll pay Debbie out of my own pocket. But if you make me press the play button, then you gotta pay me. It's your call."

With a sinking heart, I looked down at the tape recorder. Christ, it was an evil little instrument! So small it was, so tiny...so very fucking deceptive! It was the bearer of bad news, the bringer of bad karma. "It can't be that bad, Bo, can it?"

Bo shrugged. "Like I said, Bo: *in vino veritas.*"

I shook my head slowly, the saddest of smiles on my face. Then I let out a short chuckle that so much as said, "It serves me right!" And a chuckle that also said, "So this is it: the end of the line, the end of a marriage, the end of all my false hope." My marriage is a coffin, I thought, and this is the final nail in it. I looked Bo in the eye and said, "Play the fucking tape!"

Bo nodded and hit the play button.

All I could hear at first was a low hum and some background noise, then a mumbled exchange with a waiter. Bo said, "I cued it up to the good part. They're in Buckram Stables, about to make a toast. Listen. . . ."

I nodded and put my elbows on the edge of the dining-room table and crossed my arms, one atop the other. Then I rested my troubled brow on them, staring at the evil tape recorder from a side angle. It was all so terrible. I had bugged my own wife–*the mother of my children!* And what had Bo said? A woman's secret thoughts . . .

Just then I heard the Duchess's all-too-happy voice: "Here's to breaking the cycle!" And now the actress's surprisingly believable response: "Yes! To breaking the cycle of codependency!" Then the unmistakable clink of wineglasses.

"Can you believe this shit?" muttered Bo. "I never even heard of this codependency shit before. It's fucking mind-boggling."

I nodded in agreement without lifting my head. Now the Duchess started talking again. She was bitching about me, saying that I had slept with hookers while we were married. Well, what had she expected? She had been my mistress, for Chrissake! She knew what I was up to *well* before she married me–and now she was holding it against me.

All at once I was jerked alert: "Well, I've been having the best sex of my life lately; I'll tell you *that* much! I mean, the last few years with my husband were so boring–you know, the same position over and over again."

Whuh–how could she? She was emasculating me in front of Debbie–a total stranger! Someone in my employ! How could the Duchess say I sucked in bed? I didn't! I used to rock her world! She used to call me her little prince. . . .

Against my better judgment, I snuck a peek at Bo, to gauge his reaction. Was he staring at me? Was he smiling? No. He wasn't. He was staring at the recorder, his face a mask of concentration. He was nodding his head slowly. And gritting his teeth, the way a person does when they're trying to make heads or tails of something. Suddenly he looked up. I opened my mouth, to defend myself against the Duchess's baseless accusations. No words came out. I couldn't think of anything to say. The Duchess had emasculated me in front of Bo too. To deny it would only make me seem guiltier.

Just then Bo smiled and shook his head. "It's all bullshit, Bo! Every wife says her husband sucks in bed. It's par for the fucking course." He shrugged. "But if you happen to get another crack at nailing her, you should take some *Viagratation* before you stick it in; then you'll teach the girl a lesson!" With that he winked and looked back down at the recorder. I rested my brow back in my arms and prepared for more pain.

"Anyway," said the voice on the tape, "I had a little thing going with my personal trainer for a while, and that was pretty good"–*I knew it!*–"but then I got sick of him, so I started dating Michael Bolton. You know him? The singer?"

Debbie's surprised voice: "Yeah, of course! What was *he* like?"

The Duchess's voice: "Oh, he was nice. Very romantic, actually. We spent a weekend together in the Plaza Hotel. We stayed in the Presidential Suite, and he filled the whole room up with fresh flowers." The voice on the tape giggled. "Like I said, he was very romantic."

I looked up at Bo. "That ungrateful bitch!" I snarled. "You know how many times I filled up the Presidential Suite with flowers for her? She forgets that!"

Bo nodded in understanding and then pointed back down at the recorder. "Listen to this, Bo; this is where it gets good." I shook my head in disbelief and looked down at the evil little recorder. Bring on the pain, I thought.

The voice of the Duchess, twisting the knife: "Anyway, there's been some others too: I met a golf pro while I was up in Pennsylvania, learning about codependency, and then I was with one of my old boyfriends for a while, although that was only for old time's sake." Then, much happier: "But now I'm involved with a guy who owns a big garment-center company! I kind of like him, actually, although he's a bit closed off emotionally. I'll have to wait and see."

The voice of the actress: "So you think your husband's gonna buy you the house?"

A suddenly weary Duchess: "Well, I'm still working on him.

He's very slick, so I have to handle him a certain way. See, I know he still wants to get back together with me, so I'm kind of using that to my advantage, you know, hinting that there's still a possibility." A pause, then: "I know it's not the nicest thing to do, but I don't have much of a choice anymore. I won't lead him on any longer than I have to, though; once I get him to buy me the house, I'll file for divorce the next day. Then I can move on with my life. Maybe fall in love with one of the local contractors or an electrician. That would be–"

Bo hit the stop button. "You heard enough, Bo?"

I looked at Bo, speechless. The Duchess had buried me on tape. Yet, of everything she's said, it was the comment about doing it over and over again in the same position that had wounded me most. There had to be some words I could say to Bo to offset that poisonous comment. I racked my brain for them. They didn't exist. I had been officially emasculated. The most important thing was to make sure that Debbie was sworn to secrecy. *What must she think of me!*

"You all right, Bo?" asked Bo.

I nodded slowly. "Yeah, I'm all right. I'm fine." I took a deep breath and forced up a smile. "Anyway, it sounds like she still hasn't made up her mind yet, you know, Bo? Maybe there's still hope, right?" I started chuckling.

Bo smiled warmly. "That's the spirit, Bo. You just gotta laugh it off."

I nodded and smiled sadly, and then I looked around my beautiful home, marveling at its very splendor... and how little it all meant. The happiest I had ever been was with Denise, when we had nothing.

Just then Bo reached across the table and rested his massive hand on my forearm, squeezing it gently. In a dead-serious tone, he said, "Listen to me, Bo, because I'm not gonna bullshit you. What's happened to you over the last six months should happen to no man. There's no sugarcoating it. It sucks. It all sucks." He shook his head slowly. "But you gotta take a deep breath now and pick up the pieces. It's time to be a man. You understand, Bo? To be a man?"

I nodded. "Yeah," I said softly. "I do."

He squeezed my arm tighter now. "No woman can get the best of you, Bo, no wife, no girlfriend, no mistress, no one. Except one. You know who that is, Bo?"

I nodded slowly, fighting back tears now. "Chandler," I said softly.

"That's right, Bo: Chandler. She's the only one who counts now; the rest of them will come and go out of your life. And you owe it to her to stiffen your upper lip and hold your head high, and you owe it to that little son of yours too." Bo smiled nostalgically. "I remember when he was first born and almost died of meningitis. I'll never forget how my heart dropped when Rocco called me that night from the hospital and told me what was going on. I went to church and said a prayer for him that night."

I nodded, wiping a tear from the corner of my eye. "Well, it worked. He's a good kid. He's growing strong."

Bo smiled. "Yes, he is, Bo, and he's gonna keep growing; then he's gonna look to you one day to show him what it means to be a man and to show him that no matter how much shit comes his way, in the end, he can always come out on top." Bo shrugged his broad shoulders. "And that's it, Bo, that's the way it goes. Your kids are your constants; they're the only ones who can keep you going through shit like this.

"Anyway, you're about to find out who your true friends are and who was just along for the ride. Remember, friendships bought with money–"

"–don't last very long," I said.

Bo nodded. "And loyalty bought with money–"

"–isn't loyalty at all," I added.

"Exactly, Bo." And with that he reached down to the tape recorder, hit the eject button, and removed the tape and held it up in the air. Then he said, "As far as I'm concerned, this whole thing never happened." He slipped the tape into his inside suit-jacket pocket. "You don't owe me anything for this, Bo. All I want is your friendship, because, I, for one, am truly your friend. And I always will be."

And I knew he was.

CHAPTER 16

WHEN A MAN LOVES A WOMAN

The next morning I woke up to:

Broooo!–Broooo!–Broooo!... Broooo!–Broooo!–Broooo!

I opened my right eye and, without lifting my head even an inch off the white silk pillowcase, I rolled my neck to the right and made eye contact with the phone of the future—a chrome-plated technological marvel, with two dozen red blinking lights and the world's most annoying ring, the latter of which sounded like a tiny sparrow caught in an electrical wire. The phone was resting on a fabulously expensive end table—part of a matching set, of course.

Broooo!–Broooo!–Broooo!... Broooo!–Broooo!–Broooo!

"Jesus," I muttered. I was so sleepy... couldn't move. My head seemed to weigh a thousand pounds.

Broooo!–Broooo!–Broooo!... Broooo!–Broooo!–Broooo!

Christ! Who was calling at this hour? *The audacity!* I popped upright and took a deep, troubled breath. The white silk comforter was draped over my legs now, covering my loins, and in spite of being alone, my vanity caused me to look down at my bare torso and run my fingers over my abdominal muscles. They felt good; I was in fabulous shape. That was important now, especially if I wanted to attract another Duchess, but it wasn't nearly as important as being rich.

Well, at least I still had my mansion for a while. A shabby-chic mansion could be a very powerful aphrodisiac. I looked around the bedroom. The ceiling was thirty feet above the $150,000 tan and taupe carpet, and my bed was fit for a king. Thick bleached-wood poles, carved to resemble pinecones, rose up at all four corners of the bed, where they supported a canopy of tan and taupe Indonesian silk that matched the carpet perfectly. The Duchess loved her fucking canopies! And she loved her silk too. The mansion had seven bedrooms, and each one had a silk fucking canopy!

Broooo!–Broooo!–Broooo!... Broooo!–Broooo!–Broooo!

Fuck it! I reached over and picked up the chrome-plated phone.

"Hello?" I mumbled, in the sort of overly sleepy tone that implies you've been called at an inappropriate hour.

Alas, what I got in return was the bright and cheery voice of my least favorite codependent. "Rise and shine, sleepyhead!" declared the Duchess. "It's eight-thirty! We have an appointment with the real estate broker in two hours!" Cheery, cheery, cheery!

Why, the impudence! I was speechless! At a complete loss for words! What would she say next, that she was going to wear my favorite perfume today? *Christ!* If I hadn't promised not to blow Debbie's cover, I would be giving the dirty Duchess a piece of my mind right now.

The Duchess, still happy: "Wake up, sleepy-boy! Today's the first day of the rest of your life!" Then: "Why don't you have Gwynne make you some coffee?"

"Gwynne doesn't get here 'til nine," I said tonelessly. "And I'm not in the mood for coffee."

The Duchess, picking up my tone: "Well, *someone* seems awful grumpy this morning! Why don't you open the shades and let some light shine in? It's beautiful outside."

I clenched my teeth in rage and slowly turned my head to the left, to the fabulous taupe shades. Must be twenty feet high, those fucking shades, and they must've cost a fortune! God–how I'd love to have that money right now in *cash*!

Suddenly–a brainstorm! "You know what?" I said happily. "You're right! I could use some light in here. Hold on a second, sweetie," and I leaned over to the end table and grabbed the remote control of the future, which controlled everything in the bedroom, from the shades to the recessed lights to the twelve-foot-high entertainment center just across from the bed, with its forty-inch high-definition TV and $75,000 Fisher stereo system, which included, among other things, a three-hundred-CD disc changer.

First, the shades: Remote in hand, I hit a one-inch LCD square marked SHADES, and just like that, the shades slowly slid open, revealing a pair of twelve-foot-high French doors that opened onto a reddish mahogany deck looking out over the Atlantic. "Ah, light!" I said to the backstabber. "Hold on another second, sweetie," and then I hit a button marked CD SEARCH–causing a new menu to pop up. I punched in the letters *B–O–L–T–O–N*, and an instant later *Michael Bolton's Greatest Hits* popped onto the screen. This was accompanied by a rather annoying picture of him (with his big nose, narrow face, and ridiculous ponytail), along with a list of all seventeen of his ridiculously syrupy love songs, most of which he'd stolen from other, more talented artists and all of which were meant to manipulate the hearts and minds of unsuspecting females.

My teeth were still clenched in rage when I placed my index finger over the song "When a Man Loves a Woman," and pressed it gently. Then I moved my finger to the button marked VOLUME UP, and I pressed that too and held it for a few seconds.

The still-happy Duchess: "What are you doing over there?"

"Nothing," I said, staring at my shabby-chic entertainment center and hearing a few clicks and clacks as the CD changer did its thing. "I'm just putting on some music to start my day."

"Really?" she said, a bit confused. Then: "Okay! I'm heading out to the beach soon. I figured we'd spend the day together."

"Well, before you get in the car, Nadine, I think you should know that I'm having second thoughts about the Hamptons thing. In fact, I think you should stay put for a while in Old Brookville."

Not so happy suddenly: "What are you talking about? I thought we already discussed this."

Just then I heard the opening notes to the song. I took a deep breath, determined not to tip my hand. "Yeah," I said icily, "but you're already set in your ways out there. You know, you've got all your activities lined up–all the Mommy and Me classes, the cooking classes. And I know how much you like having Alex as your personal trainer. Alex..." I paused for a moment, letting the Romanian dirt-ball's name hang in the air. "I couldn't imagine Alex spending an extra hour and a half driving out to the Hamptons. Know what I mean?"

"He doesn't train me anymore," she said nervously.

"Oh, really? What happened?"

"Nothing; we had, uh, a little bit of a falling-out."

Well, that's what happens when you fuck your personal trainer! I thought. But I couldn't just come out and say that, because that would compromise Bo. So I said, "Well, that's what happens when you fuck your personal trainer! You have a falling-out!" *Sorry, Bo!*

"What are you talking about?" she said defensively.

With venom: "Oh, you're gonna deny that you fucked that slime-bucket of a Romanian?"

"I...I didn't."

"Oh, save it, Nadine! I know that smelly fuck was sleeping in my bed. I heard all about it."

Just then I heard the repulsive voice of the ponytailed bastard: *"When a man loves a woman, can't keep his mind on nothin' else."*

I help up the phone to the ceiling for a second–to the 80-watt Bose surround-sound speakers–and then I put it back to my ear and heard the Duchess say, "...you please turn down the music!"

"It's not that loud," I snapped, and I held the phone back up to the speakers again. Then I put it back to my ear and heard her scream, "...with you, *Jordan*! Stop! Why are you doing this?"

"Doing *what*?" I asked innocently. "Blasting Michael Bolton or talking about the Romanian slimeball? Which one?"

Calm panic: "Who's telling you all this?"

With a hiss: "Oh, please, Nadine! Who do you think you're dealing with? I've known about this shit for months!"

The Duchess struck back: "Yeah–well–who the fuck are *you* to throw stones? Like you've been a fucking angel out there? You slept with that disgusting Jewish girl who gave you all the blow jobs!" A moment of silence, then the Duchess continued, "I also know about all those crazy Russian girls. You'll never change! You're a whoremonger!"

"Yeah, you're right," I snarled, "and you're a fucking codependent, who fucks her fellow codependents–like that washed-up golf pro from Pennsylvania. What did he offer you: free golf lessons with every lay?"

The Duchess, incredulous: "I... I don't know what you're talking about."

Through clenched teeth: "I'll never forgive you for what you did, Nadine. You left me on the courthouse steps, you fucking bitch!"

Right back at me: "And you kicked me down the stairs, you fucking drug addict! I hope you die in jail!"

"Oh, yeah?" I snapped. "Well, I hope you die of codependency!" And I slammed down the phone. "Fucking whore!" I muttered to the phone of the future. I took a deep breath and tried to calm myself. Then the phone rang: *Broooo!–Broooo!* I picked it up in a millisecond: "What the fuck do you want *now*?"

"Well, fuck you too!" snapped my attorney. "What, are you having a bad morning over there?"

"Oh, hey, Greg!" I said happily. "What's going on?"

"Nothing," he replied. "What's going on with *you*?"

I thought about that for a second. "Oh, nothing really. Just a little spat with my soon-to-be ex-wife."

"I see," said Magnum. "And can I ask why you're blasting Michael Bolton at eight-thirty in the morning? The guy sucks!"

"Oh, shit! Hold on a second." I pressed pause on the remote control. "Sorry about that. I'm not a Michael Bolton fan; trust me. In fact, I'm gonna toss that fucking CD right in the microwave, just as soon as I get off the phone with you."

"And why is that?" asked my attorney.

"Is this conversation privileged?"

"All our conversations are privileged."

"Fair enough," I said. "Well, I just found out that the Duchess was fucking Michael Bolton. Can you imagine?"

"Really?" said Magnum. "The guy's a loser! She could do better."

"Oh, thanks a lot, Greg. Maybe you're not catching my drift here: Michael–Fucking–Bolton was porking my wife!"

"While you were together?"

"No! Not while we were married! Afterward!"

"So what are you so upset about? You haven't exactly been sitting on your hands out there. Anyway, can you come into the city today?"

"Why? Did something bad happen?"

"I wouldn't say bad," he replied, "but it's not the *best* news in the world. I worked out your deal with Joel."

"How long can I keep the houses for?" I asked quickly.

"Well, it's different for you and Nadine," he answered cautiously. "But I'd rather discuss it in person. Take a ride into the city, and we'll order up some sandwiches and have a working lunch. I'd like Nick to be a part of this too."

I thought for a moment, deciding whether or not to press for more details, but then he said, "And I have some good news for you too, and it concerns your friend Joel. So keep your chin up and I'll see you in a few hours, okay?"

I smiled into the phone. "You got it!" I said heartily. "I'll be there by noon." And I hung up the phone of the future, knowing that Magnum could mean only one thing: The Bastard was leaving the U.S. Attorney's Office.

My towering attorney was sitting behind his desk, the starchy Yaleman was sitting to my right, and I was sitting directly across from Magnum at *just* the right angle to sneak peeks at a photograph of him and Judge Gleeson, which had been taken when they worked together at the U.S. Attorney's Office. And as the three of us engaged in idle chatter about the deficiencies in our golf swings, I found myself tuning in and out–focusing on the picture of Judge Gleeson instead and praying that when the time came he would remember that Magnum and he were good friends.

"...causes me to shank the ball," Magnum was now saying. "That's why I keep my right elbow close to my hip." He shrugged knowingly. "It's the key to any good golf swing."

Who gives a shit! I thought. "Yeah, that's true," I said, and *can we please get down to my case, for Chrissake?*

The Yale-man chimed in. "It is," he added, "but that's not your problem, Greg. It's your grip. It's much too weak; that's why you keep hitting off the hozzle." He shrugged. "It's simple geometry, really. When you cut across..."

Oh, Jesus Christ! Save me! I tuned out again. I had been in their office for fifteen minutes, and so far so good. As I'd suspected, the Bastard was planning to leave the U.S. Attorney's Office. Just when, Magnum wasn't so sure, although he'd heard from "reliable sources" that the Bastard would be gone before the year was out. The *good* news was, that meant someone else would be writing my 5K letter, and, chances were, they'd be more benevolent than the Bastard.

The bad news, however, was that the Bastard would want my cooperation made public before he resigned. There were a multitude of reasons for this, Magnum explained, not the least of which was that my guilty plea (and subsequent cooperation) was a big-time feather in the Bastard's cap, which he would use to secure a partnership at a major law firm. In addition, there was an emotional component involved, inasmuch as the Bastard wanted his fifteen minutes of fame, where he would get to hold a press conference and say: "Not only have I brought the Wolf of Wall Street to justice, but I've also turned him into a world-class rat—thereby making unprecedented leaps toward the eradication of small-cap securities fraud in America."

What the Bastard wouldn't say, however, was that small-cap securities fraud was more prevalent *now* than in Stratton's heyday. In fact, with the proliferation of the Internet, stock scams had been elevated to an entirely new level, and God only knew how many millions were being lost each day as a result of puffed-up e-mails, fraudulent message boards, and dot-com mania.

Still, there was no denying that the Bastard's departure was good news for me, so the three of us had felt entitled to spend the last few minutes congratulating ourselves. My lawyers seemed to be chalking it up to some clever legal strategy on their part, although I was convinced that it had more to do with my long-term value as a rat exceeding the Bastard's patience to work for the federal government at near slave wages. Whatever the case, this information was strictly on the QT, and I was not to breathe a word of it to anyone.

Now the Yale-man was saying, "...inside-out swing plane, above everything. That's *my* secret for keeping the ball in the short grass." He offered Magnum and me a single nod, to which Magnum nodded back accordingly.

I smiled and said, "You know, my problem with this conversation is that all three of us suck in golf"–I raised my chin toward Magnum–"especially you, Greg. So, if you don't mind, I would appreciate it if you guys would stop fucking torturing me and tell me when I have to forfeit my houses."

My towering attorney smiled. "Of course: *Your* house has to be forfeited on January first, and Nadine's the following June."

"That sucks," I said. "What happened to four years from now?"

Magnum shrugged. "Like I've always said, Joel is not an easy person to deal with–especially now, while he's getting ready to leave the U.S. Attorney's Office. He wants to extract as much blood as possible before he departs."

The Yale-man said, "In fact, things were even bleaker yesterday."

"Indeed," added Magnum. "As of yesterday morning, Joel wanted Nadine to forfeit the Old Brookville house on the same date as you, but we convinced him to back off because of the children. So, in that sense, it was somewhat of a victory."

"Yeah," I said sarcastically, "a victory. And it *still* sucks!" I took a deep, troubled breath and let it out slowly. "And how much money do I get to keep?"

"Eight hundred thousand dollars," replied Magnum, "plus you each get to keep a car, your furniture, and all your personal possessions, and you get to keep the IOUs you listed. Are any of them collectible?"

I took a moment to run them through my mind. There were three, the biggest of which was with Elliot Lavigne, who owed me $2 million. Back in the day, Elliot had been my primary rathole, kicking me back millions of dollars in cash. At the time he had been a garment-center legend, ascending to the presidency of Perry Ellis while still in his thirties. But he'd also been a world-class drug addict, a degenerate gambler, and a serial whoremonger (which was why we'd gotten along so well), and ultimately he had lost everything, including his job. We hadn't spoken since I'd gotten sober, and there was no way, I knew, he could ever pay me back. He was completely broke.

The second biggest IOU was Wigwam's, which was a quarter of a million dollars. Alas, Wigwam was even broker than Elliot, and there was no chance there either. And then there was Dr. David Schlesinger, a Long Island ophthalmologist, who'd married the Duchess's childhood friend Donna. David was a pretty good guy, although Donna was, for the most part, a wench. Nevertheless, he *could* pay me back, and I had no doubt that he would. After all, I had lent him $120,000 to start his own medical practice, and now he was raking it in.

Still, the greatest shame in all this was Elliot Lavigne. If he still had money he would *definitely* pay me back! We'd been like blood brothers, the two of us. I had even saved his life once, after he almost drowned in my pool. Ironically, OCD and the Bastard had never shown much interest in Elliot, despite the cash kickbacks. But that was fine with me; if they didn't press the issue, I wasn't about to bring it up.

I said, "I think one of them is; but it's only for a hundred twenty thousand dollars. The rest are worthless. Anyway, it doesn't really matter. At the rate I burn through money, I'll be broke in six months either way."

"Well, you gotta cut back," snapped Magnum. "And you gotta tell Nadine to cut back too! This is no joke, Jordan. It's time to hunker down."

I shook my head no. "I'm not breathing a word of this to Nadine. As much as I hate her, I don't want to worry her. Anyway, I have more than a year to figure out where she and the kids are gonna live, and, believe me, by hook or by crook I'll make sure it's somewhere beautiful."

Magnum pursed his lips and nodded, as if he were an oncologist about to give a patient a terminal diagnosis. "Well, unfortunately, you're gonna have to let her know a little bit sooner than you'd like. You see, Joel wants her to sign off on this."

"Well, that sucks too!" I snapped. "In fact, everything about today sucks!" I shook my head in disgust. "When do I gotta tell her?"

With a hint of a smile: "Today."

When I first called the Duchess and told her that I needed to stop by to talk to her about something, I was shocked that she didn't just tell me to go fuck myself. She was a Brooklyn girl, after all, and given the nature of our last conversation, to tell me to go fuck myself was the Brooklyn equivalent of saying, "I think it would be best if we communicated through our lawyers for a while." And then, a few hours later, when I walked through the front door at a little before five and the kids came running into my arms, screaming, "Daddy's here! Daddy's here!" I was even more shocked at how genuinely happy the Duchess seemed over our children's love for me.

She was a complicated woman, and despite all my grudges and resentments, there was a part of me that would always be in awe of her. She had educated herself, improved herself, and, for better or worse, had aspired for perfection in all aspects of her life. In many ways, she was everything I could never be: perfectly gorgeous, utterly self-confident, and shrouded by an impenetrable cloak of emotional armor that protected her from hurt; in other ways, I was everything *she* could never be: street-smart, financially self-sufficient, and emotionally vulnerable to a fault.

Perhaps in a different time and place we could have made beautiful music together, for, in the end, it wasn't a lack of love that had gotten the best of us but all that had preyed upon it—the money, the drugs, the jet-set lifestyle, the false friends. And, of course, there was Stratton, the poison tree from which only poison fruit could grow, including the fruit of our marriage. Only the children had made it out unscathed, a fact for which I would always thank God.

We were sitting at the kitchen table, and I had just finished giving her all the horrific details about the forefeitures–the dates, the amounts, and everything else.

Her response shocked me.

"I'm really sorry," she said calmly. "I know how much that beach house meant to you. Where are you gonna live now?"

I stared at her, astonished. Could she really be serious? I mean, after everything I'd just told her, she was worried about where I was going to live? What about where *she* was going to live? And what about the *kids*?

I was about to lace into her when suddenly it hit me: It wasn't irony; she had simply walked through life's raindrops for so long that she assumed she always would. Everything would end up okay for her, she knew, and, odd as it seemed, I knew she was right.

I forced a smile and said, "Don't worry about me, Nae, I'll be fine. And don't worry about yourself and the kids either." I looked her dead in the eye. "You'll always be taken care of–no matter what."

She nodded in understanding, although just what I'd meant by that I don't think either of us knew. With the utmost sincerity, she said, "I know you'll take care of us the best you can. Do you know how long you'll have to go away for?"

"I'm still not sure," I said. "Joel is leaving the U.S. Attorney's Office, which is a good thing for me, but I'll still have to do a few years, I'm sure." I shrugged my shoulders, trying to make light of it. "And this is the end of the line, Nae: You're gonna move on with your life and I'm going to fucking jail." I smiled and winked. "Feel like changing places with me?"

"Nope!" she answered, with a few exaggerated headshakes. "But I promise you that the kids will always know that their father is a good man." She reached over and grabbed my hand, the way a friend would. "Your kids will always love you, Jordan, and they'll be waiting for you the second you get out."

I squeezed her hand gently, and then I rose from my chair and walked over to a floor-to-ceiling window at the back of the room. I leaned my shoulder against it and took a moment to relish the beauty of my property. It was gorgeous this time of year. The lawn was as green as any rain forest, and the pond and waterfall looked like a painting. How different things could have worked out. If only I would've done things right.

After a few seconds the Duchess joined me by the window and stared out. "It's beautiful," she said. "Isn't it?"

"Yeah, it is. It's hard to believe another family's gonna live here one day, you know?"

She nodded but said nothing.

Suddenly a pleasant memory: "Hey–remember what we did the day we went to contract on this house?"

She started giggling. "Yeah! We snuck onto the property and had sex in the backyard!"

"Exactly!" I said, laughing. "Those were some funny days back then, right?"

"Yeah, but they weren't my favorite."

I looked at her, surprised. "Oh, really? Which were?"

"The first days," she answered casually. "In that tiny apartment in the city. I loved you *so* much back then. If you only knew, Jordan. But you never let yourself trust me, because of how rich you were when we met." She paused for a moment, as if searching for the right words. "I want you to know that I was always faithful to you when we were together. I never cheated on you even once! And, well, what happened this morning on the phone"–she stopped and shook her head quickly, as if she was disgusted with herself–"well, it was a bad showing on my part, and I'm sorry for it."

"So am I," I said quickly. "It was a bad showing on my part too."

She nodded. "And I want you to know that I wasn't trying to manipulate you with the Hamptons." *Yeah, right!* "I mean, yeah, maybe at the end I was, but not at the beginning. When I first came up with the idea, I thought there was a chance for us." She paused for a moment. "But then over the last few weeks, well, I knew there wasn't. Too much had happened: too much hurt, too much pain, too many bad memories. I'm not gonna offer you any cheap clichés here, but I think we definitely broke the record for insane relationships, you know?"

I smiled sadly, knowing she was right. "Yeah, I guess we did," I said, "but it was definitely fun for a while, at least in the beginning." I perked up my tone. "Anyway, we got two great kids out of the deal, and I'll always love you for that." I offered her my hand, palm upward, as if she were truly a Duchess. "So, come on, Duchess; why don't we go upstairs and give the kids a kiss? Then I'll get going." She smiled, then took my hand and off we went–out of the kitchen, through the dining room, through the grand marble entryway, and then up the sumptuous spiral staircase that led to the mansion's second floor.

When we reached the top of the stairs, I turned east, toward the kids' rooms, and she turned west, toward the master bedroom. We were still holding hands, so we looked like two sailors leaning into opposing winds. I smiled playfully. "What are you doing?" I asked.

She just stared at me, with her lips compressed into a tight line, as if she were a child thinking about doing something naughty. Then she gave her head a tiny jerk in the direction of the bedroom. "Come inside with me," she said mischievously.

My eyes popped opened like a pair of umbrellas. "*What?* You want to make love to me *now*, after I just told you I lost the houses?"

She nodded eagerly. "Yeah, it's the perfect time. I was never really in it for the money! It just seemed . . ." I narrowed my eyes suspiciously; she backtracked. "Okay, I won't deny that the money definitely helped, but I could have married a lot of rich guys. I chose you because you were *cute*. And you still *are* cute!" She winked. "So, come on! Let's do it one last time before we get divorced, okay?"

"You lead, I follow!" I said happily, and a second later the bedroom door was slamming behind us and we were jumping onto the fabulous white silk comforter, with its thousands of tiny pearls.

We began kissing deeply. *Such wanton passion! Such sexual ferocity! Like never before!* The Duchess smelled so good it seemed almost impossible. I *wanted* this woman, to literally *possess* her, for all eternity.

"I love you," I groaned.

"I'll always love you too," she groaned back.

Bitch! I thought. "Me too," I said lovingly, and we began wriggling out of our shirts, and–*yes*–the Duchess was braless! And I pushed my bare nipples against her bare nipples and my bare stomach against her bare stomach–*and such softness I felt! Such heat!* The Duchess was a raging inferno! Overcome by passion! *Couldn't even think straight!*

Suddenly she broke off our kiss and looked at me nervously. Through tiny pants, she muttered, "I hope"–*pant, pant*–"you don't think"–*pant, pant*–"you're sleeping over tonight." *Pant, pant.* "I just can't"–*pant, pant*–"bear the thought"–*pant, pant*–"of waking up to you tomorrow morning!" *Pant, pant.*

Bitch! I thought. "Of course not." *Pant, pant.* "I have a meeting in Southampton"–*pant, pant*–"first thing in the morning!" *Pant, pant.*

"Oh, good!" she muttered. "Make love to me"–*pant, pant.*

And off came our pants, and the Duchess's legs–*perfection!* So soft they were! So supple! Like never before! Those luscious thighs, those slender ankles, *those heavenly hips*! My nervous system was on sensory overload, and I loved it.

"Kiss me softly," moaned the Duchess. "The way you used to..."

Yes, I thought, I would kiss her softly, just the way I used to, and then I would make love to her, just the way I used to, with myself on top and her luscious legs clamped together, for added friction. The Duchess loved it that way!

With great tenderness, I placed my hands on her cheeks and put my lips to her lips, and I kissed her softly, breathing in every last molecule of her. Her lips smelled utterly delicious, utterly *frisky*–just like they used to!

So we just lay there, kissing, for what seemed like a very long time.

Finally I broke off our kiss and looked my gorgeous Duchess in her fabulous blue eyes and decided to give it one last college try. "I still love you," I said softly, praying that she would return my words.

She nodded quickly. "I love you too," she said. "Now make love to me, sweetie!"

She still loved me!

Then–a shock, as she said, "Wait a second: Let me turn around so we can do it from behind." Faster than it seemed possible, the Duchess had wriggled out from beneath me and was crouching on her knees now, with her back to me. Then she crossed her arms over her breasts and arched her back, like a cat, pushing her butt out. She said urgently, "Hurry up and grab my arms and hug me from behind!"

Bitch! I thought. *She had learned a new trick in my absence!* Of all the insults! Who had taught her this . . . doggie-style cross-armed maneuver? Was it the ponytailed bastard? Or the sleazoid golf pro? Or even *worse*—the Romanian slime-bucket?

Just then she swung her blond head around and stared at me quizzically. "What are you waiting for?" *Pant, pant.* "Take me now or lose me forever!"

I stared back at her, speechless.

She smiled coyly. "Oh, come on, silly! You'll like it this way!"

Bitch! I thought. And then I smiled.

We ended up making passionate love that Thursday evening, and, in retrospect, I think we both knew it would be for the last time. Just why it had to happen I would never know, although I suspected it had something to do with closure, which both of us desperately needed. We had been to hell and back together, and now it was time to move on. In some way, I knew, we would always love each other.

BOOK III

CHAPTER 17

THE ART OF SELF-DESTRUCTION

Three Months Later

We were somewhere over Staten Island near the New Jersey border when it first hit me that I wouldn't be making it back to Southampton tonight for curfew. I remember reaching down to my left leg and lifting up the hem of my tan gabardine trousers and saying something like, "Uh, I haven't been totally honest with you, Kiley. This thing on my ankle isn't really a beeper–" and then suddenly I heard this horrific wailing sound and the pilots up front were pointing nervously at the orange lights on the instrument panel of the Sikorsky S-76 helicopter, which was screaming westward at a hundred forty knots with a tail wind to Atlantic City.

Then the wailing stopped. Kiley was sitting to my left, seat-belted to one of the Sikorsky's sumptuous tan leather seats, and she looked on the verge of tears. "I–I've never been in a helicopter before," mumbled Kiley, wearing a $2,000 red silk minidress that I'd just purchased at a trendy clothing store in Southampton. "Is it supposed to make noises like that?"

"Yeah," I said casually, "it happens all the time." I had just met

Kiley a few hours ago, so I hardly knew anything about her—other than that she was twenty-two years old, had been raised in Vancouver, British Columbia, and had come to New York to pursue a modeling career, only to have it cut short by an eating disorder, which caused her weight to balloon up and down thirty pounds in either direction. Today she was tipping the scales at a buck-thirty, which was a bit too fleshy for a five-foot-eight-inch model, so Kiley was having trouble finding work. Nevertheless, she was still gorgeous, with perfectly chiseled features, honey-colored skin, full lips, high cheekbones, and liquid brown eyes shaped like almonds.

All at once the helicopter began executing a sharp right turn and going into a steep dive. Kiley's slanted eyes popped open. "Oh, my God!" she screamed. "What's wrong *now*? Why are we going down?"

I grabbed her hand reassuringly. "I'm not sure," I said calmly, but what I didn't say was, "Things like this just tend to happen to me. You know, things you usually see only in the movies—like crashed planes, crashed cars, sunken yachts, exploding kitchens, helicopters that need to be pushed into the ocean to make room for air-to-sea rescues—but have no fear, Kiley, because I always seem to make it out alive!"

Just then the copilot turned around in his seat and slid back a thin Plexiglas partition that separated the orange-glowing cockpit from the passenger cabin. With a confident smile, he poked his nose through the slot and said, "We're having some mechanical problems, so we need to make an emergency landing at Teterboro." He winked at Kiley. "No worries, young lady. Teterboro is only a few miles away. We'll be *just* fine." Then he slid the partition closed and turned back around in his seat and started saying something to the pilot.

I looked at Kiley—who up until now had been fairly beaming—and every last drop of color had disappeared from her fabulous skin. So I put my hand on her bare shoulder and said, "Relax, Kiley; I've been through this before and it always ends up okay." I squeezed her hand again. "Besides, you're only twenty-two years old, and that's no age for a young girl to die!"

She shook her head sadly. "But I *lied* to you! I'm only seventeen!" And that's when I knew I was fucked.

I was pretty sure that the age for statutory rape differed by state, so as the Sikorsky made its descent into Teterboro Airport, I found myself wondering which state would have jurisdiction over me if I decided to violate Kiley: New York or New Jersey? In point of fact, we had taken off from Southampton, which was in New York, and the legal age there was seventeen, but we were heading to Atlantic City, which was in New Jersey, where the legal age was . . . I wasn't sure. And that was my problem, because it was there, in a glitzy hospitality suite in Trump Castle Casino, where I was planning to do the evil deed. So what was Jersey's legal age? I wondered.

Obviously this wasn't the sort of question I could just come out and ask the pilots, especially with Kiley right next to me. Upon closer inspection, Kiley now appeared to be in the latter stages of puberty. In fact, that thin coating of fat that I had previously attributed to an eating disorder was now giving off the troubling whiff of baby fat, belonging to a still-blossoming teenager.

Still, none of this was my fault, because when I first laid eyes on Kiley she was standing naked in one of my downstairs showers, and she had hair in all the right places, as well as a set of perky C-cups that looked old enough to vote. And she wasn't even alone! Standing right next to her was *another* naked girl—this one a blue-eyed blonde named Lisa, who, like Kiley, also looked old enough to vote—and the two of them were engaged in a passionate kiss, relishing the final moments of an Ecstasy binge.

Still, the scene wasn't as strange as it seemed—two young models whom I'd never met before, sneaking into my house to take a shower together—because, by mid-July, it was common knowledge in the Hamptons that there was this fabulous house on Meadow Lane where any young model could show up, flash a concupiscent smile, and stay as long as she desired. And while I would be the first to admit that this sort of model-mongering behavior was utterly detestable, I figured with my life on the verge of implosion, I might as well go out with a bang!

So that was how I had decided to pass my final summer on Meadow Lane: model-mongering while the Duchess and I split the kids on alternating weekends.

Chandler, being a daddy's girl, loved the action, although what she enjoyed most was torturing the young models that her daddy had hooked up with–assuring them that they meant absolutely nothing to him and that any restaurant he took them to or any clothing store he bought them a dress in was the same restaurant or store that he'd taken a dozen other girls just like them. Chandler's point being: *You're a worthless slut, and someone younger and more beautiful than you will be replacing you next week.*

Carter, on the other hand, couldn't have cared less. He was too busy passing his summer in the outdoor Jacuzzi, which, in Carter-speak, was an *outdone Hacuddi.* And when he wasn't there, he was in the TV room, watching Power Rangers videos, as half-naked models sat next to him and rubbed his bare belly and told him they would do whatever he pleased if he would just lend them his eyelashes for a photo shoot. One day, I knew, Carter would be very upset when he found out that he had waved off all these young beauties because they had interrupted the flow of his beloved Power Rangers videos.

On a separate note, it was somewhere in late July when I began hearing about someone named John. Chandler had brought the name up first, describing him as "Mommy's new friend from California." John. John. At first I didn't think much of this, although a little voice inside my head said, "This could be trouble." Not the Duchess having a boyfriend–I was fine with that. What I wasn't fine with, though, was that he lived on the other side of the country. After all, if she were to fall in love with him, she might want to move there.

I didn't know too much about this guy, other than that he was a bit older than me, he was very wealthy (*gee, what a surprise*), and he owned a large garment-center company in Los Angeles that manufactured children's clothes. I had resisted the urge to have Bo do his thing–deciding, instead, to leave well enough alone. The way I figured it, the Duchess had been doing her fair share of dating this summer, so the chances of her falling in love with John were slim.

The only thing troubling me as of late—besides the fact that I was burning through cash faster than a Latin American country—was how doggedly OCD was now pursuing the Chef. In fact, I had been to New Jersey two times in the last four weeks, trying to get the Chef to discuss our past dealings on tape. But both times he had refused. Yet OCD was certain that eventually he would. He was a born crook, reasoned OCD, and he wouldn't be able to resist the temptation forever.

Ironically, it was because of those two recent trips to New Jersey that I had been predisposed to Kiley's idea of going to Atlantic City. It was around eleven this morning, as I was cooking her and Lisa breakfast, when Kiley had her brainstorm: "Would you take me to Atlantic City one day and teach me how to gamble?" Complicating matters was the fact that I found Kiley wildy attractive, and not just her looks but her personality too. She was bubbly and vivacious—oozing a certain childlike innocence that, at the time, I had chalked up to her Canadian upbringing, rather than the fact that she was still a child.

"So you've never been to Atlantic City before?" I said to her.

"Nooo," she replied innocently. "Would you take me there?"

In retrospect, I remember thinking that her tone was that of a young child asking her grandpa if he would be willing to take her to the zoo one day. When I asked Kiley how old she was, and she said, "I'm twenty-two; how 'bout you?" I was inclined to believe her. And that was when I went about calculating the risks of taking an unapproved helicopter trip to Atlantic City while under house arrest.

In the end, I had it narrowed down to two distinct risks: first, leaving New York State without approval from my pretrial-services officer (my PO), and second, the possibility of getting stuck in Atlantic City and violating my twelve o'clock curfew. As to the actual gambling, I wasn't so concerned, because gambling wasn't illegal. I wasn't too concerned that I would have to bring along $50,000 in cash to convince Donald Trump to dispatch a helicopter either. After all, I had twice that much in my bedroom safe, which, by sheer coincidence, happened to be the very cash that I was supposed to have forked over to the government as part of my forfeiture (they simply hadn't gotten around to picking it up yet). So what was the harm, I figured, if I just borrowed a few dollars from them?

None, I thought; so I called the casino, ordered the helicopter, took Kiley clothes shopping, and then took a short-term loan from the federal government and headed for the heliport.

Now, however, six hours later, I was stranded at Teterboro, in a dilapidated hangar, with an underage girl, and about to break curfew. Being in Jersey, I figured, was the least of my crimes.

"Does this mean we're not going?" chirped Kiley.

I looked at my watch and shook my head gravely. "I don't know, Kiley. It's nine o'clock already, and I'm supposed to be home by midnight."

With a pout: "That's sad."

"Yeah, it is," I agreed with a sympathetic nod, and then I thought for a moment, focusing on the fact that my curfew wasn't *really* a curfew. Or was it? Well, technically it was, but on a practical level it wasn't, especially on a Sunday evening where a harmless violation (like this) would likely slip through the cracks. Yes, perhaps the monitoring company would place a call to Patrick Mancini, my PO, but Pat was a pretty decent guy, and he would just assume that the bracelet had malfunctioned. I mean, the thing was always malfunctioning, wasn't it? Yes, it most certainly was, and, besides, Pat *knew* I wasn't a flight risk, didn't he? Yes, he most certainly did, and he was well aware that I *was* a cooperating witness with the federal government (on the side of righteousness).

Just then the pilot walked over, smiling. "It's only a fuel gauge," he said happily. "The good news is that we should have it fixed within twenty minutes."

Kiley grabbed my hand and started shaking it up and down, as if to say, "Yippee! Yippee! Now we can go to Atlantic City!"

"And what's the bad news?" I said, knowingly.

The pilot shrugged. "Well, we got a late start tonight, so the copilot and I are out of duty time. You have to wait for two fresh pilots to come. They'll be here in about an hour."

Kiley looked at me, confused. "What does that mean?" she asked sadly.

What I felt like saying was: "It means that this is what happens when you travel with the former Wolf of Wall Street. Anything that can go wrong *will* go wrong!" But instead I said, "It means that we're stranded here for a while."

Another pout: "So we're not gonna go now?"

I looked at Kiley and shrugged. "Let me think for a second." I ran the scenario through my mind again. Well, obviously I couldn't sleep with Kiley; she was just too young. But, on the other hand, I was a very good gambler, so perhaps I could win a few bucks! "Is there a phone around here?" I asked the pilot.

He pointed his finger in the direction of a wall phone.

"Thanks," I said, and a second later I was leaving a message on Pat Mancini's voice mail–explaining that I was stuck in "the city," without saying *which* city, and that I would be back either late tonight or early tomorrow morning. Then I hung up the phone and stared at it for a second, wondering if I had just made a big mistake. *No!* I thought. Patrick had his hands full with murderers and rapists, and I had already made the decision not to have sex with Kiley. And, with that thought, I walked back to Kiley and offered her an avuncular smile. "All right, honey, we're going!"

"*Yehhhh!*" she screamed, and that was that.

There was no denying that Donald Trump sported the worst hairdo this side of the Iron Curtain, but the bastard sure knew how to make money! In Atlantic City, he owned three casinos: Trump Plaza, the Taj Mahal, and Trump Castle. I preferred the Castle because it had a heliport on the roof, which allowed for quick entrances and exits. And that's important in a town like Atlantic City, where the sheer decadence of it can throw a down-and-out gambler into an emotional tailspin when he's already on the verge of jumping out a window.

But something was bothering me now.

I unbuckled my seat belt and leaned forward and slid open the Plexiglas. "Excuse me," I said to the evening's second copilot, pointing to the roof of the Castle as it grew smaller in the distance. "Why aren't we landing on the roof tonight?"

The pilot shrugged. "I'm not sure," he replied. "We were told to land on the pier. That's all I know."

"Hmmm," I muttered. "Maybe the roof is closed for repairs."

"Not that I know of," answered the copilot, and a few minutes later Kiley and I were sitting in the back of an electric golf cart, with a driver from Trump Plaza behind the wheel. Sitting next to the driver was a sharply dressed casino host, also from Trump Plaza. He had a terrific shock of gray hair and a slick demeanor. I leaned forward and said to him, "I don't get it: When I called information this afternoon, I specifically asked for the number for Trump Castle."

He smiled a toothy smile. "Well, they must've made a mistake; it happens all the time. Anyway, we're *all* part of the Trump family, right?"

"Is everything okay?" asked Kiley. "You seem upset."

I grabbed her hand and held it. "No, everything is fine, sweetie. It's just a slight mix-up. It's par for the course when you travel with me."

Kiley giggled like a schoolgirl.

"By the way," said the sleazy casino host, "I saw your old friend Elliot Lavigne down here. He was knocking 'em dead at the tables!"

"You mean *gambling*?" I said incredulously.

"Yeah; why are you so surprised? He *is* a compulsive gambler, no?"

I nodded slowly. "Yeah, of course he is. But last I heard he was broke."

The host shook his head and smiled. "Not anymore!" he said knowingly. "He's making millions again. He's got some hip-hop line called uh, Fat Farm, or maybe Fubu."

Kiley, the budding fashionista: "Oh! I know Phat Farm!"

I looked at Kiley and couldn't resist: "Why've you been to a fat farm?"

She released my hand and smacked me in the shoulder. "It's not that kind of fat farm, wise guy! The *fat* is spelled *P-H-A-T*. And it's slang, for cool or good-looking. You know, like you'd say, 'That girl is *phat*!' or 'This casino is *phat*!'"

"I think she's right," said the casino host.

"I think so too," I agreed, and I smiled at Kiley, who was fairly beaming. Then she said, "Who's Elliot Lavigne?"

The casino host and I exchanged a look. "Oh, he's just an old friend of mine," I said casually–*who happens to owe me two million fucking dollars, which I can now collect!* "He's kind of a colorful guy."

"Oh," said a clueless Kiley. "He sounds very nice."

With that, the host and I exchanged another look, and five minutes later Kiley and I were walking through the casino arm in arm, like two young lovers. She was looking this way and that, staring at all the gaming tables and slot machines and mirrors and strobe lights, with the sort of awestruck expression that you would normally find on the face of a five-year-old girl from Dubuque, Iowa, who was walking through Times Square for the first time.

With a confident gait, I led her to a craps table.

There were six people surrounding it, all bearing the desperate expression of craps degenerates. "Watch this," I said to Kiley, and with a devilish smile and a knowing wink I opened my blue Nike gym bag and poured out $50,000 in cash on the craps table. Then I looked up at the towering Box-man, a six-and-a-half-footer with a handlebar mustache that seemed to defy gravity, and I said, "Chips, please!"

There was a moment of silence while the rest of the table looked on, astonished. *Oh, yes! The Wolf was back! And wait until they see him gamble!* Ohhh . . . I was good, all right! Like James-fucking-Bond!

The towering Box-man smiled and said, "Give Mr. Belfort twenty thousand dollars to play with while we count him out." And just like that I was handed twenty thousand in chips.

Kiley seemed impressed. "How do they know you?" she whispered.

Oh, please! I thought. Everyone knows me in these parts! I used to be the Wolf of Wall Street, for Chrissake! "That's nothing," I said confidently. "Watch me take these bastards to the cleaner's!" And I quickly started gambling.

Five minutes later, most of my chips were gone and Kiley was saying, "Why do they keep taking your chips away?"

I shook my head sadly, as I stared at $18,000 of the government's money now being stacked on the wrong side of the craps table. "I'm having a bad run," I mumbled. "I'll have to get even with the other thirty."

Just then the towering Box-man walked over holding a clipboard. "Sign here, Mr. B." And he handed me the clipboard and then a pen.

With a sinking heart, I signed a $50,000 chit, which looked like a certified bank check. Then I took a deep breath and handed it back to him. The Box-man nodded a single time. "I just need a copy of your driver's license," he added, "and you're good to go."

"No problem," and I reached into my back pocket and... "Eh, shit!" I muttered. "I forgot my damn license." I looked up at the Box-man and smiled. "I'm sure you guys got a copy on file, right?"

He shook his head. "Actually, we don't, Mr. B. You never gambled here before."

"Hmmm," I mumbled, "you're right. Let me think... How about calling the Castle and have *them* fax over my license? That should do the trick, no?" I looked over at Kiley and winked. The Wolf of Wall Street was a *master* at working through problems!

Alas, the Box-man began shaking his head again. "It doesn't work that way. Once you show ten thousand in cash, we need to see ID. That's the law."

I cocked my head to the side and said, "So let me get this straight: You take fifty thousand of *my* cash, you count it, you give me chips, you let me gamble away twenty grand, and now you won't give me a chance to win my money back?"

The Box-man shrugged. "That's about the size of it, Mr. B."

Mr. B? *Mr. B!* What a fucking mockery! If this guy weren't twice my size, I would sock him one–right in that obnoxious fucking mustache! I took a deep breath and said, "All right, can I speak to your boss, please? There's gotta be some way to resolve this."

"Absolutely!" said the Box-man, happy to pass the buck.

Five minutes later, not only was his boss there but he had five other Suits accompanying him, and they all looked like they belonged in the Corleone crime family. The Suits turned out to be very nice, very helpful, and very patient, but after a great deal of chin-scratching, the Suit of all Suits—namely, the shift manager—finally said to me, "I'm sorry, Mr. B, but there's nothing I can do, other than send a few bottles of champagne up to your suite for you and the pretty young lady to enjoy." He winked.

"All right. I'll just take my chips and cash out." I looked over at Kiley. "Come on, sweetheart, it's time to go now."

"Okay," she said, oblivious. "Where are we going?"

With a demented smile: "First we're going to cash out, and then we're flying home." I looked at the shift manager. "Will you do me a favor and call the chopper for us?"

"It's too late," he replied, seeming to fight back the urge to smile. "The chopper is already on its way back to Long Island. But don't worry: We have a beautiful suite for you, and we're gonna send you up some Dom Perignon and beluga caviar."

"Oh, good!" chirped Kiley. "I love beluga caviar!"

I stared at her, speechless.

"Okay, then!" mused the shift boss, feeling my pain. "Let's head over to the cage, so you can cash out."

Yeah, I thought, it's time to put this nightmare to an end.

"What the hell are you talking about?" I nearly screamed at the sixtyish old hag on the other side of the bulletproof glass. "How could you not give me my money back?"

"I'm very sorry," came the toneless response, through a series of shiny aluminum slits. "I can't cash you out unless you show ID. It's the law."

I was baffled. Shocked. In utter disbelief.

Here I was, standing inside "the cage," which was the size of a bathroom at Denny's, accompanied by an underage girl, a shift boss who was probably a shill for the mob, and a stack of $32,000 in multicolored casino chips, which I was now stuck with because this old hag on the other side of the bulletproof glass was a stickler for details. It was mind-boggling.

I turned to the shift boss and said, "You gotta do something here. This–is–not–right." And then I clenched my teeth and shook my head slowly, as if to say, "Someone's gonna pay for this when all is said and done!"

The shift boss threw his palms up in the air and shrugged. "What can I do?" he said innocently. "The *lawr* is the *lawr.*"

With frustration in my heart, I looked at Kiley and said, "Do you know why this shit happens to nobody but me?"

She shook her head nervously.

"Because I bring it on my-fucking-self. That's why! I'm a glutton for fucking punishment." With that I turned back to the bulletproof glass and stared at the old hag suspiciously. Then I rolled my neck, like a man on the brink. "Listen," I said logically, and I leaned forward and placed my elbows on a black Formica countertop on my side of the glass. "I'm a sane guy, usually, so let me just give you a recap of the night's events, then you tell *me* if I deserve to get my cash back, okay?"

The hag shrugged.

"Fine," I said, "I'll take that as a yes," and then I went about telling her my tale of woe–starting with the malfunctioning helicopter and finishing with the forgotten-license debacle, while carefully omitting all references to my ankle bracelet, my spurious phone call to Patrick Mancini, Kiley's age deficiency, my interest-free loan from the federal government, and lastly (but not leastly) the fact that I was out on bail and wasn't authorized to be in Atlantic City in the first place. I said, "I think it's pretty obvious that I am who I *say* I am. So why don't you just cash me out and let me go in peace, okay?" I smiled my most reasonable smile at the hag. "Is that too much to ask?"

The old hag stared at me for a few seconds longer than good manners called for. Then came her toneless response, though the slits: "I'm sorry. I *can't* cash you out unless you show *ID*! It's the *lawr.*"

"Yeah," I said, "I thought that's what you would say. . . ." And those were the last words I said to the old hag that night. In fact, those were the last words I said to anyone that night, with the exception of Kiley, who turned out to be fine company for an ill-fated trip like this. Of course, I never laid so much as a finger on her, and, in retrospect, it had less to do with the statutory-rape clauses and more to do with my own sense of right and wrong. After all, the way I had chosen to pass my last summer on Meadow Lane was an embarrassment. I knew that better than anyone, but I just couldn't seem to control myself. It was as if I were determined to self-destruct–no, it was as if I *needed* to self-destruct.

Perhaps I was thinking that if I literally ran myself into the ground–burning through every possession I had, both physical and emotional–then I could somehow turn back the clock to a time before Stratton, before the tainted tree had sprouted. Maybe. Or maybe I had just completely lost my mind.

Either way, there were certain lines that even *I* couldn't cross: One had been Dave Beall, and another had been Kiley. And while the two were entirely unrelated, each in its own way had allowed me to hold on to one of my last vestiges of self-respect.

When I arrived back in Southampton the next morning, I called Kiley a cab, kissed her on the cheek, and then sent her on her way. I knew that one day I would run into Kiley again and that I would probably kick myself in the butt for not taking advantage of her that Sunday evening. After all, you don't come across girls like Kiley every day, especially in the real world, and especially if you're a guy like me, with one foot in the slammer and the other in the poorhouse.

At this particular moment, I was sitting on a club chair in my living room, staring out at the Atlantic Ocean and trying to make sense of it all. It was almost noon, and Patrick Mancini hadn't called yet, which meant that he never would. In short: I had gotten away with it.

Then the phone rang.

Oh, Jesus! I thought. I'm busted! As fast as lightning, I began racking my brain for a cover story. There had to be some explanation... I was kidnapped... I had been visiting my brother in Montclair, New Jersey, and lost my way... I was scoping out locations for my next meeting with the Chef... *Yes!*

The phone kept ringing.

I picked up the cordless. "Yeah?" I said, in the tone of the resigned and doomed.

"It's your attorney," said my attorney. "Are you alone?"

With righteousness: "I swear to *God* I never touched that girl, Greg! You can call her yourself and ask her!" I suddenly realized that I didn't even have Kiley's phone number. In fact, I didn't even know her last name! She was just Kiley–*the child*.

"What are you talking about?" asked Magnum. "What girl?"

"Forget it," I muttered. "I was just fucking around. What's going on?"

"I got a very disturbing phone call from Joel Cohen this morning."

My mouth immediately went dry. "About what?"

"He says you may have violated your cooperation agreement. He wants to meet with you first thing tomorrow morning."

I felt a wave of panic rising up my brain stem, accompanied by despair. If I hadn't been sitting, I would've fallen over. Remain calm, I thought. You've done nothing. *Nothing!* "That's impossible!" I said confidently. "Did he say how?"

"Not specifically, but I got the impression that he thinks you alerted someone to your cooperation. Any idea what he's talking about?"

Alerted. That was a strange word to use. What did it mean in this context? To alert, to let someone know that I was cooperating? Yes, my cooperation was supposed to be secret, but there were still some people who'd had to know, like my estranged wife, for one, and my parents... and George... but no one else; not even Bo had been alerted–*alerted!* Had I told any of my friends? No. The Blow-Job Queen? No. Any of the naughty Natashas? No, not one. I hadn't told a single soul, in fact. So I was in the clear.

Feeling very confident, I said, "No, I don't, Greg. I haven't alerted anybody. I promise you that. Joel is barking up the wrong tree here."

"That's fine," he said calmly. "You have nothing to worry about, then. I'm sure it's just a misunderstanding. We'll clear it up first thing tomorrow."

"I'm sure it is," I said quickly. "Where does he want to meet?"

"Downtown, at FBI headquarters. I won't be there, though. I

have to go out of town on a deposition. But have no fear; Nick will be with you."

"That's fine," I said. "Nick is a good man." And, besides, I thought, when you have nothing to hide, you have nothing to fear.

Thank God.

CHAPTER 18

THE UNTHINKABLE

With my shoulders squared, my chin held high, and the overstarched Yale-man walking beside me, I entered the debriefing room and prepared for the worst. Immediately, three things struck me as odd–starting with the fact that all four of my captors had shown up for the day's festivities, namely the Bastard, OCD, the Mormon, and, alas, the Wicked Witch of the East, whom I hadn't seen in close to a year. All four were sitting on one side of the debriefing table, waiting for the Yale-man and me to take seats across from them.

The second oddity was that everyone was dressed formally, including OCD, who seldom was. My male captors still had their suit jackets on, ties knotted to the top. Court attire. The Yale-man and I also wore suits, as did the Witch, who sported a black-on-black polyester power suit, which, like the rest of her wardrobe, was in desperate need of alterations.

And the third oddity–the most disturbing oddity of all–was that as we went about exchanging opening pleasantries, I noticed a conspicuous absence of them. The Bastard shook my hand limply and said nothing. The Mormon shook my hand firmly and said, "How's it going, guy," using the sort of glum tone that a college coach would use before he cut a player from his team and revoked his scholarship. OCD shook my hand robustly—a bit *too* robustly, in fact, as if he were a kind Roman general, sending one of his soldiers into a gladiator pit filled with lions. And the Witch wouldn't even shake my hand.

Then we took seats.

"Okay," snapped the Bastard, "let's get down to cases, then," he calmly said, "Michele..." and he extended his hand toward her, palm upward. The Witch nodded once and handed him a thick legal file she was holding. Then she placed her tiny hands on the desktop and began twirling her thumbs at warp speed.

I felt my heart skip a beat.

With great care, the Bastard laid the file down in front of him. Then he stared at it. It was closed, held that way by a light-brown thread that was looped around a thin cardboard disc the size of a dime. And the Bastard just kept staring.

I looked over to the Yale-man, confused. He rolled his eyes and shrugged, as if to say, "It's just theatrics. It means nothing." I nodded in understanding and looked back at the Bastard, who was still staring at the file—theatrically.

Finally, doing a near-perfect imitation of the spooky, stone-faced government agent from *The Matrix* named Agent Smith, the Bastard slowly unwound the light-brown thread at a perfectly even rate and in perfectly even circles. When he was finished, he slowly opened the file and stared at a document on top of the stack.

Still looking down, he said in the spooky tone of Agent Smith: "*Mr.* Belfort: You've pled *guilty* to just about every type of securities fraud we have a law for." *True,* I thought. "Stock manipulation. Sales-practice violations. Free-riding. 10B-5 violations. Currency violations"—he slowly looked up—"and, of course, *money* laundering." He slid the document to my side of the conference table. "Are you *familiar* with this document, *Mr.* Belfort?"

I stared at it for a moment and heard Agent Smith say, "Why don't you have Mr. *De Feis* examine it for you—so there's no mis*take.*"

Eager to please, the Yale-man leaned over and studied the document for a moment. "It's your plea agreement," he whispered in my ear.

No shit, Sherlock! It says it right here on top!

The Yale-man came to my rescue: "It's his plea agreement, Joel."

"I'd like to hear *Mr. Belfort* say that," snapped Agent Smith.

"It's my plea agreement," I said tonelessly.

Agent Smith nodded once, then looked back down at the file and began staring again. After a good ten seconds, he grabbed a second document from the top of the stack and slid it over to me. Then he looked up. "And do you know what this document is, *Mr.* Belfort?"

I studied it for a moment. "It's my cooperation agreement."

He nodded. "That's right. And on the bottom of page one, you'll see a sentence highlighted in yellow. Will you please read that out loud."

"The defendant agrees to be truthful and honest at all times."

The Yale-man seemed to be running out of patience: "What's your point, Joel? Are you saying that he hasn't been truthful and honest?"

The Bastard leaned back in his seat and smiled thinly. "Maybe, Nick." Then he looked at me and said, "Why don't *you* tell *us,* Jordan? Have you been truthful and honest?"

"Of course I have!" I replied quickly. "Why wouldn't I be?" I looked around the room and all four of my captors were staring at me, expressionless.

The Witch: "You're saying you never tried to deceive us, not even *once.*"

I shook my head no, confident there was no way they could have already found out about Atlantic City. After all, it had just happened last night. Okay–*two* nights ago, I thought. But, either way, I had always been truthful besides that... unless–*Dave Beall! The note!* No! It couldn't be! Not in a million years! I pushed the thought out of my mind. Don't jump to conclusions. He would never rat me out. No upside for him. And I had protected him. Saved him. Alerted him. *Alert! Alert!*

"Is there something you wanna tell us?" said OCD, crossing his arms beneath his chest.

"No!" I replied forcefully. Then, not as forceful: "I mean, of course not. I just wasn't sure what you wanted me to say about... uh, honesty." I looked at my captors one by one, my eyes settling on the Bastard. "And then, uh, truthfulness," I felt compelled to add, although I had no idea why.

He seemed to smell blood. "Let me get more specific," he said patiently. "Have you ever told anybody that you were cooperating?"

A knife through the heart! Must *bluff* it out! "Yes," I said confidently.

"Who?"

"My parents, for one. Or two, you might say." I smiled at my joke. "Is that a crime?"

The Bastard didn't smile. "No," he replied, "that's not a crime. Who else?"

"Uhhh"–my mouth was going dry–"I told my wife, of course"–my lips seemed to be vibrating–"because I had to tell her. I mean, I had to tell her for a lot of reasons. She had to sign off on the forfeitures, for starters"–*suddenly, a brainstorm!*–"and maybe *she* slipped it to one of her friends, by accident." As in Laurie Beall, if you catch my drift, who then told Dave Beall, which makes all of this one giant misunderstanding. "I mean, I don't know; I never stressed to her to keep it quiet. Maybe I should've. Is that a problem?"

The Bastard shook his head. "No. I think your wife is smart enough to know what's at stake here. Anyone else you told?"

Remain calm! "George," I said confidently.

The Bastard looked at OCD, who said, "It's his sponsor from AA." Then OCD shook his head back and forth, as if to say, "George is clean."

Finally, the Yale-man stepped in. "Can we cut to the chase here, Joel? It's obvious you think Jordan told someone he was cooperating; so why don't you just tell us who it is? Then we can get to the bottom of it."

The Bastard shrugged, ignoring the Yale-man's words with such callous indifference that it seemed he wasn't even giving him credit for going to Yale. Then he flashed me a hideous smile and said, "Have you ever passed anyone a note, Jordan?"

Good Lord! Worst fears confirmed! Can't think. Must stall for time. And deny. "You mean, have I ever passed anyone a note–ever? Like, uh, since public school or since, uh, when do you mean? Since college?"

"Since you started cooperating," said OCD, saving me from my own nonsense.

"No," I shot back. "Or, well, maybe, actually. I mean, I have to think about that, because it's, uh, an important question." I paused for a moment, desperate to flee. How many FBI agents were in the building? Too many. But this might be my only chance! OCD might slap the cuffs on me at any moment, in this debriefing room. The Bastard would snap his fingers and point to my wrists and OCD would whip the cuffs out so fast my head would spin! But could they do that without a judge? Maybe. *Probably. Definitely!* I needed to speak to the Yale-man. But, no–if I asked for privacy they'd know I was guilty. Bad choice. Must bluff it out. *Deny! Deny! Deny!*

I blundered on: "Well, there was a time in New Jersey, when I was with Gaito and Brennan, if that's what you mean. After we played golf I wrote the name of a stock on a scorecard, and I passed it to Dennis. But it's on the tape. You can check it."

"This is a waste of time," sputtered the Witch. "We know you're lying to us. We could never use you as a witness."

"Which means no 5K letter," added the Bastard.

The Witch: "And according to my calculations, you're facing upward of thirty-five years."

Now the Bastard: "But if you come clean with us right now, maybe there's a chance. Maybe." He looked at me stone-faced. "I'll ask you one last time, and that's it. Have you–ever–passed–someone–a–note?"

The Yale-man to the rescue: "I want to speak to my client in private before this goes any further." He grabbed my arm. "Come on; let's go outside for a second and have a talk."

My moronic response: "No, it's all right, Nick." I shook his arm off me. "I have nothing to hide. I haven't done anything wrong here. I swear to God. I haven't passed anyone a note, and I'm willing to take a lie-detector test." Yes, I could pass a lie detector. Sharon Stone had done it in *Basic Instinct*... although she wasn't lying. But, still... they still might not know! It could be a fishing expedition! Not a shred of proof... or... did I take the note or did Dave take it? Not certain. But don't come clean. *Can't come clean!* To come clean is to die. Besides, maybe they don't even know it's Dave? If they knew for sure they would just come out and say it. They're trying to *bluff* a confession! No two ways about it!

The Bastard's last words: "Okay, then, so you never passed anyone a note. Fair enough," and with that, he shrugged his shoulders and closed the file. Then he said to the Yale-man: "I'm sorry, Nick. I can't use your client as a witness; he's not credible. If he lies to us here, he'll lie in front of a jury."

On cue, the Witch rose from her chair–only to be stopped by the booming voice of OCD, who shouted, "This is all crap!" He glowered at the Witch. "Sit down a second, Michele!" Then he glowered at me. "Listen," he said in a tone he'd never used with me before. "I know *exactly* what happened. You went out for dinner with Dave Beall, and you slipped him a note saying, *Don't incriminate yourself! I'm wired!* Then you left the restaurant and lied to my face, telling me that you did the best you could." He paused and shook his head, but it wasn't in disgust. He was disappointed in me. I was his star cooperator and I had let him down, perhaps even embarrassed him.

There were a few moments of silence, then he said, "I've always been straight with you, since day one, and I'm telling you right now–with no bullshit–that if you don't tell the truth about this, Joel's going to break your cooperation agreement and you're gonna spend the next thirty years in jail. And if you *do* come clean, he still might break it and you'll *still* grow old in jail." He took a deep breath and let it out slowly. "But I've never lied to you before, and I'm not lying to you now. You have to come clean or there's no chance."

The Yale-man nearly jumped out of his chair. "Okay!" he said, in a voice just below a scream. "I want five minutes with my client–alone! And I want it right now." Then he softened his tone a bit. "Will everybody *please* wait out in the hallway while I confer with my client!"

"Of course," said the Bastard. "Take as long as you'd like, Nick."

On the way out, OCD locked eyes with me, and he nodded slowly. *Do the right thing,* said his eyes. And then he was gone.

"So I assume you did this," stated my attorney.

I looked around the debriefing room, at the bare windowless walls, at the cheap government-issue desk, at the cheap black armchairs, and at the empty pitcher of water off to the side, and I found myself wondering if the room was bugged.

I looked at the Yale-man and mouthed the words: "Is it safe to talk?"

The Yale-man stared at me, incredulous. After a few seconds, he said, "Yes, Jordan, it's safe to talk. Everything we say is privileged."

"Yeah," I muttered. "Well, I guess you've never been to the movies before. It's the oldest trick in the book: The cops leave the room and wait for a confession. Then they run back inside and say, 'Gotcha!' "

The Yale-man cocked his head to one side, the way you do when you're looking at someone who's just lost their mind. Then he said, "This room is *not* bugged. I worked in the U.S. Attorney's Office for many years, doing just what Joel does, so you can trust me on this. Now, did you pass Dave Beall a note?"

Deny! Deny! Deny! "What if I did?" I asked aggressively. "I mean, I'm not saying I did, but since they think I did, what if I did?"

"Then we have a serious problem," he replied. "Joel could break your cooperation agreement–which means you'd be sentenced without a 5K letter."

Remain calm! It's your word against his! "That's bullshit, Nick! How can they prove I passed Dave Beall a note? I mean, I'm saying I didn't do it, and they're saying I did. And even if Dave is cooperating, who's to say *he's* not the one who's lying?" I shook my head righteously. "I mean, really! They can't hold back my 5K letter without having proof, right?"

The Yale-man shrugged. "It's not so cut-and-dry. If they think you're lying they can still withhold it, although I doubt that's what's going on here."

"What do you mean?"

"My guess is that they *do* have proof, or at least they think they have proof; they wouldn't be coming on so strong otherwise." He paused for a moment, as if lost in thought. After a few seconds, he said, "Okay, let's just assume for a second that you *did* pass him the note. Where would you have been when you passed it to him?"

Unbelievable! I thought. Even now, at the very moment of my doom, I couldn't help but marvel at the twisted nature of the U.S. legal system. The simple fact was that if I came clean with my attorney–telling him that I *did* pass Dave Beall the note–then he could no longer represent me if I continued to lie. So, instead, we had to speak in "hypothetical terms," so my attorney could try to find out where I was most vulnerable. Then he would help me mold the best bullshit story possible that was consistent with the known facts.

"I would have probably been in a restaurant," I replied.

"And why would you say that?"

"Because that's where the meeting in question took place."

He nodded. "Okay, and what was the name of the restaurant?"

"Caracalla. It's on Long Island, in Syosset."

"And was the restaurant crowded?"

I knew what he was getting at. "No, there were only a handful of people there, and none of them was an FBI agent. I'm certain of it."

The Yale-man nodded in agreement. "You're probably right about that. You've been cooperating for a while now, so I'm sure Coleman trusts you." He paused for a moment, while his last few words hung in the air like mustard gas. Yes, I had betrayed OCD's trust. He had always been straight with me and I had fucked him over royally! But, still, I had acted like a man. I had maintained my self-respect. *And this is what happens!*

The Yale-man continued: "Okay, so for argument's sake, let's just assume that you *did* pass him the note but that no one saw you. Would anything have been said on tape that would sound incriminating–meaning, would Dave Beall have reacted to the note? You understand what I'm saying?"

"Yeah, I do"–*and what do you think, I'm stupid? I didn't just pass him the note without warning!*–"but I'm sure that that's not it. I mean, if I was gonna take a risk like that, I would have been very careful about it. I would have looked around the restaurant to make sure no one was watching, and then I would have sent him a signal–like maybe putting my finger to my lips or something like that. Anyway, there's nothing on that tape out of the ordinary, except that Dave didn't incriminate himself. But that's not so unusual, is it? I mean, I've had four or five meetings with Gaito and *he* hasn't incriminated himself. So it's really my word against Dave's, no?"

"I hear what you're saying," reasoned the Yale-man, "but there's something not adding up here." He paused for a moment. Then: "Let me ask you this: If you had passed him a note, would you have taken it back afterward or would he have kept it as a souvenir?"

I let out a great sigh. "I'm not sure, Nick. I mean, I probably would have assumed that he would just throw the note out, but I'm not really sure." I paused and shook my head ironically. It was unbelievable! I had protected my friend, and as a way of saying thank you he ratted me out! Magnum had been right all along, and so had OCD. I was a fool, and now I was about to lose my life over it. I said, "Let me ask you a question, Nick: What's gonna happen here if I don't get a 5K letter? I mean, will I really end up doing thirty years?"

"Yes," he said quickly. "Maybe even more. Joel will hit you with other charges on top of what you've already pled guilty to: You've got obstruction of justice, lying to a federal officer, and a few others too. But we *cannot* let that happen. We need to do everything possible to stop this from going beyond this room." He put his hand on my shoulder, the way a friend would. "I need to know right now–as your lawyer: Did you pass Dave Beall a note?"

I nodded sadly. "Yeah, Nick, I did. I passed him the note, and it said exactly what Coleman said it did." I chuckled softly. "You know, it's hard to believe that I went out on a limb for a friend and this is what I get in return."

The Yale-man nodded. "Can I ask you why you did it?"

I shrugged. "Why, does it matter?"

With surprise: "Of course it matters! If you were trying to protect Dave Beall because he was holding money for you or you were in the process of breaking the law with him, then this is not going to end well. But if it was simply a crisis of conscience, and you had nothing to gain other than holding on to some mistaken notion of self-respect, then there might be a way out of this. So which is it? Are you hiding something else or was it just because he's your friend?"

"The latter," I said confidently, feeling like the boy who cried Wolf. "I swear to God about that, Nick"–*shit! I had already done that today, and then lied!* "I mean, this time I *really* swear to God! I had nothing to gain here other than to help a friend. That's it. I went to that meeting with every intention of getting Dave to talk, but then something happened when I sat at the table. I don't know–I just kinda looked at him and saw everything that Stratton could've been. I felt like it was my fault for corrupting him in the first place. I ignited his greed with those stupid meetings I used to give and all that sort of shit. And, unlike the other people I cooperated against, Dave was a friend, or at least I thought he was. Now I know that there are no friends–and that there is no loyalty–and that it's every man for himself!" I shook my head angrily. "Now I'm probably going to jail for the rest of my fucking life because of it!" I paused for a moment, trying to rein in my anger. "And what about my kids?" I shook my head in disbelief. "Chandler and Carter. Oh, *God*–what did I do?"

The Yale-man put his hand on my shoulder again and patted it a few times. "Okay," he said. "Now we gotta pick up the pieces. We gotta clean this mess up."

"And how do we do that?"

"Well, for starters, you gotta come clean with them immediately. We can't let this drag on past today."

"Yeah? Well, Joel hates my guts, Nick. The second I admit to this, he's going to break my cooperation agreement. I know it." I paused for a moment, thinking of the short-term ramifications. "I have to see my kids again. I need to one more time before this goes down. Just to kiss them good-bye and tell them that I love them."

"I understand," he said sympathetically. "And I'm sure that if I go outside and tell Joel that you have something to say to him, he'll agree not to take any immediate action; he'll at least think about it overnight."

"And then what happens? What would you have done in this situation?"

He chuckled at that. "What would *I* have done?"

I looked at him dead serious. "Yeah–what would you have done? Would you break my cooperation agreement right on the spot, or would you give me a slap on the wrist?"

"There's no way I would break your agreement," he answered quickly. "The consequences are too severe; and I would say that ninety percent of the AUSAs would agree with me." He shrugged. "Unfortunately, Joel doesn't fall into that ninety percent, but that doesn't mean he'll break your agreement. It's just that most of the AUSAs aren't as hard-nosed as Joel.

"But to answer your question, what I'd probably do is give you a stern warning–or, at worst, make you plead guilty to another charge, something like lying to a federal officer or maybe obstruction of justice. My goal would be to teach you a lesson and also to send a message to the jury that you've been punished for what you did."

"What jury? I've already pleaded guilty."

He shook his head. "I'm not talking about your jury; I'm talking about the jury you'll end up testifying against. Understand: This is all going to come out under cross-examination. That's why everyone is so pissed right now! I'm sure they know that your motives weren't evil. You were just trying to help a friend.

"Anyway, give me permission and I'll go out there right now and tell them that you're ready to come clean. Then Greg and I will roll up our sleeves and go to work for you, and we're going to pull out all the stops on this one. Once Greg finds out what happened, I'm sure he'll be back here tonight; then first thing tomorrow we'll be down at the U.S. Attorney's Office pleading your case. And we'll go right to the top if we have to. We have an excellent relationship with the chief of the criminal division, and, ultimately, that's who Joel has to go to to sign off on this. In the meantime, I would suggest you speak to Coleman and ask him to put in a good word for you. I know you guys have a good relationship; I've heard from more than one source that he genuinely likes you and that he respects you."

"Yeah," I said gravely, "maybe that used to be true, but it's not true anymore. I totally betrayed the guy." I shook my head in embarrassment. "I mean, I don't even know how I'm going to face him again." I bit my lower lip at the thought. "He must be really hating my guts right now."

"Nehhh," said the Yale-man, with a hint of a smile. "He doesn't hate you. In fact, I'm sure he understands *exactly* what happened here. You know, you're not the first cooperator to do this sort of thing; it happens more often than you think. But at least your heart was in the right place. I mean, Coleman would never admit it, but he probably respects you even more now." He winked at me. "And so do I. *So,* that leaves us with Joel: We need to do everything we can to make sure he doesn't shut down your cooperation. Then we can move forward with our lives."

I nodded, feeling very lucky that I had chosen De Feis O'Connell & Rose as my law firm. Not only were they first-rate lawyers but they were also friends, which was a commodity that I was quickly running out of. Of course, there was still a better than fifty-fifty chance that the Bastard would break my cooperation agreement or at least try to, but with Nick and Greg in my corner—and, if I was lucky, OCD—I still had a fighting chance.

Five minutes later, my captors were back inside the debriefing room, and I was spilling my very guts; thirty minutes later I was done. I had told them everything.

The Bastard took it well, or at least he seemed to. He showed little emotion—telling Nick afterward that he would be in touch with him in a few days. The Witch, to my surprise, stayed out of it, as did the Mormon.

And then there was OCD, who had been unusually quiet.

At first that troubled me—no, it devastated me, because I assumed that any goodwill I had built up with him had been permanently destroyed. After all, I had completely betrayed his trust. I had looked him in the eye and lied to him, and not just when I first handed him the tape but also right here in the debriefing room when he confronted me. So, yes, he had every right to lose my phone number and to chalk the whole thing up to experience.

But I had been wrong; he was just saving his thoughts for when the two of us were alone. That happened about ten minutes later, after he had escorted the Yale-man and me up the service elevator, through the lobby with its endless sea of dark-faced grim-faced semi-illegal aliens, and then out onto the street. It was then that the Yale-man turned left and headed for the subway, and OCD and I turned right and headed for the parking lot.

We were somewhere around Broadway, with 26 Federal Plaza rising up behind us and Broadway in front of us, when OCD stopped dead in his tracks and slapped me on the biceps and said, "What the fuck is wrong with you, huh? Did you lose your mind or something?"

I stopped dead in my tracks too. "Yeah," I replied sheepishly. "I did."

OCD attacked: "Yeah—well, you're in some deep shit right now! Do you have any idea of the uphill battle you're facing with Joel? *Christ!* You don't get it! You're playing with your life here!" He compressed his lips and shook his head. "I can't believe it! And after what you've done, now I gotta go to bat for you and plead your fucking case to Joel, and to my boss, and to Joel's boss, and to everyone else around here!

"And do you have any idea how much fucking paperwork I gotta do because of this shit?" He shook his head angrily. "Unbelievable!" he muttered. "What did I tell you that night when you were all upset about wiring up against Beall? Come on, you're the one with the photographic memory! So, tell me, genius: What did I say to you?"

With my tail between my legs: "You said that if the shoe were on the other foot he would do the same thing to me. And you were right. I don't know what to say." I paused, trying to find the right words. "Would you like to know why I did it?"

"No," he answered flatly. "Don't waste your breath. I already know why you did it. That's why I'm out here talking to you and you're not sitting in jail already." He shook his head some more. "Anyway, it's your mess, and now I gotta try to clean it up. I want to thank you for that."

I didn't quite know what to say, so I said, "Well, what are friends for?"

"Yeah," he muttered, "you–my *friend. Christ!* Who needs enemies when I have cooperators like you?" More head-shaking now. "Anyway, listen to me very closely: I can't promise you how this is gonna turn out, but I'll do everything in my power to try to salvage your life. In return, I want you to step up your cooperation to new levels. You've done a good job so far, but *only* good. You could do better–much, much better. I know what you're capable of and so does Joel, and that's the biggest thing you got in your corner. Now–you know who the targets are, my friend. So I want you to go home tonight and rack your brain on how to reach out to them. This way, while I'm busy pleading with Joel to spare your life, I can tell him that you're prepared to take your cooperation to a whole new level. You understand?"

"Yeah. Clearly," I said. "You were right all along: There's no loyalty in this world. And everyone rats." And with that we shook hands and parted ways.

How odd it was that when I sat down with George that very evening, and I asked him to place a phone call to Elliot Lavigne to see if he would send me a bit of the money he owed me in my hour of need, George hung up the phone a minute later, astonished.

"According to your friend Elliot," George said tonelessly, "you don't need money in jail. Then he told me to wish you well and to go fuck myself. Then he hung up on me."

Fair enough, I thought. There were a few people in this world I'd committed crimes with who thought they had gotten away with it. Well, they were in for a rude awakening.

CHAPTER 19

SUPER RAT

It was one of those sweltering early-August days, a Tuesday, and the island of Manhattan was being smothered by a soupy air mass of such stillness and oppressiveness that by ten a.m. you could literally *feel* the atmosphere on your skin. But inside the law offices of De Feis O'Connell & Rose, *perfection*! The building's air conditioner was working overtime as the three of us went about discussing the events of the last seven days.

Unlike my lawyers, I was dressed for the weather, in a white polo shirt, tan golf shorts, and leather boating moccasins. And, of course, I also wore socks, which concealed my ankle bracelet from the casual glance of a nosy voyeur. Right now Magnum had center stage and was in the middle of explaining the outcome of his negotiations with my good friend the Bastard.

"Obstruction of justice," he declared proudly, as he leaned back in his high-back leather chair. "You plead guilty to one count and do an extra thirty months in jail. *But*"–and he held up his right index finger–"you still get your 5K letter, which means we avoid Armageddon." He nodded a single time. "It's a terrific result,

Jordan, especially when you consider the nature of who we're dealing with."

"Yeah," I agreed, "and especially when you consider the magnitude of my idiocy." I shook my head in amazement. "I'll tell you, this has to go down as the dumbest thing I've ever done in my entire life." I shook my head some more. "And there's no close seconds." I turned to the Yale-man and offered him a warm smile.

I said to him, "If it weren't for you, Nick, I don't think I would've made it through that day. You were amazing–from start to finish."

The Yale-man raised his eyebrows. "That's very nice of you to say, but are you prepared to swear to God about that?" He started chuckling. "Or are you willing to take a lie-detector test?"

"Fuck off, Nick! That's what *all* guilty people say when you put their backs to the wall. It's a biological reflex, no different than a jellyfish stinging a passing swimmer." I shrugged. "It can't be blamed."

"Who?" Magnum asked. "The jellyfish?"

"Yes, the jellyfish, and me neither, in this case. I did what any intelligent man in my position would do: I lied through my teeth until I had no choice but to confess. Then I begged forgiveness." I shrugged again. "There's no other way."

"Maybe so," said the Yale-man, "but Joel knows that too."

"Knows *what*?"

"That *all* guilty people swear to God."

"Ahhh... but do all guilty people offer to take a lie-detector test?" I gave the Yale-man a knowing wink. "You see? I'm different, Nick!"

Nothing but silence.

"Anyway, what can I say? You guys are the best! And you, Nick... well, I'm so indebted to you that I'm willing to overlook that last insult and move forward with this relationship." Now I looked at Magnum. "So, tell me, Greg: When must I plead guilty to this latest crime of mine?"

"Sometime in the fall," he answered, "although we're gonna drag it out as long as possible. Remember, the obstruction charge won't be covered by your 5K letter, so Gleeson will have to throw the book at you."

But I had acted like a man! "Well, two and a half years isn't that high a price to pay for my self-respect. In fact, one day maybe I can explain all this to Carter and he'll be proud of me"–strange looks from my lawyers–"or maybe not. Anyway, I'd rather get the whole thing over with than delay it. You know what I'm saying?"

Magnum stared at me with his lips pursed. I looked over at the Yale-man, and he was staring at me the same way. "Okay," I said, "what am I missing here?"

"*Welllll*..." declared the towering tenor, "let me start by explaining how things went down at the U.S. Attorney's Office yesterday. There were five of us in the meeting. Nick and me, and Joel, of course, and then Coleman, as well as someone named Ron White, who just became head of the criminal division."

I perked up: "Yeah, I know Ron White! He debriefed me once in another case. He's a really nice guy. Too bad *he's* not my AUSA, instead of Joel."

Magnum nodded in agreement. "Yes, that would be nice, but, unfortunately, he's not. So it's Joel we have to deal with, and, likewise, it's Joel who has to deal with you. So as nice a guy as Ron White is, he'll still defer to Joel."

"I thought Joel was leaving the office soon?"

"He is," said Magnum, "and that's why we're not rushing your guilty plea. See, if we can delay it until *after* he leaves, then we can try renegotiating with the next AUSA, who, hopefully"–Magnum winked–"will be more sympathetic to our cause."

"That's brilliant!" I exclaimed–and what a two-tiered justice system, I thought. In fact, it was absolutely mind-boggling. If I had been poor or even middle class, for that matter, I would be sitting in jail right now, freezing my ass off and facing the better part of thirty years.

The Yale-man said, "Our first goal will be to try to get the obstruction charge reduced to lying to a federal officer, which is far less serious."

"It carries no mandatory jail time," Magnum added, with a tiny wink.

"Correct," said the Yale-man, with a starchy shrug. "Of course, it would be even nicer if we could convince them to drop the whole thing, although I don't think that's realistic. Joel already let the genie out of the bottle, so it would look *indecisive* if the U.S. Attorney's Office did a complete one-eighty."

Playing devil's advocate, I said, "What you're saying sounds logical, but what if the next AUSA is even worse than Joel? Can they go back on the current deal?"

"Two good questions," answered Magnum. "Under no circumstances can your position get worse. Obstruction of justice is too harsh *as* it is, and I'm sure Ron White would agree with me on that. And, almost anyone would be better than Joel Cohen, save Michele Adelman. But she won't be the one taking over this case, because she's already got her hands tied up terrorizing Victor Wang. Most AUSAs would have let you off with a stern warning, but, for whatever reason, Joel has it out for you."

The Yale-man said, "I think Joel is just too emotionally involved in your case."

That, and he's a fucking asshole! I thought.

"In other words," continued the Yale-man, "he's chased you for such a long time that he can't help but look at you as 'the crook you used to be,' for lack of a better term, rather than the 'upstanding citizen that you are now,' which is an accurate term."

Now Magnum chimed in: "Nick is right on the money with this, and that's why it's so important to wait things out. The next AUSA will have no history with you; the only person they'll know is the Jordan Belfort who's part of Team USA."

"And what about Coleman?" I asked. "He chased me longer than everyone else combined."

Nick said, "It's different for an FBI agent, especially in a case like yours, where there's no violence involved. You had a reputation for being a brilliant guy, so Coleman respects you. You weren't just some schnook who broke the law."

"And FYI," added Magnum, "it's because of Coleman, mostly, that Joel didn't break your agreement. He stood up for you in a very big way yesterday. He made the case that, with the exception of the Dave Beall note, you'd been a first-class cooperator. And he also said that you guys are working on a very big case right now. You know what he's talking about?"

I nodded. "Yeah; Gaito and Brennan. We haven't had much luck so far, but that's about to change. I'm actually meeting with Coleman right after this, and I have a little gift for him."

"What's that?" asked Magnum.

I nodded and clenched my teeth, angry at the recent string of betrayals by men who had had the audacity to once call themselves my friends. "A little recipe on how to cook the Chef," I said coldly, because if the shoe were on the other foot he would do the same fucking thing to me.

It seemed only appropriate that we would be in Brooklyn Heights when I finally told OCD the story of how the Duchess and I first met and how she ultimately stole my heart away from Denise. After all, it was here, in this very gentrified neighborhood, with the U.S. Attorney's Office a few blocks this way and the federal courthouse a few blocks that way, where I had picked the Duchess up on our first date.

At the time she was renting a one-bedroom apartment in a town house on Joralemon Street, which was just down the block from where OCD and I were now having lunch at a Chinese restaurant. Obviously, the main topic of today's lunch was not the sordidness of my personal life, but I felt that, after all OCD had done for me, I owed it to him. After all, no red-blooded American–even a dedicated FBI agent–can resist a story like this, where the primary ingredients are sex, drugs, greed, lust, divorce, betrayal, and blondes. I was now in the middle of explaining how our paths had crossed for the first time.

"...throw these wild parties at my beach house, and there was a total open-door policy. All you had to do was show up, smile, and you were in. It was the greatest recruiting method ever." With that I paused and took a bite of a mu shu pork pancake that I had just rolled as if it were a joint, while OCD sampled a heaping forkful of his favorite chicken chow mein.

After a few seconds I said, "You were right; the food is really good here."

OCD nodded. "The prices are dirt cheap too. To tell you the

truth, I don't know how this place stays in business. It's not like the rents are cheap around here."

I shrugged and stated the obvious: "They're probably paying the waiters six cents an hour and threatening to kill their relatives in China if they complain."

"Probably," said the FBI agent. "But if that's what it takes to get chicken chow mein at $5.95 a plate, then what can you do, right?" He scooped his fork back into the food and held it in the air suspensefully. "So you were saying?"

I nodded and put down my pancake. I said, "In the beginning, the parties were relatively small, maybe a few hundred people at most, but over time they grew into the thousands. And like everything else with Stratton, each party had to be more decadent than the last."

OCD put down his fork. "Why is that?"

I shrugged. "Desensitization, mostly; you know, what seemed wild in 1989 didn't seem so wild in 1991. It was that, and also the fact that Stratton was a self-contained society. We were like ancient Rome, in that way–held together by a bloodlust to witness acts of depravity. In Rome they used to feed their slaves to the lions; at Stratton we used to toss midgets at a Velcro target." I paused and picked up my pancake and took another bite.

"Anyway, the first parties were relatively harmless: There were DJs spinning records, there were people dancing, we had an open bar, some hors d'oeuvres, maybe a little bit of drugs, but that was about it.

"But flash-forward a few years later, and it's complete and utter insanity: Thousands of people are at my house, and they're literally *pouring* out onto the street and onto the beach, and on my rear deck are so many people that it's on the verge of collapse. Dune Road is completely impassable, because it's filled with drunk and drugged-out Strattonites, and it's all being supervised by the Westhampton cops–so the party goes on, despite complaints from my neighbors.

"Meanwhile, there's a live band playing and jugglers are juggling and dancers are dancing and hookers are hooking and strippers are stripping and acrobats are doing somersaults and a midget is walking around dressed in overalls, simply for the sake of amusement. On the beach itself there are giant hog snappers and even more giant lobsters, spinning on a rotisserie, next to a suckling pig with an apple stuffed in its mouth. And to make sure no one gets thirsty, two dozen half-naked waitresses are walking around, carrying sterling-silver trays with glasses of Dom Perignon on them."

"Jesus," muttered OCD, and he took another forkful of chow mein.

"Anyway, when I first met Nadine it was July Fourth weekend, 1990, which was still relatively early in the game, so she wasn't totally freaked out when she walked in the door. I was in my living room at the time, playing pool with Elliot Lavigne"–*a wonderful thought!*–"who, by the way, happens to be making a fortune again."

"Really?" said OCD, putting down his fork. "I thought he was broke."

I shook my head. "Not anymore! I heard he's flying high again." Just how and where I heard, I chose to keep to myself. "He's got something going on in the garment center; I don't know all the details, but rumor has it he's making millions."

"It's amazing," said OCD, "considering the guy is a complete degenerate."

"Yeah," I agreed, "and if I know Elliot, he's probably still smuggling cash over from Hong Kong." I shrugged my shoulders. "You know, I'm surprised you and Joel never went after him. I mean, he kicked me back more cash than everyone else combined."

OCD shrugged. "It's a difficult case. We subpoenaed his bank records a while ago, and there was just too much cash going in and out to find a pattern. In that sense, he was a good choice for a rathole."

"Yeah?" I countered. "Well, I remember a time when his secretary loaded up a gym bag with seven hundred thousand dollars in cash and then gave it to my old driver, George, to deliver to me. And I know for a fact that all the money was withdrawn from the Bank of New York on the same day, and it went straight from the bank to his secretary, then to George, and then to me."

OCD twisted his lips. "And how do you know that?"

"Because his secretary called and told me she'd just taken the money out of the bank and to have George come pick it up before Elliot gambled it away. And when George dropped the money off, he was sweating bullets and giving me this sort of strange look. He never said anything to me directly, but he did say something to Janet, and then she said something to me. Apparently George got curious and opened the gym bag and almost keeled over." I shrugged. "Anyway, all you have to do is subpoena Elliot's secretary, George, Janet, and the bank records, and the rest is history."

OCD stared at me for a second. Then he took another forkful of chow mein and started chewing. The unspoken message: "I'll check it out. Get back to your story."

I took a deep breath and said, "So, anyway, Elliot and I were in the middle of playing pool when the Blockhead came running over all out of breath, and he said, 'You gotta see the girl getting out of this Ferrari. She's off the charts,' and, of course, since it was the Blockhead I took it with a grain of salt. But then he literally dragged me to the front door.

"And that's when I saw Nadine for the first time." I smiled at the memory.

"I felt like Michael Corleone in *The Godfather,* when he sees Apollonia for the first time; she was walking through the olive fields in Sicily, and when Michael sees her he gets hit by the thunderbolt. Well, that's how I felt: I was totally blown away by her." I paused and looked down at my pancake, considering whether or not to take a bite. I looked back up, realizing that I'd lost my appetite. "It was her legs I remember most. I always loved the Duchess's legs, and her ass too. It's rounder than a Puerto Rican's, in case you've noticed." I winked.

OCD started laughing.

"Anyway, we said only a few words to each other, because she showed up with a date, and then the Strattonites immediately started torturing her."

"How so?" asked OCD.

I shrugged. "Mostly they just ignored the fact that she showed up with someone else, and they started coming on to her, as if the guy didn't even exist. It finally came to a head when the two of us were being introduced. We were standing by the pool table and she said something like, 'This is a really nice house,' and I said, 'Thanks,' and then suddenly I saw her face drop, so I turned around and saw Mark Hanna, who was one of my brokers at the time. He was standing a few feet behind me, staring at her and jerking off.

OCD recoiled in his seat. "What do you mean?"

I shrugged. "He had literally dropped his pants to his knees and he was pulling on his own pud. And then his wife, Fran, came running over, and she was screaming, 'What the fuck is wrong with you, Mark! Pull your pants up!' So Mark pulled his pants up, and Fran started smacking him. Then, when I turned back to Nadine, I expected to see a look of astonishment on her face or maybe even fear, but, instead, I saw stone-cold anger. She had her eyes narrowed and her fists clenched in rage, and she was leaning forward as if she was getting ready to take a swing at him.

"Of course, I didn't know she was a *Brooklyn* girl back then; she looked like she was from Australia or Scandinavia or somewhere like that. Anyway, suddenly Denise was on the scene and sensing danger in a way that only a woman can, and then I heard Nadine's boyfriend say, 'Okay, it's time to go now.' Nadine and I were both saying, 'No, no, not yet,' and Denise started bum-rushing them out the front door. As all this was happening, the party was raging around us, with the music blasting and the champagne flowing. And just as Nadine was about to leave, she turned around and flashed me this mischievous little smile, and then a second later her boyfriend yanked her out the door like a rag doll. I saw a long trail of flowing blond hair behind her, then she was gone. It was just like you see in the movies."

I paused and took a moment to study OCD. He seemed to be enjoying my story immensely. He was still shoveling in his food, but he had this wildly expectant look on his face. Yes, I thought, despite the badge and the gun he was a man like any other man. He said, "Sooooo..." and he waved his fork in tiny circles.

I nodded. "So, to make a long story short, the second she left I began asking everyone under the sun who she was and then spent the rest of the summer trying to run into her, which I occasionally did but always when I was with Denise. Denise would always say something like, "Oh, look! There's that pretty blond girl from the party, remember her?' And I would be like, 'Oh, yeah, I think that's her...' but my tone was like, 'Who gives a shit.' But, to my own credit"–I rolled my eyes–"I made it all the way to Thanksgiving before I finally broke down and paid someone to arrange a date."

OCD's eyes popped open. "You did?"

I shrugged sheepishly. "Yeah, I know it sounds kind of lame, but that's the way it is. We didn't really have any friends in common, except for this one girl named Ginger, who was a complete mercenary. So she was pulling this shit on me, saying, 'Come on, you're *married,* Jordan; I can't get involved in this,' so I said, 'Fine, Ginger, how about if I give you ten grand in cash? Will that ease your conscience?' Of course, the next day I had Nadine's phone number and Ginger had already put in a good word for me."

"Jesus," said OCD, "what a player this Ginger is!" He shook his head, amazed. "And what did Nadine say about you being married?"

I shrugged innocently. "Well, that was the first thing she asked me when I called, so I did the only thing a married man could do: I said, 'I'm in the process of getting divorced.' "

OCD's eyes popped open again. "You didn't think you'd get caught lying to her?"

I shook my head quickly. "Nah, it wasn't really like that. I mean, I didn't say it so bluntly–like 'I'm getting divorced tomorrow.' I just kind of painted the picture that things weren't going so well in my marriage. You know, that we were *considering* whether or not to consider getting a divorce."

OCD started chuckling.

"No, I'm serious! That's exactly what I said to her. That's what every married guy says when he starts an affair." I shrugged my eyebrows. "It's what you call *standard operating procedure.* Anyway, there happened to be a bit of truth to my words; not that I was contemplating getting a divorce, but my marriage to Denise *was* feeling the effects of Stratton. The two of us were never alone–we always had an entourage of Strattonites around us–and we'd already met Elliot and Ellen; and if you think Elliot's off his rocker, you oughtta get a load of his wife, Ellen! Anyway, I don't want to place the blame on Elliot and Ellen, but any bit of magic Denise and I had left was squashed when the four of us became running partners. Before that, we hardly did any drugs, and Denise was like this young beautiful girl, but then Ellen sunk her claws into her. Before I knew it, Denise was wearing Chanel outfits and buying Bulgari jewelry and taking Quaaludes during the day.

"I mean, don't get me wrong: I wasn't upset about Denise spending money on things. My money was her money, and I was making it so fast that she couldn't put a dent in things if she tried. It was just that that wasn't Denise. You see, what made her beautiful was how *pure* she was, how she could go out to dinner dressed in a T-shirt and jeans and still look gorgeous. *That* was Denise–not the chichi clothes and the overpriced jewelry. She was much too good for that.

"Anyway, by the time I met Nadine, Denise and I were spending more time apart than together, and I was sleeping with Blue Chip hookers a dime a dozen." I shrugged and shook my head sadly. Then I said, "And when Nadine and I went out on our first date, I got a lot more than I bargained for. I was expecting a dumb blonde, who I could spoil rotten in exchange for mooring rights."

OCD cocked his head to the side. "Mooring rights?"

"Yeah," I replied, "mooring rights: like my dick is the boat and her pussy is the mooring." I shrugged innocently. "Anyway, Nadine, as it turned out, was not a dumb blonde, and by the end of the night I was totally captivated. When we pulled up to the front of her apartment, I was trying to figure out a way to seduce her, but I never got the chance, because she came right out and said, 'You want to come upstairs for a cup of coffee?' Next thing I knew I was inside her tiny apartment, saying, 'Jesus, Nae, this is a really cute place,' but what I was really thinking was: How the hell am I going to get this girl into bed?

"And then she said, 'Why don't you start a fire? I need to go to the bathroom for a second.' So I said, 'Sure..." although, in retrospect, I remember being a bit shocked that a girl as pretty as she was even went to the bathroom! I mean, she seemed way too perfect-looking to ever have to take a dump! You know what I'm saying?"

OCD started chuckling. "You're demented. You know that?"

"Of course," I said proudly, "but that's besides the point. So, anyway, there I am, crouched in front of her fireplace, searching my demented skull for the perfect line to get her into bed, and then I hear, 'Okay! I'm back!' And I turn around and there she is, stark naked, in her birthday suit!"

OCD's jaw dropped. "You're kidding me!"

"Nope!" I said. "I ended up sleeping over there that night–I told Denise I was stuck in Atlantic City–and, from there, things quickly spiraled out of control. At first we were going to see each other only once a week, on Tuesday nights. We wouldn't even speak in between. And that lasted for about a day and a half, at which point we started speaking every day on the phone–just for a few minutes, though, and just to check in to see how our days were going. But that quickly turned into a few hours a day, although I'm not sure how. So I figured that I needed to just spend a few days with her alone–you know, to get her out of my system. So I told Denise that I needed to go to California on business. And that was the end: Nadine and I fell madly in love and started speaking on the phone nonstop and meeting in the afternoons to let our rogue hormones out for a romp! It was sometime in late January when I finally told Denise that I needed space, and that's when I moved into the city, to Olympic Towers.

"Ironically, Denise still had no idea that I was even having an affair. I'd been pretty careful about things–at least in the beginning–but once I moved into the city that changed too. By mid-February Nadine and I were out dancing in nightclubs and holding hands across a table at Canastel's, which was one of the hottest restaurants in Manhattan back then. Everyone knew me there, and someone, I guess, called Denise one night to give her a heads-up that I was out for dinner with Nadine. A few hours later, when my limo pulled up in front of Olympic Towers, the door swung open, but instead of the doorman standing there, it was Denise. And, to make matters worse, I happened to be right on top of Nadine at the moment, engaged in a passionate kiss and telling her how much I loved her.

" '*You* stay the fuck in the car!' Denise screamed at Nadine. 'And *you* get the fuck out of the car!' she screamed at me. Then she did a double take at Nadine and her face dropped. 'You're the girl from the party,' she said softly. Suddenly both of them were in tears at the same time." I paused and shook my head sadly. "So I turned to Nadine, who was white as a ghost now, and I squeezed her hand reassuringly. 'I need to take care of this,' I said gently. 'Why don't you go home and I'll call you in a little while, okay?'

" 'I'm so sorry,' she said through tears. 'I didn't mean for this to happen, I feel terrible.' And that was true, of course. Neither of us meant for it to happen, and we both felt terrible about it. But it *did* happen, and the fact that we felt bad about it didn't make it any easier on Denise." I shook my head slowly, trying to make sense of it all. "In a way, you don't choose who you fall in love with, you know? It just sort of happens. And when you *do* fall in love–that all-consuming love, that lusty love, where two people live and breathe each other twenty-four hours a day–what do you do then?" I shrugged and answered my own question: "There's nothing you *can* do. You can't be without the other person for more than a few hours without going crazy. And that was the sort of love Nadine and I had. We were spending every waking moment together. Even when I went to work, which was seldom, she would drive out to Long Island with me and then keep herself busy until lunch. And when she had modeling appointments, I would drop her off and wait outside until she was done. We were obsessed with each other.

"Anyway, the limousine pulled away and it was just Denise and me. The doorman had run inside the building when he heard Denise screaming at me. She was screaming at the top of her lungs: 'How could you do this to me? I married you when you had nothing! I stuck with you through thick and thin! When you were bankrupt I cooked for you! And made *love* to you! I was a good wife! And this is how you repay me? How could you do this?'

"At first I tried to put up an argument, mostly out of instinct, but there was nothing to say, really. She was a hundred percent right, and we both knew it. So I just stood there apologizing to her over and over again, telling her I didn't mean for it to happen. Finally she said, 'Just tell me you don't love her; that's all I ask.' She grabbed me by the shoulders and looked me in the eye, and there were tears streaming down her cheeks. She said, 'Look me in the eye and tell me you're not in love with her, Jordan. *Please.* As long as you're not in love with her, we can work it out.'

"But after a few seconds, I shook my head and said, 'I'm so sorry, but I am in love with her. I didn't mean for this to happen.' And I started crying myself. 'I'll always take care of you,' I said. 'You'll never want for anything.' It was no use. She broke down and started shaking in my arms.

"I can tell you that I felt like the biggest louse on earth at that moment." I shook my head sadly. "And Denise just kept sobbing uncontrollably, right there in the street. But then, out of nowhere, her friend Lisa emerged from the shadows, and she grabbed Denise and hugged her. Lisa said to me, 'It's okay, Jordan. I'll take care of her now. She'll be all right,' and then she winked at me and led Denise away.

"I was bowled over by that. I mean, I would've expected Lisa to be shooting daggers at me with her eyes, and she wasn't. But what I didn't know back then was that Lisa was in the middle of her own affair; that would come out a few months later, when she got caught cheating with some local playboy type on Long Island. Then she got divorced too." I looked at OCD and shrugged. "And that's it, Greg. That's Lifestyles of the Dysfunctional on the North Shore of Long Island. And it's not a pretty picture."

From there we spent a few minutes talking about what happened after–my marriage to Nadine, the birth of my children, my escalating drug habit, and, finally, we turned to the subject of the Chef.

"The problem," I said, "is that people like Dennis and me get so caught up in the cover story that when we talk about the past we stick to the cover story and don't tell the truth. It has nothing to do with him thinking I'm wired. If he did, he wouldn't even be returning my call.

"It has more to do with protocol than anything–that when you discuss the past you hedge by mentioning the cover story. That's why when you listen to tapes of us, he always starts by saying things like, 'You know, there are two versions of things: our version and their version,' and then he goes on talking about juries and reasonable doubts."

OCD nodded. "It's a valid point, and, of course, I'm aware of it. But over time people tend to get sloppy. So we wait for a break."

I shook my head no. "It won't happen with the Chef. The cover story, to him, is more truthful than the truth. That's why we have to take a different tack."

"What's that?"

"Well," I said confidently, "I think it's time to leave the past behind and look to the future." And, with that, I told OCD my plan.

CHAPTER 20

ALL MEN BETRAY

This time was different.

The Nagra was my shield, the microphone was my sword, and the words rolled off my tongue with such ease and fluidity that I could have gotten John Gotti to share every last detail of how he and his crew whacked Paul Castellano in front of Sparks Steak House.

Yes, I thought, having a clear conscience is a wonderful thing for a cooperator.

A rat? No, no. I was no such thing. After all, a rat gives up his friends, and I didn't have any. I had been betrayed by everyone: Dave Beall, Elliot Lavigne, my own wife, *for Chrissake,* and, if given the chance, by the Jersey Chef too.

So now it was my turn.

It was Friday afternoon, a little past two, and the Chef and I had just arrived at a small, well-appointed office I kept in Plainview, Long Island, which was halfway between Manhattan and the Hamptons. Plainview was a boring town—*so* boring, in fact, that in the entire history of Long Island no conversation had ever begun with: "You'll never believe what happened in Plainview the other day..."

Well, *that* was about to change!

I was determined to make, before the afternoon was out, the most incriminating consensually recorded conversation in the history of not only Plainview but also of Manhattan, New Jersey, the eastern seaboard of the United States, and, for that matter, the entire world.

But, first, opening pleasantries. We exchanged hugs and hellos as I led the Chef to a small seating area. An oxblood-colored leather couch and two matching club chairs surrounded a brass-and-glass coffee table. As we took seats on the couch, the Chef said, "I didn't even know you still *had* this place!"

"Yeah," I said casually. "I didn't have the heart to get rid of it. I'm sentimental, I guess." I smiled warmly at the Chef, who, as usual, looked as cool as a cucumber in his light-gray business suit and red shepherd's check necktie. I was dressed more casually, in a pair of cutoff jean shorts and a white polo shirt, both of which were doing a fine job of concealing my sword and shield.

The Chef smiled back. "Well, it's a nice place. I always liked it."

I watched with an icy detachment as the Chef looked around the room. In the past, I had always found the Chef's presence soothing–that proud way he carried his baldness, the very squareness of his jaw, his aquiline nose, that infectious smile–yet I had also found the Duchess to be soothing, hadn't I? And where was *she* now? And where was Dave Beall now? And where was that bastard Elliot Lavigne now? All men betray, I reminded myself, and all women too. So why feel guilty? No reason to; no reason at all.

"It is," I said, smiling. "Anyway, what's the latest and greatest? How's the wife, the kids, your golf swing..." and, with that, we spent the next few minutes engaged in meaningless small talk.

Actually, it wasn't so meaningless, because ever so subtly I was making two very important points: first, that I was in fine spirits and feeling better every day, and second, that once my legal problems were resolved I was looking forward to a bright future, which included the Chef as my friend, confidant, and adviser. My demeanor said that I was calm and confident, a man who deals with his problems with strength and honor.

After a few minutes, I casually steered the conversation to the status of my court case. "It's obvious that my best option is to cop a plea, because if I go to trial and lose, I'm gonna get slammed so hard, it'll be fucking ridiculous!" I shrugged. "Each money-laundering count carries ten years, and I'm facing five of them. But, on the flipside, if I plea-bargain it'll only be to securities fraud, which carries a lot less time."

The Chef nodded. "How much time would you have to do?"

I shrugged. "Six years, according to Greg, but that's before my deductions; after good time, the drug program, and six months in a halfway house, I'm looking at closer to three, which–*believe me*–I can do standing on my head."

"I like it," said the Chef. "I like it a lot. And what about Danny?"

"The same as me, I'm sure. Our lawyers are still working together on a joint defense, but it's only for cosmetic reasons. If the U.S. Attorney's Office thinks we're going to trial, it'll make it easier to cut a deal when the time comes."

"Clearly," said the Chef. "That's always been my philosophy: You fight tooth and nail, and then–*badaboom!*–you cut a deal on the courthouse steps." He paused briefly and started nodding again. "Well, this is good, this is *real* good. How big a fine you think you'll have to pay?"

"I'm not really sure," I said, seeming unconcerned. Then I stopped, looked around the room suspiciously, and I lowered my voice to just above a whisper (no problem for the Nagra, of course) and added, "And, personally, I couldn't give a shit. I got so much money socked away, I'm set forever. And I got it here *and* there"–I swung my head toward the door–"on *both* sides of the Atlantic."

The Chef nodded in understanding. "Good," he whispered, although his tone was not quite as hushed as mine. "That's your safety net."

I nodded and whispered back, "You always told me that, Dennis. Maybe if I would've used your people in the *first* place, I wouldn't be dealing with all this shit now."

The Chef pursed his lips and nodded. "This is true," he said. "But it's not worth crying over. It's spilt milk."

"Yeah, yeah, I know all about it. And a man must *learn* from his mistakes, right?" I winked. "Well, this man *has* learned, the *hard* way. The only problem is"–I started lowering my voice again–"that I still got a ton of cash overseas. More than ten million, and I'm not too comfortable with who I got it with. It's only two steps away from Saurel, and he's the bastard who ratted me out in the first place!"

The Chef threw his palms up in the air. "*Sooo,* let's move it! What's the big deal?"

"No, uh, it's no big deal!"–and *Jesus Christ!* I thought. The Chef had just buried himself *right on tape*! "It's just that you're the only one I trust. I mean, my days of being reckless are over–seriously!"

"They better be," he said, raising his eyebrows. "What country is the money in?"

"Actually, it's in two countries: Switzerland and Liechtenstein," I answered, and my mind began double-tracking wildly. On track one, the words were coming automatically, as if on tape. "I have it spread over seven different accounts, five in Switzerland and two in Liechtenstein. . . ." As I kept on speaking, track two began organizing all the topics I needed to discuss to make sure that my tape would secure a money-laundering indictment against the Chef–he had to know that my money was the proceeds of illegal activity; he had to know that I had no intention of reporting the transaction to the government; the amount had to be in excess of one million dollars (to receive the maximum penalty); and, peculiar to this case, I had to figure out a way to tie in *my* money-laundering activities with those of the Blue-eyed Devil's. ". . . which is no problem," track one was saying to the Chef. "It's the cash Lavigne kicked me back from all the new issues, and most of it came from Hong Kong. So I know it's untraceable."

"What we need to do," said the Chef, "is set up new accounts over there, and we need to do it immediately. I got some good people for that; they're the same people I used with Bob." *Bingo!* I thought. "What I'm thinking, though, is that we should stay away from Switzerland for a while, at least until the dust settles."

"I completely agree," I said quickly. "I would hate to see my money get snatched by the feds. I had to rathole a lot of new issues to generate ten million in cash."

"Don't worry," the Chef said confidently. "They'll never find the money, not with *my* people. They're experts."

I nodded quickly, as my mind raced ahead. Clearly, the Chef had already incriminated himself in money laundering, but only in conspiracy. Could I push the envelope even further? I would try. "Let me ask you this," I said, lowering my voice, as if I were still paranoid. "What if I wanted to move more *cash* overseas? I still got five million that Lavigne kicked back to me. I would *love* to get that money out of the country."

"Not a problem," said the Chef. "I know just the guy for it."

You do? I thought. *Holy Christ!* "Oh, really? Who?" I asked, not expecting him to answer.

"His name is James Loo," answered the Chef, as if I had just asked him for the name of his carpenter. "I think you might even know the guy. Bob took him public a while back. He's as straight a shooter as they come."

I nodded eagerly, wondering what the fuck had come over the Chef. He was one of the shrewdest men I'd ever met, yet for some inexplicable reason he had let his guard down. I said, "So James Loo has connections in Switzerland?"

The Chef shrugged. "*Fuhgedabouddit!* This guy has connections everywhere! Half his family still lives over in Asia, for Chrissake! He'll get your money over to Hong Kong faster than you can get to your local Citibank. And he's got people in Singapore, Malaysia . . . you name it."

I nodded in understanding, almost too shocked to ask the next question. But I asked it anyway: "So you're saying I could actually give James Loo the cash I got from Lavigne and he'll smuggle it overseas for me without anyone finding out?"

The Chef nodded slowly, deliberately, and with the hint of a smile on his face. "Yes," he finally said. "This is not a problem for James Loo."

I decided to throw the Hail Mary pass: "And he already did this for Bob?"

The Chef nodded again. "Yes, he did, and with no problems. Bob gave him the money, and *schhhwiitttt!*" The Chef clapped his hands, with his patented sliding motion, sending his right arm flying out toward what he probably thought was Asia.

I threw an even longer Hail Mary pass: "Can I meet him?"

This time the Chef recoiled in his seat, as if I were crazy for even asking such a thing. I had expected that; after all, my question was highly inappropriate, wasn't it? Apparently not, because the Chef then said, "Of course you can! How's next week for you?"

"Next week is perfect," I replied.

Without further prompting, the Chef immediately plunged into the various ways I could filter my cash back to the United States once we had it safely tucked away in numbered accounts in Switzerland and the Orient. In fact, he seemed to relish the opportunity to explain this to me, as if the whole thing were a giant game of cat and mouse, with no serious consequences if the cat won.

Afterward, when I met OCD in yet another random parking lot, I handed him the tape and said, "You have to listen to it yourself, Greg, to believe it." I shook my head slowly, still in disbelief over the Chef's recklessness. "It's totally off the charts."

"Why–what's on it?"

"Everything," I replied, "including Brennan's head on a platter." I shrugged, not feeling so pleased with myself suddenly. I took a deep breath and let it out slowly. *All men betray! Dave Beall! Elliot Lavigne! My own wife!* "Anyway, I gotta roll. It's my weekend with the kids and I wanna beat the traffic out to the Hamptons."

"All right, I'll call you Monday and we'll see what's what."

"Sounds good," I said, although I had a sneaking suspicion we'd be speaking before that. In point of fact, he called me later that night, while I was lying awake in bed with the kids sleeping next to me.

His first three words were: "Jesus fucking Christ!" Then he said, "Has Gaito lost his mind?"

"I told you," I said softly. "It's like he has a death wish or something. I don't know, it's fucking mind-boggling. Anyway, what comes next? Do I set a meeting with James Loo?"

"Of course you do! In fact, we need to memorialize it on videotape! But we'll talk on Monday. I know you have your kids, so I don't want to keep you. Have a good weekend; you've earned it."

Yeah, I thought, another worthless weekend of model-mongering and one-night stands. *I've earned it.* It was all so sad and so very lonely. What I *really* needed was to find a nice girl and fall in love again.

Alas, only half my wish was about to come true.

CHAPTER 21

BEAUTY AND THE BEAST

It's fucking ridiculous!" I muttered to Gwynne, as she walked one step behind me through the living room. "How could she just disappear?"

"Did ya check out by the tennis court?"

"Yeah," I replied quickly. "I checked everywhere, and she's nowhere to be found."

It was Sunday afternoon, and the party was in full swing. Outside, on the other side of the plate-glass wall, a merry band of fifty or sixty people–few of whom I knew and none of whom I cared about–were scattered on my rear deck, partying like rock stars and devouring the last vestiges of my crumbling empire. Most of them were young females–tall, lean, and gorgeous–and not one of them seemed to have a care in the world.

Just then something caught my eye: *breasts*–two pair, very young, perfect in every way. One pair belonged to a lithe blonde with a dazzling head of curls; the other belonged to a curvy brunette with a luxurious mane of waves that went down to the crack of her ass. They were dancing away their afternoon–shaking their little booties, with their palms up to the sky, raising the roof, so to speak.

I shook my head gravely. "You see that, Gwynne?" I pointed to the two young girls with their gravity-defying boobs. "They shouldn't have their tops off while my kids are around. It's not fucking right."

Gwynne nodded sadly. "I think thair druhnk."

"They're not drunk, Gwynne; they're *stoned,* probably on Ecstasy. See how they're rubbing against each other? It's the first sign."

Gwynne nodded without speaking.

I kept scanning my deck, astonished. *Christ*–who were all these people? They were eating my food and drinking my wine and swimming in my pool and lounging in Carter's Hacuddi and–*another wave of panic! Carter!*

I ran into the TV room, and there he was, safe and sound. He was lying on the couch watching a video. He was dressed like me, in blue nylon swimming trunks and no shirt. He looked rather content right now, with his head resting on a young girl's lap. She was a blonde, no older than twenty. And she was gorgeous. She had on a sky-blue bikini the size of kite string. Her cleavage was terrific. Someone had dimmed the lights, probably the girl, and she was tickling Carter's back, as he relished a Power Rangers episode from a side angle.

"Carter James!" I said urgently. "Have you seen your sister?"

He ignored me and kept watching. The girl, however, looked up, and she flashed me a thousand-watt model smile. "Ohhhh," she said, twirling her finger through Carter's loose blond curls, "he's *soooo* cute, your son! I could eat him up alive!"

I smiled warmly at the young blonde. "I know. He's really beautiful," I agreed, "but right now I can't find my daughter. You haven't seen her around by any chance, have you?"

The blonde shook her head nervously. "No, I'm sorry." Then she suddenly perked up. "But I could help you look if you want!" She pursed her lips like a goldfish.

I stared at her for a moment, thinking dark thoughts. "No, it's fine," I said. "But could you keep an eye on my son, please? I'd hate to lose them both at once."

Another thousand-watt smile: "Oh, I'd love to! But he better be *verrrry* careful or I might try to steal his eyelashes!" She looked down at Carter. "Right, Carter? You gonna let me steal your eyelashes?"

He ignored her.

"Carter!" I snapped. "Have you seen your sister anywhere?"

He ignored me too.

Carter's new babysitter began rubbing his cheek softly. "*Carrrrrrter,*" she nearly sung. "You have to *answer* your daddy when he asks you a question!"

Without averting his gaze even one millimeter from the TV screen, Carter whined: "*IIIIIIIIIIIII'm* watching!"

Carter's babysitter looked at me and shrugged. "He said he's watching."

I shook my head in disbelief and walked back into the living room. I looked around–nothing but unfamiliar faces, those thousand-watt model grins. I found them wholly depressing. It was like the Roman Empire before the fall. All this would be gone soon, save the mansion, which would be the ruins and...

There! Just before the plate-glass wall, one of the towering floor-to-ceiling curtains had a suspiciously large bump at the bottom. I stared at the bump for a moment, watching, with relief, as it resolved into the shape of a mischievous six-year-old girl. I walked over and peeked behind the curtain, and there she was: my daughter. She was down on both knees, in a white bikini, staring out at the deck. I followed her line of sight... *right to the topless girls!*

"Chandler!" I snapped. "What are you doing down there?"

She looked up, her face a mask of bewilderment and embarrassment. Those fabulous blue eyes she'd inherited from her mother were as wide as saucers. She opened her mouth for a moment–as if getting ready to say something–but then she compressed her lips and looked back outside at the topless girls.

"What are you doing down there, silly? Gwynne and I were looking all over for you!" I reached down and picked her up gently and gave her a warm kiss on the cheek.

"I lost my dolly," she said innocently. "I thought it fell behind the curtain." She looked down at the curtain, searching her mind for a way to support her white lie. "But it wasn't there."

I nodded suspiciously. "You lost your dolly, huh?"

She nodded sadly.

"And which dolly was that?"

A surprisingly quick response: "A Barbie. One of my favorites."

"And you weren't by any chance doing a little bit of spying while you were down there, were you?"

At first she didn't answer; she darted her eyes around the room, to see if anyone was in earshot. Then, in the tone of the tattletale, she said, "Those girls are showing their boobies, Daddy! Look..." She lifted her arm to point to the half-naked girls.

I gently pushed it back down. "Okay, sweetie; it's not nice to point."

I was ransacking my mind for something to say, when she said, "Why do they have their boobies out in public?"

I was appalled, aghast. How could these girls expose my six-year-old daughter to such a thing? (Their fault, not mine.) There was a certain decorum, wasn't there? "Those girls are French," I said casually. "And in France, girls take their tops off when they go to the beach." It was sort of true, at least.

Wondrously: "They *do*?"

I nodded eagerly. "Yeah, they do, sweetie. That's their custom."

Chandler looked at the girls again, her lips twisted in thought. Then she looked back at me and said, "But we're not *in* France, Daddy; we're in America."

I was bowled over. My daughter was brilliant! Even at the tender age of six she knew inappropriate behavior when she saw it. With a little bit of luck, I thought, she wouldn't report it to her mother. "Well, you're right," I said, "we *are* in America, but I think the French girls might've forgotten." I kissed her on the cheek again. "Come on, let's go take a walk on the beach together. We can remind them on the way."

"Okay!" she said happily. "I'll remind them."

Outside on the deck, I beat Chandler to the punch. "Okay!" I yelled to the bare-breasted duo, as Chandler and I hurried past.

"You gotta keep your tops on while you're visiting our country! Save that for St. Tropez!"

They smiled and flashed us the thumbs-up sign, seeming to understand.

Chandler said, "They got big boobies–like *Mommy's*!"

"That's true," I said, *and it's because they all use the same doctor,* "but I think you should just pretend you never saw them." Better to discuss this with your therapist down the road, when you're a troubled teen trying to make sense of the insanity your soon-to-be-jailed father exposed you to during his final days of freedom.

With that thought, I reached down to my innocent daughter and said, "Come on, I'll carry you to the beach, silly goose!" She jumped into my arms, and off we went, father and daughter, enjoying our last days together on Meadow Lane.

As sweltering as it was on the streets of Manhattan, it was perfectly comfortable at the edge of the ocean. It was as if every last drop of humidity had been sucked out of the atmosphere, replaced by an air mass so pleasant and inspiring that it felt like a gift from God Himself. As Chandler and I walked along the water's edge, her tiny hand in mine, the insanity of my life seemed to be held in harness. Every so often a middle-aged couple or a stray jogger would pass by and smile approvingly, to which I would smile back.

There was so much I wanted to tell Chandler, and so much I knew I couldn't. One day, of course, I would tell her everything–about all the mistakes I'd made and how the greed and drugs had all but destroyed me–but not until many years from now, when she was old enough to understand. So we spoke only of simple things today–of the seashells on the beach, of the dozens of sand castles we'd built over the years, and of all the holes we'd dug to China, only to give up after hitting water a few feet down. Then she nearly knocked the wind out of me when she said, "Guess what, Daddy? My sisters are coming into town tomorrow," and she kept right on walking.

For a split second I didn't know what she was talking about, or at least that's what I told myself. Deep down, though, I knew: She had been referring to John's daughters, Nicky and Allie. Nicky was a few years older than Chandler, but Allie was exactly the same age. The perfect playmate, I thought.

John Macaluso: I was hearing more and more about him lately, and not just from the kids but also from the handful of friends the Duchess and I still shared. Thankfully, I was hearing only good things–that he was a very decent guy, that he'd been divorced twice himself, and that he didn't do drugs. Most important, however, was that my kids liked him. So I liked him too. As long as he treated them well, he would be aces with me–always.

With that thought, I said, "Do you mean *John's* daughters, sweetie?"

"Yes!" she said eagerly. "They're flying in from California tomorrow, and they're coming out to the beach!"

A lovely thought: the Duchess gallivanting around the Hamptons with another man. Then a darker thought: If, after only a few months of knowing them, Chandler was already referring to John's daughters as her "sisters," might she one day refer to John as her father? For a moment I felt very concerned–but only for a moment.

I would always be my children's *daddy,* and there could be no other. Besides, the ability to love was not mutually exclusive. So let them be loved by anyone and everyone, and let them return that love in spades. There was enough to go around for everyone.

"Well, that's great," I said warmly. "That's really great. I'm sure you'll have a ball with them this week. Maybe one day I'll get to meet them."

She nodded happily, and we spent a few more minutes walking and talking. Then we headed back to the mansion. A long mahogany walkway, bounded by thick dock ropes on either side, led you over the dunes to the rear deck. As I carried Chandler along the walkway, my spirits sank lower with each step.

The Romans were waiting.

Why did I subject myself to this? I wondered. Was all this self-torture in the simple name of getting laid? It couldn't be, could it? I mean, I wasn't *really* that shallow, was I? In fact, that was just what I was thinking when I first laid eyes on her.

She was tall and blond, and she stood out among the Romans like a diamond among rhinestones. She seemed to *sway* to the music, in perfect time and rhythm. She seemed aloof to the Scene, as if she was a casual observer and not a member.

At first glance she struck me as the sort of girl I would never dare approach in a nightclub and ask to dance. She was the better part of five-nine, and her blond hair gleamed like polished gold. She was wearing a white cotton skirt, very short, a good six inches above the knee, revealing her long bare legs, which were flawless. She wore a light-pink baby-T that hugged her luscious breasts like a second skin and exposed her perfectly toned tummy and belly button. Her feet were shod in the merest of white sandals, although it was obvious, even at a glance, that they had cost a fortune.

Then–*a terrible shock!*

From behind the blond vision emerged a horrendous-looking creature. It was short and squat and had the face of a bulldog. Its body seemed to be comprised of thick cylindrical stubs, glued together in haste by nothing but God's good humor. The Creature had burnt-orange hair, pale skin, thick fleshy features, the nose of a prizefighter, and a very wide jaw. It wore a short purple sundress, which hung on its stout frame like a printer's smock. The smock was very low-cut, exposing all but the tips of its sagging D-cups. The Creature grabbed the blond vision by the hand and came waddling. I felt Chandler recoil in my arms.

"Come, Yulichka," the Creature snapped to the blond vision, in a gravelly voice that reeked of Brooklyn, Russia, the gutter, whiskey, the Teamsters' Union, and late-stage throat cancer. "This is the owner of the house. I want you to meet him."

I was shocked–and awed. Beauty and the Beast, I thought.

"You must be Jordan," growled the Creature, who then looked at Chandler and said, "Oh, cute-cute, very cute."

I felt Chandler shudder in my arms, as the Creature grabbed her hand and muttered, "Hi, *munchkin*! I am Inna, and *this* here is Yulia." With that she nearly swung Yulia into the forefront, as if she were a blond peace offering.

It seemed clear the two came as a package.

Yulia smiled, and her teeth were as white as porcelain. Her features were fine and even and chiseled to near perfection. She had pale blue eyes shaped like a cat's, which revealed something that the rest of Yulia's appearance otherwise camouflaged: that somewhere along the way, perhaps five hundred years ago, an invading Tartar had raped one of her ancestors.

Daintily, Yulia reached forward to shake Chandler's hand. "*Alloa,*" she said with a surprisingly thick accent. "I am Yulia. What is your name, beautiful?"

"Chandler," my daughter said in a shy voice, and then I waited for her to attack–to say something like, "Oh, another stupid blonde, eh?" or, more likely, "My daddy already has a girlfriend and he cheats on her all the time!" But, instead, all she said was, "You have very nice hair, Yulia," to which we all started laughing.

Yulia said, "Well, you are very sweet, Chandler," and then she turned to Inna and started saying something in rapid-fire Russian. Her voice was soft and sweet, almost melodic, in fact, but the only word I could recognize was *krasavitza,* which meant beautiful.

We spent another minute or so making small talk, but Chandler was growing restless. In fact, just what little gem of poison she might choose to sputter in Yulia's direction was anyone's guess, so I excused myself with a wink and a smile.

As I was leaving, I said to them, "Make yourself at home. My house is your house," to which Yulia smiled warmly and said thank you. Inna, however, didn't smile at all and didn't say a word. She simply nodded her head once, as if to say, "Of course I will!" After all, in her *own* mind, she had done her job well. She had come to Meadow Lane bearing gifts, so she was entitled now to devour anything and everything in sight.

While there was no denying that Inna was a world-class eyesore, I would have never guessed how adept she was at earning her keep. Later that evening, after the Duchess had picked up the kids and the party was winding down, Inna suggested that the few remaining Romans, eight of us in all, take a ride to East Hampton to catch a movie. It struck me as a reasonable idea at first, which quickly became a fabulous idea before we even made it out of the driveway.

"Come on," Inna growled to Yulia. "Let's drive with Jordan. We'll pick up the car later."

"That's a great idea!" I agreed quickly, and indeed it was.

Amid all the madness, Yulia and I had hardly had a chance to speak. Complicating matters, her English was borderline horrific, so any meaningful conversation would have to take place in silence, without distractions. The only problem was that Inna would now be sitting in my rear passenger seat with us.

But, once again, she was one step ahead.

The moment Yulia had climbed into the front passenger seat of my Mercedes the Creature growled, "I gotta go *pischka.* You two go on ahead; I'll catch up with you at the theater." And, just like that, Inna turned on her thick, calloused heel and waddled back up the stairs.

Fifteen minutes later, Yulia and I were alone in my Mercedes, driving down a wide country road on our way to East Hampton. At eight p.m. on a Sunday night, the traffic was going the other way, so we were moving along at a pretty good clip. We had the windows open, and the sweet scent of Yulia's perfume was mixing with the earthy scents of hay and pine in a most delicious way.

Keeping one eye on the road, I was sneaking peeks at her out of the corner of my other eye, searching for even a hint of a bad angle. There was none. She was absolutely perfect looking, especially those long, bare legs of hers, which she had crossed at the thighs. She was doing something very sexy with her foot–letting her right sandal dangle from the tips of her toes and slowly swinging her foot up and down. I tried my best to keep my eyes on the road.

Through the sound of rushing air, I raised my voice and said, "So what was it like winning that contest? Did it change your life forever?"

"Yes," replied Yulia, "it is beautiful outside."

Whuh? I had been referring to the rather astonishing fact that Yulia Sukhanova was the first, last, and certain to be the only Miss

Soviet Union. After all, the Evil Empire was now residing in the failed-nation-state crapper–next to Rome, the Third Reich, the Ottoman Empire, and King Tut's Egypt–so there would only be Miss Russias going forward.

Still, Miss USSR or not, Miss Yulia was even weaker in the English department than I had originally expected. I needed to cut her some slack and keep things simple. "Yeah," I said, "it's a beautiful night for a drive."

"Yes," she replied, "it will start at nine o'clock this night."

What the . . . ? "You mean the movie?"

She nodded eagerly. "Yes, I like to go to movies."

The movies, I thought. How come these female Russkies couldn't say the word *the*? What was so fucking difficult about it? Well, whatever. The beauty queen was gorgeous, so her deficiency could easily be overlooked. Changing the subject, I asked, "So do you think Inna will show up tonight?"

That one she caught. "No ways," she said. "This is Inna for you. Always playing . . . uh . . . how do you say this in English, uh . . . *svacha.*"

"Matchmaker?" I offered.

"Da, da!" exclaimed the linguistically challenged beauty queen.

I smiled and nodded, feeling like I'd just reached the pinnacle of Mount Everest. So emboldened, I reached across the center console and grabbed Miss Soviet Union's hand. "Is it okay if I hold your hand?" I asked bashfully.

Just as bashfully, she replied, "Three months now."

I stared at her for a moment. "What do you mean?"

She shrugged. "This is last time hand held."

"Really? That long?"

She nodded. "*Da;* this is when I break up with boyfriend."

"Ohhhh," I said, smiling. "You mean Cyrus, right?"

Her blue eyes popped open. "You know Cyrus?"

I smiled and winked. "I have my sources," I said slyly.

The "Cyrus" I had referred to was none other than Cyrus Pahlavi, the shah of Iran's grandson. I had done quite a bit of checking on Yulia that afternoon. I had found out that she'd just ended a three-year relationship with Cyrus, who, two years prior, had replaced the prince of Italy as her main squeeze. A royalty-monger, I'd thought.

In essence, Yulia had come to America as an ambassador of goodwill, arriving in 1990 under the watchful eyes of Mikhail Gorbachev, Boris Yeltsin, and Mikhail Khodorkovsky, the then-head of the Komsomol, the Young Communist League, and now the richest man in Russia. More than anything, Yulia was a propaganda tool: bright, educated, cultured, classy, graceful, charming, and, above all else, drop-dead beautiful. She was meant to represent the very best of what the Soviet Union had to offer and, for that matter, Communism as a whole.

It was a *wild* tale—one of political intrigue and financial skullduggery—but everything was starting to make sense to me. There was a reason why Yulia stood out so regally among the Romans: She was supposed to. A hundred million women had vied for the job of "first Miss Soviet Union," and Yulia Sukhanova had won. She had been groomed and trained to carry a single message: that the Soviet Union was best.

Upon her arrival in America, Yulia met with Nancy Reagan, George Bush, Miss USA, newscasters, socialites, rock stars, dignitaries, and diplomats. Ultimately, she traveled around the country, doing ribbon-cuttings and hosting game shows, while she served as a proud representative of the Motherland.

And then the Soviet Union fell.

Suddenly Yulia became the reigning beauty queen of a nonexistent superpower. The once-proud Soviet Union was now a bankrupt nation-state that would go down in the history books as nothing more than a failed experiment in bogus economics and corrupt ideology. So Yulia decided to stay in the United States and become a model. Inna, at the time, was one of the only Russian-speaking bookers in the modeling industry, so she took Yulia under her wing.

There were only two things that now troubled me about Yulia. The first were some references to a man named Igor, who was vaguely connected to Yulia and followed her around, in the shadows; and the second was the fact that Yulia was a KGB agent and Igor was her master. And as far-fetched as it seemed, they *had* originally come here under the auspices of the Soviet government, hadn't they?

So here I was, five hours later, heading to East Hampton, with a female KGB agent sitting next to me, and the dreaded Igor lurking in the shadows. Igor, I figured, was the least of my worries.

"Anyway," I said to the beauty queen/KGB agent. "I didn't mean that in a bad way. We all have our sources, you know? I'm sure you have yours too, right, right?" I winked playfully at KGB. "I guess mine are just a little better than most."

KGB smiled back, seeming to understand. "Yes, you are very good cook."

"Whuh? What are you talking about? What cook?"

"You say sauces," said KGB, who apparently had slept through her English classes at the secret KGB training school. "Like this night: You make tomato sauces, on penne."

I started laughing. "No–not sauces! *Sour*ces, with an *r*." I looked KGB in the eye and dragged out *sources* for all it was worth, so it came out like *Sourrrrrrrrrces.* Then I said, "You get it?"

She let go of my hand and began shaking her head in disgust, saying something like: "Bleaha muha, stupido English! Ehhh! It make no sense!" Then she started waving her perfectly toned arms around the car, as if she were swatting imaginary flies. "*Souwwwwwsses*... *Sourrrrrrces*... *Seeeeeeesses*... Sowwwwwsses!" she was muttering. "Crazy! Crazy! Crazy..."

After a few seconds, she started giggling and said, "This English make me crazy! I swear–it make no sense. *Russian* make sense!" With that, she hit the power-window button and pointed to the side of the road and motioned for me to pull over.

I pulled beneath a large maple tree a few feet off the road, put the car in park, and turned off the lights. The radio was barely audible, but KGB reached over and flicked it off anyway. Then she turned to me and said very slowly: "I... do... speak... English. It is just hard to understand with wind"–*the wind*–"blowing. I thought you say you make sauces, like tomato sauces, because you make that tonight: tomato sauces."

"It's okay," I said, smiling. "You speak English a lot better than I speak Russian."

"*Da,*" she said softly, and she turned to face me, leaning her back against the passenger door and crossing her arms beneath her breasts. Over her pink baby-T-shirt she had thrown on a white cotton sweater, a very soft cable-knit, with a very low V-neck, bordered with two thick stripes, one maroon and the other forest green. It was the sort of old-fashioned preppy sweater that you see in old photographs of people playing tennis. She had pushed up the sleeves, revealing wonderfully supple wrists and a very classy watch, the latter of which was thin and understated. It had a pink-leather band and a pearl-white face. Her blond hair looked shiny as corn silk. It rested on either side of the front of her sweater, framing the face of an angel.

She didn't look like a KGB agent, did she? I took a deep breath and looked into KGB's liquid blue eyes and smiled warmly. Try as I might, I couldn't help but compare her to the Duchess. In many ways, they looked very much the same: blond and blue-eyed, broad-shouldered yet thin-boned, perfectly proportioned above and below the waist. And they both stood with that same imperious posture–the eager young cheerleader, with the shoulders pulled back and theirs knees locked out and their perfectly round butts stuck out–that used to drive me so wild.

"You're beautiful," I said softly to KGB, ignoring my last thought.

"*Da,*" she said wearily, "*krasavitza, krasavitza*... I know this," and she shook her head with equal weariness, as if to say, "I've been called that a thousand times, so you're going to have to do better than that." Then she smiled and said, "And you are cutie too, and you like *real* Russian man! You know this?"

I shook my head and smiled. "No, what do you mean?"

She raised her chin toward my ankle bracelet. "You steal money"–she winked–"like real Russian man!" She giggled. "And I hear you steal a lot!"

Jesus Christ! I thought. Leave it to the damn Russkies! Of course, this was not the moment to alert KGB to the fact that I hadn't stolen quite enough–and that because of that I would not be living on Meadow Lane next summer. Better to cross that bridge when I came to it, I figured.

"Yeah," I said, forcing a smile, "but I'm not exactly proud of it."

"When is jail for you?" she asked.

"Not for a while," I said softly. "Another four years or so. I'm not really sure."

"And your wife?"

I shook my head back and forth. "Getting divorced."

She nodded sadly. "She is pretty."

"Yeah, she is," I said softly. "And she gave me two great kids. I guess I'll always love her for that, you know?"

"You still love her?" she asked.

I shook my head. "No, I don't." I shrugged. "I mean, for a while I thought I did, but I think I was just..." I paused for a moment, trying to find words that KGB would understand. In truth, I wasn't really sure how I felt about the Duchess. I loved her and hated her, and I suspected that I always would. But one thing I was certain of was that the only way to get over someone was to fall in love with someone else. "...I think I was just in love with the *thought* of being in love. I wasn't actually *in love* with her anymore. Too many bad things had happened. Too much hurt." I looked into KGB's eyes. "Do you understand what I mean?"

"*Da,*" she replied quickly, "I do; this is common." She looked away for a moment, as if lost in thought. "You know, I am here nine years now." She shook her head in amazement. "Can you imagine? I should speak better, I think, but I never have American friends. My friends are all Russians."

I nodded in understanding–understanding far more than KGB probably gave me credit for. There were only two types of Russians I had met so far: those who embraced America, and those who held it in contempt. The former did everything they could to assimilate themselves into the American way of life: they learned the language, they dated American men, they ate American food, and, eventually, they became American citizens.

The latter group, however, did just the opposite: They refused to assimilate. They held on to their Soviet heritage like a dog with a bone. They lived amid Russians, they worked amid Russians, they socialized with Russians, and they refused to master the English language. And at the very heart of this, I knew, was the fact that they still longed for the glory days of the Soviet Empire, when the world marveled at the ingenuity of Sputnik and the courage of Yury Gagarin and the iron will of Khrushchev. It was a heady time to be a Soviet, with the world trembling at the Warsaw Pact and the Berlin Wall and the Cuban Missile Crisis.

Yulia Sukhanova had been a product of all that–no, she epitomized that. She still longed for the days of the Great Soviet Empire and, in consequence, had refused to assimilate. Ironically, this didn't make me respect her any less–in fact, quite the contrary: I felt her pain. I, too, had risen once, to the dizziest heights of Wall Street, becoming a celebrity of sorts, albeit in a twisted sense of the word. Nonetheless, just like Yulia Sukhanova, it had all come crashing down on me. The only difference was that *her* crash was through no fault of her own.

Still, both of us, it seemed, needed to figure out a way to reconcile a completely insane past with any possible future. Perhaps, I thought, we could do it together; perhaps, once we got past the language barrier, she could help me make sense of what had happened in my life, and I could help her make sense of hers. With that thought, I took a deep breath and went for broke:

"Can I kiss you?" I said softly.

To that, Miss Yulia Sukhanova, the first, last, and only Miss Soviet Union, smiled bashfully. Then she nodded.

CHAPTER 22

STAYING THE COURSE

And we made love.

Not that night, but the very next day.

And it was beautiful; in fact, not only was it beautiful but, thanks to some very savvy biochemists at the Pfizer drug company, I performed like a world-class stud.

Indeed, just before I picked up KGB at the Creature's Sag Harbor cottage, I swallowed fifty milligrams of Viagra on an empty stomach. In consequence, by the time we pulled into my driveway that afternoon, I had an erection that the DEA could have used to break down a crack-house door.

It's not like I was impotent or anything (I swear!), but, nonetheless, it had seemed like a prudent move. After all, to consume a blue bomber, as a Viagra was affectionately known (due to its purplish color and bombastic effect), was the equivalent of taking out a biochemical insurance policy against the most dreaded of all male complexes: performance anxiety.

I had been a biochemical stud, not just that afternoon but into that evening as well. What Pfizer doesn't advertise on the label (and what every man who's taken one knows) is that blue bombers have a way of lingering in your system for a while. So, eight hours later, while your erection might no longer be suitable as a battering ram, it's still stiff enough to hang a few pieces of dry-cleaning on.

Somewhere around the fourteenth hour, the last blue-bomber molecules have been metabolized to the point of worthlessness, turning you back into a mortal man again. It was for that very reason that, precisely fourteen hours later, I took another blue bomber, and then fourteen hours after that I took yet another.

KGB, I figured, could handle it. Yet, sometime late Wednesday afternoon, even *she* began to complain. She was limping toward my master bathroom, dressed in her Soviet birthday suit, which consisted of a commie-red ribbon in her hair and nothing else, and she was muttering, "Bleaha muha! Your thing don't go down! There is something wrong here! It crazy! It crazy," and she slammed the bathroom door behind her, muttering a few more Russian expletives.

Meanwhile, I was lying in bed, faceup, dressed in my American birthday suit, which consisted of a federally issued electronic monitoring bracelet and a Viagra-induced erection that was stiffer than steel, and I was fairly beaming. After all, it's not every day that a five-foot-seven-inch Jew-boy from Queens gets to send the first, last, and only Miss Soviet Union limping to the bathroom with her loins on fire! And while there was no denying that the boys at Pfizer had a hand in that, it was very much besides the point.

The point was that I was falling in love again.

In fact, later that afternoon, when KGB told me that she had to head back to her apartment in Manhattan, I felt my heart sink. And when she called me a few hours later, saying that she missed me, my spirits soared. And then when she called again, two hours after that, just to say hello, I immediately called Monsoir and told him to pick her up at her apartment and bring her back to the Hamptons.

So it was that she arrived later that night, carrying a very large suitcase, which I gladly helped her unpack. And just like that we became inseparable. Over the next few days we did everything together: ate, drank, slept, shopped, played tennis, worked out, rode bikes, Rollerbladed, went Jet-Skiing–we even showered together!

And, of course, at every opportunity, we made love.

Each night we built a fire on the beach and made love on a white cotton blanket, beneath the stars. And, of course, with each upward thrust, I would sneak a peak toward the dunes, checking for the dreaded Igor, who, according to her, was merely her brother-in-law who had come to the States to keep an eye on her. And while her explanation had seemed a bit thin, I decided not to press the issue.

When the weekend arrived, no partyers appeared. The Creature had seen to that–spreading the word that 1496 Meadow Lane was closed for business. The following Monday morning, I dropped KGB off at her Midtown apartment to pack up more of her belongings, and then I headed down to 26 Federal Plaza to meet with the Bastard and OCD. Not surprisingly, I was back in the Bastard's good graces again, so the meeting went quickly.

The topic was the upcoming Gaito sting, and we came to a quick decision that I would try to set one last meeting with the Chef before James Loo came into town. The goal was simple: to get James Loo to accept cash. I would tell the Chef that I wanted James Loo to know that I was serious–and to know that James Loo was serious too. I would provide Loo with a small cash deposit, as a token of good faith: $50,000, I would suggest, which he could use to get things going.

At first I was skeptical of the plan, thinking that the Chef would smell a rat. But, on second thought, I knew he wouldn't. For some inexplicable reason, something had clicked off in his mind, something related to the irrational joy he got from getting around the law.

He was a complicated man, an otherwise law-abiding citizen who would never dream of breaking "the law" as *he* considered it–which is to say, all laws not having to do with securities trading, the movement of money, and its subsequent reporting to the IRS. If you were to ask the Chef for advice on how to rob a bank or how to kite checks, he would either report you to the authorities himself or, more likely, lose your number forever.

This, however, was different. We were talking about money that, in *his* mind, we had stolen fair and square–no violence had been committed, no guns were placed to people's heads, the victims were nameless and faceless, and, most important, if we hadn't done it ourselves, someone else would have done it just the same. In consequence, we were justified to hide our dirty money from those who meant to find it.

So, in retrospect, it didn't come as much of a shock to me when the Chef and I met two days later in my office, and he thought my idea of bringing "a token of good faith" to our meeting was a fabulous one.

He went about explaining his money-laundering scheme in the most intimate detail–even mentioning the names of James Loo's overseas relatives who would be assisting us in Asia. Then he named the banks and the shell corporations we would be using–finishing with the airtight cover story we would stick to if Coleman and his boys were to ever catch wind of this.

It was an inspired plan, which involved the purchase of real estate in half a dozen Far East countries and the maintenance of a full-time staff overseas, to operate a series of legitimate businesses–clothing manufacturers in Vietnam and Cambodia, and electronics manufacturers in Thailand and Indonesia, where labor was cheap and workmanship was prideful.

Yes, the plan was brilliant, all right, but it was also wildly complicated. In fact, it was so complicated that I found myself wondering if a jury would ever be able to understand it. So I grabbed a legal pad off the brass-and-glass coffee table, ripped off a sheet of paper, picked up a pen, and began drawing a diagram.

With my voice lowered conspiratorially, I said, "So let me get this straight: I'm gonna give James Loo fifty thousand dollars"–I drew a little box with James Loo's name inside it, as well as the amount: *$50,000*–"and then James will have one of his people smuggle the money overseas to his sister-in-law, Sheila Wong,* in Singapore"–I drew another box on the *other* side of the pad, with Sheila's name inside it, and then drew a long straight line connect-

---

*Name has been changed

ing the two boxes—"and then Sheila is gonna use that money to fund accounts in Hong Kong and the Chanel Islands and Gurnsey..." and before I was even finished talking about Sheila's role in our scheme, the Chef had grabbed the pen from me and begun drawing a diagram that fairly resembled the blueprints to a nuclear submarine. And as he narrated his plan, with a mixture of pride and relish, the Nagra rolled on, recording each of his words.

When the Chef was done, he said, "Now this is a fucking Picasso—although you better throw it in the garbage!"

I crumpled the note into a tiny ball and did just that. "Better safe than sorry," I said casually. We exchanged a Mafia-style hug, a firm handshake, and then confirmed our plans to meet James Loo on Monday. I suggested the Hotel Plaza Athénée in Manhattan, where, by sheer coincidence, I explained, I would be staying for a few days with my new girlfriend. But it was no coincidence, of course. Long before Loo and the Chef arrived there, OCD and his tech team would have the room wired for sight and sound.

When I met OCD afterward, I joked that I was up to my old tricks again—passing notes and such—although I had saved this particular note for posterity.

With that I handed him a sealed envelope with the tape and the crumpled note inside. "You better go stop at Macy's and pick up a steam iron," I said jokingly. "You're gonna need it." Then I climbed into my Mercedes and headed back out to the Hamptons.

But, alas, over the next days I began feeling guilty again.

In fact, by that Sunday evening, the thought of ratting out the Chef had become wholly depressing. Apparently, falling in love with KGB had softened the sting of recent events—those terrible betrayals that had ignited flames of revenge in the glare of which I had come to view friends as enemies and enemies as friends. Now, however, I wasn't so sure again.

It was a little before nine, and KGB and I were enjoying our nightly ritual—sitting on a white cotton blanket, near the water's edge, with a small fire blazing away, struggling against the first chills of autumn. Just over the horizon, an orange full moon hung heavy in the night sky, with the dark waters of the Atlantic just beneath it.

"It looks close enough to touch, doesn't it, sweetie?"

"Da," she replied cutely. "It look like Swiss cheese."

"Looks," I said, correcting her. "It *looks* like Swiss cheese."

"What you mean?" she asked.

I grabbed her hand and squeezed it lovingly. "I mean, you have a habit of leaving the *s* off words, especially verbs. Like you just said, 'It *look* like Swiss cheese,' when you should have said, 'It *looks* like Swiss cheese.' It's no big deal, really; it's just a matter of singular or plural. You see, when you say *it,* it relates to one thing, so you would say *looks,* but if you were talking about *they,* which is plural, you would say, '*They* look like Swiss cheese.' Again, it's really no big deal, but it just kind of sounds funny. It's sort of hard on the ears." I shrugged my shoulders, trying to make light of it.

She let go of my hand. "What do you mean: hard on ears?"

"*The* ears," I said calmly, although a bit of frustration had slipped out around the edges, "and that's a perfect example of what I mean." I took a deep breath and said, "You never say the word *the,* Yulia–*ever!* And it's probably the most commonly used word in the English language! It gives a certain rhythm to things, a certain flow, and when you don't say it–like when you just said 'hard on ears' or when you say, 'I want to go to store,' it just sounds funny. I mean, it sounds like you're uneducated or something, which I know you're not." I shrugged again, not wanting to make a big deal of it, although I couldn't help myself. We were spending all our time together, and her bastardization of the English language was starting to get to me. Besides, I was in love with her, so I felt it was my obligation to teach her–or to *train* her, so to speak–and lead her gently down the road to a little village called Assimilation.

"Anyway," I continued, "if you really want to improve your English, I would start with those two things: using the word *the* and knowing when to add an *s* to the end of a verb." I smiled and grabbed her hand. "From there, all good things will follow." I winked at her. "And if you want, I could even be your teacher! Every time you make a mistake I can correct–*ow!* What are you–*owwww!* Stop–that hurts! Owww! Owww! *Owwwwwwwwwwwwwwwww!*" I screamed. "Let go of my fingers! You're gonna break them! *Stop!*"

"You little puta!" she muttered, as she bent my fingers backward in a KGB finger lock. "You and your stupid English language–ha! America think they own world! Bleaha muha! Capitalist pigs!"

Thinks it *owns the* world, I thought, as I screamed, "Let! Go! Of! My! Fingers! *Please!* You're gonna break them!"

She let go, then turned her back to me and began muttering, "Stupido Americano . . . This ridiculous!"

"Jesus Christ," I muttered. "What the hell is wrong with you?" I began shaking my fingers in the air, trying to stop the pain. "You could have broken my fingers with that fucking KGB death grip!" I shook my head angrily. "And who the hell are *you* to call *me* a little puta? Do you think I'm a little whore now? Five minutes ago you were saying how much you loved me, and now you're calling me names!" I shook my head sadly, as if I were very disappointed in her. Then I prepared for makeup sex.

After a few seconds she turned to me, ready to make friends again. *"Praste minya,"* she said softly, which I could only assume meant *thank you,* and then she started babbling something in rapid-fire Russian. Her tone was rather sweet, actually, so I could only assume she was saying that she had tried to break my fingers out of love. Then she said, "Come here, *musek-pusek*; let my kiss your *palcheke,*" and she grabbed my fingers and began kissing them very softly, which led me to believe that *palcheke* were fingers.

Feeling vindicated, I leaned back on the blanket and prepared for my reward (meaning, she would kiss my erect penis), and just like that she was lying next to me and we were kissing. It was a soft, mellow kiss, a slow kiss, a *Russkie* kiss, which seemed to last for a very long time. Then she rested her head upon my shoulder, and the two of us, lovers once more, stared up to the heavens, beholding the awesome expanse of the universe–the orange moon, the glittering stars, the fuzzy white band of the Milky Way.

"I'm sorry about before," I said, lying through my teeth. "I won't correct you anymore if you don't want me to. I mean, I don't care if the moon *looks* like Swiss cheese or *look* like Swiss cheese, as long as I'm looking at it with you." With that, I kissed her on the crown of her pretty blond head and drew her close to me.

She responded by putting her long, bare leg over mine and cuddling even closer to me, as if we were trying to become one person.

"Ya lublu tibea," she said softly.

"I love you too," I said just as softly. I took a deep breath and stared up at the moon, wondering if I'd ever been happier than I was right now. This girl was truly something special–*Miss Soviet Union, for Chrissake!*–the very catch of the century, and, most importantly, she was the perfect antidote to the backstabbing Duchess.

With a fair dose of nostalgia in my voice, I said, "You know, I remember looking up at the moon as a kid and being totally blown away by it. I mean, knowing that people had actually been up there and walked on it. In 1969 you were only a year old, so you were too young to remember that day, but I remember it like it was yesterday.

"My parents had this little black-and-white TV set in the kitchen, and we were all crowding around it, watching Neil Armstrong go down the ladder. And when he took his first steps on the moon and started bouncing around..." I shook my head in awe. "I wanted to be an astronaut that day." I let out a few embarrassed chuckles. "Boyhood dreams," I said, smiling. "Which somehow led me to Wall Street. I would have never imagined it that day."

KGB chuckled back, although her chuckles had an edge to them. "This is big American joke," she said confidently. "You knows this, right?"

"What–that every kid wants to be an astronaut?"

"Nyet," she replied quickly. "I talk about moon"–*the moon, for Chrissake! What's so fucking difficult about it?* "There is English word for this moon thing you do. It is, uh, how do you say... *falcefekaceja... ah!* Hoax! You make hoax!"

"We make *a* hoax. Are you trying to say the moon landing was a hoax?"

"Da!" she exclaimed happily, and she popped upright and stared down at me. "This is hoax against Soviet people! Everybody know this."

"Knows," I replied through clenched teeth. "Everybody *knows*

this, Yulia, and you're not actually gonna look at me with a straight face and say that you think the United States faked the moon landings to embarrass Mother Russia! Please don't tell me this!" I stared at her, incredulous.

She compressed her lips and shook her head slowly. "This landing you speak of is filmed in movie studio. Everyone in rest of world know this. Only *here* people believe. How do you think America fly to moon when Soviet Union can't? We had female in space while you were flying monkey! And suddenly you beat us to moon? Oh, please—this is hoax! Look at pictures. You see flag wave on moon, but there is no atmosphere. So how can flag wave? And day is night, when night must be day; and earth rise, when it must fall. And there is belt of radiation..." and on and on KGB went, explaining how the moon landing was nothing more than a giant hoax filmed in a Hollywood movie studio, with the sole purpose of embarrassing her beloved Soviet Union. "We will talk about this with Igor when you meet," continued KGB, "and then you will see truth. Igor is famous scientist. He tame fire."

I shook my head in disbelief, not knowing quite how to respond to that. "Well," I said, fighting back the urge to tell her that her former Soviet Union, including its defunct space program, had become nothing more than a joke, "every human being is entitled to their opinion, although I *will* tell you that to pull off a conspiracy like that you'd need a thousand people, with every last one of them keeping the same monumental secret, and in *this* country, I can assure you, if more than two people know something, it doesn't stay secret very long. And I don't want to even mention the fact that there were actually *three* moon landings, not just one. So let's just say, for argument's sake, that the government actually *had* faked the first moon landing and had been lucky enough to get away with it—why would they press their luck again? It would be like: 'Hey, gotcha once, Mr. Brezhnev! Now I want you to watch very closely as I do it again, and see if you can catch me this time!' But, hey, what do I know? I mean, maybe aliens did land in Roswell, and maybe you *were* right yesterday when you said America never actually fought in World War Two"—that was KGB's other pearl of wisdom, shared with me by the tennis court after I beat her six–love, six–love in eleven and a half minutes, at which point we play-wrestled on the grass, an activity that ended with me screaming, "Let me go! Stop! You're hurting me! You're hurting me!"–"and that America stole the plans to the first atomic bomb from Russia and not the other way around." This had tumbled from her commie-red lips as we watched a History Channel documentary discussing weapons of war. KGB had informed me that Russian people–which is to say, Soviet people–were responsible for virtually every meaningful invention, from the atomic bomb to the X-ray machine to fine literature to Bazooka chewing gum. "The truth is, Yulia–and I say this out of love, as in *ya lublu tibea*–what I'm really interested in is Igor's cure for fire. Now, tell me what *that's* all about, because *that's* what I find most fascinating!"

She looked at me for a moment, shaking her head wryly. "Wouldn't *you* like to knows!"

"Yeah," I shot back, "I would like to *knows*! So why don't you *tells* me!"

She stared at me with narrowed eyes. Then she motioned with her heart-shaped chin over to our perfect little beach fire, at the base of which rested a Duraflame. "You see flame?"

I nodded. "Yeah, what about *the* flames?"

KBG snapped her long, slender fingers, and the air went *pop!* "Just like this," she said proudly, "Igor can make flame go away."

"And how does he do that?" I asked skeptically.

"He control atmosphere," she answered nonchalantly, as if controlling the atmosphere were no more difficult than adjusting a thermostat.

I looked at her for a moment, astonished, and also trying to calculate how much money I could have made with some wacky Russian scientist willing to claim he controlled the atmosphere. It was just the sort of thing the Strattonites would have eaten up. I could have stood Igor before the boardroom dressed in a wizard's costume, like Professor Dumbledore from *Harry Potter,* and I would have said into the microphone: "Behold Professor Igor and his cure for fire. . . ." The Strattonites would have gone wild–clapping and cheering and then lighting Lake Success on fire, so Igor could show his stuff.

I said to KGB: "Ohhh, I get it now! I think I've actually seen this in the movies. It was in *Austin Powers*: Dr. Evil had figured out a way to control the weather, and he was looking to hold the world hostage. On second thought, maybe that was James Bond. Or was it Superman?" I shrugged. "I'm not really sure."

She shrugged back. "Laughs all you want, big shot, but I not joking. Igor can cure fire, and I am shareholder in company. One day he will..." and as KGB kept talking, I stopped listening. I think she actually believed what she was saying, and not just all this nonsense about Professor Igor but everything. She had grown up with a different set of history books, listening to Soviet TV, where *we* were the Evil Empire determined to rule the world. I snuck a peek at my watch: It was nine-thirty. I had to be at the Plaza Athénée by nine a.m. tomorrow morning, which meant I had to leave the Hamptons at six-thirty.

It was time to end this night, which I couldn't do until I had made love to KGB in front of the fire. It was our ritual, after all, something that both of us looked forward to each day. So now I would have to agree with her. Yes, I would say: *In spite of my earlier skepticism, I am now convinced that Igor's cure for fire shall change the world. Now, be a good girlfriend, KGB, and make love to me. I don't care that you're a closet communist. I love you anyway!*

And that was exactly what happened.

The next morning, at precisely eleven a.m., the Chef and James Loo walked into Room 1104 at the Hotel Plaza Athénée. It was a one-bedroom, two-bathroom suite, and the Chef and James Loo were likes two lambs walking into a slaughterhouse.

I greeted them at the front door, first hugging the Chef and then exchanging a hearty handshake with James Loo, who was short, thin, slightly balding, and wearing an expensive sharkskin suit with no necktie.

I led him and the Chef into the main salon, directly off the entry gallery. The bedroom was on the opposite side of the suite, and the door was closed nice and tight–and for good reason. Inside that bedroom, wearing headphones, revolvers, and some very serious expressions, were four FBI agents–namely, OCD, the Mormon, and two tech guys, both of whom were in their mid-thirties and looked liked they should be working at Circuit City, fixing computers.

We had spent the last two hours analyzing the living room–checking various camera angles and such and places to hide the bugs. It was a small space, perhaps fourteen by twenty feet. Three tall windows that looked out over 64th Street admitted a great deal of light–*too* much light, actually, according to the tech guys, so we closed the bordello-red curtains to reduce the glare.

I offered my guests seats on the couch, and then I took a seat in one of the armchairs. That was just fine with the boys in the bedroom. At this very moment, they were watching us on a twelve-inch closed-circuit TV screen that received images from a pinhole camera concealed inside a digital clock. The clock was resting on one of the side tables, placed there by the tech guys. Ironically, I wasn't wired today; only the room was, pursuant to a court order. The only thing I was concealing was a very fat envelope with $50,000 inside. It was in the left-inside breast pocket of my navy sport jacket, and I was to hand it to Loo at the appropriate moment.

After a few minutes of small talk, I said, "I want you to know, James, that Dennis has vouched for you a hundred percent. And that means more than anything to me."

James nodded dutifully. "Likewise," he said. "Dennis vouched for you too, so I am very comfortable."

"And that's very good," said the Chef, who had little capacity for ass-kissing. "And now that we got *dat ouddada* way, let's move on to the good stuff!"

"Absolutely," I agreed. "The sooner I get my cash overseas the better. And by the way, James, I want you to know that the fact that you've done a lot of business with Bob makes me that much more comfortable." I nodded respectfully. "It's like getting an endorsement from the Pope, you know?" Actually, more like Darth Vader, I thought.

James nodded. "Yes, we have very good history together. And it is also a very funny story how we met."

"Oh, really?" I said. "I'd like to hear it."

"Well," he said proudly, "I was what you call 'emergency CEO' in one of Bob's underwritings."

"Yeah–get a load of this," snapped the Chef. "Bob does a deal, makes ten million, but then the CEO kicks the bucket the day the thing goes public. So now we needed someone–or, should I say, *anyone*–to step in." The Chef looked at his Chinese friend. "No offense, James."

"None taken," he replied.

"Anyway," continued the Chef, "James was on the board of the company at the time, so he agreed to step in as CEO. Then, of course, he did the right thing afterward, which is why we're all sitting here today."

I nodded slowly, searching for a way to delve deeper into how James had "done the right thing afterward," which in Chef terms (and in Wolf terms) meant that James had continued to issue cheap shares of stock to the Blue-eyed Devil after he went public. "So how did the company end up doing?" I asked casually. "Did it go anywhere?"

"It struggled for a while," said James, "but we all did okay."

The Chef said, "The most important thing is that James can be trusted. The company had its ups and downs, but James was always solid as a rock. And that's how he'll be with you on this: solid as a rock."

Sensing an opening, I asked, "So you've helped Bob the same way you're gonna help me? You know, like"–I winked–"over there, in the Orient?"

James shrugged. "I do many things for Bob, but I do not like to discuss them. It will be the same way with you. What we do is only between us, and, of course, Dennis."

I needed to get off this topic quickly, so I smiled at James, as if I'd only been testing him to see if he were a blabbermouth. "That's exactly what I wanted to hear, James. *Exactly!* See, the most important thing to me is that no one outside this room ever finds out about this. That's crucial."

"They won't," James said confidently. "Remember, it will be just as bad for me if that happens."

"And that is indeed true," added the Chef, with a single nod. "So all that's gotta happen now is you and James gotta come to your agreement; then I'll do what *I* gotta do, and you'll do what *you* gotta do, and then James will do whatever *he's* gotta do, and *badabeep, badabop, badaboop–schwiiiitttt!*–the money'll be over *there,* and we'll still be over *here,* and we can all sleep at night like babies."

"We're all on the same page here," I said confidently, "and if it's okay with you, James, I'd like to move very quickly. I have two million in cash that I want to get out of the States ASAP, because I, uh"–I looked around the room suspiciously, then lowered my voice–"got the money from new-issue kickbacks. You know, from clients I gave units to, who then did the right thing afterward and gave me back cash." I slowly raised my voice to normal. "Anyway, then I got another ten million dollars already in Switzerland, which I'd like to wire to your sister as soon as we get all the accounts set up."

"It is no problem," said James. "She is very organized and very reliable."

The Chef said, "I can take care of all the paperwork over there or anything else you need to get done. And when it comes to making investments, I'll work as an adviser to keep you one step removed until your problems blow over."

I nodded in understanding, wondering if there was any point to sitting in this room one second longer. Both the Chef and James Loo had already buried themselves a thousand times over, plus I had the Chef on audiotape from the other day, with his diagram of the nuclear submarine.

Still, according to OCD, there was nothing more powerful with a jury than videotape, so, if possible, I should try to get the Chef to explain the entire money-laundering scheme yet again. Obviously, with the way things were going, I knew he would; it was just that I was so bored with the whole thing by this point that I couldn't bear to hear it myself again. I had already been an expert on money laundering before all this started, and I was sick and tired of playing dumb.

Nevertheless, I had a job to do; so I took a deep breath and said,

"Everything sounds great, but I'm still a little bit confused. Just so there's no crossed wires in the future, can we go through the whole thing one more time?"

The Chef shook his head quickly, as if I were a bit on the dense side. Then he said, "Yeah, of course. Grab that pen and paper over there, will you . . ." and that was it. Ten minutes later I had another nuclear submarine, this one even *more* detailed. After all, the first one had only been a prototype; this one was the second generation. All I had to do now was to pass James the envelope. Then I was done.

I patted the outside of my sport jacket, just over the left breast pocket. "I assume Dennis mentioned that I was gonna give you a little cash today to get things going."

James nodded. "Yes; that would be excellent."

"Okay," said the Chef, "well, I don't think you guys need me around for this, so I'm gonna get going." And just like that he rose from the couch. "Is that okay with you, James?"

James shrugged. "Yes, no problem."

The Chef looked at me. "Is it okay with *you*?"

No, I thought, I gotta check with the guys in the bedroom first. "Sure," I said quickly, "it's fine."

With that the Chef shook James Loo's hand and headed for the door.

And that was when it hit me: I would never see the Chef again. I had no doubt that once the Bastard saw this videotape, he would indict the Chef quickly and then announce my cooperation shortly thereafter. The end was fast approaching, and it was time to say my last good-byes to a man whom I had once trusted with my dirtiest secrets, a man whom I had once called my friend.

The Chef was a man's man, and there was no one else like him. He was the sort of Chef who could stand the heat in the kitchen, the sort of man I would want to go into battle with. How many times had I said that to myself over the years? How many times had I looked to the Chef for strength, and for answers, wisdom, and courage? And this was how it ended up.

As the Chef opened the hotel-room door, I said, "Hey, Chef!"

"Yo!" he said, smiling. "What's up?"

I smiled back sadly. "I just wanted to thank you for everything you've done for me. It's a fucked-up business we're in, and you've always been a friend to me. Don't think I don't know that."

"Yeah," he said, "well, it's times like these when you find out who your true friends are. And now you know." Those were his last words to me before he flashed me a wink and a smile and walked out the door.

James Loo would never make it out the door.

Per OCD's instructions, I would pass him the envelope and then tell him that I needed to go downstairs for a minute to get something from the doorman. Then they would arrest him. Of course, the Chef would never find out, because James Loo would also join Team USA, as would the Chef, I prayed, when *his* time came. After all, it wasn't *him* that they were really after; it was the Blue-eyed Devil.

The Chef was just a stepping-stone.

On my way back out to Southampton, I held on to that thought for all it was worth: that the Chef would roll over on the Devil, and I would be spared the guilt of having ratted out my old friend. And when I wasn't thinking that, I kept reminding myself over and over again that all men betray . . . all men betray . . . all men betray.

I would be wrong about that.

Some don't.

CHAPTER 23

TWISTS OF FATE

The only newspaper KGB ever read was *Pravda,* which was the former Soviet Union's most well-respected newspaper. In Russian, the word *pravda* meant *truth,* which was somewhat ironic, I thought, considering that when the Soviet Union was around, *Pravda* never published anything even remotely truthful. And while today's *Pravda* was substantially more accurate than the *Pravda* of old, all I cared about on September 21, the day my cooperation was announced, was that *Pravda* hadn't dedicated so much as one Cyrillic letter to the day's hot topic in America, which was: The Wolf of Wall Street had secretly pleaded guilty *months ago* and had been cooperating with the feds for over a year.

So, while ninety-nine percent of Americans were reading their morning papers and saying, "This is great! They finally brought that bastard to heel!" and the other one percent were reading their morning papers and saying, "This is bad! That bastard is going to rat us out now!" KGB was reading *Pravda* and cursing out the Chechen rebels, who, in *her* mind, were worthless Muslim dogs that deserved to be nuked.

And that was what I loved most about KGB: not her burning desire to turn the Chechens into radioactive dust (I was opposed to that) but the fact that she was completely oblivious to what was going on in my life. Better she focused on those Chechen dogs, I figured, than on the fact that she was living with a rat.

At this particular moment, she was sitting with Carter on the TV room's couch, staring at a forty-inch high-definition TV screen. Every last drop of her mental energy was focused on an ultrabrave, genetically enhanced marsupial named Crash Bandicoot, who was in the process of doing what he was always doing: running for his fucking life.

"What are you guys doing?" I asked the two videoholics.

KGB ignored me; she was too busy at the PlayStation controls, her thumbs moving up and down at a frenetic pace. Carter, however, was just observing, although he was so entranced that he ignored me too. His eyes were as wide as an owl's, his elbows resting on his thighs with his tiny chin cupped in his palms.

I walked over to Carter and said, "Whaddaya doing, buddy?"

He looked up and shook his head in awe. "Yuya's *anazin'*, Daddy. She . . . she . . . she"–he couldn't seem to get the words out–"she's on the top level. She's fighting brand-new monsters I never see before. No one has."

"Look here," KGB muttered to Carter, as she assisted Crash in his escape. "If I capture golden mask I become invincible!"

Carter looked back at the TV screen, awestruck. After a few seconds he whispered, "Invincible!"

I sat down beside my son and put my arm around him. "She's pretty good, buddy, huh?"

"Use a jump attack!" he screamed to KGB.

"No!" she shot back. "To defeat this monster I must use spin attack!"

"Ohhhh . . ." he said softly.

A spin attack, I thought. Just say the word *a, for Chrissake*! Still, there was no denying that KGB was the most proficient *videogamestress* on the entire fucking planet–Ms. Pac-Man, Super Mario, Asteroids, Donkey Kong, Hercules, and, of course, her latest obsession, Crash Bandicoot, the genetically enhanced marsupial from Wumpa Island off western Australia. She'd beaten them all, rising to levels that mere mortals, like Carter, never dared dream about.

As KGB jerked her glorious body this way and Carter jerked his thirty-one-pound body that way, I found myself wondering what the hell made Yulia Sukhanova tick. She played videogames no less than eight hours a day, spending the rest of her time either reading Russian books, babbling on the phone in Russian, or whispering sweet Russian nothings in my ear as we made love. She resided in America, yes, but only in the physical sense. Her heart and soul were still in Russia, stuck in a geopolitical time warp in the year 1989, the very year she'd been crowned Miss Soviet Union.

Intellectually, she was brilliant. She excelled at chess, checkers, backgammon, gin rummy, and, for that matter, all games of chance, which she played with a hustler's edge, and she hated to lose more than anything. Her parents were both dead, her father succumbing to a heart attack when she was only nine. They had been close, she said, and his death traumatized her. He had been an important man in the Soviet Union, a rocket scientist with the highest security clearance, so even after his death the family had always been taken care of. She had never wanted for anything. Bread lines, empty store shelves, drab clothing–things like these were as far removed from Yulia's childhood as they were from mine. Her life had been a charmed one and, by Soviet standards, one of affluence.

Her grace and beauty had come from her mother. I had seen the pictures; she was breathtaking–blond, blue-eyed, and possessing the warmest of smiles. In her day, according to Yulia, her mother was even prettier than she and held a very important position in the arts. In consequence, Yulia had grown up in a chic Moscow apartment, where a never-ending parade of famous Soviet artists–actors, actresses, painters, sculptors, singers, and ballet dancers–partied into the wee hours of the night, drinking Stolichnaya vodka and singing Russian songs.

Her mother hadn't died of natural causes: She was murdered, stabbed to death in her apartment, and that was where the story became murky. Her death had come shortly after Yulia was crowned Miss Soviet Union–and literally coincided with a dispute over who had "rights" to the gravy train that Yulia Sukhanova had become. Many were suspected in the murder, but no one was ever charged. So who murdered her? Was it the KGB? The Russian mob? A disgruntled businessman trying to extort Yulia for her modeling earnings? Or was it simply a random act of violence?

Whichever it was, this was the girl I had fallen in love with, a girl who loved her country but was reluctant to return there even as a visitor. In fact, she hadn't even flown back for her mother's funeral, and while she didn't say it, I knew it was out of fear. Igor–who she still maintained was her brother-in-law, married to her older sister, Larissa–hadn't flown back either, although in his case, she admitted, he couldn't have gone even if he wanted to. He was a wanted man in his country, but not by the law. There were "others," she said, whose toes Igor had stepped on, and it had something to do with her. And that was it. Try as I might, she refused to go any further with the story.

Insofar as *my* circumstances were concerned, I was certain that she knew more than she led on. On the day my cooperation was announced, I offered her a brief explanation of what was going on–stressing the Dave Beall incident and how, in spite of it coming back to haunt me, I still felt like I had done the right thing. I had maintained my self-respect, I told her, to which she grabbed my hand and squeezed it reassuringly. And when the Chef was indicted two weeks later, I told her about that too–how he had been my accountant, a loyal friend who seemed to get an irrational joy out of "scheming," which, ultimately, had led to his undoing–to which she said that there are no friends in business and that, if I hadn't learned my lesson with Dave Beall, then I never would.

She spent a great deal of time telling me about *the great Russian soul*–the *velikaya russkaya dusha,* she called it–and how no American could truly understand it. Honesty, integrity, sensitivity, imagination, compassion, guilt, the need to suffer in silence. Those were just a few of the words she used to describe it, thumbing through her Russian–English dictionary.

Yet, from my perspective, it wasn't her great Russian soul that was impressive, but her loyalty. We had known each other for less than two months, and it had to be plainly obvious to her that I wasn't the man she had thought I was. I was burdened with problems, my future uncertain. I was a man whose financial star was on the fall, not on the rise. Still, none of this seemed to bother her.

When I told her that I had to get rid of the beach house, she shrugged her shoulders and said that she couldn't care less about Meadow Lane. Better we should live in Manhattan, she added, and who needed such a big house anyway? And when I told her that money might get tight for a while, she assured me that any man who could make as much as I had so young could figure out a way to do it again.

Emboldened by her words, I nodded in agreement and then made a decision to start trading stocks again, albeit legitimately. The NASDAQ was flying–dot-com mania, they called it–and with the money the government had left me, I could make a few million a year in my sleep. Just why I hadn't thought of this before I wasn't so sure, although I knew it had something to do with KGB believing in me.

In that sense, she was everything the Duchess wasn't. She was willing to bet on *me,* not on what I had come to surround myself with. Yet, in the Duchess's defense, Yulia didn't have two children to worry about, nor did she have "history" with me.

Whatever the case, the Duchess was my past and KGB was my future, and here she was, about to reach the twenty-fifth level of Crash Bandicoot. All she needed to do was defeat Dr. Neo Cortex, Crash's nemesis, and then Crash would be reunited with his girlfriend, Tawna, another genetically enhanced bandicoot, who, in the world of bandicoots, was as sexy as Jessica Rabbit.

Suddenly, KGB started screaming: *"Blyad! Blyad! Nyet! Nyet!"*

"Back up!" screamed Carter. "He's throwing fireballs!"

"I can't!" screamed KGB. "I have lost power!"

"No!" screamed Carter. "Use a power crystal..." and I watched the screen with total fascination as a muscle-bound ape named Koala Kong picked up a fireball and winged it at Crash's head, causing him to burst into flames. At this point Crash screamed in agony, jumped into the air, did a three-sixty, and then landed on his tiny bandicoot butt and burned to death. Then the TV made a sound like: "*Wa, wa, wa, wa, wa... boom!*" And that was it: The screen went black.

At first, KGB and Carter just looked at each other, frozen. Then KGB shook her head and said, "*Chto ty nashu stranu obsirayesh!*"

Carter compressed his lips and nodded his little head in agreement, having no idea that KGB had said, "I just shit all over this stupid game!" Then Carter said, "Again, *Yuya,*" to which KGB nodded in resignation, took a deep breath, and hit a button on the controller, bringing Crash back to life, albeit at the bottom of Neo Cortex's castle.

And as they lost themselves in the game, I found myself wondering what kind of mother KGB would be to my children if disaster struck. Unlikely as it seemed, it was still something I had to consider–that the Duchess could die and the kids would become solely my responsibility.

KGB and Carter had a close connection based on their love of video games, but, outside that, I wasn't so sure. There was a certain *disconnect* between them, inasmuch as when they weren't sitting in front of the TV screen they said very little to each other. Of course, she was never anything but nice to him, no two ways about that, but there was a lack of warmth, I thought, a certain apathy that one wouldn't expect to find given the storied nature of the *great Russian soul.*

Chandler, however, didn't play video games; she played with Barbie dolls and she played house and dress-up and she liked to watch TV–of the American variety–so she and KGB had very little in common. And that bothered me; it bothered me that I never saw KGB reaching out to her. Indeed, as with Carter, she was always nice and always quick to offer a warm smile, but there was still that same disconnect.

In my mind it was simple: KGB was the adult and Chandler and Carter were the children, so the ball was in *her* court, not theirs. Or was I expecting too much? She wasn't the mother of my children, so perhaps it was unreasonable to expect her to be a second mother to them. Maybe a degree of casual indifference was healthy, maybe it was normal, and maybe I should just thank my lucky stars that KGB was kind. No, I thought, kindness wasn't enough. Apathy is its own form of cruelty, and children can spot it a mile away.

Meanwhile, on the other end of the spectrum was John Macaluso, the Duchess's boyfriend. Just last week he'd called me out of the blue and suggested that we meet for a cup of coffee. He was spending a lot of time with my kids, he said warmly, and he wanted to assure me that he would always try his best to be a positive influence in their lives. It was a classy move, to say the least, and when we met a few days later at the Old Brookville Diner, we hit it off instantly.

He was about my height and was thin and wiry and bursting at the seams with energy. He was handsome, with salt-and-pepper hair and prominent Italian features, but he was charismatic more than anything. We spent an hour exchanging war stories–carefully avoiding the subject of my failed marriage to the Duchess or his current relationship with her–while I resisted the urge to ask him if she moaned, "Come for me, my little prince!" while they were having sex. Yet, with all the laughing and smiling, there was one issue that hung over the meeting like a dark cloud.

Finally he brought it up.

"You know, it really sucks that I live in California and Nadine lives in New York," he said wearily. "It figures I'd fall in love with a woman who lives three thousand miles away!"

And that was it: The cat was out of the bag.

There was a major problem–he knew it and I knew it–and it wasn't about to go away on its own. Either he would have to move here or she would want to move there. And knowing the Duchess's attorney–that fat bastard Dominic Barbara, with his notoriously fat mouth and penchant for bathing his even fatter ass in the limelight–he would use my legal predicament as leverage.

John was no fool; upon seeing my reaction, he quickly added that Nadine would never do anything behind my back. She knew how close I was with the kids and was always saying what a good father I was. And, with that, we dropped it, although I think we both knew that at some point this issue would rear its ugly head again.

And the lovely KGB–where did she stand in all this?

Just watching her with Carter right now, united by their love of the genetically enhanced bandicoot, gave me hope for everything she might be. Perhaps she could *learn* to love my children, and perhaps I could *learn* to love her the same way I had once loved the Duchess and the way I had once loved Denise–for, in truth, I felt the same disconnect in my own relationship with her that I sensed between her and my children.

Perhaps, over time, the gulf between our cultures could become our greatest strength. Americans, after all, had a great soul of their own, didn't they? According to Dostoyevsky, the essence of the great Russian soul was the ever-present and unquenchable need to suffer, and, according to yours truly, the essence of the great American soul was: Why should we suffer at all when our parents and grandparents suffered for us? So, together, couldn't KGB and I unite into a perfect soul? It would be my American optimism mixed with her Russian fatalism, the sum of which would be *perfection.*

Either way, we had a few years to bridge the gulf. The new millennium was just around the corner–only eighty days away–and it would be three or four years after that until I got sentenced.

Then the phone rang.

"Blyad!" sputtered KGB. "Please pick up phone! It disturb my play."

Carter turned to me and nodded. "It disturb her play."

"Disturbs," I said to Carter, fearing KGB's influence over his language skills, and I reached over to the phone on the side table and picked it up. "Hello?"

"It's your lawyer," said Magnum, in an octave of C-minor. "How are you?"

"I'm doing good," I replied automatically, and then realized *after* the fact that I actually *was* doing good. Yes, I thought, for the first time in a long time I was approaching something close to happiness. "What's going on?" I asked.

"There's been a flurry of activity at the U.S. Attorney's today."

I felt my heart skip a beat. "Oh, really? In reference to what?"

"Are you familiar with an AUSA named Dan Alonso?"

"No," I replied quickly. "What about him?"

"Well, he's your new AUSA," answered Magnum. "He called Nick and me this morning to give us a heads-up. Joel is leaving the office next week and Alonso has been assigned to your case."

I crossed my fingers: "So what's he like? Is he a nice guy or is he a douche bag?"

"*Wellllll*..." said Magnum, "on a scale of one to ten, with a douche bag being a one and a nice guy being a ten, I would say Alonso falls somewhere between a ten and an eleven."

"You're kidding!" I exclaimed.

"Shhhh!" snapped KGB. "I cannot concentrate!"

Carter looked up and put his forefinger to his lips. Then he looked back at the screen. I chuckled and said into the phone, "Is he really that good?"

"Yes," answered Magnum, "he really is. He's tough, fair, very smart, an excellent litigator, and, above all, he's got a big heart. I've already broached the subject of reducing your obstruction charge, and he said he's willing to sit down and talk about it. He wants to meet you first, and then he'll let us plead our case. I think we're in very good shape there."

I felt a wave of relief come over me. "Well, this is great news, Greg, really great."

"Yeah, it is," he agreed. "On a separate note, though, I got a very strange call from Joel Cohen this morning. He was saying something about you being in Atlantic City a few months ago and that you refused to identify yourself. He hinted that you were trying to launder money or something. I know that's not true, right?"

My mouth immediately went dry, my gut drawing conclusions faster than my mind could come to them. "Of course not!" I sputtered. "That's total bullshit! I wasn't trying to launder money! It was a misunderstanding!"

"So you *were* there?" asked Magnum, seeming extremely surprised.

I already knew where this was going.

In the end, I could prove that I hadn't tried to launder money, but I couldn't prove that I hadn't violated my bail restrictions. I had left New York without permission. "Yeah, I was there," I said softly. "Hold on a second; let me switch rooms."

On my way out of the TV room, I took a moment to regard the innocent face of my son. He had had a rocky start, Carter, yet he had grown strong. A terrible wave of sadness came over me. I felt like I had let him down.

Inside the master bedroom, I picked up the phone of the future and sat down on the edge of the bed, then went about telling my lawyer the story, all the sordid details–starting with the luscious yet underage Kiley and finishing with the stone-faced woman in the cashier's cage who refused to give me my money back. Then I said, "They're not going to break my cooperation over this, right?"

"No," he replied quickly, "not if what you're telling me is true."

Trying to maintain control, I took a deep breath and let it out slowly. Then I started spitting nails at my attorney, swearing up and down that I was telling the truth this time. First I swore on my eyes, then I swore on my children's eyes, then I swore on my unborn children's eyes, and then I swore on Magnum's children's eyes too.

Finally, he said, "All right! I believe you! I believe you! You can stop selling me now. Jesus! You know, either way, we still have some serious damage control to do. What kind of relationship do you have with your pretrial-services officer?"

"Pat Mancini?" I replied, sensing a thin ray of hope. "He's great!" I chose not to bring up my misleading phone call to Pat, with its vague reference of being stuck in *the* city, without saying *which* city. "Why do you ask?"

"I *ask* because he's the one who can ultimately turn your lights out here. If he writes a letter to the judge about your little helicopter excursion–destination, Atlantic City; companion, underage girl; seed money for gambling, a bag full of the government's cash–it could be a problem, Jordan. It doesn't look like the behavior of a contrite man. You understand?"

And that was when it hit me: *the sheer audacity of my actions!* It wasn't so much that I had violated my release conditions (that was bad enough on its own) but how I had done it.

If I had driven to Atlantic City in a beat-up station wagon with my seventy-year-old mother and a bunch of rolled-up quarters, then Judge Gleeson would probably say, "Oh, it's just the case of a good son trying to spend some quality time with his mom," and then he would let me off with a warning. But I had stolen $100 million and was being given a second chance, and how did I show my appreciation? I took a secret helicopter ride to the Sodom and Gomorrah of New Jersey with an underage model. And to finance my trip I took an interest-free loan from the federal government!

With a sinking heart, I said, "So what happens next?"

There were a few moments of silence, then Magnum said, "Nothing, hopefully. I'll call Joel back and offer your side of the story, and then I'll tell him that I'll work it out with Alonso, although this is not exactly the best way to start a relationship with him." He paused for a moment. Then: "But what are you gonna do, right?"

"Yeah, right," I said tonelessly. "What are you gonna do."

We spent a few more minutes strategizing, but there wasn't really much we could do. The most important thing, we agreed, was to make sure this never made it before Judge Gleeson. He was a conservative man, said Magnum, an altogether rational man, who lived his life by the rules. This was just the sort of thing to raise his ire.

After we hung up the phone, I sat there on the edge of the bed for a moment, dumbfounded. I must have said a thousand times, in jest, that I was my own worst enemy, but this time it wasn't funny. Once more I had put my freedom in jeopardy, and for what? In retrospect, my decision seemed utterly mind-boggling. Was I really that self-destructive? I didn't think so, yet from the outside looking in, that's exactly what I appeared to be. What malfunction did I possess that caused me to do these things, that caused me to take these wild risks, even when there was no upside?

I took a deep breath and fought down the urge to beat myself up any further. What was done was done. If Judge Gleeson found out about this, he would throw me in the slammer on the spot—at which point I would lose Yulia, the children would be heartbroken, the Duchess would move to California, Meadow Lane would be forfeited in my absence, my furniture and clothing would be auctioned off for pennies on the dollar, and my plan to trade stocks would be thwarted. Yet my expenses with the Duchess and the children would continue–so when I finally got sentenced, three years from now, and I emerged from jail a few years after that, I would be naked, alone, penniless, homeless, and my kids would live three thousand miles away, calling John Macaluso Daddy!

CHAPTER 24

THE FATE GOD STRIKES BACK

The next seven days were gut-wrenching.

Upon hanging up with Magnum, I called Pat Mancini, who, not surprisingly, had just received a phone call from the Bastard, asking if he'd given me authorization to travel to Atlantic City. Pat, of course, told him that he hadn't, to which the Bastard suggested that he inform Judge Gleeson of my bail violation.

Pat told him that he would think about it.

Thankfully he told me that he wouldn't; in fact, he actually felt bad for me, he said. Yes, I was definitely a schmuck for taking a helicopter to Atlantic City, but in a way I had been set up for the fall. "There's only so long a man can stay under house arrest before he fucks up," Pat explained. "It's like the old saying: You leave a man just enough rope to hang himself."

Before he hung up the phone, he said something that I knew I would be hearing a lot for a few weeks, namely: "For a smart guy, Jordan, you do some pretty stupid things!" Then he hung up on me.

I passed the rest of the weekend in a state of relative calm. Then, on Monday morning, all hell broke loose.

It started when Mancini called Magnum to say that he had received a scathing letter from the Bastard, demanding that Pat write a letter to Gleeson, informing him of my trip to Atlantic City. And, just for good measure, the Bastard wrote that all the high points of my trip—the young girl, the bag of cash, the chopper—must be included in the letter to Gleeson, lest Pat be accused of painting a misleading picture for the judge.

Magnum placed an emergency phone call to Joel—to beg him to rescind the letter to Mancini—only to get a recorded message that went something like: "Hi, this is Joel Cohen, and I'm no longer with the U.S. Attorney's Office. I will be on vacation for the next two weeks . . ."

Yes, the Bastard had vanished, and this was his revenge.

He had wanted to revoke my bail over the Dave Beall incident but had been overruled. So this was payback, and it was a bitch!

Magnum, however, was not ready to go down without a fight, so he hopped on the subway and went down to the U.S. Attorney's Office to meet with Alonso, who agreed to call Mancini and tell him that he could handle this "in house." My restrictions would be tightened for a few months, and then ultimately Alonso would make a motion before Gleeson to have my ankle bracelet removed—getting me out of Mancini's hair once and for all.

Sure, Mancini said, that would be wonderful. The only problem was that he had just hit the send button on the e-mail, and right now, at this very moment, Judge Gleeson was probably reading the letter, which did indeed include all the dirty details. When Magnum informed me of this, I dropped the phone, ran to the toilet, and vomited. Then I ran back to the phone and asked Magnum what this meant—which is to say, was my goose cooked for sure now?

He told me that it wasn't; there was still a fifty-fifty shot that Gleeson would read the letter and take no action. After all, the letter had not been accompanied by a request for a hearing. With a little bit of luck, Gleeson would just shake his head in disbelief, lose a bit of respect for me, and then move on with his day.

No such luck.

On Thursday morning, at 8:30 a.m. sharp, I heard a very disturbing sound: the phone ringing.

Oh, Jesus! I thought. I looked to my left, and there was KGB. As always, she was sleeping soundly, her blond Soviet head poking out from beneath the white silk comforter.

It was Magnum. His first few words were lost on me, but his next few words weren't: "Unfortunately, I just received a fax from Gleeson, and he's ordered a hearing."

"When?" I asked, in a state far beyond panic.

"Tomorrow morning, ten a.m."

I stole a glance at KGB. Well, it was nice knowing you! I thought.

"I guess I'm dead fucking meat," I said rather calmly.

"Not necessarily," he replied. "I think there's still a way out of this. The key is that we need to approach Gleeson as a united front. I already spoke to both Mancini and Alonso. Mancini will be there too, tomorrow, and he promised he'd stand up for you. He's gonna say that it was a misunderstanding and that, in *his* mind, you can still be trusted to live up to your bail restrictions."

"And what about Alonso? What's he gonna say?"

"Like I told you, when it comes to AUSAs, Dan Alonso is about as good as they get. So, in spite of him never meeting you before, he's willing to stand up for you too. I'm meeting with him later today, and we're going to work out a package that we can sell to Gleeson. There'll be some severe restrictions for a while–no travel, in your house by six p.m., no more late nights in the city–but it's much better than going to jail right now, right?"

"Yeah, it is," I replied. "And what are the chances of Gleeson going along with this?"

"Close to a hundred percent," Magnum said confidently. "It's very rare that a judge goes against the recommendation of the U.S. attorney. And the fact that Mancini's on board pretty much seals the deal."

Excellent, I thought. There was no reason to worry.

The United States Courthouse at 225 Cadman Plaza was enveloped by an irreducible despair. No one, it seemed, really wanted to be there–from the lawyers, to the defendants, to the clerks, to the marshals, to the court reporters, to the people who swept the building's six sprawling floors, to the judges themselves. Everyone looked either bored, desperate, or on the verge of tears. And while you might find an occasional smile from someone who had just been acquitted of a criminal charge, for every broad smile there was a frown. After all, for every winner there was a loser.

Except in my case.

It was Friday morning, a few minutes before ten, and my lawyers and I were standing in a long, broad hallway outside Judge Gleeson's courtroom. Save a few wooden benches against the walls, the hallway was completely bare. The benches looked about as comfortable as the linoleum floor. Between the benches were four soundproof doors, two on each side, and each leading into a separate courtroom.

Just then Magnum looked down at the top of my head and said, "Look, here comes Alonso now," and he pointed to a tall, slender figure walking toward us. At first glance he looked more like a movie star than an assistant United States attorney. Tall, lean, good-looking, immaculately groomed, and possessing a surprisingly warm smile, he was everything the Bastard wasn't–namely, a picture of grace and gentility. He looked like the actor George Hamilton, without the tan.

"So you're Jordan Belfort," said Dan Alonso, extending his hand for a shake. "You don't look capable of causing so much commotion!"

I smiled and shook his hand warmly, wondering if he was making some vague reference to my height. After all, he was every bit of six foot two, and Magnum's head was nearly scraping the twelve-foot-high cement ceiling. I took a step toward the Yaleman, for height-protection, and I said, "Well, looks can be deceiving, right?"

Alonso nodded and shook my hand firmly.

Magnum said, "I promise you, Alonso, this is the end of the commotion. Jordan has lost his desire to fly around in helicopters with bags of money. Right, Jordan?"

And don't forget about the underage girl, I thought. "Forever," I said confidently. "I will never step foot in Atlantic City again. In fact, I have no desire to ever step foot in *New Jersey* again!"

"Who does?" reasoned the Yale-man.

Magnum said to Alonso, "I think this would be a good time to go through the particulars. I've already spoken to Jordan about his new restrictions, and he's totally fine with them. Right, Jordan?"

"Yeah," I said unenthusiastically. "I'm actually looking forward to them."

Alonso said, "Just behave yourself for a few months and we can go back in front of Gleeson and make a motion to have you taken off house arrest. I think that's the safest bet for all of us."

I compressed my lips and nodded humbly, but silently I was thinking: Alonso is the fucking best, and may the Bastard burn in fucking hell, with a pitchfork up his ass! "Thank you," I said meekly.

"No problem," said Alonso. Then he looked at Magnum and said, "I'd just as soon not bring up the Dave Beall issue today. We'll set up another hearing for that."

Magnum nodded, and then looked down at me and said, "Dan has been nice enough to reduce the obstruction-of-justice charge to lying to a federal officer."

Alonso, sarcastically: "You can thank your lawyers for that one. They've been pounding me so hard over the last few days—especially you, Nick—that I just didn't want to hear their voices anymore."

"Just doing my job," said the Yale-man.

I smiled at Magnum and the Yale-man. I said to Alonso, "I appreciate it, but, above all, I know my kids will appreciate it one day."

Alonso nodded in understanding. "All right, well, let's go inside and get it over with." He took one step, then stopped dead in his tracks. He turned to us and said, "I sincerely hope Gleeson doesn't ask too many questions today, 'cause, for the life of me, I haven't the slightest idea what really happened here. This whole thing got dumped on my lap at the last second, and I really hate to go to court not knowing all the details. I mean, why the fuck would you go to Atlantic City in the first place? You were under house arrest, for Chrissake!"

I nodded sheepishly. "Well, I think I was just–"

Alonso cut me off with a raised hand. "No, don't tell me. I'd rather not know. There's no upside in it." He shook his head. "Anyway, for a smart guy you do some pretty stupid things, you know?"

I nodded in agreement. "Yeah, I've heard that before."

"Yeah, well, I'm not surprised. Come on, let's go."

"Hear ye! Hear ye!" bellowed a kind-looking middle-aged woman wearing a nondescript maroon pantsuit. "The United States Court for the Eastern District of New York is now in session," she continued, in a surprisingly deep voice. "All rise for the presiding judge, the Honorable John Gleeson."

Like a magician, Judge Gleeson, in black robes, emerged from behind a wood-paneled door that led from his chambers into the courtroom. Without saying a word, he calmly walked up a short flight of stairs and took a seat behind a vast wooden desk that sat upon a wooden stage fit for the Phantom of the Opera himself.

To the judge's left, a court reporter took her seat in anticipation of memorializing the day's proceedings. Behind her stood a very stocky man, who was wearing a loose-fitting blue sport jacket with a giant bulge under his left armpit. He was just standing there, his arms crossed beneath his massive chest, waiting for someone to fuck with the judge. Then he would strike with the speed of a cobra.

The rest of us–including my pretrial services officer, Patrick Mancini, who at six-three, two-thirty could have played tight end for the Rams–were all standing behind the defense table. That was a good sign, I figured, because there was no one standing behind the prosecutor's table. (We're all on the same side here!) In fact, even the audience's sole spectator, a young black woman in her early twenties, whom I'd pegged as an aspiring lawyer or a reporter, looked to be on my side. She was sitting in the spectator section, holding a spiral notebook and a pen.

Magnum put his hand on my shoulder and gently pushed me into my seat. Now the kind woman who'd announced the judge's presence began muttering something to the court reporter, something about the entire United States of America being against me, Jordan Belfort. I had never really looked at it that way before, even at my sentencing, which had occurred in secret, inside Judge Gleeson's chambers.

Judge Gleeson looked rather nice, actually. Even in those flowing black robes, I could still tell that he had a kind heart. He struck me as the sort of guy who would carve a Thanksgiving turkey for his family. He was very young for a federal judge, no older than forty-five, and he had a reputation for brilliance. Hopefully he was in a good mood.

Suddenly Magnum motioned for me to stand, so I did.

"Okay," Judge Gleeson said softly. "Now, what's going on here?"

Alonso said, "If it pleases the court, Your Honor, I'd like to speak."

Judge Gleeson nodded.

"Thank you," said Alonso. "Okay, Your Honor, well, we've come to an agreement with the defendant's counsel on this matter, as well as with Mr. Mancini. The agreement consists of tightening the defendant's house-arrest restrictions to very onerous terms. The defendant will only be able to travel to work and back, and he must be home by six p.m., without exception. And on weekends, he will be on twenty-four-hour lockdown." With that Alonso nodded once, pleased with my new conditions.

"Oh, *really*?" snapped Judge Gleeson. "Well, I have questions."

And that was it; it was over before it started.

Gleeson had questions and Alonso didn't have answers, because he had just taken over the case. And even if he *did* have answers, it wouldn't have mattered anyway, because, as Magnum had said, this was *just* the sort of thing to raise Gleeson's ire–the very brazenness of it!

Suddenly I realized that Alonso was babbling something about a helicopter . . . a bag of cash . . . then an unidentified female (and, obviously, every last soul in the courtroom, especially Gleeson, knew exactly what kind of female this was), and then he started saying, "...but I really don't know all the facts here, Your Honor, because I just–"

Gleeson cut him off in a menacing voice: "Are you telling me that you've come into my courtroom unprepared, that you don't know the first thing about this case?"

I snuck a peek at Alonso, who looked like he'd just taken a bullet. The way I figured it, he had two options: The first was to blame it all on the Bastard, and the second was just to say that he was sorry and that it wouldn't happen again. Alonso said, "I'm very sorry, Your Honor, it won't happen again."

Now it was Mancini's turn. "Mr. Mancini?" said the angry judge.

Pat fumbled through some notes and began spewing out random facts, then a few contradictions, and he ended by saying, "...uh, but in spite of all that, I still think Mr. Belfort can be trusted to live up to his new release conditions." He shrugged, as if to say, "But that's just one man's opinion. Don't hold me to it."

Gleeson didn't berate him. In fact, he didn't say a single word to him; he just stared at Mancini for a few seconds too long, his eyes emitting what appeared to be an incredible shrinking ray, and I watched in fascination as Mancini, the tight end, seemed to grow smaller and smaller, until he was a midget.

Satisfied with that, Gleeson turned off his shrinking ray and then looked at his old buddy Magnum. "Does the defense counsel have anything to add here?"

Magnum stood up to his full height and said, in a very confident tone, "Yes, Your Honor..." and then he went about giving a highly accurate account of what happened. His words came out smoothly, confidently, and altogether logically–which was a total fucking disaster for me, because this was not one of those situations where *the truth shall set you free,* especially when Magnum got to the part about the helicopter malfunction being the primary cause of me not getting back before curfew. That was when Gleeson pounced.

"So, what you're saying, Counselor, is that your client's excuse is that he thought he'd get away with it?"

"Uh, not exactly," said Magnum–and *Jesus Christ!* I thought.

How the fuck could a judge who'd never broken a single law in his entire life sift through all the bullshit so quickly? What were the chances?

Now Magnum began trying to defend me again, spewing out more half-truths and some rather bold predictions (considering my track record) about my future conduct under house arrest. But I couldn't listen anymore. I knew where this was going, and I knew where *I* was going. And it wasn't home.

Finally there were a few moments of silence. I fought the urge to turn around and sneak a peek at my favorite spectator. She thought she would be sitting through a boring hearing, and now she was about to see a guy who had put up $10 million in bail have it revoked!

Gleeson started talking, and I knew that he was speaking English words, but for some reason I couldn't understand them. He sounded like the muffled teacher from the *Charlie Brown* cartoons. I felt dizzy, ready to puke. The room seemed to be slowly revolving, like a merry-go-round.

Then I heard Gleeson say, "No . . . no . . . I don't like this . . . get to the bottom of this . . . blatant disregard . . . helicopter . . . where . . . did he get cash . . ." Then suddenly more *Charlie Brown*: *"Weep, womp . . . Womp, weep . . . Weep, womp . . ."* and then: "I hereby remand the defendant to custody." Next thing I knew, Magnum was saying, "Give me your watch and your money, and your belt too."

I had only a few seconds of freedom left, and my mind immediately jumped to the kids. I was supposed to pick them up this afternoon. *Such sadness.* I had let them down again. As I removed my watch, I said to Magnum in an urgent tone, "You gotta call Nadine right now and tell her what happened. Tell her that I don't know when I'll be able to call, but to kiss the kids for me and tell them that I love them. And that I'll always love them."

"I'll take care of it right away," he said. "I'm sorry this happened."

"Not as sorry as me," I said softly. "Is there any way out of this?"

He shook his head. "Not now; we need to let Gleeson calm down for a while. A *long* while."

"How long is a long while?" I asked.

"At least a few months, probably longer."

In no time flat, the man with the bulge under his jacket was standing next to me. Rather kindly, he said, "Would you mind coming with me, sir?"

"Do I have a choice?" I asked, with a nervous smile.

"I'm afraid not," he replied, and he put his beefy hand on my shoulder and gently guided me in the direction of a secret door at the front of the courtroom.

I took a few steps, then turned to Magnum and said, "Oh, shit! You gotta call Yulia! She's at the Four Seasons Hotel. I told her I'd be back in an hour."

"I'll take care of it," he said calmly. "As soon as I'm done with Nadine."

"The room's under my name," I screamed over my shoulder.

And then I was gone–walking through a door and finding myself in a little-known area of 225 Cadman Plaza, consisting of holding cells, fluorescent lights, and desperate people. The area didn't have a name, but I had been here once before and nearly frozen to death. Now I was back.

As usual, I had no one to blame but myself.

CHAPTER 25

THE INEVITABLE

The Metropolitan Detention Center rose up nine stories from out of the gloomy groin of Brooklyn, a foreboding place that passing motorists pointed to and cringed at. Some two miles south of the federal courthouse, the building, with its towering razor-wire fence and sweeping searchlights, occupied an entire square city block, sucking out the very life force from the air surrounding it.

The marshals had taken their sweet-ass time shuttling me over here; from holding cell to holding cell, from cement hallway to cement hallway, from prison van to prisoner loading dock, I was herded, handcuffed, and shackled, like a cow, and all the while, whether by design or by accident, the average room temperature never exceeded the surface temperature of Pluto.

But now the worst was over.

Stripped of my clothing and my dignity, and then ordered to lift up my *schlong* and nut-sack and bend over and cough, I had arrived in style–that is to say, I was now in a windowless, partitionless, hopeless room known as "Pod 7N," which was on the seventh floor on the north side of the building. I was now sitting on the edge of my razor-thin mattress, engaged in a conversation with my new "bunkie," Ming, who was sitting beside me. Alas for Ming: Despite being a thirty-year-old Chinaman, he looked like a sixty-year-old ghost.

"So let me get this straight," I said skeptically. "You haven't seen the sun in six years? I find that a little bit hard to believe, Ming."

Ming shrugged his narrow shoulders, which were connected to a series of equally narrow body parts. He said, in heavily accented English, "Not six year, six and one-*half* year. Judge say I flight risk, so he no give bail."

"That sucks!" I muttered. "So we never get to go outside?"

Ming shook his head no. "Just this room. Do all here."

Christ, it seemed only logical that, since a plant needs sunlight to survive, a human being would too, didn't it? Apparently not. With a sinking heart, I took a moment to regard the room. It was a vast space, perhaps forty by eighty feet, packed to capacity with 106 inmates–or *detainees,* as the phrase went–all living barracks-style, doing everything from eating to sleeping to pissing to shitting to showering to brushing their teeth for months or sometimes *years* on end beneath a sea of buzzing fluorescent lights. Without a partition in sight, I could see from one end of the pod clear to the other.

Not that there was much to see–simply a vast sea of metal bunk beds and low-backed plastic chairs bounded at the rear by six gruesome toilets and three germ-laden showers. At the center of the room were two dozen stainless-steel picnic tables, a falling-apart Ping-Pong table, a sometimes-working microwave oven, an ancient toaster oven, and three color TVs suspended from the ceiling. Other than at mealtimes, the picnic tables were used for either watching TV (with headphones on) or for playing chess, checkers, cards, or, if you were a Dominican, a jailhouse version of dominoes, which required you to smash the dominoes onto the table while muttering strings of broken-Spanish curses.

And that was all Pod 7N had to offer–unless you included, as one must, the three pay phones affixed to a cement wall up by the guard station, where a single corrections officer now sat behind a cheap wooden desk with his finger on a panic button. The pay phones were the pod's highlight, a place where *detainees,* most of them blacks or Hispanics (less than ten percent were white or Asian), would try to stay vaguely connected to the outside world. From morning 'til night, lined up six deep, they waited to speak to their loved ones, who, for the most part, were loving them less and less with each passing day. My particular bunk was located by the pay phones.

So here I was, sitting with Ming, trying to make sense of it all.

He was blessed with a generous smile, an altogether *kind* smile. It was hard to imagine that he was a heroin dealer for the Chinese mob, a pint-size enforcer who had once lit a competitor on fire and then used his burning carcass to roast spareribs.

"What's the story with the phones?" I asked Ming the Merciless.

"Collect calls only," he answered.

Just then, three detainees came scurrying by, single file. They were rotating their hips awkwardly and swinging their arms in an exaggerated fashion. Speed-walkers, I reasoned. Like everyone else, they wore gray sweatpants, white T-shirts, white canvas sneakers, and headphones. Ming and I leaned forward and watched them grow smaller in the distance. I motioned toward the speed-walkers. "What are they doing?"

Ming shrugged. "They exercise. Walk circles all day. Pass time."

Interesting, I thought.

In fact, despite arriving in Pod 7N only five minutes ago, I had already come to the conclusion that my chief enemy was not the other detainees but the intense boredom of being detained. After all, unlike a federal prison, where activities are abundant and violence is rampant, a federal detention center is devoid of both activity and violence. They simply bore you to death.

"So there are never any fights here?" I asked Ming.

He shook his narrow head. "Everyone too scared. You face ten year, have fight, now you face twenty. Understand?"

I nodded. Ninety percent of the detainees were awaiting sentencing, so if they got into a fight or otherwise fucked up, the Bureau of Prisons could alert the sentencing judge, who could then sentence them at the high end of the guidelines.

"I need to use the phone," I said tonelessly, rising from the edge of the mattress.

Ming put his hand on my arm. "Hey, you rich guy, right?"

I looked down at him and shrugged. "Why?"

He smiled. "Cause Ming do everything for you: cook, clean, wash clothes, make bed, cut hair. I be like slave."

I stared at him for a moment in disbelief. "How much?"

"Twenty dollars a week. You pay in stamps from commissary. Give me extra ten dollars, I steal food from kitchen. We eat like kings. I make best orange chicken this side of Chinatown!"

I chuckled. "Sure," I muttered, "why not?" And I headed for the back of the line.

My first call was to Magnum's home, which, sadly enough, was a number I knew by heart. The news was not good. Alonso was on the warpath: not so much because he was mad at me but because he was mad at the situation and, most of all, he was mad at himself. He had walked into a courtroom unprepared and had paid the price for it. As a consequence, it would be many months before he would go back on my behalf. On top of that, the burden would now be on us to do the investigation–to get affidavits from the pit bosses and casino hosts and the helicopter pilots, as well as Kiley, if I could find her–to prove beyond the shadow of a doubt that my trip to Atlantic City had nothing to do with money laundering.

Magnum had already enlisted Bo, who was reaching out to his contacts in Atlantic City. Coleman agreed to help too, although Magnum thought it would be best if we did our own investigation, then presented the facts to Gleeson in the form of an affidavit; this way the judge would know we were serious.

Before I hung up the phone, I found myself doing what all detainees did: I begged my lawyer not to give up on me. "No matter what happens," I said to Magnum, with my hand cupped over the mouthpiece, "don't stop trying to get me out of here. I don't care how long it takes or how much it costs."

"I wouldn't stop for any client," he said warmly, "especially not you. Just hang in there a few months. I'll get you out, buddy."

I breathed a sigh of relief. "Were you able to get in touch with Nadine?"

"Yeah, she's fine. Maybe *too* fine, if you know what I mean."

"I do," I said gravely. "She's been praying for something like this to happen. It's all the excuse she needs to bolt to California. Did she ask you how long I'd be in for?"

"No, and I didn't bring it up, for that very reason. But I told her to accept collect calls from you, and she promised that she would."

Well, that's the least she could fucking do! "And what about Yulia?" I asked with a smirk. "She's probably back with her ex-boyfriend by now."

"I highly doubt that," said Magnum.

"Oh, yeah? Why is that?"

"Well, if she's anywhere, she's probably in her psychiatrist's office."

"What are you talking about? What happened to her?"

"What *happened* to her is that she totally flipped out on me! I called her at the hotel, like you said, and when I told her you got remanded–or, should I say, got taken to jail, because she didn't know what *remanded* meant–she completely lost it. She started crying hysterically on the phone, and she kept saying, 'OhmyGods! OhmyGods!' which, I admit, I found a bit humorous, because she kept using the plural form of *God*."

"Yeah," I said proudly, "she has a tendency to do that." Suddenly I found KGB's language deficiencies rather heartwarming. "What else did she say?"

"I'm not really sure, because she started speaking in Russian, a mile a minute. Anyway, she's a *very* beautiful girl. I can see why they made her Miss Soviet Union."

"Wait a second: You *saw* her?"

"Yeah, she showed up at my office unannounced; I guess she must have called information. Anyway, she was shaking uncontrollably. It was pretty scary, actually. Nick was about to call a doctor, but then some guy named Igor showed up and took her away. Do you know who Igor is?"

A shock! "You met Igor?" I felt a twinge of jealousy. Why did Magnum get to meet Igor before I did? Whatever. Curiosity overpowered jealousy, and I said, "What does he look like?"

"Pretty average," replied Magnum. "Tall, thin, silver hair; about fifty or so. He's very suspicious-looking, like a fox. He has excellent posture."

"What do you mean, he has excellent posture?"

"I *mean,* he has excellent posture! The guy stands as stiff as a ramrod. He was probably in the military once." A brief pause, then: "He probably still is, if you catch my drift."

There were a few moments of silence as the very obviousness of Magnum's words hung in the air. Then he said, "Anyway, he left a very cryptic message for you–something about you being under his protection now. I have no idea what he meant by that. Do you?"

Under Igor's protection? What was that crazy Russian bastard talking about? "No," I replied, "I have no idea. I never even *met* the guy!"

"Interesting," said Magnum. "Well, Yulia left you a message too, although it was a bit less cryptic."

I perked up: "Oh, really? What did she say?"

With a chuckle: "She say she *love* you and she wait as long as it *take,* even if it *take* forever." More chuckles at KGB's grammar. "I think she was very sincere."

We exchanged a warm good-bye, then I hung up the phone and headed to the back of the line. There were four people ahead of me, so I had a few minutes to think. Above all, I was astonished at KGB's loyalty. I would have never guessed it, especially after my experience with the Duchess. I had just *assumed* that KGB would fly the coop, because that's what the Duchess had done. But, now that I thought about it, KGB's attitude wasn't so astonishing.

Few women would abandon their husbands on the courthouse steps. What the Duchess had done was unconscionable. I knew that I would think that forever. I no longer cared, though, because I was in love with someone else. Where once I had felt betrayed and heartbroken, I now felt angry and apathetic. And, in truth, I wasn't even that angry. I just wanted my kids to remain east of the Mississippi.

The line moved quickly, and my conversation with the Duchess moved even quicker. Magnum had already given her the low-down, and I filled in the missing blanks. Interestingly enough, Magnum had played down the helicopter aspect of the debacle, focusing instead on what had happened with Dave Beall and how it set the stage for the Bastard's revenge. I made a mental note to thank Magnum for that.

In any event, I assured the Duchess that I would be home soon–two months at the most–and, while I didn't say it, my tone of voice so much as said, "So don't be thinking of moving to California anytime soon, lady!"

For her part, both her words and her voice betrayed nothing. She said she was "really sorry" that I had gotten thrown in jail, yet she seemed no more or less sorry than if I had told her that I'd just lost my house keys and was forced to call a locksmith.

That aside, we decided that there was no point in saying anything to the kids. At the ages of six and four, they would be easy to fool–*fool* being synonymous with *protect.* Besides, what was the point in worrying them when I would be home so soon? Hopefully, I prayed, I would.

The Duchess promised to accept all my collect calls and not to trash-talk me to the kids. I believed her on both counts, not because I thought she felt a grain of compassion toward me but because I knew she felt it for the children. And that was fine; when you're in a position like mine, you accept your victories without questioning motives. Then you say thank you.

When I spoke to the kids, I kept it short and sweet. I told them I was traveling on business, which they both found very exciting. Neither of them asked when I would be coming home, simply because they assumed it would be soon. At Carter's age, the concept of time didn't mean much. He measured things in half hours, which was the average length of a cartoon; anything beyond that was considered "long."

Chandler, however, was another story. She was in first grade and knew how to read (not too well, thank God!), so she couldn't be *fooled* for long. Eventually–within a month, perhaps–she would begin to smell a rat; then her well-deserved nickname of CIA would complicate things. She would start to investigate–eavesdropping, asking pointed questions, checking for lies, omissions, and contradictions. In essence, she would become the quintessential nosy six-year-old girl, a concerned daughter who missed her Daddy and wouldn't stop digging until she got to the bottom of things.

With that in mind, before I hung up I told her that my travels might take me to some very faraway places–*fantastic* places, I said–just like those two silly Frenchmen, Phileas Fogg and Passepartout, from the movie *Around the World in 80 Days.* We had watched it together many times, and she had always found it fascinating, especially the different ways they'd traveled.

"It'll be great!" I said to her. "You can watch the video with Gwynnie and see all the great places while Daddy's visiting them. In fact, it'll be just like we're visiting them together!"

"You're going to all the same places as Passepartout?" she asked wondrously.

"Absolutely, thumbkin! And I think it might take me the same amount of time it took them."

"Eighty days?" she sputtered. "Why would it take you eighty days? They rode on an elephant, Daddy! Can't you take an airplane?"

That little devil! She was too clever! I had to cut this conversation short. "Well, I guess I could, but that might take the fun out of it. Anyway, just watch the video with Gwynnie, and we'll talk about it then, okay?"

"Okay," she said happily. "I love you, Daddy." Then she blew me a big kiss into the phone.

"I love you too," I said warmly, and I blew her a kiss back. Then I hung up the phone, fought back the tears, and went to the end of the line and waited my turn again. Ten minutes later I was dialing Southampton.

First I heard KGB's voice: "Alloa?" Then the recorded voice of the operator: "This is a collect call from a federal prison. If you wish to accept, please press five now; if you do not wish to accept, press nine or hang up the phone; if you wish to block calls from this number permanently, please press seven-seven now." And then there was silence.

Oh, Jesus Christ! I thought. KGB couldn't understand the instructions! I screamed into the phone: "Yulia! Don't press seven-seven! I won't be able to call you back! Don't press seven-seven!" I turned around and looked for a friendly face. A towering black man was next in line. He was staring at me, amused. I shook my head and said, "My girlfriend's a foreigner. She doesn't understand the message."

He smiled warmly, exposing a conspicuous absence of central incisors. "Happens all the time, big-man. You better hang up before she presses seven-seven. If she does you're"–*beep, beep,* went the phone–"fucked."

Just then I heard a loud *click.* With a sinking heart, I held up the phone and stared at it quizzically. Then I turned to the towering black man and said, "I think she pressed seven-seven."

He shook his head and shrugged. "Then you're fucked."

I was about to hang up when he said, "You got another number at the house?"

I nodded. "Yeah, why?"

He motioned to the touch pad. "Call back, then; it don't block the whole house, just that line."

"Is it okay?" I asked nervously. "I thought it's one call at a time."

He shrugged. "Go call your girl. I got nothin' *but* time."

"Thanks," I said. What a terrific guy! First Ming the Merciless and now the Towering Black Man! These people weren't so bad, were they? Especially this guy! He was a true gentleman. I later found out he was facing twenty years for extortion.

I turned around and dialed the phone again, and this time she got it right. Her first words were: "OhmyGods! *Maya lubimaya! Ya lublu tibea!*"

"I love you too," I said softly. "Are you hanging in there, honey?"

"Hanging where?" she asked, with a confused snuffle.

Jesus! I thought. In spite of everything, it was enough to make you crazy. "I mean, are you doing okay?"

"Da..." she said sadly, "I, I okay." Then: "Oh, oh... *ohmyGods...* I... ohmyGods..." and she started sobbing uncontrollably. Try as I might, I couldn't help but find comfort in her sobbing. It was as if with each sob, with each tear, and with each gooselike snort she was reaffirming her love for me. I made a mental note to count her "I love yous" each day. When they started to diminish, I would know the end was near.

Today, however, the end was definitely nowhere in sight. The moment she stopped sobbing, she said, "I don't care how long it take, I wait for you forever. I will not go out of house until you are home."

And, true to her word, that was exactly what she did.

As my first week behind bars came to a close, she was there every time I called Southampton. According to pod rules, you could speak as long as you wanted on each call, and sometimes we would speak for hours at a time. It was rather ironic, I thought, considering we never spoke that much when I was on the outside. Our relationship had been mostly about sex; when we weren't having sex, we were eating or sleeping or arguing over whose history books were more accurate.

Now, however, we didn't have such arguments. We seemed to agree on everything–mostly because we avoided all subjects even vaguely related to history, politics, economics, religion, grammar, and, of course, the moon. Instead, we spoke of simple things, like all the wonderful dinners we'd shared together... all those fires on the beach... and how we had made love to each other all day long. But, most of all, we spoke about the future–meaning, *our* future–and how once all this was over we would get married and live happily ever after.

And when I wasn't speaking to KGB, I was reading book after book, playing catch-up after years of entertaining myself with sex, drugs, and rock and roll. For as long as I could remember, I had despised reading, associating it with boredom and tediousness rather than wonder and pleasure. I viewed myself as the product of a misguided education system that stressed reading "the classics," which, for the most part, were boring and outdated. Perhaps if I had been forced to read *Jaws* and *The Godfather* instead of *Moby-*

Dick and *Ulysses,* things would have turned out differently. (Always looking to place blame somewhere else.)

So I was making up for lost time now, averaging nearly a book a day, and writing three letters as well—one to KGB and one to each of the kids. Of course, I would call the kids each day to tell them that I loved them and that I would be home soon. And while I hated lying to them, I knew it was the right thing to do.

As expected, Carter was easy to deceive. We talked about whatever Disney movie he was currently obsessed with and then exchanged "I love yous." Our conversations lasted no more than a minute, at which point he returned to the blissful ignorance of childhood.

Chandler, however, was a different story. Our average conversation would be more than fifteen minutes, and if she was especially talkative it would last for close to an hour. Just what we could talk about for so long I'm still not sure, although as the weeks dragged on I noticed her becoming more and more obsessed with Passepartout. In essence, she was using the movie to keep track of my progress, the way an adult crosses off days on a calendar.

She kept saying things like, "Passepartout did this, Daddy, and Passepartout did that, Daddy," as if I could somehow *learn* from Passepartout's mistakes and accelerate my voyage around the world. With the help of Gwynne, she had pegged January 10 as my arrival date back in the United States from Yokohama—just like Passepartout. However, if she could help me figure out a way to travel faster or simply avoid having an accident, then perhaps I could be home for Christmas.

So when I told her I was in Paris, she said, "Be careful when you take off in your hot-air balloon, Daddy! Passepartout had to climb on top of *his* balloon, and he almost fell off!" I promised that I would.

And when I told her I was heading to India, she said, "Be careful when you're riding on your elephant, Daddy, because Passepartout got captured by headhunters! He had to be rescued." And from there the subject would turn to something completely innocuous—her new friends in school, something she'd watched on TV, the toys she wanted for Christmas. Never once did she bring up John Macaluso or, for that matter, her mother. Whether this was by accident or design I wasn't quite sure, but I could sense that she was trying to protect my feelings.

By mid-November, Alonso had finally agreed to take another shot in front of Gleeson. The only problem was that he needed to get clearance from the new chief of the criminal division, a man named Ken Breen (Ron White had switched sides too, becoming a defense lawyer). Breen was currently in trial and couldn't be disturbed.

That made no sense to me; after all, it couldn't take Magnum more than fifteen minutes to make a presentation to Ken Breen. Bo had secured all the necessary affidavits, and it was crystal clear that the only thing I had been guilty of was stupidity. I said to Magnum, "I don't care how busy someone is–they always have fifteen minutes to spare for something important." Magnum explained that it was a matter of protocol. When an AUSA goes to trial, it's like a prizefighter stepping into the ring, and between rounds he doesn't talk to his best friend. All he cares about is knocking out the other prizefighter.

And just like that, the possibility of being home for Thanksgiving vanished like a fart in the wind. Fortunately, I hadn't really expected it, so I wasn't overly disappointed. Yes, it would have been nice, of course, but it had been such a long shot that I hadn't been foolish enough to get my hopes up.

As I quickly found out, expectations could be either your best friend or worst nightmare when you're behind bars. A man facing twenty years hangs on to the hope of winning an appeal; when he *loses* his appeal he hangs on to the hope of parole; and when he gives up on that–and his life seems totally worthless and no longer worth living–he finds Jesus.

I fell into a unique category of ultrashort-timers, a detainee whose downside was measured by a matter of months. Worse came to worst, Magnum assured me, Gleeson would let me out by spring, simply out of mercy. However, if we were to file our motion just before Christmas, he couldn't imagine John denying it. He was a sympathetic man, Magnum promised, and he would be willing to give me a second chance.

Fair enough, I thought. I would have to spend Thanksgiving in jail. I dialed Old Brookville on Tuesday morning of Thanksgiving week. The date was November 23. As always, I dialed with a smile on my face, anxious beyond words to hear the voices of my children. Alas, on the second ring, I heard: "I'm sorry, the number you have called has been disconnected. If you have reached this recording in error, please hang up and try your call again. No further information is available."

At first I didn't hang up the phone. I kept it pressed to my ear. I was simply too astonished to move. And while my brain desperately searched for answers, my gut didn't have to: My children had moved to California.

Two days later, it came as no surprise when the Duchess called my parents and left her new contact information on their answering machine, and both the area code and the zip code belonged to Beverly Hills.

Without losing my temper, I wrote them down. Then I hung up the phone and headed for the back of the line. There were seven people ahead of me, so I had a few minutes to think, to figure out the precise string of curses to utter, the appropriate threats to make, and anything else a man in my position–meaning a man who had no power whatsoever over anyone or anything, including himself–could say.

I would call her a bitch and a gold digger and a . . . *who was I kidding?* If I called her any of those things, she would press seven-seven and cut off all phone communication! Not to mention the fact that she could pluck my letters out of the mailbox and cut off all written communication as well. My complete lack of power was utterly enraging! Yet what enraged me most was that, deep down, I knew she was right.

I mean, what was she to do? I was in jail and the money was running out. She had bills to pay, kids to support, and the roof over her head was on the cusp of forfeiture. And then there was John Macaluso waiting in the wings, like a knight in shining armor. He had money, a mansion, and, by sheer coincidence, he happened to be a nice guy to boot. He would support her and take care of her, and he would love her.

And he would take care of the kids.

And what about the kids? What was best for them? Should they grow up on Long Island in the dark shadow of my legacy? Or would it be better for them to make a fresh start in California? Of course, my kids belonged with me, or at least *near* me. Of that much I was certain. But where did *I* belong? What was best for me?

Having little choice, I did what I had no doubt many men who'd been unfortunate enough to be a prisoner in Pod 7N had done before me: I went back to my bunk and pulled the covers over my head.

Then I cried.

CHAPTER 26

A NEW MISSION

March 2000

Finally—freedom!

Fresh air! *Free* air! The blue dome of the sky! The orange ball of the sun! The glorious phases of the moon! The sweet smell of fresh flowers! The even sweeter smell of fresh Soviet pussy! And to think I had taken all these things for granted! *How foolish of me!* Life's simple pleasures were all that mattered, weren't they? I had been to hell and back and had survived.

So it was that I emerged from the Metropolitan Detention Center on a chilly Monday morning, with a smile on my face and a bounce in my step—and with every aspect of my life in a complete fucking shambles.

Much could change in four months, and, in my case, much had: My kids were living in California; Meadow Lane was in the hands of the government; my furniture was in storage, my money was running out, and, to add insult to injury, I was wearing an ankle bracelet with restrictions *so* Draconian that I couldn't even leave my house, except to see the doctor.

I had rented a sprawling duplex apartment on the fifty-second and fifty-third floors of the Galleria Building, an ultraluxury glass-and-concrete tower that rose up fifty-seven stories above Manhattan's Park Avenue and 57th Street. (Why not be locked up in style? I figured.)

The building was an upscale haven for Eurotrash–of both the Eastern *and* the Western variety. From the West they came from places like *Roma* and *Geneva* and *Gay Paree*, and from the East they came from countries of the former Soviet bloc–mobsters, most of them, who also kept homes in Moscow or St. Petersburg, when they weren't on the run. Not surprisingly, KGB fit in perfectly here, and one of her many Russkie friends had been kind enough to rent us this fabulous spread.

It was back in early December when Magnum asked me what address I wanted to be released to upon Gleeson approving the bail application. Meadow Lane wouldn't work, he explained, because it was due to be forfeited by year's end.

Given my circumstances, my options were few: To buy a home would be ridiculous, and to stay in Southampton would be even *more* ridiculous. What with the kids living in Beverly Hills and KGB's heart belonging to Manhattan, there was no point to living in the middle of nowhere. Moreover, I needed to stay close to the U.S. Attorney's Office, because, much to my chagrin, the Chef had refused to cooperate and was threatening to take his case to trial; if he actually did, I would be spending many nights burning the midnight oil at the U.S. Attorney's Office in preparation.

Yet, as troublesome as I found the Chef's decision, it played a distant second fiddle to my troubles with Chandler, who since mid-February had been beside herself with emotion. Eighty days had come and gone, and I hadn't made my way around the world yet. She knew something was wrong, and my excuses had run out weeks ago.

"Where are you?" she kept whining. "Why won't you come home? I don't understand! You promised! You don't love me anymore. . . ."

And that was when the Duchess and I made peace with each other. We had exchanged hardly ten words since that horrific

Wednesday morning, but we had no choice now. Our daughter's suffering eclipsed our mutual disdain for each other.

The Duchess told me that Chandler had been upset for months, keeping a stiff upper lip on the phone only for my benefit. She had cried on Thanksgiving Day and hadn't stopped crying since. Something had to be done, said the Duchess. Our strategy of *protection* had backfired on us. I suggested that she call Magnum to tell him what was happening, which she did–and Magnum headed down to the U.S. Attorney's Office yet again, this time *begging* for action. Enough delays! he pleaded. This was no longer about Jordan Belfort; it was about a child, a child who was suffering.

And just like that it happened: Motions were made, hearings were held, details worked out, and on the last Friday in February, Judge Gleeson signed the order for my release. From there, Magnum immediately called the Duchess, who immediately called Gwynne, who immediately jumped on a plane to California. She landed on a Saturday, spent two nights at the Duchess's new Beverly Hills mansion, and then boarded an early-morning flight back to New York, with the kids in tow. She was due to land at five p.m., in exactly three and a half hours from now.

With that thought, I took a deep, anxious breath and knocked on the gleaming walnut front door to Apartment 52C. I had been here once, and it was absolutely gorgeous inside. A grand black marble entryway led you to a mahogany-paneled living room with paintings affixed to the walls. The ceiling was twenty feet above a black Italian marble floor. Yet, as beautiful as the place was, it was also one of the saddest apartments in all of Manhattan–for it was here, in this very apartment, where Eric Clapton's four-year-old son had accidentally fallen out a bedroom window. I had been reluctant to rent it because of that, but KGB had assured me that the apartment had been blessed by a priest and a rabbi.

Just then the door opened, but only a foot. A moment later I saw a familiar blond Soviet head pop through the gap. I smiled warmly at my favorite communist and said, in a Russkie accent, "Open door now!"

She pushed the door all the way open, but instead of throwing her arms around me and showering me with kisses, she just stood there with her arms folded beneath her breasts. She was wearing a pair of very tight jeans. The denim was fiercely prefaded, the knees and thighs having the appropriate number of rips and holes in them. I wasn't an expert on women's jeans, but I knew that these had to cost a fortune. She wore a simple white midriff T-shirt that looked soft as mink. Her feet were bare, and she was tapping her right foot on the marble floor, as if she were debating whether or not she still loved me.

Feigning insult, I said, "Well, aren't you going to give me a kiss? I *have* been locked up for four months!"

She shrugged. "Come get if you want."

"Fine–I'll *get,* you little minx!" And all at once I charged her, like a hormone-raged bull. She gave up her pose and started running.

"Help!" she screamed. "I being chased by capitalist! Help–*Polizia!*"

A curved mahogany staircase at the center of the living room rose up to the floor above, and she took the first three steps like a world-class hurdler. I was trailing a good five yards behind her, distracted by the sheer opulence of the place. The entire rear wall was plate glass, shoving the most awesome view of Manhattan in your face. Horny as I was, I couldn't help but admire it.

By the time I hit the stairs, she was already sitting on the top step, her long legs hanging open with complete insouciance. She was leaning back casually, with her palms resting on the hardwood floor behind her. She wasn't even a bit out of breath. When I reached the step beneath her I dropped to my knees, huffing and puffing. Having been locked up for so long, I was in a weakened condition. I ran my fingers through her hair, taking a moment to catch my wind. "Thanks for waiting," I finally said. "Four months is a long time."

She shrugged. "I am Russian girl. When our man sits in jail we wait." She leaned forward and kissed me on the lips–softly, tenderly–and I *pounced*!

"I gotta make love to you right now," I groaned. "Right here on the floor," and before she knew what hit her, she was flat on her back and I was on top of her, grinding my jeans into her jeans, pelvis to pelvis. I kissed her deeply—*passionately*!

Suddenly she turned her head to the side and I was kissing her chiseled cheekbone. *"Nyet!"* she whined. "Not here! I have surprise for you!"

A surprise, I thought. Why couldn't she just master definite and indefinite articles? She was so close to perfect! Perhaps there was a course she could take, a book she could read. "What kind of surprise?" I asked, still out of breath.

She started wriggling out from beneath me. "Come," she said. "I will show you. It is in bedroom." She grabbed my hand and started pulling me up.

The master bedroom was less than ten feet from the stairs. When I saw it, I was speechless. Dozens of lit candles were scattered throughout the room. They were everywhere, on the dark-gray carpet . . . on all four sides of the black lacquer platform bed . . . on the matching lacquer headboard, with its gently curved top and gold-leaf trim . . . and then lined up end to end on the twenty-foot-long windowsill at the far wall. Plush red velvet curtains blocked every last drop of sunlight from entering. The lights were off, and the flames flickered brilliantly.

On the king-size bed was a royal-blue Italian-silk comforter stuffed with so much goose down that it looked as soft as a cloud. We hit it with a giggle, and I quickly maneuvered myself on top of her. In less than five seconds we were out of our jeans and moaning passionately.

An hour later we were still moaning.

At precisely five p.m. the doorman called and said that I had three visitors downstairs. The adult was waiting patiently, he said with a chuckle, but the children weren't. The boy had run past him and hit the elevator button, and he was still hitting it at this very moment. The girl, however, hadn't passed him; she was standing in front of him right now, and she was eyeing him suspiciously. From the sound of his voice, she seemed to make him nervous.

"Send them up," I said happily, and I hung up the phone,

grabbed KGB, and walked downstairs to the fifty-second floor and opened the front door. A few moments later I heard the elevator doors slide open. Then the familiar voice of a little girl: "Daddy! Where are you, Daddy?"

"I'm here! Follow my voice!" I said loudly, and a moment later they turned the corner and were running toward me.

"Daddy's home!" screamed Carter. "Daddy's home!"

I crouched down, and they ran full speed into my arms.

For what seemed like an eternity, none of us said a word. We just kissed and hugged and squeezed one another for all we were worth, while KGB and Gwynne looked on silently. "I missed you guys so much!" I finally said. "I can't believe how *long* it's been!" I started nuzzling my nose into their necks and taking tiny sniffs of them. "I need to smell you guys to make sure it's you. The nose never lies, you know."

"It's us!" insisted Chandler.

"Yeah," added Carter. "It's us!"

I held them at arms' length. "Well, then, let me take a close look at you. You don't have anything to hide, right?"

I pretended to study them. Chandler was as beautiful as ever. Her hair had grown out quite a bit since the summer and went down past her shoulder blades now. She was wearing a fire-engine-red corduroy dress held up by two thin shoulder straps with tiny red bows on them. Beneath it she wore a white cotton turtleneck and white ballet tights. She was a perfect little lady. I shrugged and said, "Okay–I'm convinced. It's you!"

She rolled her eyes and shook her head. "I told you!"

"What about me?" snapped Carter. "Is it still me too?" With that he rolled his head from side to side, offering me both sides of his profile.

As always, he was all eyelashes. His hair was a luxuriance of platinum-blond waves. He was dressed in jeans and sneakers and a red flannel shirt. It was hard to imagine that we had almost lost him as an infant. He was the picture of health now, a son to be proud of.

"Is it him?" Chandler asked nervously. "Or is he a robot?"

"No, it's him, all right." They ran back into my arms and started kissing me again. After a few seconds, I said, "Aren't you guys gonna give Yulia a kiss? She missed you guys too."

"No!" they shot back in unison. "Just you!"

Well, that wasn't good! I knew KGB was sensitive to such things. It had something to do with the great Russian soul, although just how, I hadn't the slightest idea. "Oh, come on," I said, in a leading tone. "*She* deserves a kiss too, no?"

"Nooooooo!" they sputtered. "Only Daddy!"

Now Gwynne chimed in: "They just miss you so much they *can't ged enough a you!* Ain't that sweet?"

I looked up at KGB. She seemed insulted. I wanted to mouth the words: *It's only because they miss me!* But I knew she couldn't lip-read English. (She barely spoke the fucking language, for Chrissake!)

"This is okay," she said, with a bit of a chill. "I will take suitcases upstairs."

Upstairs, we walked down a long narrow hallway, at the end of which were two small bedrooms. One had been converted into a library; the other had two twin beds in it. As Gwynne and KGB went about unpacking the kids' suitcases, the three of us sat on the maroon carpet, making up for lost time. There were many hints of Meadow Lane in this room—dozens of Chandler's favorite dollies lined up along the windowsill, Carter's sprawling wooden train set snaking its way around the carpet, his blue Thomas the Tank Engine comforter on one bed, Chandler's $2,200 pink-and-white Laura Ashley comforter with its white lace trimming on the other. Chandler was already busy arranging her dollies into a perfect circle around us, while Carter inspected his trains for possible damage from the move. Every so often, KGB would look down at us and smile coldly.

"Okay," I said, trying to break the ice, "here's what Yulia and I have in store for you this week. Since we missed a whole bunch of holidays together. I figured—I mean, *we* figured—we should make up for lost time by celebrating them now!" I paused and cocked my head to the side in an attitude that implied logic. "Better late than never, right, guys?"

Carter said, "Does that mean we get more Christmas presents?"

I nodded. "It most certainly does," I said quickly. "And since we also missed Halloween, we're gonna get dressed up tomorrow night and go trick-or-treating!" With the exception of me, I thought. I would be faking a backache tomorrow night, lest I step foot out of the apartment and find myself back in Pod 7N the next day.

Chandler said, "Will people still give us candy now?"

"Of course!" I said, and *no way!* I thought. In this building you would have a better chance of seeing God. The Galleria was the sort of ultrapretentious *snobitorium* in which you could travel up and down in the elevator a thousand times and never see a child. In fact, in the entire history of the building, two young mothers had never bumped into each other and said, "Oh, my God! It's so good to see you! Let's arrange a play date for our kids!" Changing the subject, I said, "Anyway, we also missed Thanksgiving and Hanukkah and–"

Chandler cut me off. "We get more presents for Hanukkah, right?"

I shook my head and smiled. "Yes, wisenheimer, we get more presents for Hanukkah. And we also missed Christmas"–Carter shot me a suspicious look–"which, as Carter previously said, you will definitely get presents for"–Carter nodded once and then went back to his trains–"and then, last but not least, there's New Year's Eve. We're going to celebrate them all."

On Tuesday night we all wore costumes–including KGB, who, to my complete shock, broke out her Miss USSR sash and rhinestone tiara, while Carter and Chandler looked on, astonished. My costume, a garden-variety Western cowboy with a hat, a holster, and a semirealistic pair of toy six-shooters, was far less inspiring and not nearly as sexy. The children did the usual: Carter dressed up as a blue Power Ranger, and Chandler dressed as Snow White. Thankfully, our downstairs neighbor was nice enough to play along and give the kids candy.

On Wednesday night I made turkey and stuffing; the former I proudly baked into shoe leather, and the latter was of the Stove

Top variety. The rest of the spread—the cranberry sauce, the gravy, the sweet-potato pie, the pumpkin pie, as well as a Russkie touch in the form of two ounces of premium beluga caviar (at $150 an ounce, from my rapidly depleting checkbook)—came from a nearby gourmet supermarket that gave new meaning to the term *price-gouging.*

On Thursday night my parents came over. We lit a menorah for the benefit of my mother, and Chandler and Carter got their Hanukkah presents (more money out of the checkbook). On Friday we went—or, should I say, *they* went—to Macy's and bought an artificial Christmas tree, and then we spent the rest of the day listening to Christmas carols and decorating the tree. And, of course, they got more presents.

On Saturday night, which was our last night together, we celebrated New Year's Eve—which turned out to be a *real* hoot, because I got to meet Igor for the first time. Magnum had been dead-on-balls accurate with his description, starting with his silver-colored hair, which looked like a thin layer of sizzling gunpowder, and even more so when it came to Igor's posture, which, to my way of thinking, could only be the result of one of two things—either he'd spent countless years standing at attention in a secret KGB training camp or someone had once shoved an electrical cattle prod up his ass.

Whatever the case, Igor could drink, although, according to him, he was simply cleansing his liver in the Russian way—using vodka.

Yes, there was no denying that Igor was smart as well as very ambitious, although, more than anything, I got the distinct impression that what he *really* wanted was to possess the ultimate doomsday weapon to hold the world hostage. And why? Not for money or power or, for that matter, even sex! All Igor wanted was for everyone to shut up and agree with him.

It was a little after eight p.m., and we had decided to celebrate New Year's Eve at the twelve-foot-long dining-room table, which like the rest of the furniture was grand, solemn, and comprised of black Italian lacquer. The room was just off the living room and shared the same spectacular view of Midtown Manhattan. At this hour of night, the lights of the city rose up behind us in a dazzling display.

In spite of me being the theoretical master-of-the-house, it was Igor who seemed determined to hold court tonight, while Chandler, Carter, and myself–all sporting glittering New Year's Eve hats shaped like dunce caps–pretended to listen. KGB wore a dunce cap too, although she was hanging on Igor's every word. It was nauseating.

From across the dining-room table, Igor said to me, "Un-der-stand! I, Igor, with one snap of finger"–and he snapped his finger, as Chandler and Carter looked on, confused–"can make fire impossible!"

Now KGB chimed in. "He can; I have seen this."

And now Chandler chimed in. "You should call Smokey the Bear, then."

And now it was my turn: "She's right, Igor. Smokey the Bear would be all over you if he knew you could make fire impossible."

Carter said, "Why is your name Igor? It's a monster's name."

KGB, who had somewhat rebonded with Carter via Crash Bandicoot, said, "Igor is like Gary. It is Russian name."

Carter shrugged, unimpressed.

Igor asked Chandler, "Who is this Smokey Bear you speak of?"

"He's a bear who fights forest fires," she replied happily. "He's on TV."

Igor nodded in understanding, then lifted a $250 Baccarat brandy snifter filled halfway to the top with 80-proof Stolichnaya vodka and downed it like it was air. Then he put the snifter down with a determined thud. "You must understand!" he declared. "Fire–may–not–exist–without–oxygen. So–he–who–control–oxygen–control–fire."

After a few moments of silence, Chandler picked up a noisemaker, stuck it in her mouth, stared down Igor, and then blew into it as hard as she could. Igor clenched his jaw and cringed. Then he poured himself another glass of vodka and downed it.

Later that evening, before he left, Igor promised to give me a demonstration of his fire-controlling abilities, but not now. First he needed to know me better; then he would prove his point to me. And with that, New Year's Eve came to a close.

The next morning, the problems started when it was time to say good-bye. In truth, I had planned on having a private talk with each of my kids before they left, but I just couldn't seem to find the words. Carter, I figured, would be easier; his age, his gender, his genetic makeup–for whatever reason, things seemed to slide off his shoulders with no ill effects.

Chandler, of course, was the opposite. She was a complicated young girl, wise beyond her years. I knew that saying good-bye to her would be difficult and that tears would be shed. What I hadn't counted on, though, was how many.

I found her upstairs in her bedroom, alone. She was lying on the bed facedown, her nose pressed deep into the pink comforter. Unlike when she arrived, when she had gotten herself all dressed up for Daddy, she was now dressed more practically, in light-pink sweatpants with a pink hoodie.

With a heavy heart, I sat down on the edge of the bed and reached beneath her sweatshirt and began stroking her back gently. "What's wrong, thumbkin? Gwynnie told me you're not feeling well."

She nodded without speaking, her face still pressed into the comforter.

I kept rubbing her back. "Are you too sick to fly?"

She nodded the same way, although a bit more forcefully.

"Ahh, I see," I said seriously. "Do you have a temperature?"

She shrugged.

"Can I feel your head?"

She shrugged again.

I stopped rubbing her back and placed the back of my hand against her forehead. She was cool. "Well, you feel normal, thumbkin. Does something hurt you?"

"My tummy," she muttered, in the tone of the infirmed.

I smiled inwardly. "Ohhhh, your tummy. I see. Well, why don't you turn over and let me rub it for you, okay?"

She shook her head no.

I placed my hands on her shoulders, and, with great care, I gently turned her over. "Come here, sweetie; let me take a look at you," and I brushed back her hair and took a moment to regard her. What I saw I would never forget: the utterly anguished face of my daughter, her eyes red and swollen, her lower lip still quivering. She had been crying into her pillow, because she didn't want me to see.

Fighting back my own tears, I whispered, "Oh, Channy, it's okay. Please don't cry, my love. Daddy loves you; he'll always love you."

She compressed her lips into a tight line and shook her head quickly, trying to fight back the tears. But it was no use. Little streams began trickling down her cheeks. And that was when I lost it. "Oh, God," I said softly. "I'm so sorry, Channy." I grabbed her forcefully and held her close to me. "I'm so, so sorry. You have no idea, sweetie; it's all my fault. Please, don't cry, honey." I completely broke down, unable to get any more words out.

After a few seconds, I heard her tiny voice:

"Don't cry, Daddy; I still love you. I'm sorry for making you cry," and then she broke down too, shaking uncontrollably in my arms.

And just like that we collapsed onto the comforter, father and daughter, crying in each other's arms. I felt like the world's greatest failure, the ultimate cautionary tale for a man's life. I was born with all the gifts, all the advantages. I could have had it all, yet I destroyed everything. My own greed and excess had gotten the best of me.

After a few minutes, I was finally able to collect myself. I said, "Listen to me, Chandler. We need to stay strong for each other. We can get through this—we *can*! One day we'll be together again all the time. I promise you that, Channy. From the bottom of my heart."

Through tiny snuffles, she said, "Come back to California with me, Daddy; *please* come back. I'll live with you there."

I shook my head sadly. "I can't, honey. As much as I'd like to, I can't."

She started snuffling again. "*Why not?* I want it the way it used to be."

I hugged her gently, gritting my teeth and shaking my head in anger. I had to make this right somehow. There was no way I would allow my children to grow up without me. I would figure out a way to move to California. That would be my sole mission in life, nothing else.

I took a deep breath and steeled myself. "Listen to me, Chandler; I want to tell you something."

She looked up.

I wiped the tears from her cheeks with the back of my hand. "Okay, sweetie; now, a lot of what I'm going to say might not make sense to you right now, but one day it will, when you're much older." I paused and shook my head, wondering if it would be better if she never realized what a scumbag I'd been. "A long time ago I did some things in my business that were very bad, and people lost money because of it. That's where I was over the last few months: I was busy paying them back. You understand?"

"Yes," she said softly. "But how come you can't move to California now?"

"Because I'm not done paying them back yet. It's gonna take me some time, honey, because there were a lot of people who lost money."

"I have twelve dollars in my piggy bank. Will that help?"

I smiled and let out a tiny chuckle. "You keep that twelve dollars, honey. I'll pay them back out of my own money. But listen to me, Channy, because I'm going to make you a big promise here. Are you ready for it?"

"Yes," she murmured.

"Okay: I promise you that no matter what happens, no matter what I have to do–even if I have to walk there!–I will move to California. You have my word on it."

Her smile lit up the room. "When are you moving?"

I smiled back. "As soon as I can, thumbkin. But you're gonna have to have some patience. But I promise I will get there."

She smiled and nodded eagerly. "Okay, Daddy."

"And no more crying!" I added with a smile.

"Okay," she said, throwing her arms around me. "I love you, Daddy."

"I love you too," I said quickly, and odd as it seemed, in that very instant, despite the odds being stacked so heavily against me, I knew I would accomplish my goal.

CHAPTER 27

THE BUZZWORD IS IRONY

The next morning I was lying in bed watching the Financial News Network, when a blond anchorwoman mentioned something about a severe "down opening" for this morning's NASDAQ. There was a massive order imbalance, apparently, with an unfortunate bias toward the sell side.

No big deal, I thought. The blonde is probably overreacting, and even if she's not, it doesn't matter anyway. After all, markets rise and markets fall, and a savvy trader can make money in any market. My plan was foolproof:

With the quarter million dollars I still had left, I would trade the high-flying NASDAQ with Wolf-like precision and make a small fortune in the process. The NASDAQ had more than doubled over the last twelve months, and who better than the Wolf himself to take advantage of the greatest speculative bubble since 1929? It would be like shooting fish in a barrel.

Alas, fate had different plans.

By 9:30 a.m., the NASDAQ was down more than four percent, and two days later it was down another five. By April Fools' Day, it had lost more than twenty percent, and the joke was on me. The dot-com bubble had finally burst, and it would continue to deflate (at an unpredictable rate) for the foreseeable future. And, yes, while it was true that a savvy trader *could* make money in any market, he couldn't do it with limited resources, lest he be wiped out with a single bad trade. So I abandoned my foolproof plan before I started it.

Meanwhile, KGB and I had gotten along fine and dandy while I "sit in jail," as she so phrased it, but now that I was out, things had become tenuous. Of course, the sex was still great, but the conversation was minimal. By the third week in April, I was certain that we had no future together. It was plainly obvious; in fact, it was so plainly obvious that on April 17–which was KGB's birthday–I got down on one knee and proposed to her. With a sinking heart, I said:

"Will you marry me, *maya lubimaya,* and be my *third* lawfully wedded wife?" What I didn't say (but what I knew would be true) was: "And do you promise to torture me and drive me crazy, and to make sure that I remain the most miserable man on the planet until death do us part?"

Not being able to read my internal thoughts, she quickly answered, "*Da, maya lubimaya,* I will be wife," to which I slipped a seven-carat, yellow canary diamond in a platinum setting on her slender Soviet ring finger and took a moment to regard it. Oh, it was gorgeous, all right, and it was also very familiar; in fact, it was the Duchess's old engagement ring, which I'd managed to maintain possession of during the split.

Was it bad luck? I wondered. I mean, it wasn't every day a man asked a woman to become his third wife and then slipped the ring from his last failed marriage onto her finger as a sign of his love and affection and commitment to permanence. Still, I had my reasons, not the least of which was that I hadn't been sure what to get her for her birthday. (Not to mention the fact that a birthday present would have set me back a pretty penny, and I was trying to play things close to the financial vest.)

But when I called George and tried to explain all this to him, he blew up at me. "What the fuck is wrong with you?" he sputtered. "You could have sold the thing for a hundred grand, you numbskull!"

Blah, blah, blah! I thought. KGB had stuck with me through thick and thin, so I *owed* it to her to get married, didn't I? Besides, what about her status as the first, last, and only Miss Soviet Union in that now-defunct nation's history? That counted for something! Then George said, "Anyway, she doesn't even get along with your children, so it'll never work."

Whatever. Worse came to worst, I would just get divorced again.

Meanwhile, the Duchess was being unusually nice. Within three weeks of the kids leaving New York, she already had them back for another visit. Moreover, she had agreed to let me have them for the entire summer. The only problem was: How could I keep them entertained in a Eurotrash-infested Manhattan apartment building while I was locked up under house arrest with an emotionally disconnected fiancée by my side who couldn't say the word *the*? It would be difficult. What with no front lawn to run around on or swimming pool to swim in or beach to build sand castles on, they would be bored to death. Not to mention the fact that on the island of Manhattan it would be a hundred ten degrees and a thousand percent humidity! How could the kids survive in that? They would wilt like tiny sunflowers in the Gobi Desert.

The city was no place for children–especially in the summer! Everyone knew that–especially me. All their friends would be in the Hamptons. How could I disappoint them again? I had put them through enough hell as it was. Yet it would be obscenely expensive to rent a place in the Hamptons, and I was trying to conserve funds. If only the NASDAQ hadn't crashed!

Once again, however, George had a solution. He called me from his cell phone while standing in a sand trap on the sixth tee of Shinnecock, and he said, "I got the inside scoop on a fifteen-acre estate in Southampton. The owner is some pint-size German prince who's long on title and short on cash, so he's looking to rent the place cheap."

"What's the place look like?" asked I, the choosy beggar.

"Well, it's not Meadow Lane," he replied, "but it's still nice. It's got a pool, a tennis court, a huge backyard. It's perfect for the kids. You've even got deer running through your backyard!"

"How much?" I asked cautiously.

"A hundred and twenty grand," he answered. "It's a steal, considering. The place looks like a Swiss hunting lodge."

"I can't afford it," I said quickly, to which George even more quickly replied, "Don't worry; I'll pay the lease up front for you. You can pay me back when you're rolling again." Then he said, "You're like a son to me, Jordan, and you could use a break right now. So take it, and don't look a gift horse in the mouth."

At first, my masculine pride urged me to resist George's generosity, but only for a second. The place would be perfect for the kids, and George was, indeed, like a father to me. Besides, to a man as rich as he (a man as rich as *I* used to be), a hundred twenty grand was nothing. At that level of wealth, money was merely a book entry on a balance sheet; you got more joy from helping people with it than watching it collect four percent in the Bridgehampton National Bank. All you wanted in return was love and respect and, of course, gratitude, all of which I already felt for George. Besides, one day I would pay him back, after I became rich again.

So I packed my bags and moved back out to the Hamptons. I felt like a fucking Ping-Pong ball! Then I received an astonishing phone call from Magnum. It was early June now, and I took the call in my new sprawling living room, which, as George had indicated, looked like a hunting lodge. Magnum said, "I thought you'd like to know that Dave Beall got indicted today for securities fraud. He was arraigned this afternoon in front of Judge Gleeson."

With a sinking heart, I sat down on a distressed leather love seat. Above me hung a giant dead moose's head. The dead moose looked outraged. "Indicted?" I muttered. "How could he get indicted, Greg? I thought he was cooperating!"

"Apparently not," Magnum answered, and then he went about explaining how Dave Beall hadn't actually ratted me out; rather, he had gotten drunk as a skunk and then told one of his *buddies* about the note. His buddy, as it turned out, was a rat in OCD's ever-expanding rat stable. And the rest, as they say, was history.

The kids spent the summer in Southampton and had a ball, and then, the day they left, Elliot Lavigne was indicted for securities fraud. He blamed it all on me, of course, which was rather ironic, I thought, considering that I had once saved his life in what I now considered a momentary lapse of judgment. In truth, I was still glad that I had saved his life, because for the entire week afterward everyone was calling me a hero, but now, half a decade later, Elliot was facing five years, and I didn't give a shit.

The Chef, however, was a different story; I *did* give a shit about him.

In what would seem like the greatest irony of all, the Chef decided to defy the conventional logic and wisdom and take his case to trial. But why? With the videotapes, the audiotapes, my testimony, Danny's testimony, James Loo's testimony, and the airtight paper trail of my Swiss cover-up–which was laden with the Chef's slippery fingerprints–as well as his two spectacular renderings of his submarine, the SS *Money Launderer,* he had absolutely no shot of being acquitted. He would be found guilty as charged and be put away for the better part of a decade.

For my part, I would suffer the public humiliation of having to testify in open court against a man whom I had once called a friend. It would be in the newspaper, in magazines, on the Internet, everywhere. And how ironic it was that what I had done with Dave Beall would go down in history as nothing more than a tiny footnote, a minor offset to a dozen acts of betrayal.

At this moment, I was sitting in the debriefing with Alonso and OCD, laughing inwardly after OCD had just said, "You know what, Alonso? You got the worst case of OCD I've ever seen!"

"What are you talking about?" snapped Alonso. "I'm not OCD! I just want to make sure the transcripts are accurate."

"They *are* accurate," OCD shot back, shaking his head in disbelief. "I mean, do you really think the jury gives a shit whether Gaito said, *'Badabeep, badabop, badaboop'* or *'Badabop, badabeep, badabing'*? They're both the same, for cryin' out loud! The jury knows that!"

Alonso, who was sitting to my right, turned his head toward me ever so slightly and flashed me a knowing wink, as if to say, "You and I both know this is important, so pay no mind to the sputterings of this FBI thug!" Then he looked at OCD, who was sitting on the other side of the conference table, and said to him, "Well, Greg, when you go to law school and pass the New York State bar exam, then *you* can be in charge of the tape recorder!" He let out a single, ironic chuckle. "But, until then, I am!" Then he pressed the rewind button again.

It was close to eleven p.m., and the Gaito trial was less than a month away. For six weeks now, since just after Labor Day, we'd been working into the wee hours of the morning, trying to "nail down" the transcripts. It was a painstaking process, during which the three of us would sit in the subbasement of 26 Federal Plaza and listen to the tapes and make corrections to what were rapidly becoming the most accurate transcripts in the history of law.

Alonso was, indeed, a good man, despite being so tightly wound that I was certain one day he would take one too many deep troubled breaths and simply stop breathing. Everyone called him Alonso. For whatever reason, he was one of those people who were never called by their first name. While I had never had the pleasure of meeting Alonso's parents (wealthy Argentine aristocrats, according to Magnum), I was willing to bet that they'd also called him Alonso since the moment he emerged from his mother's loins.

Alonso hit the stop button and said, "Okay, now turn to page forty-seven of transcript seven-B and tell me what you think of this."

OCD and I nodded wearily, and we leaned forward and began thumbing through our four-inch-thick transcripts, while Alonso did the same. Finally, when we were all on page forty-seven, Alonso hit the play button.

All I could hear at first was a low hum, then a crackling sound, and then my own voice, which always sounded strange to me when I heard it on tape. "... the risk is of James Loo smuggling my million dollars overseas," my voice was saying. "What if he gets stopped at Customs?"

Now came the Chef's voice: "Eh, whaddaya whaddaya? Don't worry about it! He's got his ways, James. All you gotta know is that the money's gonna get there. You give it him, he gives it to his people, and *badabeep badabop badaboop... schhhwiitttt*"—a sharp clap of the Chef's hands!—"it's all done! There's no—"

Alonso hit the stop button and shook his head slowly, as if he were deeply troubled. OCD rolled his eyes, preparing for the pain. I braced myself too. Finally Alonso started muttering, "*Schhhwiitttt*—he keeps using this word." He let out one of his trademark deep, troubled breaths. "I don't get it."

OCD shook his head and sighed. "We've been through this before, Alonso. It just means 'that's all she wrote.' Like, *schhhwiitttt!* That's all she wrote." OCD looked at me with desperation in his eyes. "Right?"

"Pretty much," I said, nodding.

"Ahh, *pretty* much," declared Alonso, raising his finger in vindication, "but not always! Depending on the context it could mean something different." He looked at me and raised his eyebrows. "Right?"

I nodded slowly, wearily. "Yeah, it could. Sometimes he uses it when he's looking to tie up the loose ends of a cover story. Like, he'll say *schhhwiitttt* to mean: 'And with that latest phony document we've created, the government will *never* be able to figure things out!' But most of the time it means just what Greg said."

Alonso shrugged noncommittally. "And what about the clapping sound? Does that affect the meaning of the *schhhwiitttt*?"

OCD sagged visibly, like an animal that'd just taken a bullet. "I gotta take a break," he said, and without another word he left the debriefing room, closing the door gently behind him, muttering something under his breath.

Alonso looked at me and shrugged. "Tough times," he said.

I nodded in agreement. "Yeah, especially for Gaito. I still can't believe he's taking this to trial. It makes no sense."

"Nor to me," he agreed. "I don't think I've ever *seen* a more airtight case than this. It's suicide for Gaito. Someone's giving him some *very* bad advice."

"Yeah, like Brennan," I said. "It's gotta be."

Alonso shrugged again. "He has something to do with it, I'm sure, but it's gotta be more than that. Ron Fischetti is one of the best defense lawyers in the business, and I can't believe he would let Gaito go through with this just because Brennan told him so. I feel like I'm missing something here. You know what I'm saying?"

I nodded slowly, resisting the urge to tell him what I truly thought–that the Blue-eyed Devil was going to try to bribe one of the jurors. And that was all Gaito needed: one juror to hold out, and then Gleeson would be forced to declare a mistrial.

Of course, I had no proof of this, but stories like this had swirled around the Blue-eyed Devil for years–disappearing files, witnesses recanting testimony, judges making surprise rulings in his favor, prosecutors quitting on the eve of trial. But I kept those thoughts to myself and said, "My guess is that Fischetti is gonna try to focus on me, not the facts. Like, if he can get the jury to *truly* hate me or, better yet, to literally *despise* me, then they'll acquit on general principles." I shrugged. "So he's gonna try to paint me as a drug addict, a whoremonger, a compulsive liar, a born cheater–you know, all the good things in life."

Alonso shook his head. "He won't get the chance, because I'm gonna do it first. And don't take it personally when I do; I'm going to be *pretty* tough on you when you're up there. I won't pull any punches, especially when it comes to your personal life." He cocked his head to one side. "You know what I'm referring to?"

I nodded sadly. "Yeah, what happened on the stairs with Nadine."

He nodded back. "And what happened afterward too, with your daughter. I'm gonna bring up everything–all the dark stuff. And you can't try to minimize it or rationalize it. You just say, 'Yes, I kicked my wife down the stairs,' and, 'Yes, I drove my car through a garage door with my daughter in the front passenger seat, unbuckled,' because, trust me, if you do try to minimize it, Fischetti will rip you a new asshole during cross-examination. He'll say, 'Oh, so what you're saying, Mr. Belfort, is that you *didn't* actually kick your wife down a flight of stairs, because she was only on the third step as opposed to the top. And, wait, forgive me, Mr. Belfort, you didn't actually *kick* her; you *pushed* her, which is a whole other story. So, to sum it up, what you're saying is that it's all right for a man to push his wife down *three* individual steps and then risk his daughter's life by *throwing* her into the passenger seat of his ninety-thousand-dollar

Mercedes and driving through a garage door while high on cocaine and Quaaludes?' " Alonso smiled. "You get the picture?"

"Yeah, I got it, but I don't want it."

"None of us wants it," he agreed, "but those are the facts we're stuck with."

I nodded in resignation. Alonso continued: "But, on the bright side, we'll get to spend some time talking about how you went to rehab and got sober. And then you can also bring up how you go to high schools now and give antidrug lectures to the kids." He smiled reassuringly. "Believe me, as long as you're honest, it'll work out fine. Drug addiction is a disease, so people will forgive you for it." He shrugged. "Now, if only whoremongering were a disease too, then we would *really* be in business!" He started laughing. "Funny, right?"

"Yeah," I said, smiling–*fucking hysterical!* I would have to admit, under oath, to banging a thousand hookers of all shapes and sizes. The only question was if it would end up in the newspaper. It was just the sort of tawdry gossip that the *New York Post* lived for.

Alonso reached into his pants pocket and pulled out a fresh pack of Marlboros and a cheap Bic lighter. "You know, I don't make it a habit of breaking the law," he said, "but in spite of this being a smoke-free building I'm gonna light up anyway." And he did just that, taking a rather shallow, halfhearted pull that so much as said, "I'm not really a smoker; I just do this when I'm stressed out."

I remained silent and let him smoke in peace. I understood this was important–to be able to partake in a simple manly pleasure without being interrupted by idle chatter. My father, one of the world's all-time great smokers, had explained this to me on numerous occasions. "Son," he'd say, "if I want to kill myself with these fucking cancer sticks, then at least let me kill myself in fucking peace, for Chrissake!"

Alonso smiled at me and said, "Sooo . . . how are you, Jordan?"

I cocked my head to the side and stared at him for a moment. "How am I?" I asked. "Are you being sarcastic, Alonso?"

He turned the corners of his mouth down and shook his head slowly. "No, not at all. I just want to know how you are."

I shrugged. "Well, it's been a long time since someone's asked me that, so I need to think about it for a second." I paused for about a tenth of a second, then said, "Uh, I suck! How you doin', Alonso?"

He ignored my last few words and said, "Things will get better; you just gotta give it some time. After the trial is over, we can make a motion to get your ankle bracelet taken off." A brief pause, then: "I'm sure Gleeson will approve it once he hears you testify. It definitely comes through how remorseful you are."

I nodded. "Well, I am remorseful. More than you can imagine."

He nodded. "I know that; I've been doing this long enough to know when someone's full of shit. But that aside, you still haven't answered my question."

"About what: How am I?"

"Yeah. How are you?"

I shrugged. "I got problems, Alonso. I'm facing years in jail, I'm engaged to a woman I'm not in love with, I have no career path, my kids live on the other side of the country, I'm wearing a fucking ankle bracelet, I've betrayed my closest friends, they've betrayed me, and, to top it all off, I'm on the verge of running out of money and I don't have a way to make any more right now."

"You'll be rich again," he said knowingly. "I don't think anyone in their right mind would bet against it."

I shrugged. "Yeah, well, you're probably right about that, but I won't be rich for a long time. I'm in the middle of a bad luck streak, and until it runs its course, there's nothing I can do. Anyway, my real goal here is to move out to California to be near my kids. That's it. I swore an oath to my daughter that I would do that, and I'm not going to let her down. I'd like to move out there before I get sentenced. You think that's realistic?"

"Yeah, I think it is. I'll do what I can to help you, but you have to be patient for a while. The next year is going to be hectic; there are trials pending, indictments looming; a lot of things are still up in the air. But there should be a window toward the end. From a logistical standpoint, though, I don't know how much sense it makes to move before you do your time. I mean, what are you going to do: rent a house and then go to jail right after you rent it?"

I smiled and winked. "You bet your ass I am! Before I go to jail, I want my kids to know that I officially moved out to California; this way, they'll know I'll be coming back there when I get out. And I want to spend my last night of freedom with them in a house that's ours, not in a hotel. And we're all gonna sleep in the same bed that night, one of them under each arm." I paused for a moment, relishing the thought. "That's how I want to spend my last night of freedom."

Just then the door swung open, and in walked OCD. He took a few suspicious sniffs and then looked at the metal wastepaper basket, where Alonso had tossed his cigarette. Then he looked back at Alonso and said, "So how far did you guys get without me? It's getting kinda late here."

With great enthusiasm, Alonso said, "No, we're still in the same spot. We got sidetracked." Alonso compressed his lips, suppressing a cackle.

I suppressed my own cackle as the last traces of color left OCD's face.

Unlike *Law & Order,* where the excitement is heart-palpitating and the tension is so thick you can literally cut it with a knife, the real-life happenings in a federal courtroom are quite the opposite. Judge Gleeson, for example, sits high on his bench, sometimes looking interested, sometimes looking bored, occasionally looking amused—but always in complete control. There are no outbursts or arguments or people questioning the wisdom of his decisions or anything that might cause him to rise out of his chair and lean forward over his vast desk and point his finger and scream, "You're out of order, Counselor! Now sit back down or I'm holding you in contempt!"

I testified for three days—three unremarkable days—during which I found Fischetti to be fairly competent, but not overly so. Oh, he looked pretty spiffy, in his $2,000 gray silk suit and fancy gray necktie, but that was about it. His lines of questioning seemed boring and long-winded. If I had been sitting in the jury box, I would have fallen asleep.

Alonso, however, had been brilliant: organized, eloquent, persuasive, thorough. He had left Fischetti nowhere to go but in circles, double-talking and triple-talking, and the more he talked, the guiltier his client seemed. Danny testified too, as did a handful of others, although just who and how many I wasn't sure. The less I knew, the better, explained Alonso. I was not on trial, after all; I was only a witness.

A month later, I was sitting in my Swiss hunting lodge beneath the outraged moose's head when a call came in from an even more outraged OCD. "It's a mistrial," he sputtered. "I can't fucking believe it! How could that jury not convict? It makes no sense."

"Did you poll the jury afterward?" I asked.

With disgust: "Yeah, why?"

I said, "Well, let me guess, there was only one holdout, right?"

Dead silence at first, then: "How the fuck did you know *that*?"

"Just a hunch," I said. "And you want to hear my second hunch?"

"Yeah," he replied cautiously.

"The holdout was that bastard in the front row, the one with the handlebar mustache, right?"

"It was, actually," said OCD. "You're just *guessing,* though, right?"

"Not exactly," I replied, and I told him my thoughts–namely, that while I had no proof of it, this very mistrial had the Blue-eyed Devil's fingerprints all over it.

"No shit!" he snapped. "You really think so?"

"Yeah, I really do. Again, I have no proof, but, I don't know–I mean, did you see Gaito just sitting there so calm, cool, and collected? He looked almost *smug* about the whole thing, and Gaito is not a smug man. If anything, he's humble. Maybe I'm crazy, but the whole scene just struck me as odd, especially that juror; he seemed disinterested, like he'd already made up his mind beforehand."

OCD agreed–as did Alonso when I shared my thoughts with him a few minutes later, via conference call. Still, there was no way to prove it, and Alonso refused to investigate, considering it to be the act of a sore loser. Besides, he hadn't actually *lost*; a mistrial simply meant that Gaito would have to stand trial again, which he did, precisely six months later.

And during those six months, from December 2000 to May 2001, I burned through most of the cash I had left, as well as what little patience I had with KGB. She, I was certain, held me in as much contempt as I held her. Unfortunately, I'd never been good at getting out of relationships, and, apparently, neither was she. So we remained engaged, passing our days having angry sex and bitter arguments, the latter of which had to do mostly with moon landings and such.

Sadly, Gaito was convicted this time, with the jury reaching a verdict in only a single day. I was home when I got the news, and at that very moment I felt like the lowest scum on earth. I had betrayed a friend, who would now be going to jail for the better part of a decade because he refused to betray one of his friends.

Danny, meanwhile, had already gone to jail; in fact, he never even had a chance to testify at the second trial. He had gotten himself arrested in Florida on an unrelated charge–something about telemarketing fraud with sports memorabilia–and Gleeson remanded him in early April.

When the summer came, I blew what few dollars I still had left on the kids. That was appropriate, I thought, considering they were the only good thing in my life, anyway. And when I kissed them good-bye on Labor Day, I cried inwardly, because I knew I wouldn't be seeing them again for a long time. In spite of Alonso keeping his word–getting me off house arrest and granting me unrestricted travel to California–I could no longer afford to go there.

That, however, was about to change.

CHAPTER 28

FROM OUT OF THE ASHES

It was less than a week after 9/11, as the country readied for war, when my bad luck streak finally ended. I was glued to the TV set when an old friend called from out of the blue and started asking me for advice about something he kept referring to as the *refi boom.*

Home-mortgage rates had just fallen to record lows, and Americans were refinancing in droves.

"Can you do me a quick favor?" he asked.

"Yeah," I said. "What is it?"

"I need you to write me a cold-calling script. There's a *fortune* to be made telemarketing for refis right now."

Interesting, I thought, but that was all I thought. I was so down on my luck at this point that his words, in regards to my own plight, blew past me like a gust of wind. "All right," I said. "Tell me a little bit about your business, and I'll write you one this afternoon." And, with that, he went about explaining the ins and outs of refinancing to me.

It was elegantly simple. Virtually all homeowners currently held mortgages with rates between eight and ten percent, while today's rates were hovering near six percent. So all a mortgage broker had to do was secure a new loan (at the lower interest rate) to pay off the old loan, and a person's monthly mortgage payment would plummet. And while there were some minor costs involved–the so-called closing costs–you could roll them into the new mortgage by making it slightly larger than the old one, which meant no out-of-pocket fees for the borrower. Better still, the closing costs were a mere pittance compared to the long-term savings, which could be hundreds of thousands of dollars, depending on the size of the loan.

"Hmmm," I muttered, "it sounds pretty basic. You got leads to call?"

"Yeah, I bought a list of homeowners who are paying eight percent or higher. I'm telling you–it'll be like taking candy from a baby!"

"All right," I said. "Give me a few hours, and I'll e-mail you a script." Then, as an afterthought: "And why don't you send me over a few leads while you're at it to test it out with–just to make sure it flows."

And that was how it started.

He e-mailed me the leads, I wrote a script, and halfway through my first sales pitch, a very animated Haitian woman cut me off in mid-sentence by saying, "This sounds too good to be true! When can you come over to do the paperwork?"

Right this damn second! I thought. Although, not wanting to sound like a desperate salesman, I replied, "Well, it just so happens I'm going to be in your area tomorrow"–I looked at her address and noticed she lived in the Bushwick section of Brooklyn, a *dangerous* place. Why would I be in her area? What plausible explanation?–"refinancing one of your neighbors," I quickly added. "I can be there around noon. Does that sound okay?"

"Perfect!" she answered. "I'll make snacks."

The next day I found myself driving through the war zone of east Brooklyn, marveling at how a lack of money can make a man brave. The woman's house was a two-story frame affair on a grimy two-way street. From the outside it looked like a crack den. Inside, it smelled like boiled fish and mildew. There were no less than twelve Haitians living there.

She offered me a seat at her turd-green Formica kitchen table, where she immediately began serving me beans and rice and boiled fish—refusing to talk about her mortgage until I cleaned my plate. Meanwhile, I kept hearing an ungodly shriek coming from one of the upstairs bedrooms. It sounded like a small child. "Is everything okay up there?" I asked, forcing a smile.

She nodded slowly, knowingly, as if to say, "Everything is just as it should be." Then she said, "That is my grandson; he has the fever."

The fever? What did she mean by that? From her tone of voice she seemed to be implying that foul play, in the form of supernatural forces, was involved. "Well, I'm sorry to hear that," I said sadly. "Did you call a doctor?"

She shook her head no. "I am all the doctor he needs."

I felt a shiver run down my spine. Obviously this woman had not attended medical school; she was a female witch doctor, or Moomba, as the phrase went. Whatever the case, once the Moomba and I finally got down to business, I grossed $7,000 in commission in less than thirty minutes and saved her $300 a month in the process. Or at least that's what I *tried* to do. What ended up happening was slightly different.

The Moomba flashed me a smile, which exposed a gold central incisor, and she said, "I do not give a shit about lowering my mortgage payment, Jordan. I just want to take cash out of my house." She winked at me. "You know, a little *mad money*? Didn't you ever get the urge to spend a few dollars?"

Her name was Thelma. I smiled and held back from saying, "Well, Thelma, there was this one time when I was high on Quaaludes and decided to extend my yacht to make room for my seaplane!" Then I said, "How much cash would you like, Thelma?"

As I would soon find out, Thelma's answer was typical of many American homeowners, the majority of whom would eventually fall behind on their mortgage payments and end up in foreclosure. She so much as said, "Listen, Jordan, get me as much fucking cash as possible, and I don't give a shit if the rate's exactly the same as it is now. I just want to redecorate my home and travel to exotic places and buy a new sewing machine and a flat-screen TV and a twin-engine speedboat, and then I want to pay off the balances on my credit cards so I can run them back up again in six months and refi once more!

"And, by the way, Jordan, if you can figure out a way to get me approved for one of those newfangled adjustable-rate mortgages, where the payment is supercheap for the first few years and then explodes to a level that I won't possibly be able to afford, then that's what I want too. I'll worry about the payment when I'm living in a homeless shelter!"

Ahhhh, the refi boom. It was everything my friend had made it out to be. One day, of course, there would be hell to pay for all these newfangled mortgage products–products that allowed anyone with a pulse and a Social Security number (regardless of credit rating and income) to borrow 110 percent of the value of their home and worry about being able to afford the payment at some murky point down the road. But, still, for today it was wonderful; and all the homeowners and builders and bankers and mortgage brokers and real estate brokers and appraisers and retailers of luxury items and, of course, all the Wall Street hedge-fund managers who were buying these wacky mortgages to lock in *perceived* profits–which they could then tout to investors to support the notion of their continued mastery of the universe–couldn't be happier. And, of course, I was happiest of all.

Within a week I had grossed $50,000 in commission, and the week after that I doubled it. And just like that my money problems were over. The dark cloud that had followed me around since that horrific day on the courthouse steps had finally evaporated.

At first KGB didn't notice anything. That was no shock; after all, she spent the bulk of her day playing Crash Bandicoot III (*Crash Super Smash,* she called it), and what few words we *did* exchange were in the form of grunts and groans, during sex.

Nevertheless, she *was* my fiancée, so I figured it was only right to tell her the good news–which was that, in thirty days, when the loans began to close, I would be rolling in dough again. Then we could resume the semblance of a normal life.

"Good!" was all she said. "Then you can take me to store again."

In the eighteen months we'd lived together, the girl had uttered the word *the* only once, and it had been at the wrong time. That momentous event had occurred while we were still living in the city, while I was under house arrest. *Such happy times, those were!* She had said to me: "It is nice day outside. I will go to the Central Park now to take walk."

KGB and I were living together on borrowed time, and we both knew it. In fact, I wasn't the least bit surprised when, after my first loan closed and I booked a flight to California, she wasn't offended when I didn't invite her to come along. In fact, she seemed relieved.

And what a trip it was! I couldn't remember ever being happier.

For $79 per night I rented a tiny room at the Manhattan Beach Hilton, and for an additional $29 per day I rented the cheapest car Hertz had to offer. And how had I flown? *Coach!* I had also flown through Boston, to save a few extra dollars. *The new me!*

And the kids? Well, apparently the Duchess had told them that I was having money problems, because when we went toy shopping they refused to buy anything other than candy. At first I was devastated–no, worse; I was embarrassed. I had always tried to be a larger-than-life character to my kids, a daddy who could buy them anything and take them anywhere. After all, it was a daddy's job to show his children only the *best* in life, wasn't it?

Apparently not, because as the week progressed, I began to realize something very important, something that my prior life of wealth and affluence had entirely camouflaged: My children couldn't care less about all the pomp and circumstance. All they wanted was their father. And all they wanted to know was that he loved them unconditionally and that he always would. Those were simple truths, yet they had also been the most difficult for me to grasp.

And as I went about meeting their new friends, eating in their favorite restaurants, and playing in their favorite parks, I found a new peace in my life. I began thinking that this might have been God's plan all along: a rise and fall of biblical proportions, only to be resurrected once more with a newfound ability to appreciate things.

Before I flew home, I promised the kids I would come back in two weeks and that I would do that every other week until I finally moved there. And then we said good-bye, with laughs and smiles instead of tears. Without saying it, we all knew that Daddy was back.

When I landed in New York, I went straight to work–finding the refi boom accelerating at an exponential rate. In 2000, Americans had dot-commed themselves to death; in 2001, they were mortgaging themselves to death. A real estate bubble was forming right before my eyes. When would it burst? It was as if every person I spoke to either wanted to refinance or had just done so. I brought in thirty loans in two weeks and hopped back on a plane to California.

Obviously, with all the loans, it only made sense to take a slightly larger room in the Hilton (a suite, actually) and rent a slightly better car from Hertz (a Lincoln, actually). By my third trip, the loans were closing so fast that I decided to fly first class out of JFK. I mean, what was the harm? I was making my money legitimately now, and at the rate I was going I would be a millionaire in no time flat!

When I landed in L.A., my limo driver (yes, to save time I had a limo waiting for me) said he was surprised that a man of my means would choose to stay at the Hilton. "Why not stay in the Beach House?" he asked nonchalantly. "It's only a few steps from the sand, and every room has a view of the Pacific. I mean, the place ain't cheap, but it's definitely the best!"

"Well, what the hell are you waiting for?" I said to the driver. "Take me to the Beach House, for Chrissake!" And just like that I found my new home away from home: the Beach House. It was quaint and gorgeous and less than two miles from my kids. By our third stay, Chandler and Carter were like little celebrities there. Everyone knew us, and we knew everyone.

Life seemed wonderful.

There were only two things eating away at me now.

The first was my beloved fiancée, KGB.

We hated each other.

Just why we were still living together I don't think either of us could figure out, although it had something to do with inertia. Her clothes were in my closets, her panties were in my drawers, her sheets were on my bed, and no one, including Mary Poppins, likes to pack. But, alas, as 2001 came to a close, the sex began to fade away—which meant there was no reason to be living in the same zip code anymore.

It was Valentine's Day, 2002—which was as good a day as any to break off the most ill-conceived engagement since Johnny Depp and Winona Ryder. In fact, why not end it right here at dinner? We were sitting at a table for two at the American Hotel in Sag Harbor. It was a classy establishment, and, most important, it was the sort of establishment where someone as refined as KGB would think twice before she poured that glass of 1992 Louis Jadot Montrachet over my head. The sommelier, dressed in an immaculate black tuxedo and black patent-leather shoes, had just uncorked it for the bargain-basement price of $350.

KGB's fabulous blue eyes were staring at me with contempt from just a tiny table's width away. She was hanging on my every word, disgusted by each of them—already!—just fifteen minutes after we'd sat down. But I was only getting started; I mustn't rush it. This had to be more than one of our typical fights to instigate a Soviet bag-packing. From her communist-red lips, luscious as always, came the words:

"On polny mudak!" You little fucking testicle! "You think you win Cold War? Oh—please! It is all money with America! Money, money, money!" Contempt dripped off the word. "You spend my country into bankruptcy! Your Ronald Reagan call us Evil Empire and make Star Wars! And who save you in World War Two? We do! We lose twenty million people to defeat Nazis. How much you lose—ten people? Unbelievable! Fucking America... *Pizda mudak!"* Fucking pussies!

I shrugged, unimpressed with her latest anti-American tirade. "Well, if you hate this country so much, Yulia, then why don't you"–I started raising my voice–"get the fuck out and go back to your *own* fucking country, or whatever's left of it!" Other couples began to stare. "But before you *leave* us"–I reached down to the bread plate and lifted up a French baguette and offered it to her–"here, take a piece of bread with you so you don't have to wait in line when you get home." I shook my head contemptuously. "Fucking Russia! What a mockery! Once a superpower, and look at you now! You can't even defeat Chechnya, and they're throwing fucking rocks at you!"

"Blyad!" she sputtered. "Who you think you are? You'll never get girl like me again! Look at you and look at me. You will be sorry."

Alas, she had a point there. She definitely had me beat in the looks department. It was time to humor her. I looked her straight in her face and blew her a tender kiss.

She scrunched up her little model nose and muttered, *"Mudilo!"* You shrunken testicle! *"Idi na khui!"* Go suck your own penis!

"Yeah, well, looks aren't everything, Yulia." I offered her a sarcastic smile. "And I want to thank you for teaching me that. See, my problem was that I got lucky with my first two wives, so I just assumed that beauty and personality came together as a package." I shrugged innocently. "Now I know better."

"Ha!" she snarled. "Go back to ex-wife who leave you on courthouse steps. Some woman this one is."

In spite of everything, I still felt the need to defend the Duchess. I said, "My marriage to Nadine ended long before I got indicted; but that's neither here nor there. All that matters is what's going on with us–with *our* relationship. And it's not working."

"*Blyad!* You do not have to tell *me* this. You are nightmare to live with. All you talk of is kids and mortgages; that is it. You big bore." With that she looked away, muttering more Russkie curses under her breath.

I took a deep breath and said, "Listen, Yulia, I really don't want to fight anymore. You were very good to me at a time when I *really* needed someone to be good to me." I shrugged sadly. "But we're different people, you and I. And we're from different worlds, with different history books. It's not our fault that we don't see eye to eye on things. We couldn't even if we wanted to!" I shrugged again. "Besides, my heart's in California; that's where I need to be now, near my kids. There's no other way for me." I shook my head and let out a few chuckles. "Trust me, you'll be better off without me. I still have to go to jail one day, and I have no idea for how long. I think you should move out this week. I'm leaving for California tomorrow, and I won't be back until Sunday."

With great pride: "I already make plan to. Igor will come tomorrow and pack my things. You will never see me again."

I nodded sadly. What she said was true: I would never see her again. Ours, after all, was not the sort of relationship where you remain friends afterward. (We hadn't been friends while we were together.) She would immerse herself back into the "scene," and I would move out to California just as soon as possible and build a new life there. I would rent a house on the beach–just like I'd sworn to Alonso–and I would see my kids every day and make up for lost time.

I caught a glimpse of KGB's engagement ring–the Duchess's engagement ring. I stared at it for a moment, a flood of memories washing over me. That ring was one of my final possessions left over from the old days. Everything else was gone. Most of my furniture had been stolen from storage, and I'd hocked my gold watches just before I'd stumbled upon the refi boom. In fact, other than a few Gilberto suits, the only thing I still had left was my black four-door Mercedes. Everything else had been purchased with mortgage money, which is to say, with money I'd earned honestly.

Apparently KGB saw me staring at the ring, because she said, "Ohhh, so you want ring back now?"

I turned the corners of my mouth down and shook my head slowly. "No. You can keep it; sell it, hold it, wear it–I don't give a shit what you do with it. That ring's cursed, as far as I'm concerned. Maybe it'll bring you better luck than it brought me."

We cut dinner short, and ten minutes later we were back in the

Mercedes, on our way home. We were cruising down Noyack Road, a long, dark, winding country road that led from Sag Harbor to the village of Southampton. It was cold and damp outside; the roads were slick. I would keep it under forty.

KGB was staring out the front windshield. She wore a full-length Russian sable coat and a matching sable cap, the latter of which had an oversize brim and a long, fluffy tail dangling from the back. It was the sort of over-the-top fur ensemble that only a wealthy Russkie woman who had once been voted Miss Soviet Union could get away with without looking completely ridiculous. Her engagement ring was turned inward, the stone resting in the palm of her own balled-up fist, which was clenched as tight as a drum.

Apparently she wouldn't have given it up without a fight anyway.

I leaned forward and turned on the radio and hit the search button. A love song. *Fucking Cupid!* Why doesn't someone just shoot that little bastard right in his diapered ass with one of his own arrows? I hit the search button again–another love song.

"Watch out!" screamed KGB. "There is animals on road!"

I looked up–*fuck!* Deer–three of them–twenty yards away and closing fast. *A surge of adrenaline....* I smashed on the antilock brakes and screamed: "Hold on!" I jerked the wheel to the right, trying to steer the car into the woods, but the Mercedes began to fishtail.... *No!... Come on, you German bastards!...* I smashed the horn–*beeepppp!*–but the deer just looked at the car, confused. I flashed the brights in desperation. The deer were less than ten yards away. I honked again. No effect, so I cut the wheel hard left... more fishtailing.... I smashed the brakes even harder.... I felt the antilock mechanism kick in.... *The Krauts!... Come on, you Krauts!...* My heart was beating a mile a minute.... I was holding my breath... no... it's too late... gonna hit... Such helpless faces on the deer... a terrible waste.... I locked my arms and braced for impact. "Hold on!" I screamed. "We're gonna hit..."

Suddenly, as if by magic, the car came to a complete stop, five inches from the deer. KGB and I sat there speechless, mouths agape, staring at the deer, which were still frozen in the headlights. In the background, Cupid was still torturing me with a duet by Lionel Richie and Diana Ross:

"And I'll give it all to you, my love, my love, my love, my endless love."

"Jesus Christ," I finally muttered, still staring at the deer. I shook my head slowly, as the deer stared back. They seemed annoyed. I flicked off the radio and looked over at KGB. *Nice fucking hat!* I thought. "God, that was close! I can't believe it!"

SMASH!

The impact from the fourth deer was so profound that the two-thousand-pound German Mercedes seemed to fly up a foot in the air and then fall back to earth in slow motion. Without even having to look, I knew the entire rear passenger side was completely totaled. And the deer, of course, was dead. I turned back to KGB and her hat.

"You all right?" I asked.

She nodded slowly, dreamily. She was too astonished to speak. Out of the corner of my eye, I saw the three deer scatter into the woods. At that very moment, it hit me that they were a small family, probably out looking for food. I was certain I'd killed the mother. *How sad.* I told KGB to wait in the car.

Outside, it was sheer carnage. A large deer with a very gentle face was lying on its right side, motionless. I felt a shiver run down my spine. I turned up the collar of my sport coat against the cold and took a moment to regard the deer. How very odd; it still looked beautiful. There was no external damage. Its eyes were open and lifeless. Its body was completely still. Must've broken its neck.

I looked over at the Mercedes. It was completely totaled. From the rear door to the wheel well, the entire right side had buckled. It looked barely drivable. Fair enough, I thought. It was my last tainted possession. Tomorrow I would have it junked, along with KGB.

I turned back to the deer, to take a closer look. Was it dead? It didn't look dead. All at once a terrible fear came rising up my brain stem. A dead animal was the bringer of bad tidings, a sign from below. With a sinking heart, I crouched down and placed my hand on the deer's throat. I checked for a pulse, and suddenly the deer's eyes blinked! I jumped back, astonished.

Slowly, *very* slowly, the deer rose up onto all fours and began shaking its head back and forth, as if it were trying to get out the cobwebs. Then it began limping away. After a few steps it started trotting–right back into the woods, to reunite with its family. I breathed a great sigh of relief.

Now there was only one last thing eating away at me.

CHAPTER 29

JUDGMENT DAY

July 5, 2003
Seventeen Months Later

The proceedings were going just the way I had thought they would. They made me want to bolt out of Judge Gleeson's courtroom to the bathroom so I could regurgitate my breakfast in private. Still, it was time to get this madness over with, to put it all behind me. I had been out on bail for far too long, and everybody in the courtroom knew it. Everybody–not only Judge Gleeson but also Magnum and the Yale-man, who were standing beside me, and Alonso and OCD, who were standing beside them. Everyone looked rather dapper on the day of my doom.

For good measure, the spectators' section was packed to capacity, filled with friends and enemies alike. They sat behind a thick wooden balustrade with a curved top, the so-called Bar of Justice, and were as quiet as church mice. Among them were a dozen assistant United States attorneys (the friends, believe it or not), half as many journalists (the enemies, of course), a handful of complete strangers who were there simply to observe a man's sentencing (sadists, I figured), and my own beloved parents, Mad Max and Saint Leah, who were there for moral support.

We were now ten minutes into the proceedings, and Magnum was making the case to Gleeson that my fine should be much less than Danny's. Gleeson had hit him with $200 million in restitution, payable in installments of $1,000 per month. On that basis, he would fully be paid off in a little over sixteen thousand years, which would be well into the next Ice Age, when money wouldn't mean as much. Either way, I still found $200 million in restitution to be entirely outrageous. Not that I didn't deserve it, but how the hell was I supposed to pay it back? Actually, I wasn't, according to Magnum; it was symbolic more than anything. Yet he still felt compelled to make the case to Gleeson.

Gleeson cut him off and said, "Sorry to interrupt, Mr. O'Connell. Sometimes restitution *is* almost a symbolic act, but not in this case. Mr. Belfort is an earner, for a lack of a better way of putting it. He's going to earn a lot of money after he gets out of jail."

"I understand that," said Magnum, "but the amount ordered in the Porush case was far outside..." *Oh, shit!* Why was Magnum picking a fight with Judge Gleeson? What was the fucking point? Just let him slam me with a symbolic fine and go light on my jail time. "...looking to negotiate," Magnum continued. "I just don't want to agree to something that might be off by a hundred million dollars."

There were a few moments of silence as I waited for Gleeson to explode with something like: "HOW DARE YOU QUESTION MY JUDGMENT IN THIS COURTROOM! I'M HOLDING YOU IN CONTEMPT, MAGNUM!" But to my surprise, he reduced my restitution to $110 million, without seeming even a bit perturbed. Then he said, "Would you like to be heard with regard to sentence, Mr. O'Connell?"

Magnum nodded. "Yes, Your Honor"–*and keep it brief! Alonso promised to make an impassioned plea on my behalf, so don't steal his thunder!*–"but only some very brief remarks." *Thank God.* "This is a case that we fully understand involves a serious offense, and one that is broad both in terms of the time period involved, the number of victims, and the very large amount of losses sustained by them."

Well, thanks a lot. Magnum. What are you going to do next, bring up my penchant for hookers and drugs and midget-tossing? Move on, God damn it!

"First," continued Magnum, "Mr. Belfort recognizes that he was motivated by selfishness and greed during this period of activity, and he saddled himself with a serious drug problem, which I think dovetailed with his guilt over the crimes in which he was engaged and his struggle to..." I tuned out; it was just too painful to listen.

Of course, I knew Magnum was doing what he *had* to do; if he were to try to minimize my crimes, Gleeson wouldn't consider anything positive he had to say. Yet, in truth, the only person who could really help me in these proceedings was Alonso. Anything said by Magnum would be suspect because he was my paid mouthpiece, and anything said by me would be construed as the words of a desperate man, saying anything necessary to get myself off the hook.

"...and in Mr. Belfort's case," concluded my paid mouthpiece, "despite the seriousness of the offenses, I genuinely believe that a lenient sentence would be appropriate."

"Thank you," said the judge, who was smart enough to know that Magnum would have felt leniency was appropriate for pretty much anything, short of rape or murder.

Now Gleeson looked at me. "Mr. Belfort?"

I nodded humbly and said, "Your Honor, I'd like to apologize to"–*Don't do it, you ninny! Don't apologize to the world! It sounds disingenuous!*–"all the people who lost money..." and I was off and running, apologizing to everyone, knowing that, despite the fact that I was truly sorry, my words rung so hollow that I was all but wasting my breath. But I couldn't seem to stop myself; my mind began double-tracking a mile a minute. On one track I was gushing out more apologies–

"...make a list of all the people and apologize to them, but the list is so big that I can't possibly..."

–and on the second track I was thinking how much better off I'd be just saying something like: *You know what, Judge? I fucked up something awful here, and I wish I could say it was because of all the drugs, but the truth is that it wasn't. I was just a greedy little bastard, and not just greedy for money but also for sex and for power and for the admiration of my peers and for just about anything else you can imagine. And what makes it even worse, Your Honor, is that I was blessed with some wonderful gifts, and instead of using them in an honest, productive way, I used them to corrupt other people, to get them to do my evil bidding–*

". . . that when I first started Stratton, I didn't intend it to be this way, but very quickly I knew exactly what I was doing and I just kept doing it until I was stopped. I take full responsibility for my actions. I can only blame my greed–greed for power, greed for money, greed for recognition. I have a lot of explaining to do to my children one day, and hopefully they'll learn from my mistakes. I would just like to put this all behind me and start paying people back. That's the best I can do." I lowered my head in contrition and shook it sadly.

There were a few moments of silence, during which I refused to look up. I felt my speech had been terribly lame.

I heard Gleeson say, "Mr. Alonso?"

Alonso said, "Your Honor, you've just heard the defendant talk briefly about how sorry he is and about how he thinks about honesty and ethics and how he tries to do the right thing every day, and if I were sitting where you're sitting, I would have to be somewhat skeptical of a defendant who has done what this defendant has done. However, I spent many hours discussing honesty and ethics with this man. It's possible that I'm a pollyanna, but I think that he truly gets it. I believe that he really, really has tried to move on from some point in the last few years and has tried to change his life.

"I don't know if you're aware, but the first time I met him was on the day you threw him in jail for the helicopter trip to Atlantic City." *For Chrissake, of all the things to bring up, why that?* "And over the next few months, when he finally got released, I think there was a marked change in this man. I think that he really did think to himself what it was that he had done and, more importantly, what he had to do as a cooperator. I think that he got it. Is it possible that we should be skeptical? Sure. But do I think that there is good reason to believe him when he says what he just said? I do.

"And when he testified at the Gaito trial, he spent more than a hundred hours prepping with me, and it was the worst time of his life. It was a very arduous time, but we spent a lot of time talking about what he did and his past deceptions and fraud, and I do want to add my own two cents that I think there is good reason to believe him about his intention to do what he says he is going to do."

I snuck a peek at Gleeson, who was nodding. Was he nodding in agreement, though? It was difficult to say. This judge was a cool cat. He wouldn't tip his hand.

"Thank you," said Gleeson. "I think everyone has demonstrated good judgment in not speaking as long as they might have given the extremes of this case–the extreme criminal contact involving Mr. Belfort, and the extreme cooperation. It is extraordinary cooperation, I recognize that." He looked me dead in the eyes. "It's knocked many, many, many years off the jail term you otherwise would have gotten, but balanced against that are many years of brazen, arrogant fraud." Now he turned on his incredible shrink ray, and I found myself growing smaller and smaller, as he said:

"You victimized thousands and thousands of innocent people who trusted you, who trusted the people who worked for you. You thought the regulators were a joke and you took them to the cleaner's. You lived the high life"–*oh, shit!*–"the *highest* of the high life, and not because your talents got you there–I have no doubt that you are a talented man–but because you were willing to lie, cheat, and steal. Your competitors were placed at a disadvantage, certainly not all of them, but most of them did what most people do, and tried to conduct their business honorably and honestly without basically stealing the money from so many people where you can't possibly apologize to all of them.

"It's important to the sentence I'm imposing that you have apparently turned your life around. What I've read about you in the 5K letter, what Mr. Alonso said about you, has sunken in to me. It does seem to me as though you've turned a corner. I guess the most important and hard-to-predict question in this entire process is what that translates into by way of how much punishment you deserve." He paused and let out a great sigh, the sort of great sigh King Solomon would have produced if he had been faced with sentencing a redeemed Wolf of Wall Street.

I clenched my ass cheeks and said a prayer to the Almighty. He had sentenced Danny to four years, which after deductions, amounted to a bit less than two. The way Magnum and I had figured it, Gleeson would have to sentence me to less.

"It's a very, very difficult decision. I've thought about it long and hard, and I have determined that a prison term of four years is appropriate, and that's what I'm imposing."

A sudden surge of murmurs from the spectator section.

My stomach began churning before my mind could put it all together. The kids–what would I say? More tears. I dropped my head in defeat. I couldn't believe it. It was the worst end of the spectrum, exactly what Danny had gotten. My brain began whizzing through the calculations. Forty-eight months was how much after deductions? There was fifteen percent off for good time, which was 7.2 months, plus eighteen months for the drug program, equaled 25.2 months total, deducted from forty-eight–between twenty-two and twenty-three months in jail.

Then Gleeson said, "I'm imposing restitution in the amount of $110 million"–*no big deal,* I thought–"payable in the amount of fifty percent of his gross income." Holy shit!

A rigoletto of murmurs from the spectator section! Were they laughing at me? It couldn't be, but it sounded like it. What were my parents thinking?

Time seemed to slow down; I could hear Magnum asking Judge Gleeson to recommend me for the drug program.... Gleeson agreed.... Now Magnum was asking for a delay in reporting... Gleeson recommending ninety days. Although Magnum and I had spoken beforehand about delaying it until after the New Year, he now said that it shouldn't be a problem. He was asking Gleeson to allow me to serve my time in California, to be near the kids. Gleeson, of course, agreed.

Suddenly I noticed Gleeson rising from his chair, and that was it; it was over just like that. There would be no appeals, no Hail Mary passes, nothing. I was going to jail for almost two years. And the fine–fifty percent! A nightmare! Could I ever pay it back? Maybe. I would have to hit a home run. In the meantime, I would be forced to make twice as much as everyone else to live the same life. Fair enough, I thought. I could do that easily.

Outside the courtroom, the whole crew was gathered in the hallway–Alonso, OCD, the Mormon, Magnum, the Yale-man, and my parents. It was still all a blur to me. I hadn't recovered from the shock yet. There were lots of glum expressions. Apologies from Alonso and OCD and the Mormon, wishing it would have gone better. I thanked them, promising to keep in touch. I knew OCD and I would. As different as we were, we had learned much from each other. In spite of everything, I considered myself better off from the encounter.

Then I turned to Magnum and the Yale-man, and we exchanged hugs. They had done an amazing job, especially when it had mattered most. If someone I loved were in trouble, I would recommend the law offices of De Feis O'Connell & Rose and never look back. We would certainly keep in touch.

Now I hugged my parents, my father first.

Mad Max was cool as a cucumber, the proverbial Rock of Gibraltar. But that was to be expected; after all, nothing calmed him down more than a good catastrophe. Inwardly, I knew he was crying for me, but I think we both knew that that wasn't what I needed from him now. With the saddest of smiles, he extended his arms toward me and held me by the shoulders. Then he looked me in the eyes and said, "We'll get through this, son. Your mother and I will always be there for you."

I nodded in understanding, knowing that they always would. They were good people; perhaps the only good thing to ever come out of Stratton was the financial security it left them with, a result of my father's salary when he had worked there. They would grow old with grace, with dignity, and with gentility. They would not be burdened with financial worries. I was proud of that.

My mother had tears in her eyes as I hugged her, and I could feel her crying in my arms now. And that was exactly what I needed from her. I needed to know that there was one person in the world who hurt more than everyone else combined. My mother was a brilliant, complicated woman. Leah Belfort was a woman of the highest moral fiber, who had watched her son live the sort of life that stood for everything she detested–hedonism, ostentation, and a lack of regard for others. Yet she still loved me anyway, perhaps now more than ever, simply because I needed her to.

With great care, I held her by the shoulders, the same way my father had held me. Then I forced a smile and said, "It's all right, Mom. Four years isn't really four years; after deductions it's less than two. The time will fly by. It'll be okay."

She shook her head, perplexed. "I just don't understand how you got the same time as Danny. That's the only thing that doesn't make sense to me."

"Yeah," I agreed. "I guess it seems a bit unfair. But that's how life is sometimes, you know?"

She nodded. In fact, at the age of seventy-one she knew this better than I.

"Anyway," I continued, "Gleeson was right, Mom. *You* know it." I shrugged. "I think everyone *knows* it. I was the mastermind behind the whole thing, not Danny, and after everything that went down, how could I not go to jail for a while? Besides, Gleeson's a smart guy: He knows all about the drug program and about good time. So he really only sentenced me to two years, which is just enough to send me a message but not enough to ruin my life." I winked. "It'll give me a chance to catch up on some reading, so it's not *all* bad, right?" I forced another smile.

"When are you and Nadine gonna tell the kids?" asked my father.

"We're not," I said tonelessly, "at least not yet. Why worry them now? We'll wait until before I go; then we'll tell them together. Anyway, I gotta get going. I got some packing to do."

"Oh, you're going to California?" asked my mother.

I smiled proudly. "No, Mom, I'm not *going* to California; I'm *moving* there."

They looked at me, incredulous. "Now?" asked my father. "Do you think that makes sense with this sentence hanging over your head?"

"No," I answered nonchalantly, "I'm sure it doesn't, but I'm still doing it. See, I made a promise to my little girl once, and I'm not about to let her down." I shrugged, as if to say, "Sometimes love outweighs logic, you know?" Then I said, "You understand, right?"

No words were necessary; they were parents too.

So it was that I became a resident of the state of California, whether the state liked it or not. Within a week, I found myself a beautiful home on the water, less than a dozen blocks from the kids, and I went about doing just what I had sworn to Alonso that night: I made up for lost time, quite content to spend my last three months of freedom lost inside ordinary life–cooking for the kids, watching TV with them, driving them to school, soccer practice, volleyball practice, and play dates.

And then, after a three-month extension, time ran out.

It was New Year's Day of 2004, a sunny Thursday, and I was due to report to jail the next morning. The way I figured it, I had two options: Either I could show up on my own or make the marshals come look for me. And while neither option thrilled me, I had resigned myself to the former. The kids, of course, hadn't the slightest idea of this, but they were about to find out.

At this very moment, they were walking down the stairs, all smiles, while a nervous-looking Duchess trailed behind them. John and I were sitting in their living room, which, in one last dose of irony, bore an odd resemblance to Meadow Lane's: the rear plate-glass wall with its awesome view of the ocean, the shabby-chic furniture (a bit more formal here, though), the dozens of throw pillows and doilies and overpriced knickknacks scattered this way and that, and the sandstone fireplace rising up to the ceiling. All revealed what I had suspected about the Duchess all along: She liked her beach houses decorated a certain way.

"Don't worry," said John, who was sitting across from me on the couch. "I'll treat your kids as if they were my own."

I nodded sadly. "I know you will, John. I trust you more than you can imagine." And, indeed, I did. I had come to know John well over the last six months, come to know him for the man he was–kind, generous, responsible, charismatic, self-made, and, above all, a man who, true to his words, treated my kids as if they were his own. They would be safe with him, I knew, and they would want for nothing.

"Hey, Dad," Chandler said happily, as she took a seat next to me on the couch. "What's up with the family discussion?"

Carter, however, didn't *sit* down; when he was twelve feet from the couch he executed a sliding maneuver, whizzing along the terra-cotta floor on a pair of white sweat socks. He grabbed the top of the couch and vaulted over the back, like a high jumper, and landed right next to me without incident. "Hi!" he chirped happily, and then he leaned back and put his feet up on an Australian zebrawood coffee table.

John, ever the disciplinarian, shot him a look, to which Carter rolled his blue eyes and put his feet back down. Meanwhile, the Duchess had taken a seat on the Hepplewhite armchair next to John's. She still looked beautiful–a bit older, perhaps, but considering what the two of us had gone through, she looked pretty damn good. She was dressed casually, in jeans and a T-shirt, as were John and I. The kids had on shorts, and their skin glowed with youth and health.

I took a deep breath and said to them: "Come here, guys. I have something I need to talk to you about, and I want you to be sitting on my lap when I do." I extended an arm toward each of them.

Carter, all fifty-five pounds of him, immediately jumped onto my lap and maneuvered himself onto my right thigh, his legs dangling between mine. Then he put his arms around me. Only eight and a half years old, he sensed nothing.

Chandler moved more slowly, more cautiously. "Is somebody sick?" she asked nervously, easing herself onto my other thigh.

"No," I said softly, "nobody is sick."

"But it's bad news, right?"

I nodded sadly. "Yeah, honey, it is. I have to go away for a little while, and while it's not really that long a time for an adult, it's still gonna seem like a very long time for you guys."

"How long?" she asked quickly.

I squeezed her and Carter close. "About two years, honey."

I saw the first tears welling up in her eyes. "No!" she said urgently. "You can't go away again. You just moved here! Don't leave us!"

Fighting back tears, I said, "Listen to me, honey–I want both of you to listen to me closely: A long time ago, back when I was in the stock market, I did some things that were very wrong, things that I'm not very proud of now, and there were a lot of people who lost money because of it. And now, all these years later, I have to make up for what I did, which means I have to go to jail for a while and–"

She collapsed in my arms. "Oh, no, Daddy, no... please..." She began to cry hysterically.

I had tears in my eyes. "It's okay, Channy. It's–" and now Carter collapsed in my arms and started to cry hysterically. "Oh, Daddy, don't go! Please..."

I squeezed him closer, as he sobbed on my shoulder. "It's okay," I said, rubbing his back. "It's gonna be okay, buddy." Then, to Channy: "It's all right, sweetie. Trust me, the time is gonna fly by!"

Now the Duchess popped out of her armchair. She ran over and sat on the edge of the couch and hugged the kids too. "It's okay, guys. It's... it's gonna be fine." I looked at the Duchess and she was crying too, her words coming out through tiny snuffles. So now I started crying, at which point John popped out of his own armchair. He sat on the edge of the coffee table and wrapped his arms around the kids too, trying to console them. He wasn't crying yet, but he looked on the verge of it.

There was nothing to do now but let the kids cry. I think we all knew that, and I think even the kids knew it. There were a certain number of tears that needed to be shed before they could try to make sense of it all or at least accept it.

Finally, after a few minutes of rubbing their backs and stroking their hair and telling them about visiting days and how we would still be able to talk on the phone and write each other letters, they began to calm down. Then I went about trying to explain to them how all this happened–how I'd started Stratton at a very young age and how it quickly spiraled out of control. Then I said:

"Now, a lot of it had to do with the drugs, which made me do things that I would never normally do. And it's very important that you learn from that–from Daddy's mistakes–because, when you're older, you might find yourself in a situation where people are using drugs and they're telling you how cool they are and how great they make you feel, and all that sort of stuff. In fact, they might even try to pressure you to use them yourself, which would be the worst thing of all." I shook my head gravely. "And if that happens, I want you to think of Daddy, and all the problems drugs caused for him, and how they almost killed him once. Then you'll know not to do them yourself, okay?"

They both nodded and said yes.

"Good, because it's very important to me that you understand that, and it's going to make my time away from you much easier knowing that you do." I paused for a moment, realizing that I owed them more of an explanation than your basic insanity plea centered on drug abuse. I said, "Now, there were other reasons I made mistakes too, guys, and while they might not be as bad as drugs, they were still pretty bad. You see, what happened with Daddy was that I didn't grow up with a lot of money, like you guys have"–I motioned to the plate-glass window, with its breathtaking view of the Pacific–"and I really wanted to be rich. So I cut a few corners along the way, which made me get rich very quickly. Do you know what that means, to cut a few corners?"

Carter shook his head no. Chandler said, "You stole money?"

I was flabbergasted. I looked at the Duchess; she had her lips compressed, as if trying to fight down a giggle. I looked at John, who shrugged as if to say, "She's *your* daughter!" Now I looked at Chandler.

"Well, I wouldn't say that I actually stole money, Channy, because it wasn't really like that. Here, let me give you an example: Let's just suppose your friend called you and told you that there was this really great toy she wanted to buy, and she asked you to chip in with her for it. And then let's just say you did, because she made the toy sound really fun–like it was the best toy in the world. But then you found out later that the toy didn't cost as much as she said, and she used the money you gave her to buy candy for herself, which she didn't even split with you." I shook my head gravely. "You see what I mean? Wouldn't that be bad?"

Chandler nodded accusingly. "She stole from me!"

"Yeah," added Carter. "She stole!"

Unbelievable! I thought. Yeah, maybe I'd stolen, but at least I had done it with a bit of panache! I mean, I hadn't used a gun or anything! But how was I supposed to explain high-pressure sales tactics and stock manipulation to my children?

Now the Duchess chimed in: "Well, it's a bit like stealing, but the difference is that when you're as old as your daddy and me, you're supposed to know better than to send your money to strangers to buy toys, you know? Like you're supposed to take responsibility for your own actions. You understand?"

"Yes," they said in unison, although I wasn't so sure they did. Either way, I was still glad that the Duchess had made the effort.

There were a few more tears that evening, but the worst of it was over.

Having no other choice, the kids quickly resigned themselves to the fact that they would be seeing me only on visiting days for a while. In the end, my only consolation that night was that I got to fall asleep just the way I had wanted, with Chandler and Carter in my arms. And, of course, I had kept my promise to my little girl and moved to California.

EPILOGUE

THE LAND OF MULLETS

What's with all these mullets?

That wasn't the first thought I had upon entering the brick administration building of the Taft Correctional Institution, but it was close to the first. My first thought was that the building looked rather benign. The reception area was open and airy, with a very high ceiling, a few too many American flags, and a small seating area with upholstered chairs off to one side. Two uniformed guards, one of each gender, sat behind a large Formica reception desk, looking bored more than anything.

Oddly enough, they both sported mullets.

The male's mullet was comprised of reddish-brown hair that had the consistency of a tumbleweed. It was very high on top, rising up a good three inches above his swarthy skull, and very tight on the sides. Yet, in the back, the mullet was as fine as corn silk and went down a few inches past the light-gray shirt collar of his guard's uniform. The female's mullet was of similar construction, although her hair was pineapple blonde and much longer in the back.

I had done a bit of intelligence-gathering over the prior week and was told by someone "in the know" (meaning, an erstwhile guest) that I should show up wearing gray sweats, a white T-shirt, and white tennis sneakers. Anything else would be confiscated and shipped back to my family in a box. The only exception was a tennis racquet, which I would be allowed to bring in. He strongly recommended I do this, because the racquets offered by the rec department were of dubious quality.

It was for that very reason that at precisely eleven a.m. on Friday, January 2, 2004, I entered the administration building wearing a gray sweat suit and carrying a brand-new Head tennis racquet under my right arm. "I'm Jordan Belfort," I said to the two intake mullets. "I'm here to start serving my sentence."

"Welcome to Taft," said the female mullet in a surprisingly friendly tone. "Take a seat over there." She gestured toward the seating area. "Someone'll be with you in a few minutes."

After a few minutes, a third guard emerged. He was short, squat, pale, and plain-looking, with childbearing hips and the sort of lumbering gait that hints at low intelligence. He wore the same gray guard's uniform as the others, although his looked heavily padded. In his right hand was a clipboard. On his narrow skull was a light-brown mullet that looked lush enough to house a bird's nest. He looked down at the clipboard and said, "Are you Belfort?"

"Yes," I answered, picking up on the fact that I was no longer Mr. Belfort or even Jordan Belfort. I was simply Belfort.

"Okay," he said wearily. "Follow me, Belfort." He led me through a series of foreboding steel gates, the last of which closed behind me with an ominous *clank.* The unspoken message was: "You are now a prisoner; everything you knew in the outside world is now gone." Then we entered a small, windowless, tableless, chairless room, at the rear of which was a large white curtain hanging from the ceiling.

"What's with the tennis racquet?" snapped the guard.

"I'm going to the camp; I was told I could bring a tennis racquet with me."

"Not anymore; they changed the rules a few years ago." He looked down at the clipboard for a moment, then looked back up and said, "Are you sure you're going to the camp? It says that you're going to the low here."

Taft had two separate facilities: the low and the camp. The low housed *real* inmates, whereas the camp housed *campers,* as the phrase went. While the low wasn't filled with murderers and rapists, it still had its fair share of violence; the camp, however, had none. In fact, it didn't even have a fence around it–you stayed there on the honor system and could walk away at any time.

Trying to remain calm, I said, "I'm sure I'm designated for the camp; the judge recommended it at my sentencing."

He shrugged, unconcerned. "You can take it up with your counselor; give me your sneakers."

"My sneakers?" I looked down at my brand-new Nikes. "What's wrong with my sneakers?"

"They have a red stripe on them. Only plain white sneakers are allowed. We'll ship them back to your family along with your tennis racquet. Now go behind the curtain and strip."

I did as I was told, and two minutes later–after pulling back my ears, running his fingers through my hair, opening my mouth, rolling my tongue around, lifting up one foot, then the other foot, and, finally, lifting up my nut-sack (as the guard referred to it), he gave me back my sweat suit and told me to get dressed. Then he handed me a pair of blue canvas slippers, the sort Chairman Mao had given to political dissidents upon entering one of his reeducation camps.

"Your counselor is Ms. Richards,"* said the guard. "She'll be here in about an hour. Until then, you can make yourself comfortable." His last few words came out with a healthy dose of irony; after all, there was nothing in the room to sit on other than the cheap linoleum floor. Then he left, locking the door behind him.

Remain calm! I thought. There was no way they were going to stick me in the low. I was camper material! I had no violence in my background, and I was a first-time offender. I had even cooperated with the government!

---

*Name has been changed

Thirty minutes later, the door opened and in walked my counselor, Ms. Richards. She was huge, the better part of six feet tall, with the shoulders of an NFL linebacker and the thick, fleshy features of a shar-pei. Her dark-brown mullet looked a mile high. She was dressed in street clothes–blue jeans and a dark-blue windbreaker. Her feet were shod in black army boots.

Before she had a chance to say anything, I popped up off the linoleum floor and said, "Ms. Richards, I have a serious problem here: The guard told me that I'm going to the low, but I was designated for the camp. The judge recommended it at my sentencing."

She flashed me a friendly smile, exposing a pair of central incisors that were so severely overlapped they looked like one giant snaggletooth. I felt a shiver run down my spine. Counselor Snaggletooth said in a rather cheery tone: "Okay; well, let's see if we can't get it sorted out. Follow me."

Snaggletooth turned out to be very nice. She escorted me to a small interview room, where she spent a few minutes looking down at my file. Finally she said, "I've got good news for you, Belfort; you do qualify for camp."

Thank God! I thought. I was, indeed, camper material. I had always known it. Why had I even worried myself, for Chrissake? So silly of me.

Then: "Wait! I spoke too soon!"

A fresh wave of panic. "What's wrong now?"

"Your probation officer never sent us your presentencing report. I can't put you in the camp until I review it. The report has all the information about your case."

Near panic: "So you're sticking me in the *low*?"

"No, no," she answered, flashing me her snaggletooth smile. "I wouldn't stick you in the low; I'm sticking you in the hole."

My eyes popped out of my occipital orbits, like hat pegs. "You're putting me in the hole? As in solitary confinement?"

She nodded slowly. "Yeah, but only until your paperwork gets here. It shouldn't take more than a week."

Panic on top of panic now: "*A week?* How can it take a week to get my paperwork here? Can't they just fax it over?"

She compressed her lips and shook her head slowly.

"Oh, Jesus," I muttered. "A week in the hole. It's not fair."

Snaggletooth nodded and said, "Yeah, well, welcome to Taft, Belfort."

First they took my clothes, then they handed me an orange jumpsuit, and then they handed me back my reeducation slippers and told me to put my hands behind my back so they could slap the cuffs on me, which they did, with a smile.

"They" were two uniformed guards from the Special Housing Unit, known as the SHU, for short. Located in the lower bowels of the administration building, the SHU was that section of the prison where they kept the serious hard cases. Handcuffed and panic-stricken, I was escorted down a long, narrow corridor with ominous steel doors on either side.

Not surprisingly, "they" were of an entirely different breed than the affable intake mullets. (*Neither of them even had mullets, for Chrissake!*) They were unusually tall, overly muscular, and had the sort of overdeveloped jaws that indicate steroid abuse coupled with a genetic disposition toward violence. As we made our way through the SHU, no words were exchanged, other than a passing comment I made about my being thrown in the SHU not for doing something wrong; it was simply one of those lost-paperwork things. (So they really ought to go easy on me.) To that, they both shrugged as if to say, "Who gives a shit?"

The guards stopped and unlocked one of the steel doors. "Step inside," one of them ordered. "After we close the door, you stick your hands through the slot in the door and we'll uncuff you." With that, they fairly shoved me into the cell, which was incredibly tiny, perhaps six by twelve feet. Two steel bunk beds were riveted into one wall, a steel seat–desk ensemble was riveted into another wall, and a steel toilet, sans toilet seat, was right out in the open for public dumpages. A tiny window, covered by iron bars, looked out over a dusty field. The lower bunk was occupied by another inmate, a middle-aged white man with a sun-deprived complexion. He was busy doing paperwork, and, to my shock, he sported the most fabulous mullet of all. In fact, it was world class–comprised of curly red hair that was so flat on top you could have used his head as a plate. The moment the guards slammed the door, he popped off the bed and said, "So what happened? What did they say you did?"

"Nothing," I answered. "I self-surrendered, and they lost my paperwork."

He rolled his eyes. "That's what they always say."

"What do you mean?"

"I mean they make extra money throwing people in the hole. Taft is not actually part of the Bureau of Prisons; they're a private corporation, for profit. You know that, right?"

I nodded. "Yeah, it's owned by the Wackenhut Corporation."

"Exactly," he said. "And each day you're in the hole, Wackenhut bills the federal government an extra hundred dollars. Anyway, I'm Sam Hausman."* He extended his closed fist toward me for a jailhouse handshake.

"Jordan Belfort," I replied, banging knuckles with him. "So what are you in the hole for?"

"I filed a lien on the warden's house and then on a few of the guards' houses too."

My eyes nearly popped out of my skull. "You put a lien on the warden's house? Why would you do that?"

He shrugged casually. "I have my reasons. I also did it to my sentencing judge. And the prosecutor too. I've basically destroyed their credit. Now I'm starting foreclosure proceedings against them. What are *you* in jail for?"

Jesus, this mullet was insane! "Manipulating stocks. A bunch of other stuff too. All of it white-collar. How about you?"

Knowingly: "I didn't do anything; I'm innocent."

Gee, what a surprise! I thought. "Well, what did they *say* you did?"

"They say I wrote bad checks, but that's a lie. I can write as many checks as I want, regardless of how much money is in my account. That's the law."

"Oh, really? Why is that?" I asked.

---

*Name has been changed

"Because the government stole my birth certificate the day I was born and stashed it in some vault in Puerto Rico. In exchange, they gave me a straw man named SAM HAUSMAN–that's SAM HAUSMAN, all in capital letters–not the legitimate Sam Hausman, which is in small letters. That's who I really am: Sam Hausman, in small letters."

He walked over to his bed, which was less than two feet away, and he handed me a book titled *Redemption in Law.* "Trust me," he said. "After you're done reading this book, you'll be filing liens against the warden too. Understand: You're nothing more than a slave, Jordan. You need to reclaim your straw man; there's no other way."

I nodded and accepted the book. Then, for nothing more than shits and giggles, I asked, "And what about the IRS? What's the story with *them*?"

He smiled knowingly. "The IRS doesn't even exist; in fact, if you can find even one law in the U.S. Constitution authorizing the IRS to collect taxes, I'll shave my head." *You mean mullet.* "There's only one amendment that even *mentions* income taxes, and it was never ratified." With that he reached over to a stack of papers on his bed and handed me one off the top. "This is a list of all the U.S. senators who ratified the Fourteenth Amendment. Go ahead and count them: You'll see there's not enough for a lawful majority."

I nodded once more and then took my required reading material and hopped up on the top bunk. I spent the next few days learning everything there was to know about redeeming my straw man. When I wasn't reading about it, Sam was lecturing about it, as barely edible meals were slid through a tiny slot on the steel door thrice daily, to which Sam insisted that whatever I didn't eat I flush down the toilet–including half-consumed apples and unopened packets of ketchup. After all, the evildoers at Wackenhut would recycle whatever was left over, in an attempt to cut costs.

Each morning, Sam would smile and say, "It's time to feed the warden!" Then he would take a world-class dump and flush the toilet with a nod.

I managed to write two letters a day, one to Chandler and one to

Carter. I decided it would be best to lie to them—telling them how wonderful camp was and how I was playing tennis all day and working out in the gym. The only reason I hadn't called was that it took a bit of time to get a phone account set up.

And as one day melted into the next, Sam gave me the full lowdown on the camp, which was, indeed, a cushy place to do time. For a nominal fee, he explained, I could live like a king; a cook, a butler, a maid, a masseuse, and someone to do whatever job my counselor assigned to me could all be secured for a total monthly cost of less than a thousand dollars, payable either in stamps, cigarettes, food I'd purchased from the commissary, or simply by having one of my friends on the outside send a money order to another inmate's commissary account. And while this latter strategy was slightly against the rules, everyone was doing it, he assured me.

Finally, on the morning of my seventh day in solitary, the steel door swung open and I heard the most glorious ten words in the entire world: "On your feet, Belfort. It's time to go to camp."

"Thank God," I muttered, nearly springing tears. I jumped off my top bunk with the speed of a jackrabbit and turned to Sam, taking one last look at his breathtaking mullet. "Good luck redeeming your straw man," I said.

He winked. "I got these bastards right where I want them."

It sure as hell looks like it, I thought.

Then I left the cell.

"I'm gonna ram this right down your throat!" barked Tony the meth dealer, who had five years left on an eight-year sentence.

"Go ahead and try," I barked back. "It's coming right back at you."

It was two hours later, and Tony the meth dealer was standing approximately fifty feet away from me, on the other side of a tennis net. It was a mild winter day—sunny, in the low sixties—and Tony was preparing to serve. I was doing my best to keep my eye on him, but it was difficult. After all, there was a lot going on at the camp. Behind Tony was a soccer field, where a game was now in progress; to his right was a basketball court, where a game was also in progress; and beyond the basketball court was a grassy field where two dozen Mexicans sat at wooden picnic tables, rolling tacos and burritos for a Friday-night fiesta.

But that was only the beginning: Behind me was a baseball field; to my right were a running track, a horseshoe pit, a volleyball court, and a red-clay bocce court; and, off to my left, in the distance, were concrete walking paths that led to a handful of low-slung concrete buildings—the dining hall, the rec hall, the library, the quiet rooms, the music room, the infirmary, and the camp administration building. Scattered along the perimeter were little white signs—*Out of Bounds*—and beyond the signs were the flat dusty plains of the city of Taft, bordered by a rather unimpressive mountain range.

Suddenly a booming voice came over the loudspeaker: "Count time, count time! The yard is now closed. All campers return to the unit for the four p.m. stand-up count."

I was about to drop my racquet when I noticed that none of the other campers were paying attention to the announcement; rather, they kept doing what they were doing. It wasn't until the *next* announcement, which came ten minutes later, that everyone began moseying on over. The unit was a vast space, about the size of a football field. It was crammed with a seemingly endless sea of cinder-block cubicles, bounded on one side by bathrooms and showers, on another side by TV rooms and quiet rooms, and at the front by a half-dozen administration offices, where the staff pretended to work.

I entered the unit and walked down a narrow corridor toward Bunk 12-Lower. On either side of the corridor were small cubicles, each perhaps eight by twelve feet. Like the SHU, they contained only the bare essentials—two bunk beds, two stand-up lockers, and a steel seat–desk ensemble welded to a gray cement floor.

I had briefly met my new bunkie when I first arrived, and he seemed like a decent enough guy (your typical garden-variety meth dealer). He was short, squat, dark-haired, dark-eyed, and wore a perpetually grim expression. His name was Mark, and with the exception of his two front teeth, which were missing, he seemed reasonably healthy. At this moment he was lying on his bed, reading a book. He paid little attention to me as I entered the cube and took a seat at the steel table.

I heard a snappy female voice: *"Hey, Belfort!"*

I looked up and–*a shock!* There was a sexy little number standing at the entrance to the cube, staring at me. She was no more than five foot four and had fine auburn hair that rested on a pair of delicate shoulders, which were pulled back like a cheerleader's, accentuating perky little breasts. She looked around thirty. She wore a men's pink dress shirt, untucked, and a pair of skintight Levi's. In the outside world, I wouldn't have characterized her as outright gorgeous, but inside here she looked sexier than a Victoria's Secret model.

She said, "I'm your counselor, Mrs. Strickland."

What happened to Snaggletooth? I thought. "What happened to Ms. Richards?" I asked.

"She was filling in for me last week." She stared at me for a moment, then said, "Well, you don't look like a guy who stole a hundred million dollars. You seem much too innocent."

"Yeah, I've heard that before, but I'm definitely guilty as charged."

With a chuckle: "You don't hear *that* too often around here! Everyone in Taft is innocent. In fact, speaking of that, how was your week in the hole with Sam Hausman?"

"He's a fucking maniac! Did he file a lien against you yet?"

She started laughing. "No, but I'm in the minority around here; he's done it to pretty much everyone else. I think he likes me." She shrugged. "Anyway, I'm moving you after count; your new bunk is 42-Lower. That's *Chong's* cube."

"Tommy Chong?"

"Yeah, I might as well have you both in the same place. It'll be easier to keep an eye on you." With that, Mrs. Strickland smiled and walked off without saying another word.

I had heard that Tommy Chong was in Taft; he was serving time on some ridiculous charge having to do with selling "bongs" over the Internet. From what little I knew of his case, it was a ridiculous miscarriage of justice. In fact, selling bongs wasn't even illegal; it was only because he had sold them over the Internet (thereby crossing state lines) that he'd violated the law. In consequence, he received a ten-month sentence.

I resisted the urge to calculate the comparative fairness of our two sentences; after all, if selling bongs translated into ten months in the slammer, then what should stealing $100 million from thousands of investors, smuggling millions of dollars to Switzerland, and engaging in acts of depravity that defied the laws of man and God translate into? About ten thousand years, I figured.

"What a load of crap that is!" snapped my bunkie.

"What's a load of crap?"

"That people like you get special treatment around here."

"What are you taking about?"

My bunkie shrugged. "I'm not saying it's your fault, but I've been here nineteen months and the only time Strickland ever said a word to me was when she told me to make my bed. Yet you're here a few hours and she comes prancing around in her pink shirt and moves you in with Tommy Chong. Watch: She won't even assign you to the kitchen, like every other new inmate. She'll probably make you an orderly, which is the cushiest job here." Then, in a friendly tone: "Anyway, it's all good; what I'd really like to do is be your laundry man. I'll charge you two bucks a week, plus another fifty cents for the fabric softener. You can pay me either in stamps or with cans of tuna, whatever's easier for you."

"All right," I said. "I'll pay you in tuna."

Just then a booming male voice from the front of the unit: "Count time, count time! All rise for the four p.m. stand-up count." Mark popped off the bed and faced the entrance to the cube, as did I. A hush fell over the unit.

A few moments later, two guards came walking by at an overly brisk pace, glancing in as they passed. Their pace was so brisk, in fact, that I was certain that they hadn't even counted us; they just assumed we were all here. Either way, a few minutes later the same booming voice screamed, "Clear," and the noise level picked up again and campers began strolling about the unit, like athletes in a locker room.

With a bang of knuckles, I bid my new laundry man farewell

and headed down the narrow corridor to 42-Lower. When I reached the cubicle, I found Tommy sitting on his bed, going through a stack of mail. He was much more handsome than I remembered from his movies, although I was always so stoned when I'd watched them that I might have been hallucinating at the time. He was slender and tan, with a full head of silvery gray hair and a well-trimmed beard of the same rich color.

"Tommy..." I said open-endedly.

He looked up and smiled. "Yeah. Jordan, right?"

I nodded, and we shook hands in the traditional fashion, which is to say, without banging knuckles. We then spent the next few minutes making small talk. Apparently news traveled fast here, because Tommy seemed to know as much about my case as I knew about his.

"So they actually made that *Boiler Room* movie about you?" he asked.

"Not really," I answered. "It's loosely based on the firm I owned, but it was written from the perspective of a very low-level employee. It doesn't even begin to tell the story. I mean, there was a scene where they took a bus to Atlantic City..." and as I went about explaining the many shortfalls of *Boiler Room,* my mind began to double-track.

On track one, the words were coming out automatically: "...and I can promise you that my brokers never took a bus anywhere; in fact, they would have been stoned to death if they got caught. It was all private jets and limousines..."

And on track two, my internal monologue was saying, *Jesus, I can't believe how different Tommy Chong is than I expected him to be. Just look at his face drop as I tell him about my former life of insanity. I would have thought this stuff would be second nature to him, yet he seems genuinely shocked at my depravity!*

Just then another inmate appeared at the entrance to the cube. He was in his mid-fifties and looked like a broken-down version of Robin Williams. He had a wavy gray beard, lush enough for a family of sparrows to live in. With mock formality, he said, "Mr. Belfort: David, humbly at your service." He bowed. "I would like to be your butler. I will do anything you ask of me–make your bed, clean your cube, bring you coffee in the morning; there is no task too great or too small." Now he looked at Tommy. "Mr. Chong, I'm sure, will vouch for the professionalism of my services."

I looked at Tommy, trying to keep a straight face.

"David's a good man," Tommy said. "You should hire him."

"How much?" I asked David.

"Seven books a month," he replied proudly. "And I make an excellent vanilla latte. I steal syrup from the kitchen."

"Sure, why not?" I said. After all, a book of stamps was only $7.20. So, for $50.40, I would have myself a real jailhouse butler. "You can start tomorrow."

David bowed and then walked away.

Tommy said, "Just be careful if he offers you any cooked food. He's been in jail for twenty years, and he spends most of his day catching squirrels; then he marinates them in soy sauce and cooks them in the microwave." He shrugged. "They taste pretty good, from what I hear."

I took a moment to run that scenario through my mind and found myself wondering how he was actually *catching* the squirrels. Must be setting traps, I figured. Then I heard another voice. "Hey, Jordan?"

I looked up and saw a short Mexican man standing there. "What's up?" I said with a smile.

"I'm Jimmy, the head orderly. Mrs. Strickland told me you'll be working for me." *Good old Mrs. Strickland!* "I assume you don't actually want to work, right?"

"Absolutely not," I replied quickly. "How much will it cost?"

"A hundred bucks a month, and you'll never touch a broom handle."

"Done," I said. "How do you want to get paid?"

"Have a friend on the outside send a money order to my sister each month. Then she'll send it to me."

"Fair enough," I said, and the moment he walked away, an Italian-looking guy with an enormous rack of pearly whites poked his head in. "Are you Jordan?" he asked.

I nodded. "Yeah, how can I help you?"

"I'm Russo, the guy who gets things around here. I was watching you play tennis before. You're pretty good, but I think you'd be much better with the right racquet."

"What do you got?"

"A Head, Liquidmetal. In mint condition."

"How much?"

"Seventy-five bucks."

"I'll take it. How do you want to get paid?"

He waved me off. "Don't worry about it; we'll work it out later. You and I are gonna do a lot of business together; let me go fetch the racquet." He walked off.

I looked at Tommy and said, "What a freak show this place is!"

"Oh, you have no idea," he shot back. "This isn't exactly what you call 'hard time.' In fact, at nighttime, people sneak out into the fields and pick up packages from their friends; some of them even meet their wives for sex. It's a total free-for-all."

And indeed it was.

As Tommy and I spent the next few day trading war stories, a seemingly endless stream of inmates offered their services to me. There was Miguel, the Mexican masseur ($10 for a sixty-minute rubdown with no happy ending); Teddy, the Chinese portrait master (for $200 you'd give him a snapshot of your children and he'd re-create it in watercolor); Jimmy, the redneck leather man (for $75 he'd make you a Western-style pocketbook to ship home to your wife); Danny, the gay barber (for six cans of tuna you'd get a trim, while he tried to rub his dick against your kneecap)... and on and on it went. Of course, there were all the jailhouse chefs, who, using a combination of food bought in the commissary, grown in the garden, smuggled in through the fields, and stolen from the kitchen, cooked gourmet meals in a microwave oven.

And just like that I was hooked up: living the Life behind bars.

Yet it wasn't until the fourth night of war stories that Tommy brought something to my attention that would end up changing my life forever. "I've been around some insane people," he said, "but you, my friend, definitely take the cake. I had my wife Google you because I thought you were full of shit—especially that nonsense about sinking the yacht. I mean, that's *outlandish*! Who sinks a yacht? But she said it's all on the Internet."

"Yeah," I said, with a mixture of sadness and pride. "I guess I lived a pretty fucked-up life."

Tommy shrugged. "It might be fucked up, but the stories are totally hysterical, especially the way you tell them, with all the nicknames: the Blockhead, the Chinaman, Mad Max, the Cobbler, the Drizzler, and especially the Duchess, who I'd like to meet one day."

I smiled. "Well, I'm sure I can arrange it in a few years. We actually get along pretty well these days. No more throwing things around."

Tommy raised his eyebrows. "I'll tell you what you *really* oughtta do."

"What?"

"Write a book."

I started laughing. "Write a book? How am I gonna write a book? I don't know how to write! I mean, I can write, but not a whole book. Now, if you wanna talk about *speaking,* that's something I can do. I'm a really *great* speaker, I promise you. You put me in front of a room and I'll make people cry."

"There's no difference," he said confidently. "Writing is all about a voice, and you have one of the best voices I've ever heard. Just write down your story exactly the way you tell it to me."

"I'll give it a shot," I said, and then I spent the next week trying to find a starting point for my story. Some very bizarre things had happened to me–in fact, my whole life seemed to be a series of bizarre events strung together, one after the other. I decided to make a list of them.

Before long, I found myself wondering why so many bizarre things kept happening to me. I came to the conclusion that things weren't just *happening* to me; I was bringing them on myself. It was as if I were a glutton for punishment. At the top of the list was the yacht debacle, and at the bottom of the list was midge-tossing. I decided to give writing it a whirl.

With pen and paper in hand, I sat in one of the quiet rooms and began writing my memoir. Two weeks later, I was still on the first paragraph. I read it to myself. Then I read it again. Christ–it was fucking terrible! It was some ridiculousness about men in self-constructed ivory towers wanting to jump out after the crash of

1987. Who gave a shit? I didn't. What was wrong with me? Why couldn't I write?

I decided to take a different tack: I would talk about my parents and how they liked to eat at the same diner all the time. I quickly wrote four pages. I looked at them. They were damn good, so I rushed them over to Tommy for a critique.

"Okay," he said eagerly. "Let's see what we got here," and he started reading, and reading... *and why wasn't he laughing?* There was a terrific joke in that first paragraph, and he had blown right by it.

A minute later he looked up. "This really sucks!" he said.

"Really?"

He nodded quickly. "Oh, yeah, it's really bad. I mean, it's absolutely terrible. It doesn't have a single redeeming quality." He shrugged. "Start over."

"What are you talking about? Didn't you read that first paragraph?"

Tommy looked me square in the eye and said, "Who gives a shit about the diner? It's fucking boring, and it's ordinary. Let me tell you something, Jordan. There are two things about writing you can never forget: First, it's all about conflict. Without conflict, no one gives a shit. Second, it's about *the most of.* You know what *the most of* means?"

I shrugged, still wounded by Tommy's contemptuous dismissal of my diner story.

He said, "It means you always write about the extreme of something. The most of this, the most of that, the prettiest girl, the richest man, the most rip-roaring drug addiction, the most insane yacht trip." He smiled warmly. "Now, that was what your life was all about: the most of. You get the picture?"

Indeed I did, and indeed I couldn't write it.

In fact, for a month straight, day and night, I did nothing but write–only to have Tommy review my work and say things like: "It's wooden; it's irrelevant; it's boring; it sucks moose cock." Until, finally, I gave up.

With my tail between my legs, I walked into the prison library, searching for a book to read. After a few minutes I stumbled upon

The Bonfire of the Vanities. I vaguely remembered seeing the movie, and, as I recalled, it absolutely sucked. Still, it had something to do with Wall Street, so I picked it up and read the first two paragraphs.... *What utter nonsense it was!* Who would read this crap?

I closed the book and looked at the cover. *Tom Wolfe.* Who the fuck was *he*? Out of curiosity, I reread the first few paragraphs, trying to figure out what was going on. It was very confusing. Apparently there was a riot in progress, an indoor riot. I kept reading, trying to stay focused. Now he was talking about a lady; he can't see her, but he knows by the sound of her voice what she must look like: *Two hundred pounds, if she's an ounce! Built like an oil burner!* With that, I dropped the book and started laughing out loud. And that was it. I was hooked.

I read that book from cover to cover—698 pages in a single day—and I laughed out loud the entire time. I was blown away. *Mesmerized.* Not only was it the most brilliant book I had ever read but also there was something about the writing style that resonated with my soul, or as Tom Wolfe might have put it: *With my heart and soul and liver and loins.*

I swear to God, I must have read that book two dozen times, until I knew every word by heart. And then I read it again, to learn grammar. Then I paid my trusted laundry man, Mark the meth dealer (who happened to be an avid reader), ten cans of tuna to go through the book with a fine-tooth comb and write down every simile and analogy on a separate piece of paper. Then I read it over and over again until I could recite them in my sleep. And before I knew it, a voice popped into my head: my writer's voice. It was ironic, glib, obnoxious, self-serving, and often despicable, but, as Tommy explained it, it was funny as all hell.

However, I wouldn't actually write my memoir in jail; I would simply learn how to write. In fact, when I came out twenty months later, I didn't have a single page. The date was November 1, 2005, and I was scared as all hell. I had no idea what I wanted to do with my life. I think most people write out of inspiration or desperation. In my case, it was desperation all the way. I had an unspeakable past and an uncertain future, and no way to reconcile the two.

So I sat down in front of my laptop and wrote what I thought to be the perfect opening sentence. It was how I felt while I was in jail all those months, and it was how I felt my first day on Wall Street. In point of fact, it was how I felt at that very moment, staring at the blank computer screen.

"You're lower than pond scum," I wrote.

ACKNOWLEDGMENTS

Once again, I'd like to thank my literary agent, Joel Gotler, for all his support. He's been many things to me over the years, but most of all, he's been a friend.

I'd also like to thank my editor, Danielle Perez, for all her wonderful insight. I've learned more about writing from Danielle than from all my English teachers combined–from kindergarten through college.

And, of course, I'd like to thank my publisher, Irwyn Applebaum, who helped me in so many ways that I can't even count them all, and also many thanks to Barb Burg, Theresa Zoro, and Chris Artis in Bantam Dell's publicity department.

Many thanks to Alexandra Milchan, for working so hard on the movie side of things, and, of course, to Scott Lambert as well, who's been both a friend and an adviser to me. Scotty and Alexandra are married–and what a couple they are! Going out for dinner with them is like watching two gunfighters throwing down, albeit with BlackBerrys instead of guns.

I'd also like to thank Terry Winter, who read the unpublished manuscript and signed on to adapt the book for the movies before there was any buzz on it at all. He's an absolutely brilliant writer. I felt very comfortable with him adapting the book–figuring that anyone who could make Tony Soprano seem sympathetic was the right guy for me.

And I'd also like to thank my parents, Max and Leah, for always being there for me; my two wonderful children, Chandler and Carter, who've chosen to respect their dad for the way he lives his life now, not in the past; my ex-wife Nadine (aka the Duchess) for being such a wonderful, caring mother; and to the newest addition in my life, little Bowen Boulliane, who brightens up my life with all his Bowenisms.

And many thanks to my good friends Bo Dietl, Kris Mesner, Michael Peragine, Paul Scialla, John Flynn, Todd Kissel, Bob and Toni Shottenhammer, Renne and Anne Sandera, Johnny Marine, Marc Glazier, John Macaluso, Javier Perez (the world's best soccer coach), all the boys at Starbucks–Mitch, Dr. Al, Tre, Jim T.–and to Petros at Petros Restaurant in Manhattan Beach, for all the times I've tied up his tables, writing this book, and to Milo at Shade Hotel, for the same reason. And, of course, to all my fans who bought *Wolf I,* especially the ones who wrote me letters of encouragement. They were so important to me.

And, lastly, I'd like to thank the most positive influence in my life, George Benedict, who, by sheer example, proved to me that a leopard can definitely change his spots. There is no person in my life who has ever been kinder and more supportive of me.

ABOUT THE AUTHOR

JORDAN BELFORT lives in Los Angeles. He served twenty-two months in prison and spent one month in rehab.